CONGRESSIONAL POLICIES, PRACTICES AND PROCEDURES

LEGISLATION TO ADDRESS PUERTO RICO'S POLITICAL STATUS

Congressional Policies, Practices and Procedures

Additional books and e-books in this series can be found on Nova's website under the Series tab.

CONGRESSIONAL POLICIES, PRACTICES AND PROCEDURES

LEGISLATION TO ADDRESS PUERTO RICO'S POLITICAL STATUS

ALVARO CAMPOY
EDITOR

New York

DOI: https://doi.org/10.52305/ICDN4393

Additional color graphics may be available in the e-book version of this book.

Library of Congress Cataloging-in-Publication Data

ISBN: 978-1-68507-404-3

Published by Nova Science Publishers, Inc. † New York

Contents

PREFACE

Two pieces of key legislation have been introduced in Congress to resolve Puerto Rico's political status, H.R. 2070, Puerto Rico's Self-Determination Act of 2021, and H.R. 1522, Puerto Rico Statehood Admission Act. This book discusses the legislation and re-examines the island's territory status.

In: Legislation to Address Puerto Rico's Political Status
Editor: Alvaro Campoy
ISBN: 978-1-68507-404-3

Chapter 1

H.R. 1522, "Puerto Rico Statehood Admission Act"; and H.R. 2070, "Puerto Rico Self-Determination Act of 2021," – Part 1*

Committee on Natural Resources

Legislative Hearing on H.R. 1522, to Provide for the Admission of the State of Puerto Rico into the Union, "Puerto Rico Statehood Admission Act"; and H.R. 2070, to Recognize the Right of the People of Puerto Rico to Call a Status Convention through Which the People Would Exercise Their Natural Right to Self-Determination, and to Establish a Mechanism for Congressional Consideration of Such Decision, and for Other Purposes, "Puerto Rico Self-Determination Act of 2021"

Wednesday, April 14, 2021
U.S. House of Representatives
Committee on Natural Resources
Washington, DC

* This is an edited, reformatted and augmented version of Legislative Hearing, before the Committee on Natural Resources, U.S. House of Representatives, One Hundred Seventeenth Congress, First Session, Serial No. 117–3, dated April 14, 2021.

The Committee met, pursuant to notice, at 1 p.m., via Webex, Hon. Raúl M. Grijalva [Chairman of the Committee] presiding.

Present: Representatives Grijalva, Napolitano, Costa, Sablan, Huffman, Lowenthal, Gallego, Neguse, Porter, Leger Fernández, Velázquez, DeGette, Brownley, Dingell, McEachin, Soto, García, Case, McCollum, Tlaib; Westerman, Young, Lamborn, Gosar, Graves, Radewagen, Webster, González-Colón, Fulcher, Stauber, Tiffany, Moore, Herrell, and Obernolte.

Also present: Representative Torres.

The CHAIRMAN. Thank you very much. The Committee will come to order. The Committee is meeting today to receive testimony on two bills to address Puerto Rico's future political status. Under Committee Rule 4(f), any oral opening statements of the hearing are limited to the Chair and the Ranking Minority Member or their designees. This will allow us to hear from our witnesses sooner and help Members keep to their schedules.

However, for today's hearing, we will allow main sponsors to make a statement in support of their legislation before we turn to the rest of the witnesses. I therefore ask unanimous consent that all other Members' opening statements be made part of the hearing record if they are submitted to the Clerk by 5 p.m. today or at the close of the hearing, whichever comes first. Hearing no objection, so ordered.

Without objection, the Chair will also declare a recess subject to the call of the Chair. Without objection, so ordered.

As described in the notice, statements, documents or motions will be submitted to the repository at HNRCdocs@mail.house.gov.

Without objection, the following Members from New York, Representatives Torres and Ocasio-Cortez are authorized to question the witnesses of today's hearing after permanent members of this Committee have their opportunity first.

Additionally, please note that as with in-person meetings, Members are responsible for their own microphones. And as with our in-person meetings, Members may be muted by staff only to avoid inadvertent background noise. Finally, Members or witnesses experiencing technical problems should inform the Committee staff immediately. Now let me recognize myself for opening remarks.

Statement of the Hon. Raúl M. Grijalva, a Representative in Congress from the State of Arizona

The CHAIRMAN. In the hopes of some brevity, let me just state that I want to thank my colleagues for taking the time to join us at the Full Committee hearing to discuss the legislation to resolve Puerto Rico's political status. And thank you to our witnesses today for their participation and the time commitment they have made to this hearing.

The U.S.-Puerto Rico political relationship has been the subject of past discussions in this Committee. However, recent events reinforce our responsibility to re-examine the island's territory status.

Two pieces of legislation have been introduced this Congress to resolve Puerto Rico's political status, H.R. 2070, Puerto Rico's Self-Determination Act of 2021 by Representative Velázquez, and H.R. 1522, Puerto Rico Statehood Admission Act by Representative Darren Soto.

Each piece of legislation proposes a different process to end the island's current territory status. Puerto Rico's options for non-territory status or statehood, independence and free association.

At the same time, there is existing legislation to address this issue. In 2014, Congress appropriated $2.5 million to be provided to the Puerto Rico State Elections Commission for voter education and conduct a plebiscite by which Puerto Rican voters would determine the future political status of Puerto Rico. The U.S. Department of Justice is responsible for overseeing and administering that plebiscite.

Despite the different views of our witnesses today, I hope we can all agree that Congress has a responsibility to play a constructive role in the resolution of Puerto Rico's political status. We must work effectively together with the executive branch and the island's elected officials through this process, while respecting the will of the residents of Puerto Rico.

This Committee will continue to work with the Biden administration on this important matter and expanding access to Federal programs for residents of Puerto Rico and other U.S. territories. The White House already demonstrated a willingness to expand such programs as the Child Tax Credit and the Earned Income Tax Credit in these jurisdictions. I will continue advocating for equity in Federal assistance under the Supplemental Security Income and Medicaid.

A study released by the Administration recently related to the American Jobs Plan spoke to the need for action in Puerto Rico. For decades, infrastructure in Puerto Rico has suffered from a systemic lack of investment. The need for action is clear. Puerto Rico's infrastructure received a 'D minus' grade in this report on its infrastructure report card. The American Jobs Plan would make that historic investment in our nation's infrastructure and in the needs that are very pronounced within Puerto Rico.

This 'D minus' rating, I think, further presses the effort we need to undertake to address the historic need and inequity related to Puerto Rico and its residents in terms of the support American citizens in Puerto Rico deserve and merit and have earned in terms of equity from the Federal Government.

Now I also want to, as I said, welcome our witnesses, which were suggested by the bill sponsors. Thank you for joining us. It is my hope that we will receive constructive feedback that will direct and inspire the Federal Government to act and continue today's discussion, which is a priority for the people of Puerto Rico.

[The prepared statement of Mr. Grijalva follows:]

PREPARED STATEMENT OF THE HON. RAÚL M. GRIJALVA, CHAIR, COMMITTEE ON NATURAL RESOURCES

I want to begin by thanking my colleagues for taking the time to join us for this Full Committee hearing to discuss legislation to resolve Puerto Rico's political status.

For more than a century, Puerto Rico has been a U.S. territory subject to congressional authority derived from the Territory Clause of the U.S. Constitution. The Territory Clause grants Congress "Power to dispose of and make all needful Rules and Regulations respecting the Territory or other Property belonging to the United States."

The U.S.-Puerto Rico political relationship has been the subject of past discussion in this Committee. However, recent events reinforce our responsibility to reexamine the island's territory status.

First, a series of federal cases that affirmed the Commonwealth of Puerto Rico's subordinate status. For example, Sánchez Valle in 2016 in which the Supreme Court of the United States emphasized that—as a territory—the Commonwealth continues to derive its authority to govern from the U.S. Constitution, even after Congress approved the Commonwealth's own constitution in 1952.

Second, the Federal Government's enactment of PROMESA, which authorizes the President of the United States to appoint members to an Oversight Board with extraordinary powers over the decisions of the Commonwealth and the island's elected government officials.

Third, the government of Puerto Rico's decision to conduct a statehood yes-or-no plebiscite in November 2020.

Two pieces of legislation have been introduced this Congress to resolve Puerto Rico's political status—H.R. 2070, "Puerto Rico Self-Determination Act of 2021" by Representative Velázquez and H.R. 1522, "Puerto Rico Statehood Admission Act" by Representative Soto. Each piece of legislation proposes a different process to end the island's current territory status; Puerto Rico's options for a non-territory status are statehood, independence, and free association.

At the same time, there is existing legislation to address this issue. In 2014, Congress appropriated $2.5 million to be provided to the Puerto Rico State Elections Commission for voter education and to conduct a plebiscite by which Puerto Rican voters would determine the future political status of Puerto Rico. The U.S. Department of Justice is responsible for overseeing and administering the plebiscite.

Despite the different views of our witnesses today, I hope we can all agree that Congress has a responsibility to play a constructive role in the resolution of Puerto Rico's political status. We must work effectively together with the executive branch and the island's elected government officials through this process, while respecting the will of the residents of Puerto Rico.

I am committed to continue working with the Biden administration on this important matter and expanding access to Federal programs for residents of Puerto Rico and other U.S. Territories. The White House has already demonstrated willingness to expand programs such as the Child Tax Credit and the Earned Income Tax Credit in these jurisdictions, and I will continue advocating for equity in federal assistance under the Supplemental Security Income and Medicaid.

Now, I want to welcome our witnesses, most of which were suggested by the bill sponsors. Thank you for joining us. It is my hope that we will receive constructive feedback that will inspire the Federal Government to act and continue today's discussion, which is a priority for the people of Puerto Rico.

The CHAIRMAN. At this point, let me yield to the Ranking Member for comments. The floor is yours.

STATEMENT OF THE HON. JENNIFFER GONZÁLEZ-COLÓN, A RESIDENT COMMISSIONER IN CONGRESS FROM THE TERRITORY OF PUERTO RICO

Miss GONZÁLEZ-COLÓN. Thank you, Mr. Chairman. And first I would like to offer my deepest condolences on the recent passing of Alex Lofgren from your staff. My sympathies are with you, your office, and Alex's loved ones.

First of all, I want to thank you for calling on this important hearing that addresses the results of the November election in favor of statehood for Puerto Rico. Today, we will hear the testimony on two House bills, H.R. 1522, the Puerto Rico Statehood Admission Act and H.R. 2070.

H.R. 1522, introduced by Mr. Darren Soto, Florida, and myself, representing the island of Puerto Rico, elected to do so in Congress, would end Puerto Rico's territorial status, while the other bill is another tactic to delay the decolonization process and thus perpetuate the unequal treatment of the 3.2 million Americans that live on the island.

Let me be clear. There is nothing that this other bill, or this other legislation, will offer Puerto Rico that has not been already discussed in 123 years. It is nothing new.

Status convention, as proposed by that bill, creates a cumbersome process without any kind of timeline to completion and which problematically does not recognize that the only two non-territorial and constitutional status options are statehood and independence.

Not only that—the bill shamelessly ignores the will of the voters in Puerto Rico, ignores a legitimate democratic process, and ignores self-determination despite the bill's misleading title.

Letting the losing minority deny the clear choice of the majority in a free and fair vote is not democracy, and the United States must not take part in such an egregious act. That bill is truly a slap in the face to all Puerto Rican voters.

On the other hand, H.R. 1522 respects and upholds Puerto Rico's vote for statehood with the true and only self-determination method—and that is the ballot box.

Puerto Ricans have voted for statehood three times in elections that courts upheld: 2012, 2017 and again in 2020. On March 24, this year, the certified results of the Puerto Rico State Elections Commission on voter participation showcases that voter turnout was 73.15 percent. That is a higher voter turnout than we have seen here in the United States in decades.

The bipartisan bill—and I must say thank you to all Republicans and Democratic Members who are sponsoring Darren Soto's and the people of Puerto Rico's bill, which is H.R. 1522—would constitute Congress' response to our fellow citizens on the island and provide a formal offer of statehood. The legislation outlines a clear process to enable the island's admission into the Union, should it be ratified by Puerto Rico voters in a federally sponsored, yes-or-no referendum. This is exact same procedure that was established for Alaska and Hawaii prior to their admission as states. Statehood, I know, is going to happen. It is the logical next step in our political future as Americans.

Congress has the chance to make clear that when American citizens ask for equality and justice, they will get equality and justice as American citizens, not that we will welcome a proposal to make them be separate but equal like the other bills pretend.

The status quo is unsustainable, and until it is addressed, Puerto Rico's economy and social development will continue to lag behind the other 50 states, driving many Puerto Ricans to leave the island in search of better opportunities. An example of that is that, today, as we speak, 44 percent of the island's residents live under the poverty line.

For 140 years, the people of Puerto Rico have been proud American citizens, with over 235,000 having honorably served our nation in the U.S. Armed Forces, all while being denied equal participation in the Federal decision-making process.

Only statehood provides that equal participation, guarantees U.S. citizenship, and represents a permanent and constitutional solution for Puerto Rico's status issue. And that is the reason I am proud to join Mr. Darren Soto of Florida. We together are listening to the voters on the island, to the majority, to the will of the people of Puerto Rico. I am the one elected to represent them, and I am doing so by filing this bill. With that, Mr. Chairman, I yield back.

[The prepared statement of Miss González-Colón follows:]

Prepared Statement of the Hon. Jenniffer González-Colón, Resident Commissioner in Congress from Puerto Rico

Thank you, Mr. Chairman. I'd like to first offer my deepest condolences on the recent passing of Alex Lofgren from your staff. My sympathies are with you, your office and Alex's loved ones.

Mr. Chairman, thank you for calling on this important hearing that addresses the results of the November 3 election in favor of statehood for Puerto Rico.

Today, we will hear testimony on two House bills, H.R. 1522, the Puerto Rico Statehood Admission Act, and H.R. 2070.

H.R. 1522, introduced by Mr. Soto and I, would *end* Puerto Rico's centennial territorial status, while the other bill is another tactic to delay the decolonization process and thus perpetuate the unequal treatment of the 3.2 million Americans on the Island.

Let me be clear, there is nothing that this other legislation will offer to Puerto Rico that has not already been discussed in 123 years.

A status convention, as proposed by this bill, creates a cumbersome process without any kind of timeline to completion, and which problematically does not recognize that the only two non-territorial and constitutional status options are statehood and independence.

Not only that—the bill shamelessly ignores the will of voters in Puerto Rico, ignores a legitimate democratic process, and ignores self-determination, despite the bill's misleading title.

Letting the losing minority deny the clear choice of the majority in a free and fair vote isn't democracy, and the United States must not take part in such an egregious act!

That bill is truly a slap in the face to Puerto Rican voters!

On the other hand, H.R. 1522, respects and upholds Puerto Rico's vote for statehood with the *true and only* self-determination method, the ballot box. Puerto Ricans have voted for statehood three times in elections that the courts upheld.

The March 24 certified results of the Puerto Rico State Elections Commission on voter participation, showcases that voter turnout was 73.15%. That is a higher voter turnout than what we have seen here in the United States in decades.

The bipartisan H.R. 1522 would constitute Congress's response to our fellow citizens in Puerto Rico and provide a formal offer of statehood. The legislation outlines a clear process to enable the Island's admission into the Union, should it be ratified by Puerto Rico voters in a federally sponsored, yes-or-no referendum. This is the exact same procedure established for Alaska and Hawaii prior to their admission as States.

Statehood is going to happen. It is the logical next step in our political future as Americans.

Congress has the chance to make clear that when American citizens ask for equality and justice, they will get equality and justice as American Citizens. Not that we will welcome a proposal to make them be "separate but equal."

The status quo is unsustainable and until it is addressed, Puerto Rico's economy and social development will continue to lag behind that of the 50 states, driving Puerto Ricans to leave the Island in search of better opportunities. An example of this is how today, 44% of Island residents live under the poverty level.

For 104 years, the people of Puerto Rico have been proud American citizens, with over 235,000 having honorably served our Nation in the U.S. Armed Forces. All while being denied equal participation in the federal decision-making process.

Only statehood provides that equal participation, guarantees U.S. citizenship, and represents a permanent and constitutional solution to Puerto Rico's status issue.

Thank you, Mr. Chairman and I yield back.

The CHAIRMAN. The gentlelady yields back. And let me extend my appreciation for her comments regarding Mr. Lofgren, and your comments will extend to our staff. I appreciate it very much.

The Chair now recognizes the Full Committee Ranking Minority Member, Mr. Westerman, for any statement that he may make. Mr. Westerman, you are recognized.

VOICE. Mr. Westerman is getting connected, I think, right now.

The CHAIRMAN. OK. Mr. Westerman, you are recognized.

STATEMENT OF THE HON. BRUCE WESTERMAN, A REPRESENTATIVE IN CONGRESS FROM THE STATE OF ARKANSAS

Mr. WESTERMAN. Thank you, Chairman. Thank you for your patience. And I want to also thank the witnesses for being with us today. And again, with all the technical issues that we have with these virtual hearings, and given that most of us are now vaccinated, I sincerely hope that we can return to work in person soon.

At the end of the Spanish-American War in 1898, the United States acquired Puerto Rico along with several other islands. It wasn't until 1917 that Congress, through the Jones Act, extended U.S. citizenship to those residing in Puerto Rico. In 1950, Puerto Rico gained authority over its internal governance. And in 1952, its constitution was ratified by the United States.

After approval of the Puerto Rico Constitution, the island formally became known as the Commonwealth of Puerto Rico. At the time, this was another major step for Puerto Rico, but it did not resolve the relationship ambiguity with the United States, as some held that the "Commonwealth" provided Puerto Rico a status that was beyond territory but less than a state.

Recent Supreme Court decisions and enactment of PROMESA resulted in the legal determination that Puerto Rico is a U.S. territory. Puerto Rico has tried to gain consensus from its people on how to proceed on the status issue. On November 3, 2020, Puerto Rico held its sixth non-binding status referendum that asked voters in the territory one simple question: Should Puerto Rico be immediately admitted as a U.S. state?

The results of that vote were 52 percent or 655,000 people voting in favor of statehood and 47 percent voting against it. Today, we have two bills on the agenda. The first, H.R. 1522, attempts to build upon the November 2020 election. If enacted, the Puerto Rico voters would need to ratify being admitted to the Union. If a majority of Puerto Ricans vote no, nothing would happen, and the bill would cease to be effective.

The other bill before us today, H.R. 2070, seeks to establish a status convention, which would include Puerto Rican elected delegates who would define status options for Puerto Ricans to vote on. The status option chosen by voters would require ratification by Congress. Oddly, the sponsor is well intentioned to help Puerto Ricans, but it is unclear why electing delegates to lifetime terms, to define what status options are available, is necessary or accomplishes anything.

Additionally, the delegates would have to put forward status options for the people of Puerto Rico to vote on. However, the bill does not specify how and if those choices will be narrowed before selection or if they need to be voted on or unanimous. In fact, the status convention could be stymied by the same internal disagreement that is playing out between the current Puerto Rican political parties.

If the elections for the delegates are lopsided from one particular party, the other parties may disengage and eventually boycott the referendum, as has happened in the past.

I believe that it is undemocratic that delegates elected under this provision could receive a lifetime appointment, which could result in an endless cycle of debate.

Lastly, this bill raises significant concerns as the bill sponsor's intent is for the convention to consider statehood, independence, free association or "any option other than the current territorial agreement." However, there are no other options outside of statehood, independence, or free association.

If another option beyond these were selected, Congress would be in a position to potentially bring forward a status option that isn't attainable under the Constitution.

While I have reservations about this bill, I look forward to hearing from the witnesses and continuing to engage in meaningful dialogue so Congress can make informed decisions. Thank you, Mr. Chairman, and I yield back.

[The prepared statement of Mr. Westerman follows:]

PREPARED STATEMENT OF THE HON. BRUCE WESTERMAN, RANKING MEMBER, COMMITTEE ON NATURAL RESOURCES

Thank you, Chairman and thank you to the witnesses for being with us.

With the many technical issues this Committee has experienced with virtual hearings this year and given that most of us are now vaccinated, I sincerely hope we can return to work in person soon.

At the end of the Spanish American War in 1898, the United States acquired Puerto Rico along with several other Islands.

It wasn't until 1917 that Congress, through the Jones Act, extended U.S. citizenship to those residing in Puerto Rico.

In 1950, Puerto Rico gained authority over its internal governance and in 1952 its Constitution was ratified by the United States.

After approval of the Puerto Rico Constitution, the Island formally became known as the "Commonwealth of Puerto Rico."

At the time, this was a another major step for Puerto Rico but it did not resolve the relationship ambiguity with the United States, as some held that a "commonwealth" provided Puerto Rico a status that was beyond territory but less than a state.

Recent Supreme Court decisions and enactment of PROMESA resulted in the legal determination that Puerto Rico is a U.S. territory.

Puerto Rico has tried to gain consensus from its people on how to proceed on the status issue.

On November 3, 2020, Puerto Rico held its sixth nonbinding status referendum that asked voters in the territory one simple question: "Should Puerto Rico be immediately admitted as a U.S. State?

The results of the plebiscite were 52.52% (655,505) voting in favor of statehood and 47.48% (592,671) voting against it.

Today we have two bills on the agenda.

The first, H.R. 1522, attempts to build upon the November 2020 plebiscite. If enacted, the Puerto Rico voters would need to ratify being admitted to the Union. If a majority of Puerto Ricans vote no, nothing would happen, and the bill would cease to be effective.

The other bill before us today, H.R. 2070, seeks to establish a Status Convention, which would include Puerto Rican elected "delegates" who would define status options for Puerto Ricans to vote on. The status option chosen by voters would require ratification by Congress.

While I believe the sponsor is well intentioned to help Puerto Ricans, it is unclear why electing delegates to lifetime terms, to define what status options are available, is necessary or accomplishes anything.

Additionally, the "delegates" would have to put forward status options for the people of Puerto Rico to vote on. However, the bill does not specify how and if those choices will be narrowed down before selection or if they need to be voted on or unanimous.

In fact, the Status Convention could be stymied by the same internal disagreement that is playing out between the current Puerto Rican political parties.

If the elections for the "delegates" are lopsided for one particular party, the other parties may disengage and eventually boycott the referendum as has happened in the past.

I believe that it is undemocratic that delegates elected under this provision could receive a lifetime appointment, which could result in an endless cycle of debate.

Lastly, this bill raises significant concerns as the bill sponsor's intent is for the Convention to consider statehood, independence, free association, or "any option other than the current territorial agreement."

However, there are no "other" options outside of statehood, independence, or free association.

If another option beyond these were selected, Congress would be in a position to potentially bring forward a status option that isn't obtainable under the Constitution.

While I have reservations about this bill, I look forward to hearing from the witnesses and continuing to engage in meaningful dialogue so Congress can make informed decisions.

Thank you, Chairman. I yield back.

The CHAIRMAN. The Ranking Member yields, and the Chair now recognizes a sponsor of the legislation, Ms. Velázquez. You are recognized. The floor is yours.

STATEMENT OF THE HON. NYDIA VELÁZQUEZ, A REPRESENTATIVE IN CONGRESS FROM THE STATE OF NEW YORK

Ms. VELÁZQUEZ. Thank you, Mr. Chairman, and the Ranking Member for holding this very important hearing today. The topic at hand, the political status of Puerto Rico, is one of the most serious and consequential matters the Committee will consider.

Over 100 years ago, the United States invaded Puerto Rico. Despite the fact that Puerto Ricans are U.S. citizens and certain advances like the adoption of Puerto Rico's own constitution, the reality is that Puerto Rico remains at the mercy of the Federal Government. While we may not agree on the outcome, there is widespread agreement that the present political status should change.

Let me stress that any such process needs to be fair, inclusive, and democratic. That is the true nature of self-determination. Some have tried to blur self-determination for Puerto Rico with an admission process for the island as the 51st state. This is not only overly simplistic, but it is also wrong.

The conversation should not be about a process. It should be about a process that respects the will of the people and not how to stack the deck toward a particular status option, much less using millions of dollars in public funds to skew the outcome. This is not the same conversation as the push for DC statehood.

The history of the District of Columbia and the colonization of Puerto Rico are two very different realities, and we must consider that in this discussion. So, now Congress must take responsibility and enter into a serious dialogue with the Puerto Rican people.

I am very grateful for this hearing and to hear the many perspectives of our distinguished witnesses. Much of the conversation about Puerto Rico status is understandably focused on the outcome, be that statehood, independence, free association, or any other political arrangement. But I would like to take a second to discuss the importance of a transparent and inclusive democratic process. As such, I am proud that my bill, the Puerto Rico Self-Determination Act, establishes a fair and inclusive process by giving the Puerto Rican people the opportunity to make their voices heard in two open elections.

This bill recommends Puerto Rico's legislate the creation of an established convention whose delegates will be elected by Puerto Rican voters to develop a long-term solution for Puerto Rico's status. But most importantly, it will be drafted and ratified by and for Puerto Ricans. Unlike the bill being offered by my colleagues, the Self-Determination Act does not impose one option on the people of Puerto Rico. Instead, it allows for a thorough discussion about the implications of each of the status options and what transitional plans would look like.

Puerto Ricans have never had the benefit of having any of this information up front. Congress should commit itself to following through on the self-determination process that Puerto Rican people may embark on. I am grateful that the Puerto Rico Self-Determination Act is being co-led by Representative Ocasio-Cortez and has 17 additional House co-sponsors and counting.

This bill is also being led in the Senate by Senators Bob Menendez and Republican Senator Roger Wicker, along with their distinguished colleagues, Senators Sanders, Brown, Booker, Gillibrand, Warren, and Markey. This is a historic opportunity for the people of Puerto Rico, a moment to finally chart their own course. I am leading the chart on this bill so that we can once and for all address the question of Puerto Rico's political status in a manner that truly respects their will and aspirations.

I look forward to today's hearing, and I once again thank the Chairman and the Ranking Member. Now is the time to act. And this is a step toward meaningful progress. Thank you and I yield back.

The CHAIRMAN. The gentlelady yields back and thank you. Before I introduce our witnesses, just a commentary on the side. The sponsor of the legislation, Mr. Darren Soto—I will extend a courtesy when your time comes up in terms of questioning the witnesses or making a statement, extend the courtesy of some additional time insofar as, as a sponsor, we try to keep a balance as to both pieces of legislation, try to retain that.

I didn't recognize you as a sponsor of the legislation. For that, I will extend a courtesy when your opportunity comes up. And thank you very much for your cooperation in making sure that we take the balance of Members speaking to both pieces of legislation.

Before I introduce the witnesses, let me remind the witnesses that under our Committee Rules, we must limit their oral statements to 5 minutes but that their entire statement will appear in the hearing record.

When you begin, the timer will begin. And it will turn orange when you have 1 minute remaining. I recommend that Members and witnesses join remotely to using stage view so they can pin the timer on their screen.

After your testimony is complete, please remember to mute yourself to avoid any inadvertent background noise. I will also allow the entire panel to testify before questioning begins from the Members.

The Chair notes that Senator María de Lourdes Santiago is participating with the assistance of an interpreter. To ensure that Members hear from the witnesses, I will allow some extra time for opening statements so that she can hear the translation. This practice is under the Chair's recognition, as described in Committee Rule 4(a). I would also note that Members are encouraged to ask all questions in English to the Senator so that we can avoid any complications in terms of the translation that will be required.

With that, let me now turn to our first witness, the Hon. Pedro Pierluisi, Governor of Puerto Rico. We appreciate you very much, your attendance, Governor. And the floor is yours.

Statement of the Hon. Pedro R. Pierluisi, Governor of Puerto Rico, San Juan, Puerto Rico

Governor PIERLUISI. Thank you, Chairman Grijalva, Ranking Member González-Colón and members of the Committee.

For years, Congress has entertained the idea of putting an end to the unresolved issue of Puerto Rico's political status, but has failed. Some reasons, or excuses if you will, have included that Congress should not interfere, that no option had a majority, or that Puerto Ricans needed consensus. And many Members of Congress have preferred to take no position on the future of Puerto Rico's status, hiding behind their support for self-determination.

Things are different now. On November 3 of last year, the residents of Puerto Rico voted to resolve their status. The process was straightforward, an up-or-down, yes-or-no vote on statehood. It was a referendum much like any other territories had prior to becoming states. And the majority of the voters in Puerto Rico said yes to statehood. More Puerto Ricans voted for statehood than for any candidate running in that same election.

So, today, here we are again to discuss Puerto Rico's political future. I contend that we should only be discussing how to enable the freely and democratically expressed will of the American citizens of Puerto Rico. They deserve an answer to their request for statehood.

That is precisely what the Puerto Rico Statehood Admission Act does. As a self-executing legislation, the bill sets out the terms and conditions by which Puerto Rico could be admitted as a state, and presents a formal offer of statehood to the U.S. citizens of Puerto Rico who, in turn, are given the opportunity to accept or reject the admission in a final referendum.

If the majority votes again in favor of equality, Puerto Rico will begin a transition to statehood. Let me be clear. This bill does not force or impose statehood on Puerto Rico. It only offers statehood and provides a proven mechanism and a legal means for it to happen.

When statehood is granted, the U.S. citizens of Puerto Rico will have equal rights, equal responsibilities, and full representation in the U.S. Congress, and will be treated equally under all Federal laws, policies, and programs. Puerto Rico will also be able to participate in U.S. presidential elections to select the leaders that implement the laws that they live under.

Perhaps most importantly, for the very first time, the world's greatest democracy will offer equality to the U.S. citizens of Puerto Rico, who have been unequal to their fellow Americans for well over a century.

Unfortunately, we are also here today to discuss another bill which offers a convoluted process to deal with unknown status options or status options that Puerto Rico's voters have already rejected.

Those who did not like the people's choice in the November plebiscite, many who for years had dared proponents of statehood to carry out an up-or-down vote on statehood, now choose to ignore the results, change the process, and change the questions—anything to avoid accepting the will of the people.

H.R. 2070, ironically called the Puerto Rico Self-Determination Act, is the farthest thing from self-determination. It is the epitome of colonialism. It not only ignores the people's vote, but it also aims to tell Puerto Ricans what the process to express their will should be. That is not self-determination, that is an imposed determination. If you claim to favor self-determination, then you must support what Puerto Rico's voters freely determined. And that means admitting Puerto Rico as a state. You must take a stand on their choice.

In the late 1860s, Members of Congress just like you, against great opposition, stood on the right side of history and granted all men the right to vote, including African-Americans. In the early 1920s, Members of Congress just like you stood on the right side of history and granted women the right to vote. In 1964, Members of Congress just like you stood on the right side of history and voted to prohibit discrimination and segregation.

Our nation still has much to do to become a more perfect Union and to live up to the democratic ideals that are based on equality for all.

Now, the question I pose to you is: On which side of history will you stand? Will the position of this Committee, and of this Congress, be that American citizens who want full equality should be denied it? Will you tell the thousands of soldiers and veterans from Puerto Rico who have fought and died for those democratic ideals that they have not earned their right to be equal under the U.S. Constitution, that they must defend this country in war but cannot enjoy its democracy at home? Are you OK with telling their spouses, their children, and their widows and widowers that they do not deserve to vote for the president that sent them in harm's way?

This is not about whether you support self-determination. This is about whether, as Members of Congress, you are willing to stand on the side of equality and respect the results of our vote. My people and I will never consent to inequality. Inequality is un-American. And we must all stand against it.

That is why I stand in front of you today to speak for the American citizens of Puerto Rico who spoke with their vote. We deserve equality as American citizens, and we will not stop this fight until we achieve it.

Thank you very much.

[The prepared statement of Governor Pierluisi follows:]

PREPARED STATEMENT OF THE HON. PEDRO R. PIERLUISI, GOVERNOR OF PUERTO RICO

Introduction

Chairman Grijalva, Acting Ranking Member González-Colón, and Members of the Committee: Thank you for today's hearing on one of the most important and urgent matters facing the people of Puerto Rico, ending our colonial status. This topic is also of extreme importance to the United States. America has been a beacon of liberty and a champion for self-determination throughout the world for almost three centuries. There should be no room in the American family for colonialism, especially when on three occasions in the last decade, a clear majority of the U.S. citizens in Puerto Rico have exercised their right of self-determination in favor of becoming a state of this Union.

For years, Congress has entertained the idea of putting an end to the unresolved issue of Puerto Rico's political status but has failed. Some reasons, or excuses, if you will, have included that Congress should not interfere, that no option had a majority, or that Puerto Ricans needed consensus. And many Members of Congress have preferred to take no position on the future of Puerto Rico's status and to hide behind support for self-determination.

The governing relationship between Puerto Rico and the United States has been the subject of extensive study and debate. What has emerged over the past self-determination exercises is an expression of the unmistakable desire of the residents of Puerto Rico to become a state.

Things are different now. As you know, on November 3 of last year, the residents of Puerto Rico went to the polls and voted to resolve our status. The process was clear and straightforward. An up or down, yes or no, vote on statehood. It was a referendum much like many other territories had prior to becoming states. And the majority of the voters in Puerto Rico said yes to statehood. More Puerto Ricans voted for statehood than for any candidate running in that same election.

So, we are here before this Committee again to discuss our political future. I contend that we should only be discussing how to enable the people's choice, the freely and democratically expressed will of the American citizens of Puerto Rico. We should be discussing how to best respond to their request for statehood.

This is not the time for another protracted and convoluted process to debate the options. The voters have spoken clearly, and it is time for Congress to accept the results.

After almost 125 years of colonial status as a U.S. territory, the American citizens of Puerto Rico favor equality in all respects with their fellow Americans in the 50 states and are ready to begin their own transition to statehood.

The Right to Vote as a Fundamental Human Right

This urgent issue comes before the Committee at a time when the United States is engaged in a great national debate over voting, the most important right we have to shape our political destiny. This hearing adds to that debate the fact that 21 years into the 21st century, in the United States, approximately 3.1 million U.S. citizens—the majority of whom are Hispanic and bilingual and, as such, ethnic and linguistic minorities within the United States—have no domestic legally recognized right to vote for their country's President and Vice President or any voting representation in the House or Senate. In Puerto Rico's case, this is not about the mechanism of voting but the denial of that right altogether.

The right to vote, to participate in politics, and to shape the direction of the democracy we share and to which all Americans have a duty of loyalty and a responsibility to support are internationally recognized as *fundamental human rights.* These rights are among the most important human rights because, through them, citizens are able to hold their governments accountable and help shape government policies.

These rights constitute an acknowledgment that people are entitled to be masters of their fate by participating directly in the decisions that fundamentally affect their lives. Securing and protecting these rights are the keystone for a system in which all other human rights are respected.

I come before you today to express the will of the people of Puerto Rico, to demand that Congress move forward on the statehood admission process they support, and to end the era in which Puerto Rico has been an exception to America's legacy of supporting self-determination at home and overseas.

Puerto Rico's History as a Territory of the United States

Puerto Rico has been a territory of the United States since 1898, and we have waited longer than any other territory to finally and fully resolve our status within the Union. The Treaty of Paris, which formally ended the Spanish-American War, provided in its Article IX that "[t]he civil rights and political status of the native inhabitants of the territories hereby ceded to the United States [including Puerto Rico] shall be determined by the Congress."

During the first 2 years after the end of the Hispanic-American war, the United States administered Puerto Rico as a military protectorate.

In 1900, the U.S. Congress passed the Foraker Act, which replaced the military government with a civilian one, established a Governor and an Executive Council, a popularly elected legislature, a judicial system, and a non-voting delegate to Congress called "Resident Commissioner," who remains to this day.

In 1917, the United States conferred United States citizenship on all Puerto Ricans through the passage of the Jones-Shafroth Act. The Jones Act also replaced the Executive Council with a popularly elected Senate. The Governor, however, remained a U.S. Presidential appointment.

Despite the unsettled nature of our own status over this period, Puerto Ricans have served, fought, and died for the cause of freedom and democracy in every military conflict since we became a territory and many with great distinction. But, at the national level, our Federal Government denies them the legally recognized right to vote for their Commander-in-Chief and has yet to give serious consideration to the process that will provide us with the right to voting representation in Congress and to participate in the future of our Nation.

Although I served in this House for 8 years representing the largest single constituency among my colleagues, just as our Resident Commissioner Jenniffer González does now, I had to stand by as they voted for legislation in the House that affected all Americans, including the American citizens in Puerto Rico. For many years, the reason we were given for the extension of our colonial status, was that the will of the people of Puerto Rico as to their status, was unclear. That is not the case today by any means.

The process that begins today in this Committee must be definitive. The time for debate and study about what to do has passed. Now, in this Congress is time to end the denial of these fundamental political, civil, and human rights to the United States citizens living in Puerto Rico.

The Puerto Rico Statehood Admission Act

Puerto Ricans are deeply proud to be American citizens and have contributed to this Nation in countless ways since 1898. Yet, no territory of the United States has waited longer than Puerto Rico to bring an end to its colonial status.

I ask you, both on behalf of your fellow Americans in Puerto Rico, and as a clear way to strengthen democracy for all Americans, to respond to the will of the people of Puerto Rico by approving legislation that will initiate the admission of Puerto Rico as a state.

The only acceptable response to this clear expression of a desire for permanent status as a state of the Union is the enactment of H.R. 1522, the Puerto Rico Statehood Admission Act, sponsored by Resident Commissioner Jenniffer González-Colón and Congressman Darren Soto, and S. 780, as introduced in the Senate by Senator Martin Heinrich, and others.

Under this legislation, Congress would set out the terms and conditions under which Puerto Rico would be admitted as a state and presents a formal offer of statehood to the U.S. citizens of Puerto Rico who, in turn, would be given the opportunity to accept or reject admission in a final referendum before admission is proclaimed.

The Puerto Rico Statehood Admission Act is self-executing. If the majority votes (again) in favor of equality, the territory's days would be over, and Puerto Rico would begin a transition to statehood.

Conversely, if a majority were to reject statehood, then the island would remain a territory with the option to pursue sovereignty, through nationhood, at any time in the future. Let me be clear—this bill does not force or impose statehood on Puerto Rico, it only offers statehood, as the majority wants it, and provides a proven mechanism and the legal means for it to finally happen.

When statehood is granted, the U.S. citizens of Puerto Rico will have equal rights, equal responsibilities, and full representation in the U.S. Congress, which enacts the federal laws that affect their daily lives. Puerto Rico would also be able to participate in U.S. Presidential elections to select the federal executive that implements the laws they live under. Puerto Rico would be treated equally under all federal laws, policies, and programs.

Perhaps most importantly, under this legislation, for the very first time, the world's oldest and greatest democracy would offer equality to citizens who have been unequal to their fellow Americans for well over a century.

Constitutionally, there are only two status options available: statehood and nationhood. The former embodies the equality that Puerto Ricans have voted for now in three successive referenda. The latter, however, as its supporters try to label it, would be based on a relationship outside of the Territorial Clause and the U.S. Constitution. Effectively removing Puerto Rico from being a part of the United States and the eventual loss of our American citizenship. A third option, the current territorial status—unequal, colonial, and unworthy of the United States—given that those subject to it have petitioned their Government for its rejection in favor of full equality.

When you consider this legislation, I ask you to think about how your own constituents would feel if their full rights as Americans were still in question after being a part of the United States for well over a century and after they voted three times in the past decade for statehood.

How would they feel if the response from Congress was to set aside their expressions of self-determination by favoring competing legislation that has no real purpose but to delay (rather than to respect) the clear determination of your constituents to enjoy the full benefits of U.S. citizenship? While we live and work in the greatest democracy the world has ever known, there remains some work to be done to perfect our democracy, and the appropriate way to respond to the expressed and repeated desire of the voters of Puerto Rico is to begin the statehood admission process that they have voted for.

Your support for the Puerto Rico Statehood Admission Act will reaffirm the most sacred principles upon which our system of government was founded and strengthen our democracy. It will also reaffirm to our allies and to those nations under the duress of governments that reject democracy that America lives up to the principles that it has fought to protect since its foundation.

The Puerto Rico Self-Determination Act Does Not Confer Additional Rights nor Does It Advance a Resolution to the Puerto Rico Status Question

Unfortunately, we are also here today to discuss another bill that offers a convoluted process to include unknown options or other routes that Puerto Rico's voters have already rejected. Those who did not like the people's choice in the November plebiscite, many who for years had dared proponents of statehood to carry out an up or down vote on statehood, now choose to ignore the results, change the process, and change the questions. Anything to avoid accepting the will of the people.

H.R. 2070, ironically called the Puerto Rico Self Determination Act, is the farthest thing from self-determination. It is the epitome of colonialism. It not only ignores the people's vote, but it also aims to tell Puerto Ricans what the process to express our will should be. That is not self-determination; that is an imposed determination.

While I respect those who advocate otherwise here today, I emphasize that the Puerto Rican people have made a clear, democratic choice for statehood, and there can be no doubt about where the American citizens of Puerto Rico stand. First, in 2012, a clear majority, over 54% of the voters, rejected Puerto Rico's current territorial status, and now a clear majority, almost 53%, have chosen statehood for Puerto Rico.

In some instances in our history, Congress has moved territories toward statehood without a clear expression of the popular will of the citizens living in those territories, and some territories have been forced into statehood against the popular will. But when the popular will clearly has been expressed, it is Congress' responsibility to respond to that vote and to reject proposals that would perpetuate a colonial status in the guise of promoting yet another complicated and totally superfluous process of "self-determination."

H.R. 2070 and S. 865, as introduced in the House and Senate by Representatives Velázquez, Ocasio-Cortez, and Senator Menéndez, includes the utilization of a voting method that is unknown and that has never been used in Puerto Rico.

Their proposed legislation is also non-binding, which means that even if we go through the complete set of convoluted processes included in their bill, Congress may or may not choose to approve the option chosen by voters.

Even worse, their bill does not define any of the possible status options to be voted on or say how many could be presented to voters, leaving it up to a "Status Convention." Let me be clear: However proponents of this alternative approach to label it, anything short of statehood is colonial and unequal. Within the Constitution, there is statehood, independence, and a territorial status that historically has been viewed as temporary. It is highly misleading that the sponsors of this legislation continue to hold open the possibility of Congress considering "any option other than the current territorial arrangement," even though there are no other constitutionally valid alternatives to the territory status beyond statehood or nationhood.

The Puerto Rico Self-Determination Act lacks a clear timeline for execution. It would be cruel to have our people, the constituents I represent, go through years of endless debates and back and forth engagements with Congress, only to be left out in the end with no response to their clear intention to move toward equality and statehood.

Proponents of this bill argue that Puerto Rico's case is different from the U.S. citizens living in Washington, DC. That we have a different culture and a "unique Caribbean heritage that existed long before it was forcibly seized by the United States."

By doing so, they seem to adopt the same reasoning used by racist and xenophobic Justices of the Supreme Court in the early 20th century that decided the infamous *Insular Cases*. These cases invented the concept of the "unincorporated territory"— a territory of the United States not destined for statehood—in which only those constitutional protections extended to it by Congress and/or otherwise recognized as fundamental by the domestic courts apply in the territory.

It is precisely this same school of thinking that brought the conditions—which can only be changed by Congress—which cemented Puerto Rico's second-class U.S. citizenship. That is the historical record. You cannot shy away from it. The Court went as far as stating that Puerto Rico was "inhabited by alien races, differing from us in religion, customs, laws, and modes of thought, [the result of which] the administration of government and justice, according to Anglo-Saxon principles, may for a time be impossible."

Certainly, the American citizens of Puerto Rico are no less citizens of the United States than those living in the District of Columbia or, for that matter, than those living anywhere in the United States. As such, the U.S. citizens in Puerto Rico do not deserve any less protection from this Congress than our brothers and sisters from Washington DC.

In fact, these principles, and the current colonial status, make no sense because Puerto Ricans, by virtue of their American citizenship, can simply come to the mainland and acquire the rights they are denied in Puerto Rico. Why should the rights of any American citizen be defined by location?

Moreover, despite the offensive language in the Insular Cases, we must all agree that America is made up and strengthened by the grand and vast variety of cultures and customs of its people.

Just visit the home states of the primary sponsors of the so-called "Self-Determination Act," and what do you see? People united by their love and devotion to the United States, that freely and actively celebrate their heritage they and their ancestors brought to this Nation, often under great sacrifice and duress. New York is like any American state; on any given day, you see people celebrating their heritage. The people of Puerto Rico voted for statehood because they realize that they have nothing to lose through statehood while gaining equality. Those who support any other approach would deny them the fundamental rights of our democracy.

It is highly doubtful that the original framers of the U.S. Constitution ever envisioned or would have approved a system where territories are held in perpetuity while permanently denying any voting participation to their inhabitants. After all, these imperialistic views are precisely what the 13 colonies rebelled against.

The differential treatment in voting rights between citizens of the 50 states, the District of Columbia, and Puerto Rico lacks any objective or reasonable justification. A citizen is a citizen regardless of the citizen's place of residence within the territorial jurisdiction of his or her state.

Support for Statehood Has Never Been Greater and the Time to Act Is Now

If you claim to favor self-determination, then you must support what Puerto Rico's voters freely determined, and that means admitting Puerto Rico as a state. You must take a stand and support their choice.

I hear some say that we need to wait until we reach a "consensus." Those of us who want equality can never consent to discrimination and unequal treatment. There can never be consensus for second-class citizenship—the majority rules in our democratic system. And the majority of the American citizens residing in Puerto Rico want equality, which can only be conferred through statehood.

We had the courage to hold an up or down vote on statehood, and the people voted affirmatively. Statehood received more votes than any candidate or political party in Puerto Rico (by more than 200,000 votes, a substantial number). Statehood won in every single senatorial district and in 33 of 40 house districts. We must respect this sacred mandate and abide by the will of the people.

We ask Congress to seek that same courage, to provide an answer, and to respect the will of the American citizens of Puerto Rico. The fight for equality is a matter of civil and human rights. A proposal for an entirely new process, which is not binding, with no clear options, with delegates elected in perpetuity, with no timelines for execution, because some did not like the results, shows a lack of respect to the people of Puerto Rico.

I commend Congresswoman Jenniffer González-Colón, Puerto Rico's sole representative in Congress, and Congressman Darren Soto, for introducing a status bill that actually represents and defends the will of the people.

I urge this Honorable Committee to not turn its back on us and look the other way. The source of your power to rule over Puerto Rico stems from Article IV, Section 3 of the U.S. Constitution, which reads: "Congress shall have power to dispose of and make all needful rules and regulations respecting the territory *or other property* belonging to the United States . . ."

"Other . . . *property,*" ladies and gentlemen . . .

Not long ago, a former state senator from Puerto Rico—who is not a statehood advocate—appeared before this Committee and read you that same Constitutional clause.

We demand that you start treating us as equals and stop treating us as property. Contrary to what the Insular Cases and its new modern progeny in Congress believe, we do not belong to the United States. We are an integral and fundamental part of it.

Inequality is un-American.

And we must all stand against it.

That is why I stand in front of you today to speak for the American citizens of Puerto Rico who spoke with their vote.

We deserve equality as American citizens. And we will not stop this fight until we achieve it.

Thank you.

The CHAIRMAN. Thank you very much, Governor. The Chair now recognizes Ms. Johanne Vélez-Garćıa, Vice President of the Puerto Rico Democratic Party. Ms. Vélez-Garćıa, the time is yours.

STATEMENT OF JOHANNE VÉLEZ-GARCÍA, VICE PRESIDENT, PUERTO RICO DEMOCRATIC PARTY, SAN JUAN, PUERTO RICO

Ms. VÉLEZ-GARĆIA. Thank you, Mr. Chairman, Commissioner, and distinguished Members. I have devoted my life to advocacy for equality for more than 25 years, primarily women's and LGBTQ rights. After going to New York to marry, my wife and I joined others in a Federal suit to end Puerto Rico's discriminatory same-sex marriage ban. In 2017, I was appointed President of the first Governor's Advisory Council on LGBTQ Affairs in the territory and first elected Democratic Party Vice Chair.

Puerto Rico's unequal status, denying equality to more than 3.2 million Americans, is the biggest contradiction to the U.S. status as a democracy.

Testifying in this first panel before you today are four American citizens, of which two are your equals and two are not. The Governor of Puerto Rico and myself, like our fellow Puerto Rican residents in the island, are second-class citizens since we do not live in a state, whereas the other two panelists who live in the mainland have their full-fledged U.S. citizen rights. The shameful colonial status under which the residents of the island are not recognized as equals must end.

H.R. 1522 by Representative Soto would honor the majority self-determination choice of Puerto Ricans for equality within the nation. It follows free and fair votes in 2012 and 2017 on all of the possible options that chose statehood. Because boycotts urged by the opponents who knew they would lose diminished the number of votes, our elected representatives got a simple vote in 2020 on statehood, as had been held in other territories.

The various opponents thought that together they could win and stage a big campaign. Virtually as many people voted as voted for any local office, a greater percentage than in the statehood votes of many territories. And statehood won by an unequivocal margin. Now, minority opponents want you to ignore the purest possible form of self-determination, a democratic choice in a process determined by elected representatives.

H.R. 2070 tries to pressure the territory into conducting a process that our elected government has declined to adopt and has no purpose other than a desperate attempt to embarrass the United States into accepting a status proposal that successive congressional committees and administrations of both national parties have said is impossible for constitutional and other reasons.

Accepting the results of an election in 2020 was a national issue. Democrats, and I trust most Republicans, accept fair votes. The 2016 PROMESA law, which originated in this Committee, recognized that, "Puerto Rico's right to determine its future political status," among the possible options by its own method of choice. All should now respect Puerto Rico's self-determination.

H.R. 2070 invites status proposals that are not possible under the Constitution and the basic policies of the United States. The primary authors call these "any other non-territorial status" in addition to statehood and the nationhood options. Such "commonwealth status" proposals are the exact reason that the issue of Puerto Rico's status has not been resolved and that Puerto Rico remains a colonial territory.

H.R. 2070 would authorize certain Members of Congress to tell Puerto Ricans what their culture and language should be. It would be outrageous if the entire U.S. Government tried. It couldn't constitutionally in a state or practically in a nation.

H.R. 2070 absurdly proposes to force the full Congress to vote on changes in a wide range of Federal laws proposed by Puerto Rico without consideration by committees of jurisdiction or amendment and only minimal debate. This alone should be enough to show it for what it is, a ruse to prevent democracy, equality, and self-determination for Puerto Ricans. Thank you for inviting me to testify for you today.

[The prepared statement of Ms. Vélez-Garćıa follows:]

Prepared Statement of Ms. Johanne Vélez-Garćia, Vice Chair, Democratic Party of Puerto Rico

I am pleased to today to join the Governor of Puerto Rico and so many distinguished witnesses today to discuss my views on the two pending bills today before the House Natural Resources Committee on Puerto Rico's political status.

For over 25 years now, I have been an advocate for equality. My activism has primarily addressed women's and LGBTQ rights. In 2014, 2 years after getting married in New York City, my wife and I joined five other couples in a federal court suit to end the discriminatory marriage ban for same-sex couples in Puerto Rico. In 2016, halfway through a tough at-large primary, I realized I had become the first openly lesbian woman to run for an elected position in Puerto Rico. And although I did not prevail in that run, history has its interesting turn of events, and in 2017, became the president of the first ever Governor's Advisory Council on LGBTQ Affairs in Puerto Rico and Vice Chair of the Democratic Party of Puerto Rico. So, you see, the defense of equality is activism, advocacy, public policy, legislation, and more than anything, a commitment to further the full rights of every person in our democracy.

Testifying in this first panel before you today, are four American citizens of which two are your equals, and two are not. The Governor of Puerto Rico, and myself, like our fellow Puerto Ricans in the island, are second-class citizens since we do not live in a State. Whereas the other two panelists who live in the mainland have their full-fledged U.S. citizens' rights. The shameful colonial status under which the residents of the island are not recognized as equals, must end.

During the last few months, the need to resolve Puerto Rico's unequal and undemocratic status as a territory has gotten increased attention with the introduction of Puerto Rico Statehood Admission Act and the Puerto Rico Self-Determination Act. Given the many ways that Puerto Rico's territory has become unsustainable for both the island residents and the Federal Government, all efforts to end the dysfunctional territorial status are worth considering.

The first bill sponsored by Congressman Darren Soto (H.R. 1522) is based on a response to several referendums in which Puerto Rican voters went to the polls to express their views on the preferred political status. This bill is straightforward, and it clearly defines the terms for Puerto Rico to become a state. The Soto bill offers the island a federal sanctioned Yes or No vote on statehood and if a majority chose "YES" then Puerto Rico becomes a state after a brief transition, without the need for further congressional action. If voters chose "NO" then the island remains a territory and can then choose to pursue independence or sovereignty with free association at any point in the future.

I think it is important for the members of the Committee to understand how we got to this point and real reasons we are discussing two bills today. In 2012, 2017 and 2020, Puerto Rico voters supported statehood over the other status options. In the 2012 and 2017 referendums, the supporters of Commonwealth and Independence protested the structure of the ballot and opposed how these options were defined. These two plebiscites were based on the status options approved by various congressional committees and successive Administrations of both parties which said were valid Constitutional options. The anti-statehood parties urged their supporters to boycott the referendum since they could not define their preferred options anyway they wanted. But as Congressman Soto said after the 2017 plebiscite, choosing to boycott a vote on Puerto Rico's political status is a choice in itself.

In 2020, this was not the case. Due to largely to the complaints of the antistatehood parties of the previous two plebiscites, the Governor and Legislature of Puerto Rico decided to offer the voters of Puerto Rico a clear and simple choice, "Statehood Yes or No." Virtually as many people voted in the plebiscite as voted for any local office. Many of the political leaders of Puerto Rico might disagree how to define Commonwealth or the current territorial status but generally everyone agrees what Statehood for Puerto Rico means. The Statehood Yes or No referendum was also based on similar votes that dozens previous territories held in petitioning Congress for statehood. The participation percentage on this vote was greater than similar votes in many territories.

Unlike the 2012 and 2017 referendums, the anti-statehood parties did not boycott the 2020 referendum. They officially registered in Puerto Rico to represent the "No" option. The Commonwealth and Independence parties as well as other anti-statehood parties actively campaigned and urged their supporters to vote No. Congresswoman Velázquez who is the main sponsor of the other bill which I will soon discuss came to Puerto Rico and urged voters to reject statehood.

Despite a well-run and well-funded campaign by the opposition, Statehood won nearly 53% of the vote. The statehood option received a greater percentage of the vote than even our distinguished Governor and Resident Commissioner who are with us today. For the third consecutive time, the voters clearly chose statehood as the preferred status option.

Let us spend a few minutes talking about why I believe statehood won again last year. A clear majority of people in Puerto Rico understand that the current Commonwealth territorial status has failed us. Our economy has been in decline or stagnant for decades. The only way we have been able to provide basic services to its people is by selling bonds to investors on Wall Street. In 2016, it finally became apparent Puerto Rico was borrowing well-beyond its means and Congress had to pass a new law creating a federal control board of oversee Puerto Rico's finance. The following year, Puerto Rico was devastated by Hurricane Maria and the federal response led by the Trump Administration left a lot to be desired to say the least. Even before the fiscal crisis and Hurricane Maria, the trend was for hundreds of thousands of Puerto Ricans to leave the island and move to the mainland United States. Obviously, most of the people leaving the island support Statehood since they voted for Statehood, as we say in Puerto Rico, with their feet. With the all the people moving the mainland United States, it is amazing to me that Statehood still won by such a clear majority.

So why did statehood did win again last year. The people of Puerto Rico know that the current political status no longer works for them. In order for our economy to grow, we need a permanent political status. We will never see real economic growth and stability if we have come to Congress each year asking for more federal benefits such as help for our almost bankrupt Medicaid system. We cannot depend on Congress creating tax incentives, which often change, to encourage big U.S. corporations to set up a plant on the island and provide a few hundred jobs. A majority of Puerto Ricans know that the only hope to rebuild our economy is become fully part of the United States through statehood. Only through statehood will we have full equality as Americans and sending

Senators and Congresspersons to Washington will have a chance to make sure our people to fully benefit as American citizens.

So how should the Democratic Party and its elected representatives respond to the people of Puerto Rico clearly choosing statehood once again. All the recent Democratic party platforms have clearly stated it is up to Puerto Rico to choose its own political status and once the voters choose a preferred status the Congress should respond accordingly. President Biden said during the campaign that he prefers statehood for Puerto Rico and, if voters choose this option, Congress should respond by granting Puerto Rico their preferred status option. When he gave John Lewis's eulogy last year, former President Obama said only statehood would give Puerto Rico have full equality. Senate Majority Leader Schumer said last year, "if Puerto Rico chooses statehood, I would be glad to offer it."

How can the Democrats in Congress and on this Committee ignore the will of the people of Puerto Rico? All throughout this country, we as Democrats, are fighting the efforts of former President Trump and his GOP allies to pass new voter suppression bills. I am sure every Democrat on this Committee opposes the new Georgia law and other efforts in Texas and other states to pass new state laws making it harder to vote. Would not ignoring the recent referendum vote in Puerto Rico be another form of voter suppression? All Democrats opposed President Trump's efforts after the 2020 election when he claimed there was widespread voter fraud and he tried to overturn a legitimate election. No one is claiming there was voter fraud in the 2020 referendum vote. Just like Trump did after the November vote, the opponents of statehood just cannot accept they lost so they just ask you to ignore that Statehood won. There can no purer self-determination process than the people voting on questions posed by their elected representatives.

As I see it, the Soto bill is response to the people of Puerto Rico choosing its preferred status in fair and legitimate election. As it has in the past when other territories petitioned for statehood, Congress would establish a formal process to consider statehood for Puerto Rico. If Puerto Rico again chooses statehood for the 4th time, this bill would set a process in which the President, executive branch and Congress would change the relevant U.S. laws and regulations so the island would be treated fully and equally as the other 50 states. This bill is an appropriate and equitable response the people choosing statehood and respecting long held traditions of the Democratic Party.

I would like to spend the rest of my time today addressing the details of the other bill before the Committee today. This legislation is sponsored by Congresswoman Nydia Velázquez and known as the Puerto Rico Self-Determination Act. This bill creates such an unprecedented process that it is so complicated and ambiguous it does not even say how many status options should be considered, what their definitions will be, or when voters will have a chance to vote on them. Despite its title, this bill has little or nothing to deal with true self-determination. If you carefully read the bill and understand the full meaning of many of its key provisions, it is a pro status quo bill, a pro territorial option bill and an anti-statehood bill.

This bill would ignore the free and fair votes of Puerto Ricans, upheld by the Federal Court as well as the insular Supreme Court. It attempts to pressure the territory into conducting a status process that the Government of Puerto Rico has declined to adopt for decades. While the bill recognizes the inherent authority of the Puerto Rico legislature to call for a status convention, it specifically ignores that Puerto Rico has already legislated three laws and carried out three plebiscites over the last 10 years. Specifically, it ignores that these votes have shown, with increasing clarity, that a majority in Puerto Rico rejects the current territory status and favors statehood for its future.

As we did after the 2020 election all across the country, Democrats respect democratic election results and should respect Puerto Rico's decision on how to exercise its own self-determination.

The Velázquez bill would include status proposals that are not possible which prolong the current territorial status that the voters of Puerto Rico have already rejected three consecutive times. This bill claims that the status options which should be considered are statehood, independence, free association, and "any other non-territorial status." This committee and every Administration has always made it clear that other than the current territorial status there are only three real options: statehood, independence and free association.

This bill also calls for amending many Federal laws as unilaterally drafted by a convention in Puerto Rico without the committees of jurisdiction of either House in Congress being able make any changes. How can this committee consider this bill which basically grants its authority to a convention of elected representatives on the island? Will the House Ways and Means Committee allow this Convention to rewrite all the tax laws to the island? The bill requires both the Senate and House to vote up or down on whatever this Convention decides without the right to make any changes. Why would any Congress seriously consider any bill which limits its own authority and granting its power to a territory decide what status option it prefers without any real opportunity to review the decision.

Another difference in these bills is timeline. The Statehood bill sets out a flexible yet structured timeline that would allow voters in Puerto Rico to choose in a matter of months and see the results implemented in a few months thereafter. On the other hand, the so-call "Self-Determination" bill has no start or end date for the status convention. It does not say when Puerto Rican residents will be allowed to vote on the options and even if Congress ratifies the final choice by voters, it does not indicate how long any transition out of the territory status would take. So as one prominent bill supporter said, "the Velázquez and Ocasio-Cortez legislation would start a process that could take years."

To prove to how biased this bill is against statehood it also calls for a congressional commission to make recommendations to Puerto Rico on its culture, language and other matters as a State or Nation. As we all know, the language or culture of a territory or state is not within the jurisdiction of the U.S. Government under the Constitution or international law. So why did the sponsors of this bill add this provision? It was simply included to scare the voters of the island that they could lose their identity as Puerto Ricans if they chose statehood.

The main premise of the bill is that the people of Puerto Rico should hold a status Convention of elected representatives who would serve indefinitely without ever having to run for re-election. If you understand anything about Puerto Rico politics and the disagreements of over political status, this Convention proposal is just simply ridiculous. As we saw during the 2012 and 2017 referendums, the political parties will never be able to come to an agreement on how to define the current political status. What would a Status Convention achieve? The clear answer is absolutely nothing. The Convention concept proposed sounds good in theory but is just a way to block statehood and protect the same territorial status that the voters have already rejected.

So, you might ask yourself, why cannot the political parties in Puerto Rico agree on the real status options. Despite numerous Supreme Court cases, some prominent leaders in the Commonwealth party do not even believe Puerto Rico is a territory. Some Free Association and Independence leaders claim Puerto Rico could become its own nation, but every Puerto Rican can keep their U.S. citizenship. Under the U.S. Constitution, only Congress under the territorial clause gets to decide these fundamental issues. These political fights and disagreements on status issues have been going on in Puerto Rico for over 50 years since we have our first status referendum in 1967. So, what could possibly be achieved by requiring us to hold status convention? Absolutely nothing.

I urge the members of this Committee to review both bills carefully and understand the true meaning of each bill and what process these proposed laws would establish. The Soto bill is a true response to the most recent referendum in which the voters of Puerto Rico clearly chose statehood. This bill respects the jurisdiction of congressional committees, the previous bipartisan bills approved by this committee, and long traditions of the Democratic Party to support voting rights and the will of the majority of voters in a territory or state. The Velázquez bill does the complete opposite, and creates an unfair process that Congress has never imposed on any territory petitioning for statehood.

While there could still be room for improvement in the Statehood Admissions Act, the flaws in the Self Determination bill are numerous and self-evident. If Members of Congress are serious about ending Puerto Rico's outdated colonial territory status, they must listen to what the majority of the islands voters already said, and make the most logical and effective choice to support and approve the Puerto Rico Statehood Admissions Act.

The 3.1 million Puerto Ricans living on the island are proud Americans. Polls show that over 90% of the people in Puerto Rico cherish their U.S. citizenship. Please consider legislation which only respects us as full Americans and our right to true self determination. I passionately believe that if Congress approves the Soto bill and offers Puerto Rico a real path to statehood it would be overwhelmingly approved by the voters of Puerto Rico. Thank you for allowing me to testify today and offering my own views on the most important issue facing the people of Puerto Rico.

The CHAIRMAN. Thank you very much. The Chair now recognizes Mr. José Fuentes, Chair of the Puerto Rico Statehood Council. The time is yours.

STATEMENT OF JOSÉ FUENTES AGOSTINI, CHAIR, PUERTO RICO STATEHOOD COUNCIL, WASHINGTON, DC

Mr. FUENTES. Thank you, Chairman Grijalva, Ranking Member Westerman and distinguished members of this Committee. I am honored to appear before you as former Attorney General of Puerto Rico and Chairman of the Puerto Rico Statehood Council.

I speak today in support of the Puerto Rico Statehood Admission Act, which proposes a constitutionally sound process respecting the will of the majority of voters in Puerto Rico. I last testified in Congress on this issue 23 years ago after this House passed bipartisan legislation sponsored by Congressman Don Young to hold a plebiscite in Puerto Rico offering voters the only options available to them under the U.S. Constitution. That is statehood, independence with free association, or remaining a U.S. territory. Speaker Newt Gingrich led House consideration of the bill, which died in the Senate, but kicked off over two decades of bipartisan progress toward a more complete American democracy and Puerto Rican statehood.

After the U.S. Senate failed to act on the Young bill in December 1998, Puerto Rico held a plebiscite presenting all the constitutionally viable alternatives. The Puerto Rican electorate rejected the current territorial status and all the constitutional options. That prompted President Bill Clinton to establish the President's Task Force on Puerto Rico status to clarify both the status options available for Puerto Rico and the process to realize these options.

President George W. Bush continued this initiative and consulted extensively with stakeholders. In December 2005, the Task Force published a report outlining a process to resolve Puerto Rico's ultimate status. It was the most complete analysis of the status issue under any president. Its findings remain relevant today, calling for a two-step self-determination process authorized by Congress.

First, Puerto Rico's voters would be asked whether they wish to remain a territory. If voters elected to remain a territory, then they should be asked the same question periodically to ensure continued consent of the governed, something we clearly do not have today. However, if voters opted to change, the report called for another plebiscite to choose between the only permanent non-territorial options, statehood, independence, or free association.

These options are the only viable alternatives to territory status under the U.S. Constitution, period, full stop. There is nothing else. This has been confirmed by the Supreme Court, Department of Justice, this Congress, and every White House since Ronald Reagan, a staunch supporter of statehood for Puerto Rico.

So, what's the use of a status convention? There is nothing new under the U.S. Constitution. In 2010, under the leadership of then-Resident Commissioner Pedro Pierluisi, this House again passed the bill that implemented the 2005 President Bush Task Force report recommendations. The U.S. Senate again failed to act, but Republican Governor Luis Fortuno signed legislation approving the two-part plebiscite in 2012 with 78 percent participation. Fifty-four percent of voters rejected continuing under the current territorial relationship, and 61 percent voted for statehood. In 2017, Puerto Rico held another plebiscite under local law, this time between territory, statehood, and independence in its two forms. But when polls showed statehood leading, opponents boycotted. So, even though statehood received 97 percent support, turnout was not high.

To remove any remaining doubts, in 2020, Puerto Rico legislated a simple statehood yes-or-no vote, just as Alaska and Hawaii did 70 years ago. With 73 percent of affected voters participating, statehood won by a clear majority of 52½ percent and garnered more votes than any candidate on the ballot, clearly cutting across local party lines. Yet, here we are today, after 123 years under U.S. rule, six commissions, three Presidential Task Force reports, 65 hearings, over 100 failed bills and 18 definitions of "commonwealth" with no change.

H.R. 2070 would cause further delay, disempower voters, and put future status in the hands of local political party elites by imposing a Federal mandate for a local status convention to recycle impossible options when people know what the options are, and statehood has won in three separate plebiscites.

Puerto Rico has self-determined you should pass H.R. 1522 as soon as possible. Thank you very much.

[The prepared statement of Mr. Fuentes follows:]

PREPARED STATEMENT OF HON. JOSÉ FUENTES AGOSTINI, FORMER ATTORNEY GENERAL OF PUERTO RICO & CHAIRMAN OF THE PUERTO RICO STATEHOOD COUNCIL

Chairman Grijalva, Ranking Member Westerman, and distinguished members of the Committee, I am honored to appear before you today to discuss the "Puerto Rico

Statehood Admission Act" (H.R. 1522) and the "Puerto Rico Self-Determination Act of 2021" (H.R. 2070).

The last time I testified before Congress on the issue of Puerto Rico self-determination—in 1998—I urged Congress to acknowledge Puerto Rico's status as a U.S. territory, and I sought congressional leadership to confirm constitutional parameters on alternatives for Puerto Rico's future status.

Almost 25 years later, it is now well established that Puerto Rico is indeed a U.S. territory, and it is further recognized that this colonial relationship is no longer acceptable. The question for consideration by the Committee today is what should Congress do next and how to get there.

With respect to the two proposals before the Committee, only H.R. 1522 represents true self-determination. The bill respects the voices of the U.S. citizens of Puerto Rico and recognizes Puerto Rico's history of local plebiscite votes. The measure provides a Democratic process to resolve the issue of Puerto Rico's status with a clear, up-or-down ratification vote on an option with 50 precedents: statehood.

On the other hand, H.R. 2070 seeks to create a federally imposed structure that ignores Puerto Rican votes, Puerto Rican history and Puerto Rican voices. The bill proposes a new process with no accountability and no end date. H.R. 2070 provides no explicit guidance on constitutional parameters and creates a new federal commission. The proposal is not true self-determination, and it is not a solution to the legal, political and moral problem we are discussing today.

History & Background

The "United States-Puerto Rico Political Status Act" & the 1998 Plebiscite

In 1998, under the leadership of Speaker Newt Gingrich (R-GA), the House of Representatives passed the "United States-Puerto Rico Political Status Act," H.R. 856, led by Rep. Don Young (R-AK). That bill called for a local referendum in Puerto Rico in which voters could choose from among three ballot options: (1) statehood, (2) independence or free association, or (3) remain a U.S. territory. The bill passed by a bipartisan vote of 209 to 208 but died in the Senate.

In the face of congressional inaction, later that year, Puerto Rico Governor Pedro Rossello (D) proceeded to hold a local plebiscite vote in Puerto Rico with five options on the ballot: (1) statehood, (2) independence, (3) free association, (4) continued territory status, or (5) none of the above.

Statehood was the clear winner among the four defined options with 46.5% of the vote, followed by independence (2.5%), free association (.1%) and the current territorial status (.06%). Yet just over half of all voters (50.3%) chose none of the above.

Given four constitutionally valid options, a slight majority of Puerto Rican voters held out hope for something different which they were being told locally was possible.

What they were looking for was known at the time as "Enhanced Commonwealth," an unconstitutional mixture of sovereignty and federal entitlements. This make-believe status, which former Rep. José Serrano (D-NY) called "a letter to Santa Claus," requires the U.S. Congress to cede power to Puerto Rico in a permanent agreement and makes accessible a package of federal benefits to Puerto Ricans that go well beyond the rights and responsibilities of any other U.S. citizen.

The 1998 "Enhanced Commonwealth" platform as ratified by the Commonwealth (PDP) Party of Puerto Rico can be found at the conclusion of this testimony along with a related explanatory graphic as published by the San Juan Star.

For additional background, please see attached list of "Commonwealth" proposals debated in Puerto Rico from 1952 to 1998 and a Congressional Research Service (CRS) history of "Commonwealth" ballot options from 1967–1998. The CRS footnotes document the changing definitions of "Commonwealth," often with constitutional implications.

President's Task Force on Puerto Rico's Political Status

In 2000, in response to the "none of the above" vote in the 1998 plebiscite, President Bill Clinton issued Executive Order 13183, establishing the President's Task Force on Puerto Rico's Status. The purpose of the Task Force was to "clarify both the status options available to Puerto Rico and the process by which those options can be realized."

President George W. Bush continued the initiative, consulted extensively with stakeholders, and in December 2005 published the first President's Task Force on Puerto Rico's Status report, an authoritative study containing an analysis of the constitutionally viable status options and a proposed process to resolve Puerto Rico's ultimate status.

The report recommended a two-step plebiscite. First, a vote would ask Puerto Rico's electorate "whether they wish to remain a U.S. territory." If voters chose to remain a territory, then this question would be presented periodically to voters to ensure continued "consent of the governed."

If voters decided they wanted change, the report called for another plebiscite to enable voters to choose between statehood or independence.

In 2007, the Bush administration issued a second report of the President's Task Force on Puerto Rico's Status, confirming the previous report's findings and reinforcing its recommendations.

President Obama released the most recent report of the President's Task Force on Puerto Rico's Status in 2011. That report was consistent with the two previous reports in expressing a "marginal preference" for a two-plebiscite system. Recognizing the ongoing definitional dispute over status options, the report also clarified:

"[C]onsistent with the legal conclusions reached by prior Task Force reports, one aspect of some proposals for enhanced Commonwealth remains constitutionally problematic—proposals that would establish a relationship between Puerto Rico and the Federal Government that could not be altered except by mutual consent. This was a focus of past Task Force reports. The Obama administration has taken a fresh look at the issue of such mutual consent provisions, and it has concluded that such provisions would not be enforceable because a future Congress could choose to alter that relationship unilaterally."

The "Puerto Rico Democracy Act of 2010" & the 2012 Plebiscite

In 2010, the House of Representatives passed the "Puerto Rico Democracy Act," H.R. 2499 under the leadership of then Resident Commissioner Pedro Pierluisi (D-PR) by a bipartisan vote (223–169). Unfortunately, the legislation, which was modeled on the two-part structure endorsed by the Bush and Obama Task Force reports, again failed to advance in the Senate.

To continue making progress on the issue, in 2012, Puerto Rico Governor Luis Fortuño (R) proceeded to hold a vote on a two-part plebiscite based on the Bush Task Force recommendation. The first question asked voters whether or not they "agree to maintain the current territorial political condition" of Puerto Rico. The second question instructed voters to select—irrespective of their answer to the first question—their preference from among three non-territorial status options: (1) statehood, (2) independence, or (3) free association.

The plebiscite results indicated that nearly 54% of voters (53.97%) rejected Puerto Rico's territorial status and that among those who selected a non-territorial option in the second question, a majority (61.16%) preferred statehood over sovereign free association (33.34%) and independence (5.49%).

Support for ending the current territorial status and progress toward statehood were clear despite sources of ambiguity in the plebiscite that possibly dampened support for statehood. For example, free association was simply described as a "voluntary political association, whose specific terms would be agreed between the United States and Puerto Rico as sovereign nations."

In the three current U.S. free association relationships (Republic of the Marshall Islands, Palau and Federated States of Micronesia), nationals do not have U.S. citizenship or any representation in Congress. The U.S. has sovereignty in free association relationships over the other nation's defense and national security, and freely associated nations do not qualify for Medicaid or almost all other federal programs currently available in Puerto Rico. Given the vague "free association" definition on the ballot, it is unclear whether voters fully understood the limits of free association.

PDP Proposes and Then Rejects a Status Convention

As part of the pro-Commonwealth Party (PDP) platform that Governor Alejandro Garcia Padilla (D) used to get elected in 2012, his party proposed a "status convention" as the mechanism that they would use to help resolve Puerto Rico's political status. The PDP had also included this proposal in their previous general election party platform in 2008. However, even though the PDP party controlled the Governorship and both chambers of Puerto Rico's legislature during the 2013–2016 term, once in office the PDP led government did not act toward that end. Specifically, in 2013 prominent PDP members of the House and Senate proposed legislation to hold a referendum to ask the electorate whether or not the legislature should to convene a status convention (P.C. 210 & P.S. 694), and another bill to set up the convention and elect its delegates (P.C. 1334 & P.S. 693). Ultimately, Gov. Garcia Padilla and the top PDP leadership in the legislature did not support that effort. Having had the inherent authority as well as the legislative majority necessary to enact what H.R. 2070 proposes, the Puerto Rican legislature rejected that course of action.

The $2.5 Million DOJ Appropriation & the 2017 Plebiscite

In 2014, under the leadership of Rep. Serrano (D-NY), Congress legislated an appropriation of $2.5 million for a plebiscite on "options that would resolve Puerto Rico's future political status" premised on the approval of ballot definitions by the U.S. Department of Justice (DOJ).

In response, Gov. Garcia Padilla promised to use the funds to hold a "fair process." Yet after repeated unsuccessful attempts to convince the DOJ to approve a ballot that included an "Enhanced Commonwealth" option, in August 2014 Gov. Garcia Padilla withdrew his proposal and the PDP attempted to reach an internal consensus on a new "Enhanced Commonwealth" definition. After a year of internal debate, they disbanded the effort.

Having run and won on a platform of resolving the political status issue and advancing the statehood cause, in 2017 incoming Governor Ricardo Rossello (D) passed legislation and presented a proposal to the DOJ for the utilization of the $2.5 million appropriation. Relying on the appropriations language that sought to "resolve" Puerto Rico's future political status, a plebiscite was proposed between statehood, independence and free association, leaving off the—unresolved— territorial status.

After amending the local plebiscite legislation to incorporate DOJ feedback the DOJ declined to review the amended language because of "insufficient time." The Government of Puerto Rico decided to move forward with the plebiscite in June 2017 without using the $2.5 million available.

Weeks and days before the plebiscite public polls showed statehood leading by a clear majority, so opponents decided to "boycott" the election with PDP leaders passing a resolution to tell their followers that the plebiscite was not fair because no version of

"Enhanced Commonwealth" was on the ballot. Support for statehood was overwhelming at 97%, Independence/Free Association obtained 1.5% and current territory status 1.3%. Yet those who were unwilling to even try to win at the ballot box then turned around to argue that the statehood victory was not legitimate because of low-voter turnout. The victory for statehood was certified by the State Elections Commission of Puerto Rico, and turnout statistics on "effective voters" showed a participation rate of 31% (*See Voter Turnout Certification Attached*) consistent with those of previous non-general election electoral events on the Island (22.5% in 2005 and 35% in 2012).

The 2020 Plebiscite

In 2020, recognizing the rejection of the current territory status by Puerto Rico's voters, the Government of Puerto Rico legislated a simple statehood "YES" or "NO" vote. DOJ approval was requested, and again the DOJ failed to approve the ballot irrespective of clear historic and legal precedent for its design and word choice. Instead, DOJ insisted that the current territory status be included despite the intent of Congress in the 2014 appropriation, which sought a permanent solution to "resolve" the current territory status.

Given that Congress has also made clear in federal statute (Pub. L. 114-187 § 402) that Puerto Rico's right to determine its future political status can be exercised with or without the use of a federal appropriation that requires DOJ approval, the Government of Puerto Rico decided to proceed with the vote. Its purpose was simple, to determine definitively whether or not a majority of Island voters support statehood. Its precedent was clear: Alaska, Hawaii and multiple other territories became states after polling voters on statehood without any federal authorization or approval.

In the case of both Alaska and Hawaii, the results of the non-federally approved statehood referendums served to demonstrate to Congress that voters sought statehood. The locally sponsored votes helped educate and compel Congress to enact admission bills which in turn contained a final statehood ratification vote. In both cases support for statehood grew significantly between the territory's first locally sponsored "non-binding" statehood vote (58% in 1946 for Alaska & 67% in 1940 for Hawaii) and their final ratification vote after Congress enacted admission legislation (83% in 1958 for Alaska and 94% in 1959 for Hawaii).

The Puerto Rican government's decision to proceed with the locally sponsored statehood "YES" or "NO" vote last November was consistent with this history.

The plebiscite was held concurrent with the general election, and the voter participation rate was initially estimated at 52%. The Puerto Rico State Elections Commission later certified that among the "effective voters" in Puerto Rico participation in the plebiscite reached 73%. So, any claims of low-voter participation are simply inaccurate.

Additionally, no registered political party in Puerto Rico called for a "boycott" of this plebiscite. In fact, all political parties actively campaigned for either the "YES" (New Progressive Party) or the "NO" (Popular Democratic Party and Puerto Rico Independence Party) options, and the Citizens Victory Movement had some of its candidates campaigning for "YES" and others for "NO." No one was excluded from the vote.

Out of 1.2 million ballots cast, statehood won with 52.5% of the vote. This percentage represents 655,000 ballots, more votes than were received by either the prostatehood Governor (33.24% with over 427,000 votes) or pro-statehood Resident Commissioner (41.18% with over 512,000 votes), both of which who also won the election. The result demonstrates that support for statehood in Puerto Rico cuts across all party lines and that voters differentiated between the ballots cast on the status issue and those for individual candidates running for office.

This vote marks the third time in less than a decade in which the U.S. citizens of Puerto Rico rejected the current territory status in favor of statehood and shows definitively that an unquestionable majority of voters support immediate admission as a state.

Implications of Puerto Rico Statehood

Under the U.S. Constitution, new states to the union are admitted on "equal footing" with existing states. The "equal footing" doctrine makes it clear that when Puerto Rico becomes a state, full constitutional rights will apply to its residents, including constitutional U.S. citizenship and the Bill of Rights. As a U.S. territory, the Bill of Rights does not fully apply in Puerto Rico, and a 1917 statute, not the U.S. Constitution, grants U.S. citizenship.

Statehood is a responsible ballot option because there are no variations on its definition. Each of the 50 current states is treated equally under federal law. The meaning of "state" is well established and consistent; there is a sense of certainty in the definition.

There are, however, three implications of Puerto Rico statehood that are subject to much conjecture in Washington and often misunderstood: (1) predictions of Puerto Rico's partisanship as a state, (2) the economic implications of Puerto Rico statehood, and (3) the impact of statehood on Puerto Rican culture. Contrary to assertions that Puerto Rico would be a deep blue state with a struggling economy, Puerto Rico is poised to be a purple state with a strengthened economy, and Puerto Rican culture would thrive as a result.

The Perils of Political Forecasting

While many in Washington speculate about how Puerto Rico's admission would impact the political balance in Congress, the reality is that this speculation is not a legitimate basis upon which to deny three million U.S. citizens the full voting rights that they are demanding at the federal level.

First, historically past predictions of partisan leanings have missed the mark. When Hawaii and Alaska were admitted into the Union, the pair was approved on the assumption that Alaska would vote Democratic and Hawaii would be Republican.

Second, instead of assuming what voter preferences on the Island will be based on Puerto Rican voter preferences in the states, observers should look át actual election results in Puerto Rico. Currently, the most popular elected official in Puerto Rico is a Republican. As a matter of fact, at the time of the November 2020 election, all of the top government officials in Puerto Rico—Governor Wanda Vázquez, House Speaker Johnny Méndez and Senate President Thomas Rivera Schatz—identified as Republican.

Members of this Committee may also recall former Resident Commissioner and Republican Luis Fortuño, who served in Congress from 2005–2009 before being elected Governor of Puerto Rico from 2009–2013.

Republicans have a clear and active voter base in Puerto Rico due to the Island's large socially conservative population. In fact, last year the James Madison Institute reported that Puerto Ricans living in states such as Florida continue to vote Republican in meaningful numbers for socially conservative candidates and are even more likely to vote for Republican candidates who are clear that they favor Puerto Rico statehood.

We cannot know the partisan makeup of a congressional delegation for the state of Puerto Rico until the U.S. citizens there are afforded full voting rights. What is obvious is that the party that is viewed as being responsible for including Puerto Rico fully in the America's national democratic process will be remembered by Puerto Rican voters for many years to come.

Economic Growth under Statehood

While some may argue that Puerto Rico must improve its economy and fiscal situation before statehood can be considered, this perspective is based on a flawed understanding of the interplay between a jurisdiction's political status as a territory and its prospects for economic development. Economic underperformance is not uniquely attributable to Puerto Rico as a territory; indeed, throughout history all U.S. territories have underperformed and been in an arrested development compared to after they became states.

Inherent Limitations of Territorial Economics

Territory status prevents Puerto Rico from being fully integrated into the U.S. economy inhibiting investment and generating uncertainty because of the fear of a possible change in political status, or arbitrary treatment by Congress in federal laws and programs. Puerto Rico's lack of representation on the Federal level also severely limits its ability to impact Federal legislative and rulemaking processes which further hampers its integration into the broader U.S. economy.

At its core, the current territory status represents an inherent limitation on Puerto Rico's economic development because it creates an unequal playing field with a distinct disadvantage from which the local economy cannot escape. It also creates incentives for deficits and debt spending as a way to make up for underinvestment by the Federal Government when local elected officials are faced with the public demands of a local electorate who see the higher quality of life and higher incomes stateside and can easily relocate to obtain better economic opportunities.

Ticking Timebomb of Population Loss

Federal underinvestment under territory status will always hamper Puerto Rico's aggregate demand and cause residents to relocate stateside making sustainable economic growth difficult if not impossible. According to the U.S. Census, the relocation of Puerto Ricans stateside has led to a population decline from 3.9 million in 2000, to less than 3.2 million in 2019. That is absolutely devastating for the Island's economy because it diminishes the consumer base, tax base and the workforce, and increases per capita debt. This trend makes it crystal clear why a gamechanger like the definitive resolution to the political status issue is urgently needed, and why further delay by Congress could be catastrophic.

History Shows that Statehood Stimulates Economic Growth

Economic data from the transition of Alaska and Hawaii into statehood shows that economic progress is massive as a former territory converges into the national economy through statehood. Both states averaged growth rates two times greater than the U.S. average after admission.

Following statehood, Hawaii's economy skyrocketed—quadrupling in size by 1989. In Alaska, the wages for the average non-agricultural worker increased 28% in the 10 years following statehood. The University of Alaska Institute of Social and Economic Research found that after becoming a state, production of goods and services in Alaska increased, employment expanded, gross state product more than doubled, and the state's population grew.

Similarly, economic data in the first decade after statehood also showed consistent growth patterns in Montana, Washington, Idaho, Wyoming, Utah, Oklahoma, New Mexico and Arizona. These economic results were quick and dramatic, and they have been enduring, demonstrating that economic growth follows statehood, not the other way around.

Statehood will provide Puerto Rico the equality, stability, access and certainty needed to attract long term investors. It will increase interstate commerce by boosting consumer demand. Statehood will also help speed up debt restructuring by promoting the economic growth needed to support debt repayment and to regain access to capital markets for making responsible public investments in infrastructure that can generate more growth in the future.

Statehood Would Respect and Strengthen Puerto Rican Culture

The course of Puerto Rico's history changed in 1898, when the United States acquired the Island in the aftermath of the Spanish American War. At the time Puerto Rico already had a rich identity and cultural history with a mixture of Spanish, African and Taino native influences. And while some like to raise concerns about Puerto Rico retaining its unique cultural identity as a state, this again is a false dichotomy. In the United States, every state has its own culture and identity. There is no reason to believe that Puerto Rico would be any different.

The reality is that Puerto Rican culture and identity has already been shaped in undeniable ways from its current territorial relationship with the United States, and American culture has also been shaped by Puerto Rico. There are simply no requirements under statehood that would prevent Puerto Rico from maintaining its culture and identity.

Preserving American Citizenship & Puerto Rican Identity

In 1917, the U.S. Congress enacted legislation granting U.S. citizenship to the people of Puerto Rico, further including Puerto Ricans in the American political family. The overwhelming majority of Puerto Ricans treasure their U.S. citizenship. Puerto Rico is already included in the United States, travel is seamless and no passports or visas are required. Statehood will provide a constitutional guarantee of U.S. citizenship for current and future generations born on the Island, allowing us to keep a critical connection, access to and mobility with the six million Puerto Ricans living stateside.

The stateside population of Puerto Ricans is itself the greatest proof that one can continue to carry and cherish one's culture and identity as Puerto Rican while also enjoying the full and equal rights of U.S. citizenship under statehood. There is no contradiction in being proud to be Puerto Rican and proud to be American at the same time.

Language

Puerto Rico is predominantly Spanish speaking, but with a large bilingual population that also speaks English. The official languages in Puerto Rico today are both Spanish and English. Under statehood there would be no limitation on the capacity of Puerto Rico to retain both Spanish and English as its official languages. As a state that right would be reserved to Puerto Rico under the 10th Amendment to the Constitution. Examples of states with more than one official language include Alaska, Hawaii and New Mexico. And for those concerned that Puerto Rico would be alone as a state with a large Spanish speaking population, Census data shows there would still be more Spanish speakers in

California (10 million), Texas (7 million) and Florida (6 million) than there are in Puerto Rico (3 million). Past public polling has also shown that an overwhelming majority of parents (95%) support requiring that all public schools in Puerto Rico teach English so that students can become fully bilingual. Parents realize that being fully bilingual preserves Puerto Rican culture while opening doors to better educational and professional opportunities.

Population

When I testified before Congress in 1998, I referred to the 3.8 million U.S. citizens of Puerto Rico. Census data today indicates that Puerto Rico's population has decreased to under 3.2 million. The people of Puerto Rico are voting for statehood with their feet. The heart of Puerto Rican culture is Puerto Rico. The best way to strengthen Puerto Rican culture is by strengthening Puerto Rico.

Today, there are more Puerto Ricans living in the states than Puerto Ricans who live in Puerto Rico. We have experienced population loss and brain drain for years, as the next generation of talented Puerto Ricans are leaving home in favor of Florida, Pennsylvania, Texas, and countless other states. Puerto Rico's most important cultural resource is its people, and under the failed territory status people are leaving Puerto Rico.

If Puerto Rico's relationship with the United States posed an existential threat to Puerto Rican culture we would know that by now. The damage would be done. After all, Puerto Rico has been a territory of the U.S. for 123 years. The so-called "annexation" that, ironically, appears to be feared most by people who do not call Puerto Rico home, occurred in 1898 and was fully enacted in 1917.

Puerto Rican culture continues to endure despite its long colonial history—and its colonial status today. An economically vibrant Puerto Rico under statehood would be much more able to retain and further develop local talent in arts, music, dance, cuisine, sports and other cultural fields than under the deteriorating territory status where top talent is often times forced to leave the island to be able to fully develop and grow.

Puerto Rican Participation in the U.S. Military

U.S. citizens from Puerto Rico have served proudly in all branches of the U.S. Armed Forces, and historically, Puerto Rico has ranked alongside the top states in terms of per capita military service.

Estimated wartime deployment contributions include: Over 18,000 during World War I; Over 65,000 during World War II; Over 61,000 during the Korean War; Over 48,000 during the Vietnam War; Over 10,000 during the Gulf War; and over 25,000 during Operations Enduring Freedom & Iraqi Freedom.

In 2016 Congress awarded the Congressional Gold Medal to the famed 65th Infantry Regiment, known as the Borinqueneers, which was composed mostly of soldiers from Puerto Rico and served as the only Hispanic segregated unit in the Korean War. While nine members of the Armed Forces from Puerto Rico have received the Medal of Honor, our Nation's highest award for military valor.

Puerto Ricans continue to serve today, with tens of thousands in active duty, and reserves, and thousands more in the Puerto Rico National Guard. Indeed, more than 90,000 veterans call Puerto Rico home.

Most poignantly, 1,900 U.S. citizens of Puerto Rico have been casualties of war paying the ultimate price in defense of America's freedom, while lacking full voting rights and equality at the federal level. Only the granting of full rights and equality under statehood would fully honor the sacrifices of blood, sweat, tears and lives made by all the Puerto Ricans who have served and continue to serve in the military to this day and by their families.

The Fallacy of the Puerto Rico Self-Determination Act of 2021 (H.R. 2070)

The biggest fallacy of the Puerto Rico Self-Determination Act, H.R. 2070, is that it ignores all of the previous efforts at locally led self-determination that Puerto Rico has engaged in over the past several decades. It engages in explicit election denial regarding the indisputable reality that a majority of voters in Puerto Rico favor statehood. It disrespects those voters and all election processes, wrapping itself in the language of "fairness," but instead seeking to discard their suffrage to start a new process as if their votes had not happened and didn't matter. That is not how democracy works, and I strongly urge the Members of this Committee to reject this approach.

The other fallacy is that in the name of "inclusion" H.R. 2070 seeks to re-open a debate about what status are possible that has already taken place over decades, and where definitive conclusions have already been reached. Presidents and Members of Congress from both political parties have examined the status issue for decades, and they have come to the same conclusion: clear constitutional parameters are in order when presenting status options on a plebiscite. H.R. 2070 fails to do that.

Instead, H.R. 2070 re-opens the door to endless debate on an undefined number of options when its proponents say that beyond statehood, independence and free association, the bill would consider "any option other than the current territorial arrangement." Inevitably this includes proponents of the fantasy "Enhanced Commonwealth" option—an impossible mix of the best features of sovereignty and statehood. In doing so, H.R. 2070 would spoil the potential to resolve the island's ultimate status and would hurt self-determination efforts which ultimately must be a real choice by Puerto Rico's voters among the constitutionally valid options.

The final insult to the majority of voters in Puerto Rico is that H.R. 2070 proposes a convoluted convention that the people of Puerto Rico have not requested with an "uninterrupted space of dialogue," and no timeline or end date. As one prominent bill supporter described it recently, "Velázquez and Ocasio-Cortez's legislation would start a process that could take years . . ." This is simply disrespectful and wrong, because justice delayed is justice denied.

After almost 70 years of Puerto Ricans wrangling to get out of the "Commonwealth" and "Enhanced Commonwealth" myths, it is time to say enough. Puerto Rico has a legislature and a governor with authority to hold a convention. When they have had a chance to do so, they have chosen not to. Compelling Puerto Rico to hold a convention against the wishes of its governor and legislature is not self-determination, it's an example of the same paternalistic colonialism that the authors of H.R. 2070 say they are against.

Instead, the duly elected governor and legislature of Puerto Rico have decided to self-determine by holding multiple plebiscite votes, and millions of voters have cast their ballots. The U.S. Constitution grants Congress the power to "make all needful rules and regulations" regarding U.S. territories. With that power comes a responsibility. In this case, Congress has the responsibility to consider and respect Puerto Rico's plebiscite history, and the most logical next step is to move forward with the ratification vote set forth in H.R. 1522, the Puerto Rico Statehood Admission Act.

Conclusion

Puerto Rico's territorial status represents the unfinished business of American democracy. The resolution of Puerto Rico's ultimate political status is not only vitally important to the three million U.S. citizens who call the islands home and the nearly six million Puerto Ricans stateside, but to all Americans.

Democracy is the soul of America. In 1980, then-Presidential candidate Ronald Reagan wrote in the Wall Street Journal about Puerto Rico, "we cannot expect our foreign policies to be enjoying prestige around the world . . . when we are having serious problems with our closest neighbors." His words still ring true today.

Congress does not have to take a position on statehood today, but the Constitution and fundamental American principles compel Congress to at least provide a dignified path forward. I urge the Committee to listen to the messages that the majority of the people of Puerto Rico have sent in the recent plebiscites and pass H.R. 1522. It is time to put an end to the decades of misleading information that will continue to spread in Puerto Rico if left unchecked by Congress.

There is a new window of opportunity before us today. History will judge us by what we do or fail to do to correct the historic wrong of America's colonial legacy in Puerto

Rico. I am deeply hopeful that 2021 will be the year that Congress provides clear direction to finally resolve Puerto Rico's ultimate political status, and unleash our enchanted island's full potential for the benefit of Puerto Rico, America and the world.

ATTACHMENTS

Explanatory Graphic Related to the 1998 "Enhanced Commonwealth" Platform as Published by the San Juan Star, 1998

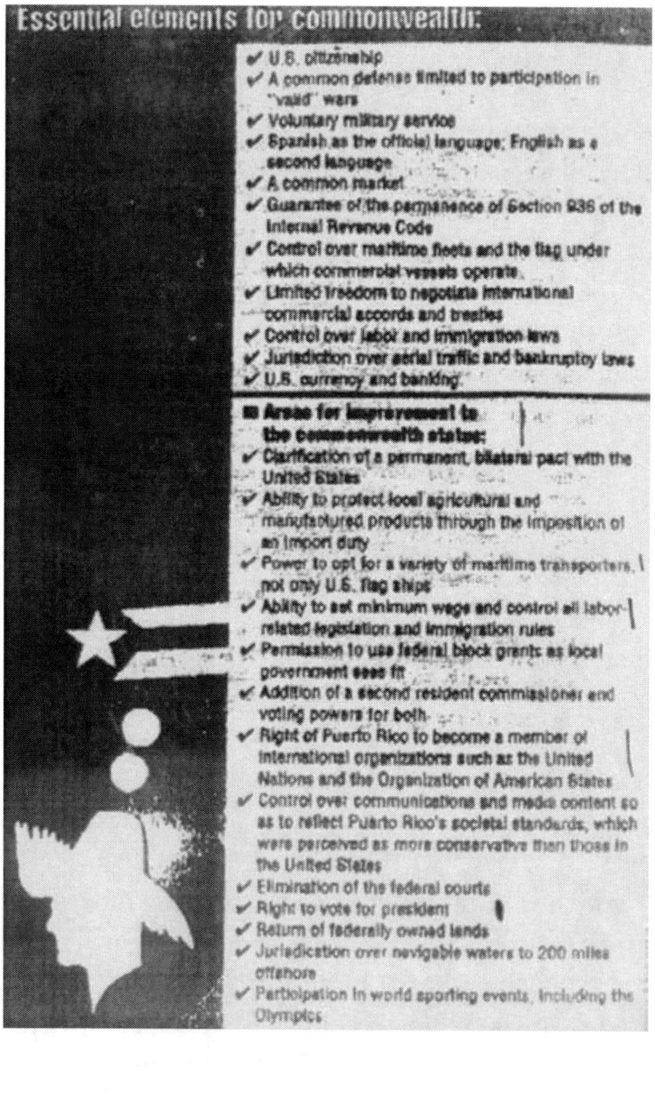

1998 "Enhanced Commonwealth" Platform as Ratified by the Commonwealth (PDP) Party of Puerto Rico

POPULAR DEMOCRATIC PARTY
DEVELOPMENT OF THE COMMONWEALTH

The people of Puerto Rico, in the exercise of their sovereignty, their natural right to self government and their free will as ultimate sources of their political power, hereby reaffirm the validity of the Commonwealth established as an autonomous political body, that is neither colonial or territorial, in permanent union with the United States under a covenant that cannot be invalidated or altered unilaterally and proposes its autonomic development. The relationship between Puerto Rico and the United States will continue to be based on common defense, market and currency and on the irrevocability of the U.S. citizenship, acquired by birth and protected by the U.S. Constitution.

This relationship guarantees the autonomous development of Puerto Rico based on the democratic precept of government with the consent of the governed and the recognition that Puerto Rico is a nation with its own history, idiosyncracy, culture and Spanish language.

To achieve its maximum economic progress and well-being, the people of Puerto Rico propose to develop Commonwealth retaining all the powers that are not delegated to the United States. Under Puerto Rico's fiscal autonomy, economic development areas will be identified in which joint action can produce jobs and other benefits for both parties, including the flexibility in the use of federal funds, providing that programs of direct aid to individuals will continue as they are present. The Commonwealth will be able to enter into commercial and tax agreements, among others, with other countries, and belong to regional and international entities, consistent with the common interests of defense and security between the United States and Puerto Rico, as agreed to in the covenant.

Once the request for the development of the people of Puerto Rico is approved, a Constituent Assembly will be called to negotiate with the U.S. government the terms and conditions of the covenant, which will include a mechanism to approve the application of legislation approved by the U.S. Congress.

ARTICLE I – PUERTO RICAN IDENTITY

A. PUERTO RICAN NATIONALITY

Puerto Ricans have a common history, idiosyncracy, culture and language that constitute a specific nationality separate from that of any other nation.

B. PUERTO RICAN CITIZENSHIP

Persons born in Puerto Rico are Puerto Rican citizens by birth and their Puerto Rican citizenship is transmittable to their descendants as determined by the Commonwealth and would have the rights, privileges and obligations that derive from it.

ARTICLE II – BASIS OF THE UNION

The union between Puerto Rico and the United States will continue to be based on the following fundamental elements determined by Puerto Rico freely and in agreement with the United States:

A. COMMON CITIZENSHIP

People born in Puerto Rico will continue to be citizens of the United States by birth and this citizenship will continue to be protected by the Constitution of the United States and by this Covenant and will not be unilaterally revocable.

B. COMMON DEFENSE

The United States will maintain authority and responsibility over defense matters. This will include: the same responsibility for the defense of Puerto Rico and its people as the United States and its people; denying and limiting military or strategic access to Puerto Rico to any foreign power, maintaining the bases or other military installations currently operating in Puerto Rico as well as the National Guard; stipulating that the case of the Municipality of Vieques will be the object of the highest attention in agreement with the legitimate call of its residents; and, any additional need would be considered and dealt with through specific and separate agreements.

C. COMMON CURRENCY

The U.S. dollar is and will continue to be the currency in Puerto Rico.

D. COMMON MARKET

A common market will continue to exist between Puerto Rico and the United States, by which the free flow of goods and services between the two countries will continue.

ARTICLE III – DISTRIBUTION OF POWERS

A. SELF GOVERNMENT

The Commonwealth emanates from the power of the people to govern themselves, and for that reason, the people of Puerto Rico retain all the powers that have not been delegated to the United States.

B. DELEGATION OF POWERS

The powers related to the Federal laws related to defense, currency, U.S. citizenship, Social Security, Medicare, unemployment insurance, banks and brokerage, Postal Service and the programs for providing social and educational assistance to citizens and veterans are delegated to the United States. In addition, international relations are delegated to the extent consisted with this Covenant.

C. SHARED POWERS

Areas of special cooperation will be identified in which the United States and the Commonwealth will exercise shared powers for the benefit of both people through the process established in Article XII.

ARTICLE IV – RIGHTS OF CITIZENS

A. CONSTITUTIONAL RIGHTS

The U.S. citizens residing in Puerto Rico will be protected by all the rights, privileges and immunities granted by the Constitution of the United States and the Commonwealth.

B. ECONOMIC BENEFITS

The Federal programs that provide social and educational assistance directly to Puerto Rico's residents, such as the Nutritional Assistance Program, Pell Grants and educational loans, among others, will continue and be guided by the applicable Federal and State regulations.

The United States recognizes as acquired rights Federal programs for veterans and Social Security, Medicare, and unemployment insurance benefits for which Puerto Rican workers and employers have made and will continue to make the corresponding Federal contributions.

ARTICLE V – ECONOMIC DEVELOPMENT

A. WITH THE UNITED STATES OF AMERICA

To promote Puerto Rico's economic development, and considering the present and future relations between Puerto Rico and the United States, the U.S. commits to provide the Commonwealth an annual block grant adjusted for inflation, so the Government of Puerto Rico can continue to provide social assistance, develop public works and infrastructure, and provide incentives for the creation of jobs and socioeconomic development.

The U.S. and Puerto Rico will identify and agree on areas of economic development in which joint action will produce jobs and other economic benefits for both parties, including the creation of special incentives programs for investment in the islands.

B. INTERNATIONAL

The Commonwealth will have control over international trade and will establish a policy to promote its maximum economic development. To that effect, it will have the capacity to enter into commercial and tax agreements, among others, with other countries, consistent with the common interests of the defense and security of Puerto Rico and the United States.

The Commonwealth will be able to enter into international agreements and belong to regional and international organizations consistent with the common interests of the defense and security of Puerto Rico and the United States.

The United States commits to support the participation or membership of Puerto Rico in the agreements and organizations to which this article refers.

ARTICLE VI – FEDERAL LANDS

The Government of the United States will transfer to Puerto Rico the lands that now it has in Puerto Rico with the exception of those lands that are used for common defense or that are necessary to exercise the powers delegated in this Covenant.

ARTICLE VII – AREAS OF SPECIAL COOPERATION

Puerto Rico and the United States will establish other areas of special cooperation intended to guarantee the quality of life of Puerto Ricans and to continue nourishing from the collective experiences of institutional and local development of both peoples.
For the sake of an orderly and calm future and development in harmony with the cultural, spiritual, psychological, and economic nature of both peoples, Puerto Rico and the United States commit to jointly determine strategies to: control drug trafficking; regulate communications; protect the borders from illegal immigration; protect the environment and recognize guarantees of mutual benefit consistent with international rules; promote a new basis for cooperation between workers and management; deal with natural disasters; share technological advances in the sectors of agriculture, medicine, pharmacology, criminal justice, and other disciplines in the areas of Natural and Social Sciences and Humanities.

ARTICLE VIII – FEDERAL COURT

The Federal Court will have jurisdiction over matters that arise from: provisions of the Constitution of the United States and of the Federal laws that apply to Puerto Rico consistent with this Covenant and not in violation with the laws of the Constitution of Puerto Rico. Spanish and English will be the official languages of that court.

ARTICLE IX – RESOLVING DISPUTES

A. NEGOTIATION COMMITTEE

Any controversy about the interpretation of this Covenant will be resolved through negotiations between the parties to this Covenant, that is the United States and the Commonwealth of Puerto Rico. In all negotiations, the Commonwealth of Puerto Rico will be represented by a negotiating committee of three (3) members appointed by the governor and confirmed by seventy-five percent (75%) of each of the two (2) legislative houses of Puerto Rico.

At least, two (2) of the three (3) members of the committee should believe in the political philosophy described in this Covenant, that is, be Commonwealthers. In the same manner, the United States of America will be represented by a committee of three (3) members appointed by the President of the United States.

B. COMMISSION TO RESOLVE DISPUTES

If it is not possible to resolve a controversy through a negotiation between the parties, the controversy will be submitted to the Commission to Resolve Disputes. This commission will have five (5) members, two (2) appointed by the Commonwealth of Puerto Rico, two (2) appointed by the United States of America and a fifth member appointed by majority of these four (4). The five (5) members will select a chairman from their membership.

Decisions of this Commission in disputes between the Governments of the Commonwealth of Puerto Rico and the United States of America regarding the interpretation of this Covenant will be final and firm.

ARTICLE X – LEGALITY

The agreement between the people of Puerto Rico and the government of the United States of America will have the force recognized by the constitutional and international rights in force as a bilateral covenant that recognizes rights and delegates powers, based on mutual consent, that cannot be unilaterally renounced or altered.

ARTICLE XI – SYMBOLS

The symbols, flags and hymns of the Commonwealth of Puerto Rico will continue to be as at present.

ARTICLE XII – OTHER INTERNATIONAL ASPECTS

The Commonwealth of Puerto Rico will retain the authority to ratify cultural, educational, scientific and sports agreements.

ARTICLE XIII – NEGOTIATION

a. Once this development proposal is approved by the people of Puerto Rico, a Constituent Assembly will be called that will negotiate with the Government of the United States the terms and conditions of the association between Puerto Rico and the United States and the specific drafting of such agreement on behalf of the people of Puerto Rico. This Constituent Assembly will not be able to adopt proposals that undermine or cancel the mandate expressed by the people of Puerto Rico or that undermines the precepts of common citizenship, market, currency and defense, or against the Puerto Rican national identity.

b. The Constituent Assembly will design and propose to the Government of the United States a mechanism for a specific agreement regarding the application of legislation approved by the Congress of the United States after the adoption of the covenant and that the people of Puerto Rico wish to have extended to Puerto Rico. The people of Puerto Rico will elect a Resident Commissioner who will represent Puerto Rico before the Government of the United States and who will be considered a Member of the U.S. House of Representatives for purposes of all legislative matters that have to do with Puerto Rico, but whose role will also be extended to representing Puerto Rico before the Executive Branch of the United States.

c. The main political parties of Puerto Rico will be represented in the Constituent Assembly and will be able to nominate candidates to be part of the assembly.

d. The Covenant will take effect after it has been negotiated and approved by the Government of the United States and the Constituent Assembly, and it has been approved by the people of Puerto Rico in a referendum called for that purpose.

e. Any change to the terms of this Covenant will have to be approved by the people of Puerto Rico in a special vote conducted consistent with its democratic processes and institutions.

f. The Constituent Assembly will not have authority to alter, modify, amend, and/or change the Constitution of the Commonwealth of Puerto Rico.

Approved by the Governing Board of the Popular Democratic Party
On October 15, 1998

LIST OF DEFINITIONS PROPOSED OR DISCUSSED FOR COMMONWEALTH OF PUERTO RICO

1. Relationship as established under Law 600 in 1952
2. The Fernós-Murray Bill of 1959
3. The Status Commission (STACOM) Bill of 1964
4. The 1967 local plebiscite
5. Aguas Buenas Declaration (1971)
6. 1972 U.S.-Puerto Rico Ad-Hoc Committee
7. 1975 U.S.-Puerto Rico Commission (Nixon-Hernández Colón)
8. The New Pact (1976)
9. The New Thesis (1979)
10. The New ELA ("Estado Libre Asociado" – Commonwealth) 1989
11. Vizcarrondo Amendment to New ELA
12. 1991 Democratic Rights Referendum (calling for amendments to the Puerto Rico Constitution)
13. The 1993 local plebiscite
14. The Young Bill (H.R. 856)
15. The definition proposed by Former PDP Senate President Miguel Hernández Agosto in 1997
16. The definition proposed by PDP Senator Eudaldo Báez Galib in 1998
17. The definition proposed by PDP Party President and Representative Aníbal Acevedo Vilá in 1998
18. 1998 PDP official party platform

CONGRESSIONAL RESEARCH SERVICE (CRS) SUMMARY OF RESULTS OF PUERTO RICO PLEBISCITES HELD FROM 1967–1998

Political Status of Puerto Rico: Options forCongress

R. Sam Garrett
Specialist in American National Government,
June 7, 2011

Appendix. Puerto Rico Status Votes in Plebiscites and Referenda, 1967-1998

Table A-1. Puerto Rico Status Votes in Plebiscites and Referenda, 1967-1998

		Votes	
Ballot Options		**Number**[a]	**Percent**[b]
	July 23, 1967[c]		
Commonwealth[d]		425,079	60.5%
Statehood		273,315	38.9%
Independence		4,118	0.6%
Registered voters	*1,067,000*		
Total votes	*702,512*		
Percent turnout	*66%*		
	December 8, 1991[e]		
Against the reclamation of democratic rights (No)		660,267	53.6%
In favor of the reclamation of democratic rights (Yes)		559,163	45.4%
Registered voters	*2,052,537*		
Total votes	*1,219,430*		
Percent turnout	*59%*		
	November 14, 1993[f]		
Commonwealth[g]		826,326	48.6%
Statehood		788,296	46.4%
Independence		75,620	4.4%
Registered voters	*2,100,000*		
Total votes	*1,700,000*		
Percent turnout	*81%*		
	December 13, 1998[h]		
None of the above [option five]		787,900	50.3%
Statehood [option three]		728,157	46.6%
Sovereignty [option four, independence]		39,838	2.6%
Free association [option two]		4,536	0.3%

Table A-1. (Continued)

		Votes	
Ballot Options		**Number[a]**	**Percent[b]**
Limited self-government [option one][i]		993	0.1%
Registered voters	*2,197,824*		
Total votes	*1,561,424*		
Percent turnout	*71%*		

a. Table excludes blank or null and void ballots.

b. Number of registered voters, total votes, and percent turnout derived from sources of results (noted below), except for registered voters in 1991 calculated by CRS.

c. Number of votes for independence calculated by CRS based on data presented in: Arturo Morales Carrion, Puerto Rico: A Political and Cultural History, (New York: W.W. Norton & Co., Inc., 1983), p. 306. [Total number of registered voters was 1,067,000, according to Surendra Bhana, The United States and the Development of the Puerto Rican Status Question, 1936-1968, (Lawrence, KS: The University Press of Kansas, 1975), p. 185.] See also Roberta A. Johnson, "The 1967 Puerto Rican Plebiscite: The People Decide," Revista/Review InterAmericana, vol. 5, spring 1975, pp. 27-46.

d. The votes in favor of the 1967 Commonwealth option arguably demonstrated support for an expanded form of self-government for Puerto Rico, in that the ballot proposition included text referring to the "inviolability" and "indissoluble link" of Puerto Rican citizenship and would have required approval of changes in the political status in a referendum.

e. Results taken from Representative Robert J. Lagomarsino, "Certification of Puerto Rico Referendum Results," remarks in the House, Congressional Record, vol. 138, Feb. 7, 1992, p. 2141. A "yes" vote, generally urged by commonwealth and independence supporters, expressed support for legislation that would have amended the Constitution to support the right of Puerto Ricans to determine a political status not subordinated to Congress and respective of the unique culture and identity of Puerto Rico. A "no" vote, generally urged by statehood supporters, rejected the proposed constitutional amendment.

f. Results taken from Ivonne Garcia, "Final Status Plebiscite Results Released," San Juan Star, Dec. 10, 1993, p. 12.

g. The text of the ballot for the "Commonwealth" option in 1993 included provisions that arguably exceeded the relationship established in 1950, included "irrevocable U.S. citizenship," "fiscal autonomy for Puerto Rico," and a legislative agenda to be considered by Congress.

h. Results taken from U.S. Congress, House Committee on Resources, The Results of the 1998 Puerto Rico Plebiscite, committee print, 106th Congress, 1st session (Washington: GPO, 1999), p. 10.

i. The text of the ballot arguably presented the commonwealth option in that it referred to the political status set forth in P.L. 600, the plenary authority of the Congress in the territorial clause of the U.S. Constitution, and other characteristics generally associated with the political status of Puerto Rico.

VOTER TURNOUT CERTIFICATION—PLEBISCITE 2017

State Elections Commission
Office of the PNP Election Commissioner

Analysis of the Results of
Plebiscite 2017* held in Puerto Rico

Plebiscite 2017	Votes for Statehood	Total Voters	Percentage Obtained
	502,616	517,216	97%

Plebiscite 2017	Votes for Statehood	Effective Voters	Percentage Obtained
	502,616	1,622,237	31%

Plebiscite 2017	Votes for Statehood	Registered Voters**	Percentage Obtained
	502,616	2,260,804	22%

Data source, Puerto Rico State Elections Commission webpage, http://ceepur.org/
* Preliminary Results Report of the 2017 Plebiscite Night of the Event.
http://resultados2017.ceepur.org/Noche_del_Evento_78/index.html#en/default/CONSULTA_DESCOLONIZACION_Resumen.xml
** By decision of the Federal Court the State Elections Commission (SEC) is required to remain in the General Register of Electors those who did not vote in the General Elections of 2016.

The CHAIRMAN. Thank you, Mr. Fuentes. And now let me recognize Dr. Christina D. Ponsa-Kraus, Professor of Law at the Columbia Law School. Doctor, the time is yours.

STATEMENT OF CHRISTINA D. PONSA-KRAUS, PROFESSOR OF LAW, COLUMBIA LAW SCHOOL, NEW YORK, NEW YORK

Dr. PONSA-KRAUS. Thank you, Mr. Chairman, Ranking Member Westerman, and members of the Committee. I am a law professor at Columbia University and an expert on Puerto Rico's constitutional status. And I am the author of a letter to congressional leadership signed by 47 legal and constitutional scholars supporting the Admission Act and opposing the Self-Determination Act. The letter has been introduced into the record.

I am also Puerto Rican myself. I was raised on the island from my infancy until I graduated from high school. I am a native speaker of Spanish. My parents and extended family live in Puerto Rico. I appreciate the Committee's attention to the urgent matter of Puerto Rico's future and the invitation to speak today.

Puerto Ricans reject territorial status, which denies them a guarantee of local self-government and Federal representation. Last November, a majority chose statehood in a referendum on the island. The Admission Act responds to that vote, and it is crucial to be clear about how. It does not automatically admit the island into statehood. It does not impose or force or grant statehood to Puerto Rico. Instead, it offers statehood to Puerto Rico. But first, Puerto Ricans must vote in a second referendum in which they can accept or reject the offer. Only if they accept does the Act provide for Puerto Rico's admission into statehood. This is a careful and constitutionally sound process.

The contrast with the Self-Determination Act could not be more stark. This Act contradicts its own title by completely ignoring the referendum in a thinly veiled attempt to delay and, therefore, defeat an offer of statehood. It sends Puerto Ricans back to the drawing board to have a debate they have been having for 70 years, and it requires Congress to ratify whatever option they choose, something Congress cannot constitutionally bind itself to do.

The Act requires convention delegates to "debate and draft definitions on self-determination options for Puerto Rico, which shall be outside the Territorial Clause." If this language means Puerto Ricans should debate the pros and cons of statehood and independence, it is gratuitous and dilatory. Puerto Ricans do not need a congressional invitation to debate these options, and they can keep right on debating them even after Congress offers statehood.

If this language means what its principal sponsors have said it means, then the problem gets worse. They have explained that a convention would consider "statehood, independence, free association, or any option other than the current territorial arrangement." This gets wrong a basic point of constitutional law. There are no other options.

Statehood is non-territorial. Independence is non-territorial. Free association has been described as a third option. But to be clear, it is a form of independence with a treaty or compact of free association between two sovereign nations. In short, there are two and only two non-territorial options for Puerto Rico, statehood and independence with or without free association. By inviting Puerto Ricans to define other territorial options, this bill revives a debate Puerto Ricans have already had.

When the island became a Commonwealth in 1952, many Puerto Ricans believed it had ceased to be a U.S. territory, become a separate sovereign, and entered into a binding compact with the United States. If there were a compact, Congress would no longer have the power to modify Puerto Rico's government unilaterally, and the island would at least no longer be a territory. But they were wrong. As the Supreme Court recently confirmed, even as a Commonwealth, Puerto Rico remains a U.S. territory, and Congress retains the power to modify the island's government unilaterally as it did, for example, when it created the Financial Oversight and Management Board in 2016. The myth of non-territorial commonwealth has long prevented Puerto Ricans from reckoning with the constitutional reality that the only alternatives to being a territory are statehood and independence. The last thing Puerto Ricans need is to debate options that are no longer debatable.

The Self-Determination Act invites Puerto Ricans to have a debate they have been having for seven decades and for which they need no congressional invitation. Yet, it deprives them of an offer of statehood which they have never had, they just asked for, and only Congress can deliver. Congress should pass the Admission Act without delay. Thank you.

[The prepared statement of Dr. Ponsa-Kraus follows:]

Prepared Statement of Christina D. Ponsa-Kraus, Law Professor at Columbia University

Good afternoon. My name is Christina D. Ponsa-Kraus. I am a law professor at Columbia University and an expert on Puerto Rico's constitutional status, and I am the author of a letter to Congressional leadership signed by 47 legal and constitutional scholars supporting the Admission Act and opposing the Self-Determination Act. The letter has been introduced into the record.

I am also Puerto Rican myself. I was raised on the island from my infancy until I graduated from high school. I am a native speaker of Spanish. My parents and extended family live in Puerto Rico. I appreciate the Committee's attention to the urgent matter of Puerto Rico's future and the invitation to speak today.

Puerto Ricans reject territorial status, which denies them a guarantee of local self-government and federal representation. Last November, a majority chose statehood in a referendum on the island. The Admission Act responds to that vote, and it is crucial to be clear about how. It does *not* automatically admit the island into statehood. It does *not* impose or force statehood on Puerto Rico. Instead, it *offers* statehood to Puerto Rico. But first, Puerto Ricans must vote in a *second* referendum, in which they can *accept* or *reject* the offer. Only if they *accept* does the Act provide for Puerto Rico's admission into statehood. This is a careful and constitutionally sound process.

The contrast with the Self-Determination Act could not be more stark. This Act contradicts its own title by completely ignoring the referendum. In a thinly veiled attempt to delay, and therefore defeat, an offer of statehood, it sends Puerto Ricans back to the drawing board to have a debate they have been having for 70 years. And it requires Congress to ratify whatever option they choose—something Congress cannot constitutionally bind itself to do.

The Act requires convention delegates to "debate and draft definitions on self-determination options . . . outside the Territorial Clause." If this language means Puerto Ricans should debate the pros and cons of statehood and independence, it is gratuitous and dilatory. Puerto Ricans do not need a congressional invitation to debate these options, and they can keep right on debating them even after Congress offers statehood.

If this language means what its principal sponsors have said it means, then the problem gets worse. They have explained that a convention would consider "statehood, independence, free association *or any option* other than the current territorial arrangement."[1] This gets wrong a basic point of constitutional law: There are no "other" non-territorial options.

Statehood is non-territorial. Independence is non-territorial. "Free association" has been described as a "third option," but to be clear: It is a form of independence, with a treaty or compact of free association between two sovereign nations. In short, there are two, and only two, non-territorial options for Puerto Rico: statehood, and independence with or without free association.

By inviting Puerto Ricans to define "other" non-territorial options, this bill revives a debate Puerto Ricans have already had. When the island became a "commonwealth" in 1952, many Puerto Ricans believed it had ceased to be a U.S. territory, become a separate sovereign, and entered into a binding compact with the United States. If there were a compact, Congress would no longer have the power to modify Puerto Rico's government unilaterally, and the island would at least no longer be a territory.

But they were wrong. As the Supreme Court recently confirmed, even as a "Commonwealth," Puerto Rico remains a U.S. territory, and Congress retains the power to modify the island's government unilaterally—as it did, for example, when it created the Financial Oversight and Management Board in 2016.

The myth of non-territorial commonwealth has long prevented Puerto Ricans from reckoning with the constitutional reality that the only alternatives to being a territory are statehood and independence. The last thing Puerto Ricans need is to debate options that are no longer debatable.

The Self-Determination Act invites Puerto Ricans to have a debate they have been having for seven decades and for which they need no congressional invitation. Yet it deprives them of an offer of statehood, which they have never had, they just asked for, and only Congress can deliver. Congress should pass the Admission Act without delay.

---

[1] Rep. Nydia Velázquez & Rep. Alexandria Ocasio-Cortez, *Puerto Rico, Not Congress, Must Determine Its Future. Our Bill Enables It To Do So*, nbcnews.com, Aug. 25, 2020.

The CHAIRMAN. Thank you very much. The Chair now recognizes the Speaker of the Puerto Rico House of Representatives, the Hon. Rafael Hernández. Sir, time is yours.

STATEMENT OF THE HON. RAFAEL HERNÁNDEZ MONTAÑEZ, SPEAKER, PUERTO RICO HOUSE OF REPRESENTATIVES, SAN JUAN, PUERTO RICO

Mr. HERNÁNDEZ. Thank you, Chair Grijalva, Ranking Member Westerman, Resident Commissioner González-Colón, and distinguished members of the Committee. I am the speaker of the House of Representatives in Puerto Rico. I stand today representing the people of Puerto Rico. I fully endorse H.R. 2070, introduced by Chairwoman Nydia Velázquez and Congresswoman Alexandria Ocasio-Cortez, a Senate companion bill introduced by Chairman Bob Menendez. This bicameral and bipartisan legislation is long overdue.

It will empower Puerto Ricans with an inclusive, transparent, and democratic process to determine our own political future and relationship with the United States. Under H.R. 2070, a political status convention would be created and delegates would be elected to discuss options with Federal representatives in Congress and the Federal Department of Justice and, therefore, create an official, legitimate, and comprehensive bilateral conversation on status.

On Election Day 2020, the people of Puerto Rico undeniably forged a historically diverse legislature with representation of five local political parties. I am both humbled and honored to have been elected by multiple sides of the aisle. This reality entrusts me with the responsibility of defending a fair and inclusive self-determination process. Puerto Rico treasures their identity and the benefits of their American citizenship. Trade, currency, defense, and common citizenship are assets that we enjoy today, and as such, are non-negotiable. A vast majority, some 85 percent of Puerto Ricans greatly value their citizenship and favor a permanent relationship with the United States.

On March 2, with support for a stable, free association, independence, and commonwealth, we approved Concurrent House Resolution No. 1 to demand that Congress clearly and affirmatively establish their alternative. It is willing to consider a solution to the political relationship. It also requests that Congress promote a binding, inclusive process with all ideological sectors.

I support H.R. 2070 because voters will be given a realistic definition of each viable option, avoiding political grandstanding. It is time we build a relationship based on dignity and respect. The Puerto Rico Self-Determination Act ensures a fair process that provides certainty to our people and to their political aspirations.

International law recognizes four alternatives. It is respective for H.R. 2070 to reaffirm that Estado libre asociado has the legal and practical viability of developing in a political model that our people can freely choose. It is the interest of Puerto Rico and the United States to promote this process. Previous, non-binding exclusionary electoral events managed by partisan extremists have wasted both our time and limited resources. Puerto Rico deserves a legitimate and truly binding self-determination process. Legitimacy is essential for credibility and veracity in the eyes of our people. These standards can only be achieved with equal participation.

Democracies evolve. That is why we legislate. The United States has changed throughout its history. Just as it was over a hundred years ago that women were given their right to vote, I sit today before your Committee to testify in support of legislation led by women that will enable our government to evolve the relationship within Puerto Rico and the United States. I urge this Committee to approve H.R. 2070. I thank you for this opportunity.

[The prepared statement of Mr. Hernández follows:]

PREPARED STATEMENT OF THE HON. RAFAEL HERNÉNDEZ MONTAÑEZ, SPEAKER, PUERTO RICO HOUSE OF REPRESENTATIVES

Chairman Grijalva, Ranking Member Westerman, and distinguished Members of the Committee, I am Rafael "Tatito" Hernéndez Montañez, and I am respectfully here as Speaker of the House of Representatives in Puerto Rico. I fully endorse H.R. 2070, legislation introduced by Chairwoman Nydia Velázquez and Congresswoman Alexandra Ocasio-Cortez, which has 73 co-sponsors to date. The Senate companion bill, introduced by Chairman Bob Menendez, has 7 co-sponsors.

This bicameral and bipartisan legislation is overdue. It will empower Puerto Ricans with an inclusive, transparent, and democratic process to determine our own political future and relationship with the United States. Under H.R. 2070, a political status convention would be created, and delegates would be elected to discuss options with federal officials, and therefore create an official, legitimate, and comprehensive bilateral conversation on status. I am thankful for the leadership of Chairwoman Velázquez, Congresswoman Ocasio-Cortez, and Chairman Menendez, and to all of those who have joined them as co-sponsors.

On Election Day 2020, the People of Puerto Rico unequivocally forged a historically diverse Legislative Assembly with representation from five (5) local political parties. That same day, Pedro Pierluisi-Urrutia of the New Progressive Party (NPP or "PNP" for its Spanish acronym) was elected as Governor of Puerto Rico; Jennifer González-Colón of the NPP was reelected as Resident Commissioner; and the people chose a Popular

Democratic Party (PDP or "PPD" for its Spanish acronym) majority in both the House and the Senate. However, after an in-depth analysis of this issue, other more relevant, pertinent data regarding the self-determination mechanisms before us arises.

The Governor of Puerto Rico was elected with 73% of party-line votes, 3% of mixed votes, and 24% of per candidate votes. The Legislature, on the other hand, was chosen with 67% of party-line votes, 14% of mixed votes, and 19% of per candidate votes. This data reveals that a third (1/3) of the Puerto Rican electorate does not identify itself with traditional parties. Most importantly, this data shows that Puerto Ricans have their own criteria when choosing partisan ties with their democratic institutions. This reality may explain why electors identify themselves as statehooders, but do not feel represented by the NPP; why commonwealth supporters may not see themselves as members of the PPD; or the reason why plural pro-independence voters do not support the Puerto Rican Pro-Independence Party ("PIP").

I was elected as the Speaker of the Puerto Rico House of Representatives with affirmative votes from the complete NPP delegation, the Representative from the newly founded Dignity Project ("Proyecto Dignidad") and the complete PDP delegation. Given our historical reality, I am both humbled and honored to have been elected by multiple sides of the aisle. This reality entrusts me with the responsibility of defending a democratically participative and inclusive self-determination process. Only through collaborative, honest dialogues may we see clear results that guarantee participation from all ideological sectors. This congressional hearing's inclusiveness honors our diversity.

Puerto Ricans treasure their identity and the benefits of their relationship with U.S. Trade, currency, defense, and common citizenship are assets that we enjoy today and, as such, are non-negotiable. A vast majority, some 85% of Puerto Ricans greatly value their American citizenship and favor a permanent relationship with the United States. These aspirations are already guaranteed by our current political arrangement, i.e., the Commonwealth of Puerto Rico.

On March 2, 2021, the House of Representatives approved Concurrent House Resolution No. 1 ("R. K. de la C. 1," or "RKC1") seeking to demand that the U.S. Congress, clearly and affirmatively, establish the alternatives it is willing to consider as a solution to the political relationship between Puerto Rico and the United States of America. It also requests that, in its expression, Congress promotes a binding, inclusive and participatory process with all of our ideological sectors.[2] Its main purpose is to ensure further discussion as to statehood, independence, sovereign association, and a new political model for the Commonwealth as viable solutions. Steps like today's hearing are necessary to achieve concrete results. However, we will only succeed if all ideological sectors feel and are indeed represented.

---

[2] See attached.

We support Congresswomen Velázquez and Ocasio-Cortez' H.R. 2070 because it convenes and calls upon a status convention, which genuinely promotes the participation of all parties while simultaneously collaborating with Congress and the Federal Department of Justice in analyzing all legal possibilities. For the first time, the electorate will be given a realistic definition of each viable option, preventing that a democratic exercise becomes a popularity contest, as has historically happened.

Without falling into scare tactics of politicians from all parties (NPP, PPD and PIP) on the island, Puerto Ricans identify only two alternatives of permanent union: Statehood and the Commonwealth. Therefore, if this self-determination process created by Congress does not allow for the continuing legal life of the Commonwealth outside of the territorial clauses, the process becomes one similar to the intention of H.R. 1522 in that we are excluded from the process.

I affirm that those of us privileged enough to speak here on behalf of the People of Puerto Rico aspire to some sort of political relationship with the United States. We must build a relationship based on dignity and respect, safe from any single party's unilateral modification. This effort's result must ensure a fair self-determination process that provides certainty to the people of Puerto Rico as to their political relationship with the United States. International law recognizes, according to United Nations Resolution 2625 (XXV) of October 24, 1970, "the establishment of a sovereign an independent State, the free association or integration with an independent State or the emergence into any other political status freely determined by a people constitute modes of implementing the right of self-determination by that people." It is from this international perspective, as H.R. 2070 reiterates, that the Commonwealth has the legal and practical viability of developing in a political model that our people can freely and voluntarily choose.

Previous, non-binding exclusionary electoral events managed by partisan fanaticism have wasted both our time and limited resources. Puerto Rico's present and future condition critically deserves a legitimate and truly binding self-determination process. Legitimacy is essential for credibility and veracity in the eyes of our people. These standards can only be achieved with equal participation.

Democracies evolve. That is why we legislate. The U.S. has changed throughout it's history. Just think that it was just over 100 years ago that women were given the chance to vote in the United States. And I sit here today before your Committee to testify in support of legislation, led by women no less, that will someday enable my government and yours to evolve and to realize a relationship for Puerto Rico and the United States that is more perfect in nature that what exists. Let's not close our minds to progress.

I thank you for this opportunity to testify.

The CHAIRMAN. Thank you very much, Speaker. And let me now recognize the Hon. Aníbal Acevedo-Vilá, former Governor, former colleague of mine on this Committee, the Popular Democratic Party Governor. The time is yours.

STATEMENT OF THE HON. ANÍBAL ACEVEDO-VILÁ, FORMER GOVERNOR, POPULAR DEMOCRATIC PARTY, SAN JUAN, PUERTO RICO

Mr. ACEVEDO-VILÁ. Thank you, Mr. Chairman and Ranking Member. I think I know what is the question in the mind of many of you today. Should Puerto Rico become a state? Let me be clear: I strongly oppose statehood. Like many in Puerto Rico, and many Members of Congress, we recognize that statehood is not good for Puerto Rico, nor will it be good for the United States. Our opposition is based on historical, cultural, national identity, and economic realities.

But let's examine today a more immediate question. Is there a mandate to grant statehood to Puerto Rico? The answer is no.

Yes, the people of Puerto Rico voted with a close margin in favor of statehood in November. That was a non-binding referendum rejected by the U.S. Department of Justice and by four of the five political parties in Puerto Rico.

On election day, Puerto Ricans elected new anti-statehood majorities in the House and the Senate, and most of the mayors elected that day are also anti-statehood. The truth: we remain deeply divided. Any attempt to move forward a petition to make Puerto Rico a state will further divide our people, without solving the underlying problem of our colonial relationship.

In my written statement, I have shared some data from a poll conducted by Hart Research in August of last year. When all of the options are given to the people of Puerto Rico, statehood support goes down to 41 percent, Commonwealth gets 38 percent, Free Association 8 percent, and independence 6 percent.

Making Puerto Rico a state is an irrevocable decision that will affect present and future generations. The most important information that comes from the Hart Research is the limited support a state would have with the younger generation. Within the 18- to 34-year-old bracket, the support for statehood goes down to 35 percent, the support for free association goes up to 20 percent, and for independence to 15 percent.

Contrary to all other status bills introduced within the last 30 years, H.R. 2070, the Puerto Rico Self-Determination Act, was not drafted nor pushed by any of the local political parties in Puerto Rico. That is a good way to start this contentious process.

For the first time, this bill gives the opportunity for Congress to talk directly to the people of Puerto Rico. H.R. 2070 is not a colonial imposition. It doesn't order anything, nor precludes any type of outcome. No one is excluded nor favored. If our legislator decides to call for a status convention, all status options will have a fair opportunity to participate and elect delegates.

Actually, if the statehood in reality are the majority, then the majority of the delegates elected to the convention will support that option. The most important component of this bill is the creation of the Congressional Negotiating Commission. This Commission will have to answer and clarify many of the legal constitutional language, cultural, and economic questions that for more than 100 years our people have attempted to answer, but Congress has failed to address.

Included now, how will the different status alternative be affected or impacted by the ongoing process established by PROMESA and the restructuring of the debt? Everything will then be in the hands of Puerto Rico.

Under H.R. 2070, the people will freely vote two times, initially to elect the members of the convention, and later to select the preferred status option. The only limitation is that any definition presented to the people for a vote after the negotiation with the commission must be outside of the Territorial Clause. That will guarantee that we really put Puerto Rico on the path for decolonization.

The first time I testified before this Committee on this issue was in 1997. All congressional attempts have failed precisely because they have no consensus in Puerto Rico and were based on the agenda of the Puerto Rico Statehood Party to tilt the process in their favor.

Before us today you have two paths, one that will repeat the same mistakes of the last 30 years, or you can finally try a different approach, inclusive and unbiased toward any alternative.

The Puerto Rico Self-Determination Act is a creative and fair process to avoid the mistakes of the past. The path toward decolonization is not going to be easy, but it has to start now. I urge this Committee to approve H.R. 2070.

[The prepared statement of Mr. Acevedo-Vilá follows:]

PREPARED STATEMENT OF GOVERNOR ANÍBAL ACEVEDO-VILÁ, FORMER GOVERNOR OF THE POPULAR DEMOCRATIC PARTY

I am grateful to Chairman Raúl Grijalva and the House Natural Resources Committee for holding this important hearing and for this opportunity to testify. I come to you in my personal capacity as a former Member of the House of Representative and this Committee and as former Governor of Puerto Rico. I have also directly or indirectly participated in every political status process that has been held over the last 30 years regarding the relationship between Puerto Rico and the United States. Recently I began working collectively with a group of puertorriqueños, from diverse backgrounds and political views, and help to establish a new non-partisan political advocacy group, *Frente Puertorriqueñista*,[3] to advocate and educate the public regarding the urgent need for the

---

3 *A new group to address political status*, El Nuevo D′ıa, March 30, 2021, https://www.elnuevodia.com/english/news/story/a-new-group-to-address-political-status/. See attachment 1.

U.S. Congress to enact and adopt a fair and inclusive process of self-determination to decolonize Puerto Rico, and to defend the national and cultural identity of the Island. One of the core positions of the *Frente Puertorriqueñista* is to support H.R. 2070, The Puerto Rico Self-Determination Act, introduced by Chairwoman Nydia Velázquez and Congress-woman Alexandria Ocasio-Cortez.

I want to start with what I believe is the question at the forefront in the minds of the Members of this Committee and more broadly in the House and Senate— should Puerto Rico enter the Union as the 51st or 52nd state? Let me be clear— I strongly oppose statehood for Puerto Rico, a position shared by the members of the *Frente*. Like many of you, we recognize that statehood is not a good option for Puerto Rico, nor would it be good for the United States. Our opposition to statehood is based on historical, cultural, national identity and economic realities. But this is not the reason I'm here today. Let's examine a more appropriate question today: Is there a mandate to grant statehood to Puerto Rico?

The answer is NO.

Yes, the people of Puerto Rico voted 52.5% to 47.5% in favor of statehood in a non-binding referendum held on Election Day 2020. But that was a referendum rejected by the U.S. Department of Justice, and by 4 of the 5 political parties in Puerto Rico, because all the other options for the future political relationship between Puerto Rico and the U.S. were excluded from the ballot. The referendum's result has to be analyzed within the following context:

1. The pro-statehood candidate for Governor won with only 33% of the votes, while the other 67% voted for a candidate for Governor who did not promote making Puerto Rico the 51st state.
2. On Election Day, Puerto Ricans elected new anti-statehood majorities in both the Puerto Rico House of Representatives and the Senate. A majority of mayors elected in Puerto Rico also oppose statehood.
3. The referendum was held even after the U.S. Department of Justice refused to sanction the referendum and formally rejected using federal funding to conduct the vote. DOJ ruled that the statehood party-designed plebiscite did not comply with the Constitution, federal law, or standing public policy. The DOJ, in 2017, rejected another statehood party designed referendum for similar reasons.
4. Only the pro-statehood movement was actively campaigning and spending money for a yes vote. That means it was basically a one-sided campaign with only statehood on the ballot, therefore excluding pro-independence, pro-Commonwealth, and pro-free association voters from the ballot.

Any objective look at Puerto Rican reality and the facts on the ground lead to one conclusion: Puerto Ricans remain deeply divided on the statehood question. And any attempt to move forward with a petition to make Puerto Rico the 51st or 52nd state will further divide our people without solving the underlying problem of our colonial relationship with the U.S.

This division raises another important question that needs to be answered: Do Puerto Ricans support other options or is statehood the only option?

I am here to tell you that Puerto Ricans certainly do support other options—and statehood is not the only option for Puerto Rico, or for the United States.

I'm sharing with the Committee the results of a poll conducted during the period of July 20 to August 9, 2020 by the prestigious D.C. based firm Hart Research.[4] Their results were extremely accurate regarding the final outcome in November, and included very relevant questions related to the statehood referendum.

The Hart Research poll had statehood wining by a close margin, 48% to 45%, in early August. This was nearly the exact result in November. Interestingly, 54% of those polled thought the referendum was not a serious proposal, even though they were willing to participate.

The most interesting data from the Hart poll was when the real political status questions were asked. In Puerto Rico, the issue about our relationship with the USA, the "status" issue as we call it, is not only regarding "statehood" (it is really annexation.) There is complete agreement there are other options, like a new non-colonial, non-territorial Estado Libre Asociado, some form of Free Association with the USA, and Independence. One of the complaints of the local political parties was that those of us who believe in those other options were not afforded (some might say silenced from) real participation in the referendum.

The Hart Research poll did ask that question. When all the options are given, annexation ("statehood") support goes down to 41%, Commonwealth gets 38%, Free Association 8% and Independence 6% (with 7% undecided).

Beyond the fact that the support for statehood in that poll goes from 48% when it is a yes or no question, to 41% when the other options are included, it is more interesting that the options of a relationship with the USA other than statehood are the majority (Commonwealth + Free Association = 46%).

Making Puerto Rico the 51st state is an irrevocable decision that will affect future generations, well beyond that 52% of individuals that actually voted for that option. Perhaps the most important piece of information that comes from the Hart Research poll is the limited support that statehood has with the younger generation. Within the 18–34-year-old bracket, the support for statehood goes down to 35% and the support for Free Association goes up to 20% and for independence to 15%.

So why did statehood eventually get 52% in the November referendum? The Hart Research poll also gives us some explanation. When only given the yes or no to statehood

---

[4] See attachment 2.

option, 15% of those who vote yes, really support one of the other options not given to them (especially Commonwealth) in the question that included all the options. Having been deprived of their alternative, they voted for statehood. It is clear that it is only the lack of options and not that they really want statehood.

The answer to the two previous questions is obvious: there is no mandate from the People of Puerto Rico to make the island the 51st state and we do request a fair and inclusive process of self-determination that will finally bring decolonization. And there is where H.R. 2070 comes to play.

I, as well as the *Frente Puertorriqueñista* support H.R. 2070 because it's a serious, fair and inclusive process.

Contrary to all the other status bills introduced in Congress during the last 30 years, H.R. 2070 was not drafted nor pushed by any of the local political parties in Puerto Rico. That's a good way to start this contentious process. This new approach could also facilitate an eventual consensus here in Congress as well as in Puerto Rico. For the first time, this bill gives the opportunity for Congress to talk directly to the People of Puerto Rico, without the need to use local political parties as intermediaries. The political diversity of those from Puerto Rico testifying today in support of H.R. 2070 is a clear showing of its potential for consensus.

H.R. 2070 is not a colonial imposition by Congress on Puerto Ricans. It doesn't order anything, nor precludes any type of outcome. No one is excluded, nor favored. If enacted, the start of the process will be completely in the hands of the elected officials in the Island. It doesn't even have status definitions so as to avoid a process that could be challenged as biased and in favor or in opposition to any of the status options from the very beginning.

If the Legislative Assembly in Puerto Rico decides to call for a Status Convention, all status options will have a fair opportunity to participate and to elect delegates to the convention. Actually, if statehood is really the favorite option of the people, the majority of delegates elected will support that option.

The most important and creative component of this bill is the creation of a Negotiating Commission. If Puerto Rico calls for a Status Convention, a bipartisan commission, with Members of the House and the Senate and with representation from the executive branch will be created with the specific duty to have dialogue and negotiations with the delegates of the different status alternatives. The Negotiating Commission will have to answer and clarify many of the legal, constitutional, language, cultural and economic questions that for more than a hundred years our people have attempted to answer, but Congress has failed to address. Is Congress willing to accept as a state a nation with Spanish as the official and only language in the state courts, legislature and public schools? What effect will federal income taxation have on the economy and the budget of the government of the "State of Puerto Rico? Can the state of Puerto Rico keep the triple tax exemption that the current bonds (and that are being renegotiated right now) enjoy? Under what constitutional underpinnings can a non-territorial Estado Libre Asociado be established? What agreements regarding U.S. citizenship can be established under free association? What transition agreement toward independence is Congress willing to offer? How will all the status alternatives be affected or impacted by the undergoing process established by PROMESA and the restructuring of the debt? H.R. 2070 has for the first time established a process that could finally give the people of both our countries the necessary answers we deserve.

After the negotiating process, the members of the Status Convention will deliberate and present to the people the different options for a vote. This will be the first time that we will vote on status options with clear information of what Congress is willing to offer and what are the consequences of the different options. Everything will then be in the hands of Puerto Rico. Under H.R. 2070 the people will freely vote two times, initially to elect the members to the Status Convention, and later to select their preferred status option. The only limitation imposed by H.R. 2070 is that any definition put forward by the Negotiating Commission and presented to the people for a vote must be outside of the territorial clause of the U.S. Constitution. That will guarantee that we will really put Puerto Rico on the path for decolonization.

The first time I testified before this Committee on this issue of the status of Puerto Rico was in 1997. I have lost count how many times I have walked the halls of Congress over the last 30 years to discuss different bills on this important issue. All prior attempts have failed precisely because they had no consensus in Puerto Rico and were based on the agenda of the Puerto Rico statehood party to tilt the process in their favor. During that same period, the statehood party has called for plebiscites in Puerto Rico, without any federal support, in five occasions (1993, 1998, 2012, 2017 and 2020). Those local initiatives have failed for the same reason.

Puerto Ricans deserve that this time be different. The U.S. Congress and the Biden Administration have a moral, legal and political responsibility to enact H.R. 2070. Before us today are two paths. One that will repeat the same mistakes of the last 30 years. Or we can finally try a different approach. One that is inclusive, and unbiased toward any alternative. The Puerto Rico Self Determination Act of 2021 is a creative, inclusive and fair process that avoids the mistakes of the past and offers a new way forward. The path toward decolonization is not going to be easy. But it has to start now. I urge this Committee to approve H.R. 2070.

The CHAIRMAN. Thank you, sir. Let me now introduce the Honorable María de Lourdes Santiago, Senator of the Puerto Rico Independence Party. Senator, the time is yours.

STATEMENT OF THE HON. MARÍA DE LOURDES SANTIAGO, SENATOR, PUERTO RICO INDEPENDENCE PARTY, SAN JUAN, PUERTO RICO

[The following statement and answers were delivered through an interpreter.]

The CHAIRMAN. Gracias. Over to the interpreter.

Ms. SANTIAGO. Mr. Chairman and members of the Committee, at the outset, it is important to put this hearing in its right context. We are here today because of the refusal by the United States to exercise its responsibility toward Puerto Rico, the territory it claimed 123 years ago as a war booty.

The continuance of the U.S. colonial domination of our nation, notwithstanding the many occasions and diverse methods by which we have demanded an end to colonialism, contravenes both legal and historical mandates, provoking a situation that is oppressive for us and shameful for the United States. Regarding the status problem, Puerto Rico has been the victim and the United States the perpetrator.

The only serious initiative undertaken by Congress to promote the exercise of the right to self-determination by the Puerto Rican people was the consideration between 1898 and 1991 of the Johnston Bill. Though it was defeated, there was three important outcomes that deserve careful examination by this Committee: the impossibility, recently ratified by the three government branches of the U.S. Government, to upgrade the existing colonial status to a truly bilateral relation amongst equals; the need to elaborate a transition plan for independence; and, finally, the resistance to make an offer of statehood to a Caribbean and Latin American nation in which the vast majority of the population, even those who favor annexation, do not think of themselves as Americans. And many of those that promote statehood wield as the main reason for their political aspiration their ambition to perpetuate the financial dependence on Federal funds.

Of the two bills before this Committee, only H.R. 2070 provides the means to avoid a similar dead-end as the Johnston Bill. In contrast with H.R. 1522, H.R. 2070 contains the elements that make it a potentially effective instrument to promote decolonization by enabling the Congressional Bilateral Negotiating Committee included in the bill to answer the essential question as to what Congress is really willing to offer Puerto Rico.

Contrary to the case of Washington, DC, Puerto Rico is financially bankrupt as a result of the failure of the colonial relationship. Neither is there an overwhelming support for statehood in Puerto Rico. On the contrary, we are deeply divided as to our future relation with the United States. More importantly, the national identity of the inhabitants of Washington, DC, is unmistakably American, and in this critical respect, indistinguishable from the residents of other states. That is not the case of Puerto Rico. Our nationality was forged and established before the U.S. invasion. And even after 123 years of colonialism, most of the population does not have a working knowledge of the

English language. Ours is not the struggle for full individual civil rights. It is one for the collective right to self-determination of a colonized nation.

Furthermore, we are all aware that the leadership of both parties in the U.S. Senate have anticipated that H.R. 1522 is destinated to failure, which translates as another path to congressional inaction and to the continuation of the colonialism.

Finally, we must emphasize that for H.R. 2070 to be successful, it is critically important that Congress be unyielding in its requirement that the status options be outside the Territorial Clause.

The Puerto Rican Independence Party welcomes H.R. 2070 and looks forward to proposing modifications to the bill in order to improve its efficacy. The enactment of H.R. 2070 would represent a much-needed return to the principles that once guided the nation that first raised the flag for freedom and independence in America.

[The prepared statement of Ms. Santiago follows:]

Prepared Statement of María De Lourdes Santiago, Vice President and Senator, Puerto Rican Independence Party

Mr. Chairman and members of the Committee: We are here today because the United States has never exercised its responsibility toward Puerto Rico, the territory it acquired by conquest in 1898. Puerto Rico's status problem cannot be attributed to Puerto Rico. Puerto Rico has been the victim and the United States has been the perpetrator. Such an egregious breach of fiduciary duty throughout the 20th century and until today by a nation that thinks of itself as a beacon of democracy can only be described as stunning and shameful.

It was the United States who demanded Puerto Rico as a war booty at the conclusion of the Spanish American War, and it has been—since then—the United States who has maintained Puerto Rico as a colony, subject to the plenary powers of Congress under the Territorial Clause.

During the last 123 years the people of Puerto Rico—on innumerable occasions and by different methods—have requested that the United States put an end to the colonial regime in Puerto Rico. Yet, never once has the United States provided the people of Puerto Rico—a distinct Caribbean and Latin American nation—the opportunity to enter into a process that would permit the exercise of the right to self-determination and independence as required by international law in order to put an end to colonial rule. This responsibility is incumbent upon the United States not only through the International Covenant on Civil and Political Rights which was ratified by the U.S. Senate in 1992 and is part of the "supreme law of the land," but also by virtue of the United Nations General Assembly Resolution 1514 of 1960.

The only serious congressional initiative in the direction of self-determination was that undertaken from 1989 to 1991 (as the fall of the Berlin Wall put an end to the cold war) by Senator Bennet Johnston (S. 712). It attempted to negotiate with the Puerto Rican leaders definitions and transition measures for different status alternatives such that a final vote by Puerto Ricans would take place between alternatives that had the prior approval by the Congress.

After 2 years of intense work by various Senate committees and by the political parties in Puerto Rico (including the PIP), the bill was defeated in Senator Johnston's own Committee on Energy and Natural Resources.

What happened in that failed attempt bears careful examination. For the Puerto Rican Independence Party the results were bittersweet. On the one hand there were three positive outcomes, all of which we had predicted and which amply justified our strong participation in that legislative process; on the other hand it turned out the bill was destined to fail.

The first important outcome was that it became absolutely clear, especially to those who had hoped differently, that the existing colonial status of unincorporated territory (titled "Commonwealth") could not be upgraded to a truly bilateral relation amongst equals because Congress could not effectively abdicate any of its powers over Puerto Rico under the Territorial Clause unless it disposed of the territory, in which case Puerto Rico would be a separate sovereign.

This conclusion was subsequently formally ratified in this century by the Congress, the White House under different administrations, and the Supreme Court.

The second important outcome was the elaboration of an economic transition plan for the independence alternative that put to rest old mythologies which equated national liberation and Puerto Rican sovereign status to a form of collective suicide and as a recipe for isolation from the U.S. market and from the millions of Puerto Ricans who resided in the United States.

The third decisive outcome of the Johnston process was that it quickly and clearly emerged that resistance to statehood (particularly in a bill that, at least initially, purported to be self-executing) would lead to the defeat of the bill, as it did. In the end the worry by most Republicans and many Democrats was that the inclusion of statehood in any plebiscite sponsored by the Congress would be interpreted as a commitment to granting statehood if it should win such a vote.

These three outcomes are pertinent today. The problem with the Johnston initiative however was that its defeat only served to place the issue of Puerto Rico's status in the back-burner for 30 years thus assuring that the existing colonial relationship—ever more dysfunctional—continued by default.

At this moment, if we are to avoid a similar outcome, it is indispensable for Congress to speak out openly in a clear and strong voice as to its true parameters concerning the future of its relation to Puerto Rico.

Of the two bills before this Committee, H.R. 2070 is the only one that has the potential of promoting a process that will lead to decolonization. H.R. 1522, on the contrary, will lead us back to another dead end. H.R. 1522 will either not be brought to a final vote, at least in the Senate, and if it were, the leadership of both parties in the Senate have already anticipated their opposition. H.R. 1522 is therefore another path to congressional inaction and to the continuation of colonialism.

The possibility of statehood is a pipe dream concocted by a toxic combination of colonialism induced dependency and insecurity in Puerto Rico (a tropical form of the Stockholm Syndrome), with the well-intentioned but superficial sympathy of some U.S. liberals who believe that not to support statehood would be to think of Puerto Ricans as "non-deserving." Thinking that to become a state of the U.S. is an exalted and privileged condition to which everyone should aspire, they don't want to be singled out as excluding Puerto Rico. What they forget or ignore is that Puerto Rico's problem is a colonial problem, not one of the equality denied to a minority under the laws and Constitution of the United States. While Puerto Ricans who live in the United States, being a minority, struggle for full individual civil rights, the problem of Puerto Rico is one of national liberation where the collective right to self-determination and independence of a colonial people is an inalienable and universally recognized human right.

The comparison with Washington DC is illustrative of why the case for statehood for Puerto Rico cannot prevail, and why it is objectively contrary to the interests of the United States.

DC is financially viable as a state, being a net contributor to the U.S. Treasury, and support for statehood is overwhelming. More importantly and this is crucial— the inhabitants of Washington DC are citizens whose cultural and national identity is American, who have no conflict of loyalties with the United States and are indistinguishable from the residents of the different states in this critical respect. There are no reasons of substance to exclude them from full participation at this period in history other than circumstantial and cynical considerations of partisan advantage.

Puerto Rico, on the contrary, is financially bankrupt as a result of the failure of the colonial relationship, and deeply divided and wary of political integration. Those of us who believe in independence—and those to come—will continue our struggle under any circumstance and never renounce our inalienable right to independence. The immense majority of the population—including most who favor statehood— though U.S. citizens, do not think of themselves as Americans and allude principally to considerations of economic convenience as reasons to prefer statehood. More than two-thirds of the population (for complex reasons including historical resistance to foreign imposition) does not have even working knowledge of the English language.

Puerto Rico, as a Caribbean and Latin American nation distinct from the United States, is a non-compatible donor to the organism of U.S. federalism: the opposite of Washington DC. The challenge before Congress in the case of Puerto Rico is to face up to these truths at the same time that it insists that colonialism in Puerto Rico must be terminated.

H.R. 2070, in principle, and in contrast with H.R. 1522, contains the elements that make it a potentially effective instrument to promote decolonization by enabling the congressional leadership (through the Congressional Bilateral Negotiating Commission included in the bill) to answer the essential question of what Congress is really willing to offer Puerto Rico. Other than independence— which is an inalienable right and can never be off the table, even if Puerto Rico were a state—both statehood and a sovereign free association require the consent of Congress. Congress therefore has a right to grant or not to grant either statehood or a Treaty of Free Association, and to define their terms and conditions.

Since the U.S., although it recognizes cultural diversity, is not and does not wish to be a multi-national federation, the Bilateral Negotiation Committee proposed by H.R. 2070 will inevitably lay out the truth—either directly or by imposing impossible conditions—regarding the possibility of statehood. Moreover, why would the U.S. admit a state that will become the problem Quebec represents for Canada, Scotland for the UK, or Catalonia for Spain? If marriage is not possible, the suitor, no matter how deluded, has a right to know as soon as possible.

Furthermore, it is critical and indispensable that for H.R. 2070 to be successful Congress be unyielding in its requirement that the status options be outside the Territorial Clause. It must also, of course, chart out the alternatives of independence and sovereign free association in terms that do justice to Puerto Rico and that protect the legitimate interests of both countries by duly taking account of the consequences and entanglements of 123 years of enforced colonialism.

In light of the above, the PIP welcomes H.R. 2070 and looks forward to working with the proponents and the Committee to make such modifications in the bill (including its Findings) that improve its efficacy and clarity as well as its opportunities for congressional approval.

When Senator Johnston in 1989 brought up the question of self-determination for Puerto Rico one can say—looking back—that the matter was important to the U.S. but it certainly was not urgent.

Today, the reality is otherwise. This time Congress cannot afford to fail. Puerto Rico is constitutionally a failed colonial state; it is literally bankrupt, has 50% of the population under the poverty level, the lowest labor participation rate in the world, 15 years of continuous economic contraction, a rapidly diminishing population, and a growing sense of collective desperation.

It is incumbent upon Congress to exercise its responsibility to put an end to colonialism and at last to promote and make possible the exercise of the right of self-determination of the Puerto Rican nation to which Puerto Rico is entitled. That is the historical debt owed by the United States to the People of Puerto Rico.

It would also be a much needed return to first principles by the nation that first raised the flag of the struggle for freedom and independence in America.

The CHAIRMAN. Thank you very much. Much appreciated. And let me now turn to our last witness. Let me recognize the Honorable Manuel Natal, President of the Citizens Victory Movement. Mr. Natal, the time is yours.

STATEMENT OF THE HON. MANUEL NATAL-ALBELO, PRESIDENT, CITIZENS VICTORY MOVEMENT, SAN JUAN, PUERTO RICO

Mr. NATAL-ALBELO. Thank you, Chairman Grijalva and members of the Committee. My name is Manuel Natal-Albelo. I am a former member of Puerto Rico's House of Representatives, and as of last Sunday, I serve as General Coordinator of Movimiento Victoria Ciudadana, a recently created, people-powered, community-oriented, progressive political party in Puerto Rico.

I must stress from the outset that Puerto Rico has been a colony of the United States since 1898 and legally defined as an unincorporated territory, a possession but not part of the United States, under the plenary powers of Congress. Although Congress has reorganized the territorial government over the years, the colonial nature of the relationship has remain unchanged.

Since 1898, Congress has never—let me repeat that again—never consulted the Puerto Rican people in a binding plebiscite or referendum on whether to retain the present status, become independent, or a state of the Union. Having retained its plenary powers, Congress should assume its responsibility for a territory it claims as a possession, yet it has avoided doing so for 123 years.

Today, we have an opportunity to change that. This Committee, and eventually Congress, is presented with a unique choice between two paths. The first path is one that we have traveled many times before. Plebiscites or referenda promulgated unilaterally and without consensus by a political party on the island, devoid of informed public deliberation, and usually designed to be slanted toward the outcome favored by the ruling party, the final results of which have lacked democratic legitimacy, whether the prevailing options receives 97 percent of the votes or 0 percent of the votes. That path of exclusion and subordination is currently represented by H.R. 1522.

The second path is one that, although it has been historically promoted by diverse and well-respected groups in Puerto Rico, it has never been supported by Congress or by any previous administration in Puerto Rico. A binding self-determination process, in which all non-colonial, non-territorial options can compete on a level playing field, and in which the people of Puerto Rico get to cast an informed vote, and Congress must act upon the will of the majority. That path of inclusion and empowerment is currently represented by H.R. 2070.

We choose the latter and urge Congress to do the same. We, a political movement that promotes real change in all aspects of our lives as Puerto Ricans, including ending the colonial relationship. We, the only political movement in Puerto Rico that has elected officials from all three non-colonial, non-territorial options. That is statehood, independence, and some form of free association.

How have we managed to achieve what the two-party system in Puerto Rico has not in more than 70 years? By focusing on finding common ground and not on how we can cancel each other's efforts on the status question.

In this particular case, we have focused on building a fair and inclusive process, rather than trying to predetermine the outcome. This is why we propose and support the Constitutional Status Convention, Asamblea Constitucional de Status, as the best means for decolonizing Puerto Rico.

Puerto Ricans, yes, are U.S. citizens. But we are also a nation, a people with our own identity and culture under U.S. colonial rule since 1898. Sometimes these facts generate confusion.

Should Puerto Rico aspire to become a state of the Union? Should they become independent? Should they become a sovereign freely associated state with the United States? A democratic response from the U.S. Congress should be that it is for them, not us, to decide. The first step in that process shall be done by ourselves, los puertorriqueños y las puertorriqueñas, in a true, binding exercise of self-determination.

We are ready to do our part. It is your moral responsibility to fulfill yours. Thank you very much.

[The prepared statement of Mr. Natal-Albelo follows:]

PREPARED STATEMENT OF MANUEL NATAL-ALBELO, GENERAL COORDINATOR, CITIZENS VICTORY MOVEMENT

My name is Manuel Natal-Albelo, a former member of Puerto Rico's House of Representatives and as of last Sunday, the General Coordinator of *Movimiento Victoria Ciudadana* (Citizens Victory Movement), a recently created, progressive, people-powered, and community-centered political party in Puerto Rico. I was invited by the Committee to testify before the Full Committee Legislative Hearing on H.R. 1522, "Puerto Rico Statehood Admission Act" and H.R. 2070, "Puerto Rico Self-Determination Act of 2021."

I must stress from the outset that Puerto Rico has been a colony of the United States since 1898 and legally defined as an unincorporated territory, a possession but not part of the United States, under the plenary powers of Congress. Although Congress has reorganized the territorial government over the years leading up to the creation of the present Commonwealth status in 1952, the colonial nature of the relationship has remained unchanged. Since 1898, Congress has *never* consulted the Puerto Rican people in a binding plebiscite or referendum on whether to retain the present status, become independent, or a state of the Union. Having retained its plenary powers, Congress should assume its responsibility for a territory it claims as a possession. Yet, it has avoided doing so for 123 years.

Today we have an opportunity to change that. This Committee, and eventually, Congress, is presented with a unique choice between two paths. The first path is one that we have traveled many times before: plebiscites or referenda promulgated unilaterally and without consensus by a political party on the island, devoid of informed public deliberation, and usually designed to be slanted toward the outcome favored by the ruling party, the final results of which have lacked democratic legitimacy, whether the "prevailing" option receives 97% of the votes or 0%. That path of exclusion and subordination is currently represented by H.R. 1522, the "Puerto Rico Statehood Admission Act." The second path is one that, although it has been historically promoted by diverse and well-respected groups in Puerto Rico, has never been supported by Congress, or by any previous administration in Puerto Rico: a binding self-determination process, in which all non-colonial non-territorial options can compete on a level playing field, and in which the People of Puerto Rico get to cast an informed vote and Congress must act upon the will of the majority. That path of inclusion and empowerment is currently represented by H.R. 2070, the "Puerto Rico Self-Determination Act of 2021."

We chose the latter and urge Congress to the same. We, a political movement that promotes real change in all aspects of our lives as Puerto Ricans, including ending the colonial relationship with the United States. *We*, the only political movement in Puerto Rico that has elected officials from all three non-colonial non-territorial options. That is: statehood, independence, and some form of free association. How have we managed to achieve what the two-party system in Puerto Rico had not in more than 70 years? By focusing on finding common ground and not on how we can cancel each other's efforts on the status question. In this particular case, we have focused on building a fair and inclusive process, rather than trying to predetermine the result. This is why we propose the Constitutional Status Convention (*Asamblea Constitucional de Status* in Spanish) as the best means for decolonizing Puerto Rico. Our proposal provides for the following course of action:

1. The Legislature of Puerto Rico will call a Status Convention (SC).
2. The People of Puerto Rico will elect delegates to the convention, representatives of all three non-colonial non-territorial options (statehood, independence, and some form of free association).

3. The delegates will draft definitions on self-determination options for Puerto Rico, which shall be outside the Territorial Clause of the United States Constitution, and will draft transition plans for each self-determination option.
4. These self-determination options and the transition plans will be negotiated with Congress, and the results of this process will be binding upon Congress.
5. The People of Puerto Rico will vote for all the self-determination options drafted by the Convention and adopted by Congress in a referendum. The winning option will be enacted. If in the first referendum no option obtains more than 50% of the vote, a second-round will be held between the two options that obtained the most votes in the first round.[5]

As proponents of the Constitutional Status Convention as a means of exercising our right of self-determination, we reject the argument made by some that this mechanism places the solution of the status question in the hands of a minority or a few people or in "small rooms" and not in the hands of the people. With this process, the People of Puerto Rico elect the delegates to the Status Convention, and the people, through a referendum, also determine which self-determination option they prefer. Nobody decides for the people. The delegates to the Convention have the task of elaborating the options to be presented to the people in a referendum. This is the task performed in the past by the legislators who drafted the legislation for the five previous status plebiscites conducted in 1967, 1993, 1998, 2012, and 2017. In our case, we propose that this task be carried out by a special body, the Constitutional Status Convention, elected for that specific purpose, in negotiation with Congress, and the people will vote at the end of the drafting and negotiation process.

Thus, we oppose H.R. 1522, "Puerto Rico Statehood Admission Act." Puerto Rico's colonial condition requires a fair and inclusive self-determination process in line with international law that considers all non-colonial, non-territorial options, and not merely an admission bill. On the other hand, we are optimistic about the proposals included in H.R. 2070, "Puerto Rico Self-Determination Act of 2021." It is high time for Congress to recognize the right of self-determination for the People of Puerto Rico and act expeditiously to put an end to the existing colonial relationship.

Puerto Ricans are U.S. citizens as well as a nation, a people with their own identity and culture, under U.S. colonial rule since 1898. Sometimes these facts generate confusion regarding Puerto Rico's relation with the United States. Should Puerto Ricans aspire to become a state of the Union? Should they become independent? Should they become a sovereign freely associated state with the United States? A democratic response from the U.S. Congress should be: that is for them, not us, to decide. The first step in that

---

[5] We note that H.R. 2070 promotes the use of ranked-choice voting for the final referendum, and we recognize that it is another legitimate electoral mechanism for reaching a majority mandate on a self-determination option.

process shall be done by ourselves, *las puertorriqueñas y los puertorriqueños*, in a true, binding exercise of self-determination.

The CHAIRMAN. Thank you very much, and let me thank the witnesses for their testimony, and we will go to questions now. Under Committee Rule 3(d), it imposes a 5-minute limit on the questions by Members, with the noted exception that I made regarding the sponsor of the legislation, Mr. Soto, who didn't have an opportunity at the beginning to speak to his legislation.

The Chair reminds Members that under the Chair's right of recognition, as described in Committee Rule 3, will provide some reasonable additional time for any Member that has a question for Senator María de Lourdes to account for the interpreter.

The Chair will now recognize Members for any questions they may wish. And on the Majority side, that process is going to be by seniority. On the Minority side, it is the names that were submitted to us by the Minority, in that sequence.

I will forego at this point my initial questioning and recognize Mr. Costa. I will alternate back and forth for his 5 minutes. Mr. Costa, the time is yours. Mr. Costa?

Let me now recognize, in order of seniority, the next Member, Vice Chair of Consumer Affairs as well, Mr. Sablan. Sir, the time is yours.

Mr. SABLAN. Chairman Grijalva, thank you very much, and I want to thank all of the witnesses for their testimony. I have learned enough over the years that I will stay out of Puerto Rico's political status issues. I will stay away from this until when I have no choice but to cast the vote in Committee.

I yield back. Thank you.

The CHAIRMAN. Let me now recognize the Ranking Member of the Full Committee, Mr. Westerman. The floor is yours. Mr. Westerman, you are recognized.

We will go back to Mr. Westerman when he connects with us.

Let me now recognize the gentleman, Mr. Hice, for your time. Sir, you are recognized.

[No response.]

As recommended by the Minority, let me now recognize Miss González-Colón for her 5 minutes. Miss González, you are recognized.

Miss GONZÁLEZ-COLÓN. Thank you, Mr. Chairman. First of all, I want to say thank you again to all the witnesses that are here with us today, and I want to say thank you to the Governor of Puerto Rico for traveling to DC.

My first question is going to be for him. Many people are saying that the statehood votes in November of last year were not enough or the percentage was not big enough to establish the vote for the decision of the people of the island. And I just want to point out that 52 percent of the vote was for statehood, which is an absolute majority, and just 47 percent against. It is almost 5 percent difference.

And if we compare that to the result of the general election in the United States where President Biden got elected by 51 percent versus 46 percent, I think it is less than

4.4 percent, which means that for some people elections in the United States were a landslide or bigger margin, but those margins are not good enough for the people of Puerto Rico to establish their vote for statehood.

I think that is something that the Governor of Puerto Rico is the only one elected to pursue the will of the island. And I want just to say on the record the status of statehood got more votes than any elected official, the Governor, myself, mayors, and state legislators. So, that is something that even between party lines on the island statehood got more votes than anyone else.

Governor, do you think the percentage to support statehood and the mandate that you have—the request of the state, of the Governor of Puerto Rico to Congress for statehood was made as an official petition last year. Do you support that?

Governor PIERLUISI. Yes. Thank you, Resident Commissioner. As in any democracy, in Puerto Rico the majority rules. That is how democracies work across the world. To put this in context, I publicly have been calling for an up-or-down vote on statehood for years. And the reason was that I realized that the plebiscites we had been conducting, providing multiple options for the public, for the people of Puerto Rico, were not working, and let me explain why.

Always you had a sector, a faction of Puerto Rico complaining that the options were not inclusive, that we had left out one option or another, that the options were not well defined. It is the never-ending story. That beauty or wisdom of an up-or-down vote, in this case for statehood, but it could have been for the current territorial status, it could have been for independence, it could have been for free association, the beauty or wisdom of this vote is that it is all-inclusive. All those who support statehood could say yes, and all those who oppose statehood, for whatever reasons—they support another option or they are not yet ready for Puerto Rico to become a state—could say no, and that is precisely what happened here.

Puerto Rico had no offer from Congress. There was no Federal legislation providing for this plebiscite. But in accordance with the principle of self-determination, Puerto Rico always has the right to conduct a plebiscite or a referendum like we did. And there was no boycott this time around, and we got an absolute majority against all odds. Even the Justice Department under the Trump administration objected to this vote. And even then the people requested statehood, so the least that Congress should be doing is responding to this vote, answering to this vote.

And your bill, Resident Commissioner, Congressman Soto's bill, is the right approach. Again, it does what Hawaii and Alaska did; it basically tells us, tells the people of Puerto Rico, this is statehood. These are the terms and conditions: Hold a referendum; if you ratify it, the President will proclaim it, and it provides for a year-period for a transition.

So, I fully support your bill. It is democratic. It is fair because, again, all those for statehood will have a chance to support it, and all those against, for whatever reason, will be able to say no.

Miss GONZÁLEZ-COLÓN. Thank you, Governor.

I yield back.

The CHAIRMAN. Thank you very much. Let me recognize Chairman Huffman for your 5 minutes of questions, comments. Sir, you are recognized.

Mr. HUFFMAN. Mr. Chairman, I simply want to say hello to our dear friend and former colleague, Governor Pierluisi. It is great to see you again. Pedro, we miss you at the Natural Resources Committee, and I want to thank everyone for this great discussion. It has certainly helped me prepare for what I hope will be an important and helpful vote in the weeks and months ahead.

Governor PIERLUISI. Thank you.

Mr. HUFFMAN. I yield back.

The CHAIRMAN. Mr. Young.

Mr. YOUNG. Mr. Chairman, I thought Mr. Huffman had something to say. I am up?

The CHAIRMAN. You are up, sir. Thank you.

Mr. YOUNG. Thank you, Mr. Chairman. And thank you, Governor, and all of the witnesses. This is an issue I have been involved in for many, many years. We had the Young bill that did pass the House one time by one vote. I am proud of that. And, of course, I believe in statehood. I believe in Jenniffer's bill. I think it is time—as far as the plebiscite, we have three of them. Each time I believe we have actually been victorious in the sense of being a state. It is long overdue.

You know, we talk about this all the time, but I am part of that. Puerto Rico was supposed to be a state after Alaska, even before Alaska. And because of circumstances, the delegates who were in Congress at that time, we came by and then, of course, instead of Puerto Rico becoming a state, Hawaii became a state. Anybody there from Hawaii, I apologize, but it was the wrong pecking order. Now, I think Puerto Rico has a decision to make. They have said before, and I think we ought to keep going. I like Jenniffer's bill. I don't expect anybody else has another bill, but let's not take and plow fields that have been plowed before. The people have spoken. Let's have the vote. Let's become a state, the 51st state.

And although I have some opposition on my side about they will all be Democrats, they said the same thing about Alaska, and now we are all Republicans. So, everybody has the right to decide what they are going to be, but don't rethink what they are going to be because it doesn't work out that way. Hawaii was supposed to be Republican.

So, Mr. Chairman, and Jenniffer, and all of the people involved, you have a person here who is going to work very hard with you to try to achieve the goals of what this bill really tries to do.

Governor, very frankly, do you think that H.R. 2070 ignores the will of the voters of Puerto Rico?

Governor PIERLUISI. Of course not. Congressman Young, are you referring to H.R. 1522 or H.R. 2070?

Mr. YOUNG. H.R. 2070.

Governor PIERLUISI. The problem with H.R. 2070 is the following: it clearly ignores the vote that just happened. And when I hear people talking about that that wasn't a fair vote, that it wasn't inclusive, what are they talking about?

By definition, by design, it couldn't be fairer. It couldn't be more inclusive, because a yes-or-no vote allows everybody to express themselves. And that is what happened in Puerto Rico. All of those now opposing H.R. 2070, or at least most of them, campaigned against statehood before the plebiscite in Puerto Rico.

They had to turn it back, and they can now continue lobbying Congress against it. But they shouldn't be stopping this process from happening because Congress should be responding. Congress should be allowing this process to go forward, not start a whole new process, providing for the election of delegates, a bipartisan or joint commission that is going to engage in a dialogue with these delegates to talk about options that nobody knows what we are talking about, including non-territorial options other than statehood and independence, which is clearly unconstitutional.

That definitely is a never-ending story. It has no deadlines on it, and actually it has constitutional problems because it is only Congress that can offer any status to Puerto Rico or bind itself to offer any status. Congress has never appointed a commission that all of a sudden speaks for Congress and binds Congress in terms of particular status options for Puerto Rico.

One option, one undeniable option, is statehood. I agree that independence is an option. I say it with respect. I agree that Puerto Rico could try to negotiate or have a compact or a pact of free association, such as the one that Palau and the Marshall Islands have. Those are options, I agree, but those options have never gotten majority support in Puerto Rico.

And if anybody wants to hold an up-or-down vote on them, I welcome them to do it, because they will end up getting a very small vote on them. Statehood has the majority support in Puerto Rico, and it only will grow if Congress offers it to the people of Puerto Rico and subjects it to a vote once again by the people of Puerto Rico.

Mr. YOUNG. Thank you, Governor, and you spoke very well about it. It was what I was going to say, but you said it so well. Thank you for your support and for testifying before the Congress.

Mr. Chairman, if I have any time left, I will yield it to the Congresslady, Miss Colón. And with that I yield back.

The CHAIRMAN. Unfortunately, Mr. Young, you have no time left. But I am sure she appreciates the gesture, and thank you.

Let me now turn to and recognize Chairman Lowenthal for any questions or comments that he might have.

Sir.

Dr. LOWENTHAL. Thank you, Chairman Grijalva. And before I actually get into this debate, I just wanted to send to you and to the family and your staff member, Mr. Lofgren's family, my sincerest condolences. I know this is a difficult time suddenly, the loss, and I just send my best wishes and my sadness for what you are going through.

The CHAIRMAN. Thank you, sir.

Dr. LOWENTHAL. I am here to listen. I don't really have too many questions. I am trying to understand and I think it has been an excellent hearing providing the alternatives.

The only questions that I have may be for Governor Pierluisi. And I think also it is good to see you back on the Natural Resources Committee as one of the old timers. Glad to see you, as Jared also mentioned.

Governor PIERLUISI. Thank you.

Dr. LOWENTHAL. I just want to know, from your point of view, you have made your case I think because the will of Puerto Ricans is that the majority have voted for statehood now, and that is what they want. What are the consequences if we wait longer to resolve the status? If the Congress does not act, do you have any idea what is going to happen? What are some of the consequences of not acting?

Governor PIERLUISI. Yes, I will tell you. I live through them right now as Governor. And I know Resident Commissioner Jenniffer González suffers through them every day in her tenure in Congress.

I tell you, Jenniffer González is doing a remarkable job as a Resident Commissioner. She is only one, and she doesn't have a vote on the Floor. I know what she has to go through when she is seeking support for Puerto Rico, for the Medicaid Program, for the SSI Program, for our nutrition assistance.

She needs to go and talk to all of you and use her persuasion, her personality, to convince you to go along with her, because she cannot vote on your bills. She cannot negotiate, like get this done in Congress every day, on our behalf. And she is only one in the House. Because of the size of our population, we would have two Senators and four Representatives at bat for us, for Puerto Rico. And I know that would make a difference.

We suffered a huge hurricane. We went through a huge hurricane back in 2017. We went through incredible earthquakes early in 2020. And now we are facing the pandemic. And we went through all of that, and unfortunately, when the time came to assist Puerto Rico, using existing disaster management programs of the Federal Government, we were facing all kinds of requirements that states do not face, because it is so easy to treat Puerto Rico differently.

Actually, the Supreme Court has said that Congress can treat us differently, that the Federal Government can treat us differently. Our request is always treat me the same. We are American citizens. Give me the same treatment in all Federal programs, and give me representation in the Congress that approves the laws that affect me on a daily basis. Allow me to vote for the President. Allow me to vote for the Commander in Chief.

Our men and women are wearing the military uniform, are losing their lives on behalf of this nation, yet when they come home they have no say in our democracy. That is the quandary. That is the fight, and definitely we want to put an end to it.

And I say this again with respect, I say it with respect because the situation of Puerto Rico is not the same as the other territories. Because of our size, because of everything that we have been dealing with in the past, and because of the vote that just happened, we need to address this issue and do it for the benefit of all, for the benefit of the nation at large, and for the benefit of Puerto Rico. And let's do it fairly. Let's hold it for a vote once again. We just held a vote. Let's have another one once Congress offers equality—statehood—to the American citizens of Puerto Rico.

Thank you.

Dr. LOWENTHAL. Thank you. And I yield back, Mr. Chair.

The CHAIRMAN. Thank you, Mr. Lowenthal. And thank you for your kind comments. I appreciate it very much.

Let me now recognize the gentleman from Arizona, Mr. Gallego— no, excuse me. Let me recognize the Ranking Member of the Full Committee, Mr. Westerman, for your comments.

Sir.

Mr. WESTERMAN. Thank you, Chairman Grijalva, and also a big thank you to all of the witnesses. This is a very informative hearing that we are having today, and it seems to me it is obvious we have two proposed processes to move forward. And it is great to be able to put those two processes side by side and to debate the merits of each one.

Dr. Ponsa-Kraus, according to Representative Velázquez's summary of H.R. 2070 on our website, where she talks about the status convention, there has been a lot of talk about how there are three options to consider: statehood, independence, or free association. But the status convention offers a fourth option, or actually I would say a Pandora's Box of options. And you say in your testimony that there are only three options, and no room for other options. Will you explain that again?

Dr. PONSA-KRAUS. Yes, of course. Thank you for the opportunity to explain it. My emphasis, and the emphasis you have heard from other speakers, on the fact that there are only—I said two options, but you are right that there is one that is described as a third—it is statehood and independence, with or without free association. So, let's call them three: statehood, independence, and free association.

Free association is a form of independence. And the reason it is so critical to emphasize that is because the people of Puerto Rico were led to believe that there was another alternative. It was non-territorial, and that turned out not to be true. And what is so urgent is for the people of Puerto Rico not to be led along, not to be misled, not to be offered options that they can't have. That doesn't respect them or the process of self-determination.

So, to say you can't have this is not to disrespect them. To say you can't have this is to respect them. So, that option that they were offered repeatedly that was not constitutionally possible was non-territorial commonwealth.

And let me just try to explain, what are the stakes of this debate? I think one statistic, one figure that has been lost in all of this—I don't think I have heard this—is that Puerto Ricans have had an overwhelming consensus, and I am talking on the order of 90 percent, for decades, since the mid–20th century.

Those same 70 years we have had a consensus that people want to remain U.S. citizens and have a guarantee of citizenship for themselves and their posterity, and they want some form of union with the United States, which is absolutely consistent with being Puerto Rican.

Mr. WESTERMAN. Do you believe that——

Dr. PONSA-KRAUS. We want these two things. And if you want a union with the United States and citizenship for yourself and your posterity, well, then, statehood is your only option because the other options don't guarantee you either of those things. So, that is what this debate is all about. How do we maintain citizenship for ourselves and our posterity and a union with the United States? If there were other ways to do it, that would be OK.

And I, too, want to say what the Governor said. I respect the option of independence. I respect the option of free association. But I also respect the expression of the Puerto Rican people's desire for a union with the United States of some form and guaranteed citizenship for themselves and their posterity. And if that is what they want, then it respects them at the very least to offer statehood, which is all the Admission Act does. It offers them statehood.

Mr. WESTERMAN. Thank you. And Section 6 of H.R. 2070 binds Congress to pass the joint resolution in the future. I know you are a constitutional lawyer. Can Congress bind itself to pass a joint resolution in the future?

Dr. PONSA-KRAUS. No, it cannot. That is yet another promise that shouldn't be made to Puerto Ricans because Congress can't bind itself to pass a joint resolution in the future. So, H.R. 2070 says Congress shall enact a joint resolution ratifying the people's choice in a referendum following the Constitutional Convention.

That sounds, once again, like you are giving them what they want. You are hearing them out, and then you are giving them what they want, and you are promising to do it. But Congress shouldn't make promises to the Puerto Rican people that it can't keep.

Mr. WESTERMAN. Well, what would happen if the bill passed, the Convention puts forward options, the people vote, and then send an option to Congress; would Congress have to act?

Dr. PONSA-KRAUS. Congress would not have to act. So, if the people choose a constitutional non-territorial option, Congress should act, but Congress wouldn't have to act and that ought to be clear as well.

Mr. WESTERMAN. Do you think this bill would be or is misleading to the Puerto Rican people?

Dr. PONSA-KRAUS. It is. It invites them to debate options that they can't have, along with the ones they can. It invites them to debate options that they can't have, that they have already debated, that we know are unconstitutional. And then it invites them to send that choice to Congress and promises Congress will act when Congress can't promise to do that. The Puerto Rican people have been led along long enough.

Mr. WESTERMAN. Thank you, Dr. Ponsa-Kraus. I am out of time, so I yield back.

The CHAIRMAN. Thank you, Mr. Westerman. I am going to now recognize the gentleman from Arizona, Mr. Gallego, for your time.

Sir.

Mr. GALLEGO. Thank you, Mr. Chairman. It weighs on my mind knowing right now that President Biden is talking about our movement out of Afghanistan, and of course, reminds me that there have been a total of 77 Puerto Ricans from down in Puerto Rico that have died both in Iraq and Afghanistan as well more than 1,700 injured.

So, this is actually very important to me. I've never understood why the Puerto Ricans I served with were treated as second-class citizens and that their citizenship could be decided by their zip codes. And I am very happy to see that we are at least having a debate about where and how we should proceed with the statehood question of Puerto Rico.

I do find it odd that some Democrats are arguing that this last election, that Puerto Rico had a referendum is somehow illegitimate after we just had a huge January 6 fight with our colleagues across the aisle who are trying to call that election illegitimate. I think that is something that I don't know how we can reconcile. The referendum that was put forward was put forward by duly elected members of the Statehouse of Puerto Rico, that's a language, it was supported. I don't understand where somehow there's a mandate that has to be hit by a number that is above, I guess, that 52 percent is not acceptable somehow in normal American mainland politics. If you get fifty plus one, that's a mandate. Heck, sometimes we've had presidents that have not even hit 50 percent of the population and they have the popular vote and they have won. Yet, we have considered that a mandate.

And now, the other argument I'm hearing that also does not make sense, there are multiple parties that were elected last cycle to the Statehouse and State Senate. I understand that, but I also know Puerto Rican politics is not just about statehood and about statehood questions. There are a lot of other reasons why people vote for different members of the Statehouse and State Senate over there, and it is not just statehood.

And lastly, just as an Arizonan, the 48th state that did get accepted into Congress, if we were living by the standard right now, I'm actually fighting in Arizona to preserve Proposition, I think, 108, which is a tax increase the majority of Arizonans voted for, but the Arizona legislature actually is controlled by Republicans, and their argument is, well, the Arizona legislature is a better reflection of what truly Arizonans want instead of the referendum that we passed.

So, it would be extremely hypocritical of me to somehow use those two standards. Number 1, the fact that we had a free and legitimate election last time and it should not have been questioned by our colleagues across the aisle. And Number 2, that the Arizona State Legislature should be listening to the will of the voters and then somehow turn and not support this.

So, that's my general statement. I'd also like to talk to Professor. And I apologize, my screen is going a little blank in terms of names here. Professor, what is your name? I apologize.

Dr. PONSA-KRAUS. Ponsa-Kraus.

Mr. GALLEGO. Thank you, Professor. So, the argument here is that we need to restart it, right? We need to restart this by pulling delegates together and then putting a constitutional convention together. What states actually did that in the past?

Dr. PONSA-KRAUS. Well, no states did anything like this in the past.

Mr. GALLEGO. OK.

Dr. PONSA-KRAUS. Yes.

Mr. GALLEGO. Thank you for answering that question.

Dr. PONSA-KRAUS. I mean, if you're referring to the process provided for in H.R. 2070?

Mr. GALLEGO. Yes.

Dr. PONSA-KRAUS. Yes. No territory did anything like this because no territory had this range of options and confusion and this long a debate about an option that turns out not even to have been constitutional. We spent 70 years arguing about it. There's no precedent for this.

Mr. GALLEGO. Yes, OK. And even if it was even remotely possible that this could work out, it doesn't have a time period. It doesn't sound like there is a definitive time period that this has to be decided. So, let's say they go through these elections, they elect their delegates. It sounds like the delegates get elected by popular vote I'm assuming. But when does a decision have to be made? Let's say they get the popular vote, delegates get selected. Is there a time period? Like, is there a year, 2 years? What are we talking about? Could this go indefinitely?

Dr. PONSA-KRAUS. H.R. 2070 does not contain any time limit either for the terms of the delegates or for the convention to produce a result. In fact, I can't tell you how my heart sank when I read the requirement that certain reports be submitted every 12 months. I thought, really, 123 years isn't enough?

Mr. GALLEGO. Yes. And then even how they come to a decision, is that defined? I mean, is it like, let's say for some reason the statehooders receive the majority of the votes and delegate votes. Can they just quickly call a convention together and say, OK, we're good, let's do this?

Dr. PONSA-KRAUS. The bill doesn't explain exactly how the convention itself would go about the process of debating.

Mr. GALLEGO. Right.

Dr. PONSA-KRAUS. And I certainly am a believer in all voices being heard, but I believe that all voices were heard in the referendum as well.

Mr. GALLEGO. Right. And lastly, so again, just to be clear, has the U.S. Government ever dictated to a territory exactly what they need to discuss in order for them to come back and talk to us about joining the Union?

Dr. PONSA-KRAUS. Well, what the U.S. Government has never done is sent people off—first of all, ignore a referendum in which a majority voted for statehood and say actually, no, we don't like the process you came up with; we want you to do something else and then call that self-determination. I mean, I can't put those two things together. How do you just ignore a vote on the island provided for by its own elected representatives and say no, actually, do this other thing because we respect self-determination.

Mr. GALLEGO. Right. Self-determination to me means the local state representatives and senators decide to put a language on. When people voted for these state reps and state senators, they knew what they represented and then they got on there and it was the most popular thing that was voted on. So, I think if anything, this reeks of a sort of paternalism from us stateside Members of Congress. Why am I going to over-ride the local elected officials that are closest to democracy after they have clearly spoken? So, with that, I am fully in support of Representative Soto's bill, and I yield back my time.

The CHAIRMAN. Thank you. The gentleman yields. Mr. Lamborn, you are recognized, sir.

Mr. LAMBORN. Thank you, Mr. Chairman. And this has been a very good discussion. I want to say hello to my former colleague and the governor of Puerto Rico, Governor Pierluisi. It was good to visit with you recently when I was in Puerto Rico. I visited with you and Delegate Jenniffer González-Colón. And one thing about Jenniffer that I want to say, she's not expecting me to say this, but I was astounded by the affection and the effectiveness that she brings to the table as the delegate from Puerto Rico.

I was in the Statehouse, the capital of the territory and I saw a row of oil portraits, former speakers of the general assembly there, and Jenniffer's picture was the last in the row, and I was very impressed with it. In fact, I took a picture, you can see it here on my phone. That's the oil portrait of the former speaker of the Puerto Rico legislature.

I'm going to yield the rest of my time to my friend and colleague, Jennifer González-Colón.

The CHAIRMAN. Ms. Colón, you are recognized. The gentlelady is recognized.

Mr. SABLAN. Jenniffer, you are on mute.

The CHAIRMAN. Thank you, Mr. Lamborn.

Miss GONZÁLEZ-COLÓN. Thank you. First of all, I want to say thank you, Mr. Lamborn. I mean, I'm humbled by your words and I really appreciate your willingness always to work with our Governor and everything you've been doing in the Committee. My gratitude to you for visiting the island and visiting certain places that are the jurisdiction of this Committee, like the national parks in terms of how they were recovering. Thank you, Mr. Lamborn.

And I want to say thank you as well to Mr. Don Young, Mr. Lowenthal, and Mr. Gallego, who just made brilliant questions. And I will take it where you leave it. This question is to Professor Ponsa-Kraus. First of all, thank you for your willingness to be a witness here and to answer direct questions. My line of questions will now be yes or no, in terms of saving time, so if you can just tell me yes or no, I would really appreciate that.

Will the Admission Act that Darren Soto and I submitted in this Congress impose statehood for Puerto Rico, would voters of the island always have the last say on that?

Dr. PONSA-KRAUS. No, it will not impose, and yes, they will have the last say.

Miss GONZÁLEZ-COLÓN. Thank you for that. Some argue that the result of November of last year was an invalid or illegitimate mandate for statehood because the vote wasn't federally sponsored or sanctioned by Congress or the Department of Justice. Others claims that an absolute majority of 53 percent isn't enough as Congressman Gallego just established. First question, are these constitutionally sound arguments, yes or no?

Dr. PONSA-KRAUS. No.

Miss GONZÁLEZ-COLÓN. Does the U.S. Constitution require a specific level of majority support for statehood in order to admit a territory as a state?

Dr. PONSA-KRAUS. No.

Miss GONZÁLEZ-COLÓN. Is it required to have a federally sponsored referendum as a prerequisite for Congress to act?

Dr. PONSA-KRAUS. No.

Miss GONZÁLEZ-COLÓN. Did we have that requirement before for Alaska and Hawaii?

Dr. PONSA-KRAUS. No.

Miss GONZÁLEZ-COLÓN. Was any other state required when they were a territory to have an absolute majority or a specific percentage to be admitted to the Union?

Dr. PONSA-KRAUS. No.

Miss GONZÁLEZ-COLÓN. Should Puerto Rico require that?

Dr. PONSA-KRAUS. No.

Miss GONZÁLEZ-COLÓN. Does our bill, the Puerto Rico Statehood Admission Act, address the concerns by authorizing a self-executing process that it will have ratified by voters. Do you think that is a self-executing bill? Yes or no.

Dr. PONSA-KRAUS. The Admission Act? Yes.

Miss GONZÁLEZ-COLÓN. Do you think that H.R. 2070 is a self-executing bill?

Dr. PONSA-KRAUS. No.

Miss GONZÁLEZ-COLÓN. Do you think that it is a binding bill? Dr. PONSA-KRAUS. No.

Miss GONZÁLEZ-COLÓN. Do you think the Department of Justice declining to fund a campaign would disqualify or take out any legitimacy of the voters result in November of last year?

Dr. PONSA-KRAUS. No.

Miss GONZÁLEZ-COLÓN. Thank you, Professor Kraus. With that, I yield back.

The CHAIRMAN. The gentlelady yields.

Mr. LAMBORN. I yield back.

The CHAIRMAN. Thank you, sir. Mr. Lamborn yields. Let me recognize the sponsor of the legislation, Ms. Velázquez. You are recognized. You need to turn off your mic, Jenniffer.

Ms. VELÁZQUEZ. Thank you, Mr. Chairman. First, I would like to address the issue of the binding nature of my bill. Section 7, Joint Resolution outlines a serious and structured process for both chambers of Congress to act upon the results of the referendum that my bill proposes. And let me just say this to my colleagues in this Committee. This is not an election for president. It is not an election of a Member of Congress. This is an election about decolonization—123 years of imperialism by the United States. How do we morally put an end to colonization? How do we empower the people of Puerto Rico to finally decide what is the choice made by the people of Puerto Rico. Governor Pierluisi talked about how the percentage of votes are binding of Nydia Velázquez in my own district. This is not about that type of election. This is the most consequential act that will be taken by the people of Puerto Rico and the U.S. Congress.

And let it be known to this Committee that the November 2020 plebiscite was legislated, designed, and pushed by only one party in Puerto Rico, and that is the pro-statehood party that Governor Pierluisi represents. So, if we are honest and serious about providing a path for the people of Puerto Rico for all political sectors to be able to decide their own future, why are you so afraid? My bill doesn't preclude or exclude statehood. And if you are so assured that the outcome is going to be statehood, why then oppose a process that is inclusive, that is transparent, and that is democratic.

I would like to address my first question to Governor Acevedo-Vilá. Could you please explain to the members of the Committee the steps that have historically taken place in Puerto Rico to design and implement the previous plebiscites? Could you explain to us the context on how the 2020 plebiscite came into existence, and if any voices from the opposition were taken into consideration?

Mr. ACEVEDO-VILÁ. Well, the short answer, Congresswoman, and thank you for the question, is no. Nobody was considered from the other political parties in Puerto Rico. It was approved without any votes of the other political parties in the House and in the Senate. And, actually, the whole design was precisely to be a one-sided campaign because it was together with the elections. The other parties, they were not in power. They had the control of the whole apparatus of the government. The other parties had to spend all the money that they raised for their own campaigns for elected officials, and if you compare the numbers, this was one-sided. And I would love Members who are favoring the statehood bill to see some of the ads that were put out there basically scaring people. Saying if you vote no, you're going to lose your U.S. citizenship. If you vote no, you won't get the tuition assistance program.

Ms. VELÁZQUEZ. Thank you.

Mr. ACEVEDO-VILÁ. This was totally one-sided.

Ms. VELÁZQUEZ. Time is running out, and I have many questions to ask. Thank you, Mr. Acevedo. Mr. Natal, you recently sued the Puerto Rico State Election Commission for issues arising in your bid to become mayor of San Juan. Mr. Natal, can you provide the members of this Committee with some example of how the electoral reform law affected the election results and if such reforms created a lack of transparency, voter disenfranchisement, and other electoral deterrents?

Mr. NATAL-ALBELO. Thank you for your question, Congresswoman Velázquez, and I'll go right to it. Not only did the New Progressive Party unilaterally legislate this referendum one sided, but they also changed the electoral laws in Puerto Rico 136 days before the election. So, they decided to change the rules of the game 136 days before the actual election was supposed to be taking place. And particularly when it comes to the plebiscite.

I'll give you just one example. In the case of the five precincts of San Juan, when it comes to the plebiscite, in an Act certified by four of the five parties from the electoral commission, it was found that there were close to 1,800 votes or 1,800 ballots in excess of actual voters for the plebiscite only in terms of the election in San Juan. That's just one example of the many irregularities that happened and I'll clear one more thing, Congresswoman Velázquez.

The actual percentage of what the statehood received when you take into account invalid votes and blank votes was actually 50.8 percent, not the 52 that's been said here before.

Ms. VELÁZQUEZ. And I would like to remind the members of the Committee also that the Department of Justice rejected the 2017 and 2020 referendum citing the Obama Task Force before had stated that excluding options won't call into question the legitimacy of any referendum. I yield back.

The CHAIRMAN. The gentlelady yields and the time is over. If anybody has a question about that, it is exactly the same for Members that were pro the other piece of legislation that went over a minute and 37 seconds and a minute and 26 seconds. So, there was no effort to give to Ms. Velázquez any additional time. We've only been consistent with what other people received. Let me now turn to Ms. Radewagen. The gentlelady, the time is yours.

Ms. RADEWAGEN. Thank you, Chairman Grijalva and Ranking Member Westerman, for holding this hearing. Welcome to the panel and thank you. As a fellow Member representing a U.S. territory, I want to align myself with the statements made today by Resident Commissioner González-Colón. Above all else, today's hearing is about respecting the will of the Puerto Rican people. With that, I yield my time to the Resident Commissioner.

Miss GONZÁLEZ-COLÓN. Thank you, Amata, for yielding. I really appreciate all of your support and your co-sponsorship of this bill today. And I would love to continue my line of questions to Professor Ponsa if she is available. And I would love to maintain yes or no answers so we can get hold of the time. Not without saying, my first question will be: Is a blank vote count for electing somebody to any position?

Dr. PONSA-KRAUS. No.

Miss GONZÁLEZ-COLÓN. I assumed that. In your view, H.R. 2070, the Puerto Rico Self-Determination Act, do you believe that it is problematic that this bill does not define or recognize that the only non-territorial status options available to Puerto Rico are statehood or independence?

Dr. PONSA-KRAUS. Yes.

Miss GONZÁLEZ-COLÓN. In your view, will the Self-Determination Act open up the door for convention delegates to come up with unconstitutional options?

Dr. PONSA-KRAUS. Yes.

Miss GONZÁLEZ-COLÓN. Do you think that including unconstitutional provisions in the transition plans they have to develop may be opposed by Congress?

Dr. PONSA-KRAUS. I apologize. I couldn't really follow whether that——

Miss GONZÁLEZ-COLÓN. If that constitutional convention use creates a new definition of the status that is not non-territorial, Congress and the Department of Justice can just say no to that?

Dr. PONSA-KRAUS. That's right, yes.

Miss GONZÁLEZ-COLÓN. Are there any constitutional concerns with the Puerto Rico Statehood Admission Act?

Dr. PONSA-KRAUS. No.

Miss GONZÁLEZ-COLÓN. In your testimony, you argued that the Self-Determination Act is, and I quote, "a thinly veiled attempt to delay and defeat an offer for statehood." Can you elaborate on why you think that?

Dr. PONSA-KRAUS. Absolutely. The Self-Determination Act ignores the referendum in November and displaces it with a process altogether different from the process that Puerto Rico came up with. I've heard people say Puerto Rico's Statehood Party designed the referendum. Puerto Rico's elected legislatures designed the referendum. The Self-Determination Act recognizes the inherent right of Puerto Rico to exercise self-determination, well, this is it. Puerto Rico's elected legislatures designed the referendum. They are the ones who put this process in place.

Miss GONZÁLEZ-COLÓN. Professor, you believe the Self-Determination Act engaged in election denial?

Dr. PONSA-KRAUS. Yes.

Miss GONZÁLEZ-COLÓN. Do you think that ignoring and rejecting Puerto Rico's recent vote on statehood, not just in 2020—but in the 2017 and 2012 referendums, are those actions undemocratic?

Dr. PONSA-KRAUS. Yes.

Miss GONZÁLEZ-COLÓN. In your opinion, were the November 2020 results on statehood and the yes-or-no referendum a legitimate self-determination process?

Dr. PONSA-KRAUS. Yes.

Miss GONZÁLEZ-COLÓN. Do you think that as a professor of constitutional law in American legal history, how do you respond to arguments that the Self-Determination Act has stated that the convention authorized by the bill will consider a statehood independence of free association, which is independence, and any other non-territorial options; how do you believe that is consistent with U.S. law?

Dr. PONSA-KRAUS. To the extent that it invites Puerto Ricans to debate options that are not constitutional, it is not consistent with U.S. law. To the extent that it invites Puerto Ricans to debate options at all instead of responding to the plebiscite, to the referendum in November, it is unnecessary and it is dilatory. Puerto Ricans can continue debating their options even if Congress offers statehood, and in response to the referendum, Congress should offer statehood.

Miss GONZÁLEZ-COLÓN. Thank you, Professor. I yield back.

The CHAIRMAN. The gentlelady yields. Ms. Radewagen yields back. Let me recognize Mr. McEachin.

Sir, you are recognized.

Mr. MCEACHIN. Thank you, Mr. Chairman.

I am not going to go into a long series of questions, but I am just going to state for the record my support for Mr. Soto's bill, and I look forward to the day that I can be part of the delegation welcoming the people of Puerto Rico into the Union.

With that, I yield the balance of my time to Mr. Soto.

Mr. SOTO. Thank you, Representative McEachin.

And first I want to thank you, Chairman, for hosting this hearing dedicated to Puerto Rico's political status.

After the election in November, we deserve a real debate on this, and we are getting it today finally, and I want to thank Ranking Member Westerman as well for that opportunity.

I was more than happy to have Resident Commissioner Jenniffer González-Colón begin speaking on behalf of our bill together because my motivation is to lift up voices from Puerto Rico not from the states' side. That has been the problem all along.

Yesterday, we celebrated National Borinqueneers Day, heroes who fought for this country since 1899, for many years in segregated units, and to date, Puerto Ricans enlist in the Armed Services at double the rate of those on the mainland.

Yet, none of them can vote for Commander-in-Chief, have Senators or voting Representatives in Congress. That is a national shame.

My family's native island of Puerto Rico has been through so much hardship over the last few years, and over a decade-long economic recession, deadly hurricanes Maria and Irma, terrible budget cuts from the PROMESA Fiscal Board, earthquakes, and now COVID-19.

It is clear now that two Senators and four Representatives would have greatly helped during these crises and that the territorial status is failing 3.2 million Americans there.

We see this every day in central Florida, as thousands of Puerto Ricans feel they have to leave the island to come to our region because they no longer think they can be prosperous on the island.

This is an injustice, and this is the main motivation why I am here to help lift up voices on the island.

Amidst the chaos, the Puerto Rico legislature decided to do something about it. They passed legislation to hold a vote on the future political status of the island. Unlike past elections, the ballot language was simple. There was a statehood yes-or-no question voted on during a high turnout 2020 general election, and the people voted by a majority of 52.52 percent for statehood.

This was higher than the gubernatorial candidate, our Resident Commissioner, or even any party—all of whom won by pluralities we opposed to a simple majority. The fact is the statehood vote crossed many party lines to get to the majority. The numbers just evidence that.

And this is why I filed the Puerto Rico Statehood Admission Act, along with Commissioner Jenniffer González-Colón and many others, because in democracy, when the people vote, action is supposed to occur afterwards.

Governments change. Leaders change. And political statuses change. That is the essence of our Republic. We vote, and a majority rules.

Our bill would still set up one last binding election: statehood, yes or no. And if a majority votes yes, they would be admitted to the Union after a brief transition period, and if they vote no, then it would be no.

There are other factions that I am more than happy to bring to light. A minority of Puerto Ricans on the island are pushing for a concept called enhanced commonwealth status. This is, of course, not a thing.

Dr. Ponsa-Kraus mentioned it at length today, and I am not going to belabor it other than to say it is a fictional status where Puerto Rico would get most of the benefits of statehood without any of the burdens.

Feel free to review our Constitution or the letter from the professor, as well as other top constitutional law experts, which has already been submitted for the record, but if not, Mr. Chairman, I would like to submit it.

The Constitution is clear. Puerto Rico could choose statehood, territory, or independence. Free association does not need to be on the ballot. It would be a decision if Puerto Rico decided to be independent, whether they want to be a free association like Palau or whether they would want to be independent without a relationship.

So, the choices have been clear for a long time, which brings me to the other bill. Why would we have a constitutional convention when the three options are already clear? Perhaps to create lofty demands to the United States that will never happen, but it will, in fact, cause critical delay during a limited window of opportunity for Puerto Rico to finally resolve its second-class citizenship.

Other problems with the convention bill, it creates a new legislative body when Puerto Rico already has a legislature, and it also purports to allow for meaningful debate to decolonize Puerto Rico.

But the Puerto Rican legislature has been debating this for 100 years. My time has expired.

The CHAIRMAN. Thank you. You are subject to be recognized for your own time right after our Republican colleague has his 5 minutes.

We will recognize Mr. Obernolte for his time. Sir, you are recognized.

Mr. OBERNOLTE. Thank you very much, Mr. Chairman.

And thank you to all of our witnesses. It has been a fascinating hearing on a very important topic.

My question is directed toward Congresswoman Velázquez. I had a couple questions about H.R. 2070.

The bill requires that whatever the results of the referendum are, that Congress ratify the results, including, I assume, results of a vote for independence.

However, we have heard testimony from some of the witnesses here that requiring a future Congress to ratify the results of a referendum would be illegal.

Do you disagree with that?

Ms. VELÁZQUEZ. Well, first and foremost, I am not one of the witnesses, but if you repeat your question, I would be more than happy to answer. I was not paying attention.

Mr. OBERNOLTE. Oh, I am sorry. My question was about your bill, H.R. 2070.

Ms. VELÁZQUEZ. Yes.

Mr. OBERNOLTE. The bill requires that Congress ratify the results of the referendum in Puerto Rico. However, there has been testimony here today at the hearing that requiring a future Congress to ratify the results of the referendum would be illegal.

Do you disagree with that?

Ms. VELÁZQUEZ. Yes, I disagree. Congress will create a commission. I seriously believe that under Section 7, Joint Resolution, that outlines the serious and structured process for both chambers of Congress to act upon the results of the referendum that might be a proposal.

Mr. OBERNOLTE. OK. So, presumably even if the results of the referendum is a vote for independence, there would be, I am sure, hundreds and hundreds if not thousands of issues that would have to be determined, both financial and legal status.

So, how could we require a future Congress to just blindly ratify that result?

Ms. VELÁZQUEZ. Again, Section 7 will provide and will outline a process for the commission that is going to be appointed by leaders of the House and the Senate to come into negotiation.

This is a process of decolonization, and clearly, there is language in the bill that will provide a process for that to be achieved.

Mr. OBERNOLTE. OK. I understand. Thank you.

And then lastly, if I could ask about another section of the bill that establishes the Puerto Rico Status Convention Public Matching Fund and appropriates $5.5 million to establish a four-to-one match for not just paying for the election, but paying for the campaigns of Puerto Ricans that wish to become delegates.

I personally have a problem with that. How is it fair to use U.S. tax dollars collected from U.S. taxpayers to fund the election campaigns of candidates in Puerto Rico, particularly on a four-to-one ratio?

Ms. VELÁZQUEZ. So, sir, this is decolonization, and we have a moral obligation to provide whatever it takes for the people of Puerto Rico to be well informed as to what their vote or their choosing means for themselves and their families.

And, by the way, we do that every day. We do it in New York and other states, where we provide matching funds, because we want to make sure that not only the wealthiest 1 percent, whether they are here or in Puerto Rico, have the opportunity to be engaged and participate democratically.

But you should address the same question to the Governor of Puerto Rico. Right now they are asking for millions of dollars to have shadow Representatives and Senators so that they could come to Congress and lobby for statehood. And this is money from taxpayers. This is money that we have sent to Puerto Rico for the rebuilding of Puerto Rico.

Do you support that?

Mr. OBERNOLTE. Certainly, and I also support the funding of the referendum in Puerto Rico, but I cannot support the funding of campaigns in Puerto Rico.

Ms. VELÁZQUEZ. You will support that the government will use public funds to hold this special election at a time when Puerto Rico continues to face a financial crisis and a bankruptcy process.

And, by the way, today, unanimously, the PROMESA Board voted against it because it is wrong.

Mr. OBERNOLTE. Well, to be clear, Congresswoman, I think that we have an obligation to hold elections, but I want to thank you very much for your candid answers to the questions.

And, Mr. Chairman, I will yield the balance of my time——

The CHAIRMAN. There is no balance.

Mr. OBERNOLTE. My condolences to you for the loss of your staffer. That unfortunate death occurred in my district. If I can be of any assistance to you, just let me know.

The CHAIRMAN. I know, and let me thank your staff for their inquiries and their response to law enforcement. It was very kind of them, and we are all very appreciative of that. Thank you, sir.

Let me now return to the sponsor of the legislation, Mr. Soto. The time is yours.

Mr. SOTO. Thank you, Chair Grijalva.

We talked a lot about my bill already. Just a few concerns about the competing bill.

First, we have heard at length that there are three choices: statehood, territory, or independence. Association is a type of independence, we would not need that on the ballot. If Puerto Ricans picked independence, they could decide whether or not they want to be free association or not.

The second concern is it is a critical delay of an issue that has been debated for over 100 years during a limited window of opportunity to finally resolve the second-class citizenship of Puerto Rico. And a third, it creates a new legislative body on top of the Puerto Rico legislature, which is already elected and, trust me, debates this every day.

It also purports to allow meaningful debate to decolonize Puerto Rico, but that is untrue because colonization is about ignoring elections. That is colonization, ignoring three elections in favor of statehood.

Lastly, it has to be stated that a lot of these issues are pushed by a minority of Puerto Ricans who live on the mainland who support independence, Puerto Ricans who live in states and use their clout in Congress to prevent our brothers and sisters on the island from finally resolving their political status.

I have never been opposed to independence. If I thought there was a good chance, that would be another great option, but we know independence polls in the single digits routinely on the island.

Puerto Ricans value their American citizenship. We have heard that over and over today. Being part of the United States lifts up their quality of life. They pledge allegiance to the flag, and they serve in the U.S. military in staggering numbers.

So, what do you do if you cannot win an election? You delay. Justice delayed is justice denied.

And I want to also quote our Majority Leader. Steny Hoyer just signed onto our bill this week, and, Mr. Chairman, if I may move to submit his written testimony for the record, he says, and I quote, "The people of Puerto Rico have told us time and time again through multiple plebiscites in recent years that they chose statehood. I think that we in Congress would be wise to listen to what the people of Puerto Rico are telling us."

We also have constitutional experts from the Congress supporting it, like Jamie Raskin, because he understands that there are really only three options, and we have already had a vote.

We have fellow Puerto Ricans like Richie Torres and Jenniffer González-Colón supporting our bill. We have progressives, centrists, and conservatives supporting our bill, including over 60 House sponsors, many from the Hispanic Caucus, many from the territories, as well as Senators Heinrich, Padilla, Wyden, and Schatz, because it represents the enforcement and recognition of democracy.

Ultimately, should our bill pass, Puerto Ricans will have one last election to vote to become a state or not. If they truly want to remain a territory or become independent, they could vote no, and if they want to become a state, they will vote yes.

I ask the Congress to let our people vote. Let the will of the majority prevail, and let democracy be done in these United States of America and not let this be about personalities or alliances. This should be about the vote.

I wanted to talk to some of the witnesses that we have invited today.

Ms. Vélez-Garćıa, are there a lot of progressives who support the plebiscite and statehood on the island?

Ms. VÉLEZ-GARĆIA. Yes, actually. Supporting equality across the board without being selective is at the heart of being a progressive, and as you know, within the Democratic Party, the progressive movement has gained gigantic steps.

I understand that there are progressives within the rank and file of the Democratic Party that do not support statehood certainly, and you know, we are a big house, and we are respectful of everyone's opinion.

But as you said yourself, there is no better exercise on democracy than the casting of the ballot, and we have——

Mr. SOTO. Thank you so much. My time is limited.

Ms. VÉLEZ-GARĆIA. Yes. Sorry.

Mr. SOTO. Mr. Fuentes, are there many conservatives on the island who support statehood as well?

Mr. FUENTES. As you know, the Republican Party is adamant [audio malfunction] Puerto Rico is at the highest level of home ownership in the country, at the highest level second only to Nevada in military participation. We have more churches per square mile than anywhere in the country.

So, yes, the answer to your question is an absolute yes.

The CHAIRMAN. Thank you.

Mr. SOTO. I see my time has expired.

The CHAIRMAN. Thank you very much, Mr. Soto. The gentleman yields back.

Mr. Tiffany, you are recognized for 5 minutes.

Mr. TIFFANY. Thank you, Mr. Chairman.

Once again, as with each of our meetings here in House Natural Resources, we have had glitches in technology. I am asking the Chairman to bring us into committee rooms. It is time to do that so that there is clear communication in what is supposed to be the greatest deliberative body created in the history of mankind.

I am going to yield my time to Miss González.

I just hear lots of noise from people here, some politicians in America, about this, and I wanted to hear from the person who is closest to the people, and that is Miss González.

And I know she has spoken about this issue earlier today, but I would like to hear her thoughts on where she sees this going.

I yield to Miss González.

Miss GONZÁLEZ-COLÓN. First of all, I want to say thank you, Mr. Tiffany, for yielding and for your respect and deference to the people elected from the island to manage this issue.

And as you just said, the issues of Puerto Rico have been discussed for more than 100 years. We have been discussing statehood, independence, a kind of a free association which you need to become an independent nation in order to get that kind of transition like the Marshall Islands or the Micronesia Islands, that is not what the people of Puerto Rico want.

Even in the past, when there have been several votes on this, people of the island cherish American citizenship, and that is the reason in the last three plebiscites, statehood has won those plebiscites as the will of the people of the island.

So, I want to say thank you for yielding.

Another reason, after the results of November of last year, we drafted this bill in a different way. We put the same process Alaska and Hawaii did in order to become a state, what those territories did in order to become a state, and that was a yes-or-no legislation on the island, and that was the way state houses and state senates legislated this during the last year.

And with that vote, a yes-or-no vote, we are answering to that request and that request of statehood and equality, with that stated bill.

And with that stated bill, I want to say thank you to Congressman Darren Soto and to many others, Democrats and Republicans, that are supporting this bill in the House, including the Minority Leader, Mr. Hoyer, you just included his testimony for this hearing, and I want to say thank you for sponsoring the state of Puerto Rico as well.

I will make a question to Mr. José Fuentes of the Puerto Rico Statehood Council.

I know that Governor Pierluisi a few minutes ago said that people who campaigned against statehood are now trying to discredit or trying to stop the results of last November.

My question to you is: All those people that campaigned and voted against the statehood bill in the yes-or-no questions in November, do they have the right to overcome that majority and meet a minority that were defeated in many ways, now try to impose those alternatives?

Mr. FUENTES. No, they do not. But what we have to understand is that this is a process that started with a young bill. There have been five different referendums, three of them in the last 10 years. All three have been won by statehood.

So, this is not something that happened at the last minute like they are trying to portray, but it is the same process that has been followed by 32 territories that became states, most recently Alaska and Hawaii.

What we are seeing here is the progression of the Northwest Ordinance established by our forefathers.

Now, the beauty of this last vote is that if you believed that Puerto Rico should be returned to Spain or if you believed that Puerto Rico should be part of the moon, you had a place to vote. You voted no.

So, it is all against one, and that is the final vote that statehood had to win before Congress pushes this over the line, before more people leave the island.

Eight hundred thousand Puerto Ricans have left the island in the last 20 years.

Miss GONZÁLEZ-COLÓN. Mr. Fuentes, my time is getting short.

A few minutes ago when the witnesses were saying in their testimony, some of them said that the Negotiation Committee will inevitably lay out a rejection of statehood either directly or by imposing impossible conditions.

How do you respond to that argument?

Mr. FUENTES. Well, the opposite is also the same, right? If we have another vote like your bill calls for——

The CHAIRMAN. You need to wrap up your answer, sir.

Mr. FUENTES [continuing]. Then if the people do not like them, they will vote against them, and then that will be the end of the statehood movement.

The CHAIRMAN. Let me now turn to Mr. Garćıa. Sir, the time is yours.

Mr. GARĆIA. Thank you, Mr. Chairman and Ranking Member, for this hearing.

It is 2021, and Puerto Rico is still a colony, the oldest in the world. From the annexation of the island to a century of limited citizenship, the imposition of PROMESA and our failures in disaster response, we know that Puerto Rico's relationship with the United States is rooted in the history of racism, exploitation, and oppression.

While many may disagree about the future of Puerto Rico's status, we must recognize that the decision should come from those who will be impacted most, the people of Puerto Rico.

We have an opportunity to rectify Puerto Rico's long-standing colonial status, which has resulted in its people being treated as second-class citizens, but it must be done correctly and with transparency.

I would like to explore some topics that have not gotten a whole lot of attention in this hearing yet. So, I would like to ask Governor Pierluisi—regarding the Fiscal Oversight Board, or "La Junta," the proposed cutting pension, University of Puerto Rico's budget, additional austerity measures to make room for Wall Street bank holders, I know that you have opposed some of these measures.

With respect to the present conversation about the status of Puerto Rico, given the final word is left, of course, to the Junta, my first question to you is: How does Puerto Rico's $70 billion debt restructuring work under statehood?

If you would be brief, I have some more questions I would like to ask you, sir.

Governor PIERLUISI. Well, I will be brief. That process is ongoing, and the bill, H.R. 1522, provides that basically all laws, all regulations in place remain in effect unless they are inconsistent with the legislation itself.

My expectation is that the restructuring of the commonwealth's debt will be done and over with at the latest by the middle of next year, and it could be earlier.

Mr. GARĆIA. But does not the final plan, Governor, of adjustment saddle Puerto Rico with billions in yearly debt service for 40 years? Governor PIERLUISI. Well, actually that is debt that Puerto Rico incurred, and as the legislation provides, whatever bonds or obligations Puerto Rico has, Puerto Rico keeps because that is the way it should be.

We are restructuring it, and under PROMESA, and we will be achieving incredible savings in terms of the payments that we will be making for the next 30 years.

You are talking about a very significant reduction in the debt service that Puerto Rico will be paying as a territory until it becomes a state, and then as a state thereafter.

Mr. GARĆIA. And if Puerto Rico were admitted as a state under the Puerto Rico Statehood Admission Act, how would taxation of Puerto Rico residents and companies operating in the island change?

Governor PIERLUISI. The bill provides that Puerto Rico would become a state on an equal footing with the other states. There is only one statehood. You cannot change it. That is why statehood is so straightforward.

We aspire to have the same rights and responsibilities. Obviously, you can transition Puerto Rico into the Federal income tax system. That would not be inconsistent with the tax uniformity clause of the U.S. Constitution, and that Congress can address within the time frame that the bill provides for.

Because the way this works is that once the people of Puerto Rico vote for statehood in the final referendum, and I anticipate it will be an overwhelming vote, then the President has about a year to proclaim statehood.

And within that time frame, within that year, Congress will be addressing all the different ways in which we need to conform existing laws, programs, regulations so that Puerto Rico becomes a state and a viable state.

Mr. GARĆIA. Thank you, sir.

Do I have time for another question, Chairman?

The CHAIRMAN. Yes, a quick one.

Mr. GARĆIA. Thank you.

Senator Lourdes Santiago, in your view, does the Puerto Rico Statehood Admission Act explicitly outline a transition plan?

And why is it so important for the residents of Puerto Rico to be included and made aware of this process?

Ms. SANTIAGO. The Independence Party opposes the H.R. 1522 bill. It gives us an opportunity that is completely exclusive of the other status of options.

For example, here we have been saying that Puerto Ricans have been discussing this issue of the Puerto Rican status for decades.

But this conversation is where a very critical speaker has been missing and that is the U.S. Congress. Puerto Rico is not a colony of any party of Puerto Rico. It belongs to the United States.

That is why one of the greatest values to H.R. 2070 is that it obligates us to have the conversation that the Congress has not been willing to have.

The CHAIRMAN. You need to wrap up now. Time is over.

Mr. GARĆIA. Thank you, Mr. Chairman.

The CHAIRMAN. Thank you very much, Mr. Garćıa.

Let me now recognize Mr. Moore for his time.

Sir.

Mr. MOORE. Thank you, Chairman and Ranking Member.

And those of you who are here today, thank you for being here. Sincerely, this is an important issue.

Regardless of disagreements on how to move forward, I think we all share an appreciation for our fellow Americans in Puerto Rico and hope to be able to continue these conversations and do something productive.

My first question will be for Governor Pierluisi.

Again, can you just highlight very, very briefly the biggest challenges that you face due to Puerto Rico's status as a territory rather than a state?

Governor PIERLUISI. Let's start with programs such as Medicaid. The 50 states have a Medicaid Program providing for the health services needed by their medically indigent population or low-income, moderate-income population.

Puerto Rico does not have a permanent financing for this program. In the last couple of years, because of the disasters we faced, Congress increased the amount of funding that we get for purposes of our local Medicaid Program.

But you cannot budget for your health system on a year-to-year basis or on a 2-year cycle. You need a permanent program, fair for the American citizens in Puerto Rico.

We are seriously underfunded as we speak. We do not cover 100 percent of the population falling below the poverty level in Puerto Rico in our Medicaid Program, and we are far from being able to do so. That is just one example.

The Nutrition Assistance Program, SNAP, does not apply in Puerto Rico the same way. We are $1 billion short of Nutrition Assistance System in the middle of the disaster. As it happened elsewhere in the nation, we got additional assistance, but it falls short, again.

And we do not have a permanent treatment from the part of the Federal Government with SSI, which is intended to assist people that are disabled, elderly, or low income. It does not apply at all in Puerto Rico.

Those are just examples. On top of it, I tell you that the way Federal disaster programs work in the mainland is different than in Puerto Rico.

We are always facing different requirements, and unfortunately, the Supreme Court has said that because we are a territory, we can be treated differently.

And again, it makes no sense as a matter of Federal policy because this is like geographic discrimination. Puerto Ricans are not immigrants. Puerto Ricans are American citizens. They hop on a plane if they do not get the health services that they are seeking. They hop on a plane if they do not have Nutrition Assistance as in the states.

And I should add to this that the political uncertainty caused by this status that we have discourages investment into Puerto Rico. Once Puerto Rico settles its political status once and for all, I am sure and I have no doubt our economy will prosper. We will attract more investment.

That happened in Alaska. That happened in Hawaii. That happened in New Mexico. That happened in Arizona. That is why all of those territories aspired to become states, so their quality of life and the economic level of their territories would improve.

So, that is the vision. It is an empowering vision.

And lastly, let me just say this, and again, with all due respect. A yes-or-no vote cannot be fairer. A yes-or-no vote cannot be more inclusive. We had it. We had it on statehood, and all that we are doing now is telling Congress to say yes or no on statehood for Puerto Rico.

It is the right thing to do. It is the courageous thing to do, and I welcome the debate, and I welcome all, including Puerto Ricans who want to oppose statehood, but let Congress address this issue. It is your responsibility, morally and legally.

Mr. MOORE. Thank you.

To close, if you could also just comment, with the Puerto Rico Self-Determination Act, to what extent were you or other key stakeholders brought into this for your input when it was drafted?

Governor PIERLUISI. Meaning which legislation? I am sorry.

Mr. MOORE. The Puerto Rico Self-Determination Act.

Governor PIERLUISI. The Self-Determination Act, no. This bill, as far as I know, was drafted by its original co-sponsors, and I am talking about the Resident Commissioner and Darren Soto.

If you are talking about the other one, H.R. 2070——

The CHAIRMAN. The time is up, Mr. Moore.

Governor PIERLUISI. If it is H.R. 2070, I have no idea who drafted that bill. I had no role in it.

The CHAIRMAN. Time is up, sir.

Governor PIERLUISI. It ignores the vote that we just had.

Mr. MOORE. Thank you.

I yield back.

The CHAIRMAN. Thank you.

Mr. Case, you are recognized, sir.

Mr. CASE. Thank you, Mr. Chair.

Like Mr. Lowenthal, I came to this hearing to really listen as carefully as I could. It is a critical decision not just for Puerto Rico but for our country.

I also came with a sense of personal history and responsibility having been born in the territory of Hawaii, of course, Hawaii being the last state that was given a chance by the United States to become a state, after a very, very long struggle, by the way, similar to what you have all described today.

My great-grandfather, as a matter of fact, was a delegate for statehood to this Congress probably 100 years ago. So, I understand it, and I think I certainly believe that this time has come.

Also, just from a perspective of free association, I want to emphasize since I work directly with the countries of the Pacific that are in free association with our country, I just want to drive a point home one more time that free association is an association, a treaty between two independent countries, so functionally it is independent.

So, I do not understand, in all honesty, the discussion having to do with free association. Our treaties are there. Treaties can be abrogated, and countries go about their way. So, just to make that point.

I want to say very directly something from my heart. I am strongly inclined to Mr. Soto's and Miss González-Colón's proposal, but it does trouble me, in all honesty, that the indication from the voters of Puerto Rico thus far has not been at the same level of overwhelming agreement with statehood, as, for example, Hawaii, which in 1941 was at 66 percent. The final plebiscite was 93 percent in 1959.

In the case of Alaska, in 1946 it was 60 percent, and by 1958, it had grown to 83 percent.

So, I just want to be honest. I do ask myself the policy question. Is the vote today enough to move forward with the process?

Again, I think it is, but I just leave that with all of the folks, and I don't have a question. It is just an observation.

I wish it was higher because then it would be an easier decision.

With that, I want to defer the remainder of my time to Ms.

Velázquez because I want her to have the opportunity to ask further questions.

Ms. VELÁZQUEZ. Thank you to the gentleman for yielding.

Senator Santiago, as a proponent of independence for Puerto Rico, could you please explain to this Committee the importance for Puerto Ricans to understand the implications of statehood or any other options, what it would mean for the island?

Ms. SANTIAGO. First of all, the only option that represents an inalienable right is independence. The libre association option, would have to be ratified by a treaty like statehood and requires affirmative action by the Congress of the United States.

I think that the great confusion that we see here today is because there is a great number of U.S. people allied mostly with the liberal part. They are afraid of speaking up because of fear of racism, of being considered racist. They are afraid of speaking up against the United States becoming a multi-national country, which is the fundamental question behind the statehood proposal.

Thank you.

Mr. CASE. Thank you. I yield back.

The CHAIRMAN. The gentleman yields back.

Ms. Tlaib, you are recognized for 5 minutes.

Ms. TLAIB. Thank you, Chairman.

I really want to focus today, as many of my colleagues touched base on, how we in Congress can fulfill our responsibility to the people of Puerto Rico by providing a free, open, and informed process for resolving their political status.

I know here in Michigan, especially in communities of color, we do not take self-government for granted. For years, the state imposed unelected emergency financial managers on a number of majority Black cities across the state of Michigan.

We all felt the pain of our unaccountable actions to slash city services and benefits to residents and in many cases resulted in the poisoning of Flint children with contaminated water.

My residents in Detroit still have our municipal bankruptcy fresh in our minds, the largest in the history of our country, especially for the pensioners, who saw their benefits slashed by someone they did not vote for or could not remove.

And it was not the people of Detroit who incurred the debt, but it was the people of Detroit who suffered for it.

So, I understand the pain that Puerto Ricans feel as the unelected, unaccountable Financial Oversight and Management Board has slashed budgets and services by taking away Puerto Ricans basic rights of government.

Senator Santiago, can you describe for the Committee what it is like living under both American colonial rule and by an unelected Financial Management Board and why the status quo cannot continue?

I know you talked about some of it, but talk about really the human impacts of all of that.

Ms. SANTIAGO. The colonial regime that is in place in Puerto Rico violates the human rights of all Puerto Ricans, and with the arrival of the fiscal control Junta board, which has veto power over us, elected officials.

There is no other way to call this other than a dictatorship, as Puerto Ricans claim our collective rights to free determination, and I think it is important to establish a distinction with other examples that other Congressmen have mentioned.

We are not here talking about whether to approve a tax or not, or whether we are going to have any elected official in their position for a certain number of years, we are talking about the fundamental rights of a colonized nation, and we have as part of that right to claim the opportunity to discuss all of the possible options.

In the case of H.R. 1522, it ignores the deep differences, profound differences that we have in Puerto Rico. Besides, it also allows Congress to avoid their responsibility to tell the Puerto Ricans what it is that they are willing to offer Puerto Ricans.

I am convinced, and this has definitely been my experience up until today, that the United States, when it comes to the moment of truth, they are not willing to offer statehood to a Caribbean and Latin American nation.

Ms. TLAIB. Thank you so much, Senator. And thank you, Ms. Gomez, for translating.

I have a very short time, and I just really want my colleagues to truly understand the responsibility that we all have to provide the most democratic, participatory, and more informed path forward to Puerto Ricans.

And I hope my colleagues will be guided by the goal as we continue to consider the two different bills in front of us right now, and again, really appreciate this really thoughtful conversation that we do always have to be based on the truth about the impact of those Puerto Ricans and their families that are impacted by our actions.

Thank you so much, Chairman. I yield.

The CHAIRMAN. Thank you very much.

Now let me recognize the Chair of the Oversight Subcommittee, Ms. Porter. The time is yours.

Ms. PORTER. Thank you very much, Mr. Chair.

I would like to yield my time to Ms. Velázquez.

The CHAIRMAN. The gentlelady yields.

Ms. Velázquez, you are recognized.

Ms. VELÁZQUEZ. Let me thank the gentlelady for yielding.

Governor Vilá, as a law professor yourself, could you explain how the academic argument that independence or statehood are the only true self-determination options available under U.S. law is inaccurate?

And can you please explain to the members of this Committee the current territorial arrangements allow Micronesia and the Marshall Islands to have?

Mr. ACEVEDO-VILÁ. I will quickly answer, and there was a response from all constitutional law professors from Puerto Rico answering specifically that argument and saying that precisely that is why the bill you have proposed—and this is my position—the best alternative because you have questions, yes, about how free association will work in a relationship with a territory that we are U.S. citizens now.

The cases of Micronesia and those other places, they were never, never U.S. citizens. So, that is something that the negotiating commission will have to answer. The same thing with any other non-territorial alternative.

That is the beauty of your bill. I hear people and Members asking questions to law professors. Those are the questions that the Congress has to answer in terms of different alternatives and different possibilities so the people of Puerto Rico, they will vote based on that information.

We have never had the opportunity to vote with the information of what are the conditions for the different status alternatives, even statehood.

There are a lot of things that need to be clarified by Congress before people vote.

Ms. VELÁZQUEZ. Yes, thank you.

In the past, proponents of statehood have sold a bill to the people of Puerto Rico saying that they will maintain participation in the U.S. Olympics or Miss Universe, and that that will not change if Puerto Rico becomes a state, things that might not have incredible implications or economic consequences for the people of Puerto Rico.

But it shows to you and it shows us that this is not any election. This is a most important process in our relationship of the United States keeping a colony for 123 years; that it is our responsibility to provide a process for the people to determine their own political future.

So, a lot of education needs to happen. People need to know: What does it mean supporting or voting for statehood. What does it mean? What are the implications?

Mr. ACEVEDO-VILÁ. Quickly, if I have a second, I heard Governor Pierluisi answering the question about taxes, and that was very illuminating.

He said that after we vote for statehood, and on Congressman Darren Soto's bill, Puerto Rico will become the 51st state. Then after a vote, they will explain to us what are the economic consequences and fiscal consequences of our vote.

No. Those are the things that people need to know before we vote, and that is something that only Congress can answer.

Ms. VELÁZQUEZ. And that is something that my bill does.

Mr. ACEVEDO-VILÁ. Yes.

Ms. VELÁZQUEZ. It includes a transition plan.

Mr. Natal, in any of the plebiscites that have been held in recent history, including transition plans for the options put forward, have Puerto Ricans ever received public, non-biased education about the consequences of each of the options?

Mr. NATAL-ALBELO. Unfortunately, they have not, and they have not because the plebiscites that have been legislated locally in Puerto Rico have the same default problem, that they have been legislated one-sided by the ruling party, usually trying to design the consultation in a way that it is slanted toward the outcome that is preferred by the party in power.

And that is why it is so important that with your bill the legislative assembly in Puerto Rico would be able to call for a status convention. There are different models that have been suggested. The Puerto Rico's Lawyer Association has presented one for many decades that includes 75 delegates. That is not a small group of people in dark rooms.

That is close to the same numbers of members that we have in the legislative assembly, but they will be elected specifically according to the status preferences as long as they are non-colonial, non-territorial, and in that sense they will have an equal opportunity to talk to the people of Puerto Rico about why their preferred option is the one that the people should elect.

And at the end of the day, the people will have the final decision, as it should be.

Ms. VELÁZQUEZ. Thank you.

And thank you to Ms. Porter for yielding time to me.

I yield back.

The CHAIRMAN. The gentlelady yields. Ms. Porter yields back. Let me now recognize Mr. Gosar for 5 minutes.

Dr. GOSAR. Thank you, Mr. Chairman.

I would like to yield my time to the gentlelady from Puerto Rico, Miss González.

Miss GONZÁLEZ-COLÓN. Thank you, Mr. Gosar, for yielding and always in helping Puerto Rico in many of the issues and tasks, and I really appreciate that.

I will continue with my line of questioning.

One of the issues that has been brought to this Committee is about definitions, and I would love to have Professor Ponsa, who is a constitutionalist professor and who led a letter with more than 45 constitutional professors across the nation from very prestigious universities, including universities in Puerto Rico, to support H.R. 1522 and establish the constitutionality of the other bill.

And I will make this question to you. H.R. 2070 establishes a commission of Members of Congress who will make recommendations to the status convention of Puerto Rico culture and language under its self-determination options, which we know must include statehood and nationhood.

On what aspects of Puerto Rican culture may the commission make recommendations? Are they in music or religious freedom? Will it be in our traditions and history, or will it be in the definitions of how we mix rice and beans, or any other issue. Can you answer that question for me?

Dr. PONSA-KRAUS. Well, as far as I can tell from H.R. 2070, there is no limit to what those recommendations could be. I don't consider that a good idea.

I think that if one is going to respect the people of Puerto Rico, then one should let them live their culture as they do and enjoy it as they will, which I believe is consistent with the constitutional options that are available to it.

I am not a fan of having a bilateral commission involving Congress advising Puerto Rico on its culture and language. I do think they have gotten plenty of advice. Thank you very much.

What we need is a response to the referendum and that kind of clarity from Congress that it is willing to offer the people of Puerto Rico statehood once they voted for it.

Miss GONZÁLEZ-COLÓN. Do you think that bill will be xenophobic?

Dr. PONSA-KRAUS. Which bill?

Miss GONZÁLEZ-COLÓN. H.R. 2070.

Dr. PONSA-KRAUS. I would not describe H.R. 2070 as xenophobic, no.

Miss GONZÁLEZ-COLÓN. OK. Do you think that it will be a precedent if there is an exclusion of most of the members of this Committee of the House that has direct jurisdiction over the issues of the territories, and specifically Puerto Rico, and the Senate from being able to serve on a congressional committee because that bill would allow a bilateral advice commission to negotiate with the territory of Puerto Rico, as we were an independent nation?

Do you think that that bill established that Puerto Rico is an independent nation?

And if doing so, that means that in order to get free associated state status like the Micronesia Island, like some of the witnesses are supporting here are establishing, should be negotiating without any Federal laws applying to Puerto Rico?

Dr. PONSA-KRAUS. If I have understood your question, I believe that the bilateral commission created by H.R. 2070 is expected by that bill to negotiate in ways that don't make any sense within the structure of Puerto Rico's relationship to the United States.

If Puerto Rico is going to debate the options that are available to it, it should be able to debate those without being nudged, guided, or advised.

Clarity from the Federal side is a good thing, but to call it a negotiation when you have the Federal Government on one side and a territory on the other side that is being steered in a self-determination process, to me it is a misnomer.

That is not a negotiation. That is the Federal Government guiding a process by advising Puerto Rico on issues in which Puerto Rico should make its own decisions instead of offering the kind of clarity that it is Congress' responsibility to provide.

Miss GONZÁLEZ-COLÓN. Thank you.

I have 30 seconds, and, Mr. Governor of Puerto Rico, you have had a lot of experience in Congress. You were for 8 years a member of this Committee in the House.

Do you think establishing a constitutional convention where people are elected like delegates will be the right option to be expressed?

Governor PIERLUISI. The fact of the matter is that it has never been legislated in Puerto Rico itself, and people here, some were blaming the Statehood Party. Well, we have not been in control of the House and the Senate and the Governorship always.

There have been many occasions in which the House and the Senate of Puerto Rico and the Governorship have been controlled by the other major party in Puerto Rico.

And this concept of a status convention was never legislated, and the problem I have with it right now is that we just had a vote, a majority vote. We had not had a majority vote, a clear-cut majority vote in a long time in dealing with the status of Puerto Rico.

In 2012, we had another one, 54 percent clearly rejected the current status, and now 53 percent approved of statehood.

The CHAIRMAN. Your time is up, sir. Thank you.

Miss GONZÁLEZ-COLÓN. Thank you, Governor.

I yield back.

Dr. GOSAR. I yield back.

The CHAIRMAN. Keeping track of overtime, too.

Thank you.

Mr. Webster, you are recognized, sir.

Mr. WEBSTER. Thank you, Chair.

I would like to yield my time to the Resident Commissioner from Puerto Rico.

Miss GONZÁLEZ-COLÓN. Thank you, Congressman Webster, for yielding and for always being supportive of many of the issues regarding the island.

I will continue my line of questions.

I will go now with the Governor of Puerto Rico, Mr. Pierluisi, who, as I said, was a member of this Committee of the House for 8 years and now is the one representing the island as the elected official to carry out the results of the last election.

Governor, there have been many things that have been said today here regarding how Congress is willing or not to grant statehood for Puerto Rico.

You are a lawyer as well. You were a former prosecutor and served justice locally on the island. You know the movement that gained the vote, the right to vote for women and African Americans.

Do you think statehood and equality is an issue of civil rights?

Governor PIERLUISI. Definitely. That is what we are talking about mostly. It has economic development implications, quality of life implications, but at its heart this is a civil rights issue.

Somebody said it before, and I will repeat it. Nine out of ten American citizens living in Puerto Rico are proud American citizens. I am talking about Puerto Ricans.

I know a lot of Puerto Ricans, unfortunately, left the island, and now they are pursuing their dreams in the states, but the ones remaining in Puerto Rico, they are proud American citizens and proud Puerto Ricans, and that is not inconsistent.

You can be a proud Puerto Rican American, like you have so many in the states, or we could add to this nation. This nation is diverse, and of course, we're Hispanic. This would be the first truly Hispanic state, and, of course, we would continue speaking Spanish, but we all aspire to be bilingual, and we will always treasure our heritage, and that's good for America.

It's good that we have this history, that we have these customs. That's why people come to Puerto Rico and visit. That's why people come to Puerto Rico and invest in Puerto Rico and retire in Puerto Rico. It's not inconsistent. What we're talking about here is finding a way forward, and the people of Puerto Rico express their will, and the ones here talking about that there was no debate, where are they? Where were they? Were they on the Moon? On Mars? We know how to debate these issues. We have been debating them for too long.

Everybody in Puerto Rico knows what independence is all about. Everybody in Puerto Rico knows what free association is all about. Everybody in Puerto Rico knows what the current status means. We suffer through it every day, and everybody I meet knows as well what statehood means. Enough of this debate. The ball is in Congress' court. It is time for Congress to address this issue, and I have no doubt if Congress offers statehood to Puerto Rico, you will get an overwhelming vote from the people of Puerto Rico accepting it. That's why I'm not hesitating. That's why our Resident Commissioner is not hesitating, and you will have a diverse Puerto Rico, with Republicans such as Jennifer González, and Democrats like me, and we will enrich this nation when the time comes, and we become the 51st state of the Union.

Miss GONZÁLEZ-COLÓN. Governor, one of the questions that was made a few minutes ago, and Congressman Case from Hawaii was saying about the percentage, and how Hawaii voted for statehood, and a percentage of that.

Do you have an expectation that once there is a bill approved in Congress like the one we are supporting today, and that becomes a law, that the statehood support will grow on the island once Congress makes a formal offer to the island?

Governor PIERLUISI. I have no doubt. Some of the ones participating in this hearing, they don't miss a step saying that Congress will never offer statehood to Puerto Rico. They have been encouraging the people of Puerto Rico to doubt Congress, to doubt this nation. They have been saying we don't deserve it. They are not going to give it to us.

Well, I know. I know the time will come when this offer will be made, and the people of Puerto Rico will see that it is for real, and they'll go out, and they'll vote overwhelmingly for statehood. Whatever requirement that is imposed on us that is reasonable, we will meet, because we want to become the 51st state.

Miss GONZÁLEZ-COLÓN. Thank you, Governor, and I yield back.

The CHAIRMAN. The Gentlelady yields. Let me now recognize the Gentleman from New York, Mr. Torres, who is recognized for 5 minutes.

Mr. TORRES. Thank you, Mr. Chair. Puerto Ricans on the island are citizens of the United States, and we are here today to debate whether those citizens should be equal, and the mere fact that we are even debating the legal equality of Puerto Ricans as American citizens is a tragedy for both democracy and decolonization, and history will not judge us kindly for the great harm that we have done and continue to do to the people of Puerto Rico.

If Puerto Ricans are American citizens, why not make them equal under the law? If Puerto Ricans have long been and largely wish to remain citizens, which has been borne out repeatedly, there are only two options that preserve citizenship. There's the status quo, which means colonialism, and then there's statehood, which means legal equality. The single most egregious example of colonialism is the financial control board, which represents a cardinal sin against the sovereignty and self-determination of Puerto Rico.

The fact is if Puerto Rico were a state, there would be no financial control board. Unlike colonies, states have rights under the United States Constitution. The absence of statehood has left Puerto Rico wide open to colonization at the hands of the financial control board. The U.S. Congress that gave us the financial control board is the same Congress that now wishes to deny Puerto Rico the right to exercise self-determination through a plebiscite.

And I imagine there are powerful interests that have a stake in the status quo of colonialism, but if you're a corporation that exploits Puerto Rico as a tax haven, you have a powerful incentive to sabotage statehood, but if you're an everyday Puerto Rican who seeks to become an equal citizen of the United States, who seeks to have the right to vote in presidential or congressional elections, who seeks to have your voice heard, to have a seat at the table, and to get your fair share of Federal resources and representation, then you have every reason to support statehood, and that is precisely what a majority of the Puerto Rican electorate voted to do in November 2020, and instead of respecting the will of the people, the U.S. Congress has chosen to ignore it, and not only has Congress chosen to ignore the results of the plebiscite, Members of Congress are proposing to micro-manage the process by which Puerto Ricans make decisions about their own status. The patronizing paternalism of Congress should never be mistaken for self-determination. True self-determination means that the people on the island have a right to decide not only what to decide, but how to decide.

This Congress should practice the Hippocratic Oath, and do no harm. When the people speak, the proper role of Congress is to listen. The people of Puerto Rico have spoken through a democratic process. Congress ought to listen to the people. Congress ought to legislate what the people voted for, and Congress ought to abolish the financial control board, which is an abomination. That, to me, is true decolonization. Everything else is a red herring; a distraction masquerading as decolonization.

I have a question for the Governor. I've never met the Governor, it is good to meet you.

Governor PIERLUISI. Nice to meet you.

Mr. TORRES. Governor, statehood would likely yield two U.S. Senators and five Members of Congress. Regardless of where one stands on the question of status, we all have a vested interest in securing more resources for Puerto Rico. Is it fair to say that two U.S. Senators and five Members of Congress would likely mean more resources for Puerto Rico, which is an outcome that all of us share?

Governor PIERLUISI. Of course. They would be our gladiators. They would be fighting for us whenever we face a natural disaster, whenever the nation as a whole is facing a pandemic like the one we are dealing with at the moment, we have no voice, no vote in the Senate. We have friends, colleagues in the Senate that come to assist us, but it is not the same, and we only have a great Resident Commissioner, but only one, without a vote in the House. We would have at least four, perhaps five. You don't need to know much about politics to realize that that would make a big difference, and voting for the president—presidents don't visit Puerto Rico—rarely so. Why? They don't need our vote.

I have no doubt presidents would be visiting, candidates for president would be visiting. To make commitments to the American citizens of Puerto Rico when they are aspiring to the highest office in this nation. That makes a difference. That's going to make a difference. That would be democratic. Our status is not democratic. The CHAIRMAN. Time is up. The gentleman yields back. Let me now recognize Representative Herrell from New Mexico. You are recognized.

Ms. HERRELL. Thank you, Mr. Chair. I would like to yield my time to Representative González-Colón.

Miss GONZÁLEZ-COLÓN. Thank you, Congresswoman Herrell for yielding, and I appreciate you being here the whole afternoon. That means a lot for the people of Puerto Rico knowing that Members of Congress, even when there are votes being called, are participating in this hearing. That is an answer for the November elections, so I want to say thank you.

I want to make a question to Professor Ponsa, and this is not that I'm fixated with your statement, it is that you are the Constitutionalist here, the professor, who can clarify many of the words that are being put in some bills trying to be Constitutional. You have said many times today, and I know that in the past you have argued that statehood is not just about equality, but it is also about empowerment.

Could you elaborate this idea, and how, saying here in Congress, having the leverage, and I do know about that, because I cannot vote on the Floor. I mean, I can vote on amendments, but not on the Floor on regular bills. We had that situation during the last 4 years. How do you think Puerto Rico can achieve more economic progress by having statehood?

Dr. PONSA-KRAUS. Well, I frankly can't put it better than you and the Governor have, but I can add this. It isn't only that Puerto Rico would have two Senators and four or five Representatives and a Presidential vote. It is also that statehood itself as a status would guarantee equality in legislation that the Federal Government passes to aid and address issues in the states. As a territory, Puerto Rico is subject either to exclusion from certain programs, such as SSI, or to caps in benefit programs.

So, there's no comparison between the current situation in which Puerto Rico has no voting representation whatsoever in the Federal Government. It has you, thank goodness, but it does not have voting representation through the Federal Government, and a situation in which it is empowered based proportionately to its population, like any other jurisdiction under the United States with equality on the vote.

So, that difference is profound, and it is also a constitutionally protected difference because states are treated equivalently under the Constitution. So, it is both the presence of voting representatives, and the status of statehood that would guarantee equality for Puerto Ricans.

Miss GONZÁLEZ-COLÓN. You said it well, and I'm really fighting for the inclusion of Puerto Rico in many Federal programs as Governor Pierluisi did while he was in Congress. However, some people talk about parity without statehood, and that means leaving Puerto Rico at the mercy of the decisions in Congress, not having their elected officials there to take part in that decision process, and as a territory will always run the risk that as Congress, or the administrations, should simply decide whether or not we are treated equally or not. Even President Bush established an executive order that Puerto Rico should be treated equally in all Federal quorums as a state, but yet, the administration changed, and that executive order has been interpreted in many different ways. My question will be to you. What options of status will guarantee the U.S. citizenship for Puerto Rico?

Dr. PONSA-KRAUS. Specifically as to the question of citizenship, only statehood guarantees citizenship for current U.S. citizens in Puerto Rico, and going forward under the 14th Amendment Citizenship Clause, Puerto Rico becomes a state, and birthright citizenship will exist in Puerto Rico now, and going forward. Other options, the United States has the power to grant citizenship anywhere in the world that it wants.

So, advocates of free association argue that free association should come with U.S. citizenship. The truth is that I understand the difference that Governor Acevedo-Vilá pointed to, that the other free associated states with relations to the United States weren't citizens beforehand, but it is really important to understand that the Commonwealth of the Northern Marianas had a choice to become a free associated state, or to enter into a different kind of arrangement with the United States, which ended up being territorial, and they made that choice in order to pursue citizenship. The United States could grant it that citizenship, but it didn't want to to a free associated state, and even if it didn't, this is what the people have to understand when they consider the options. The United States could always stop granting birthright citizenship going forward in a free associated state. So, even if it was preserved for some time, it could always be taken away. Only statehood guarantees it now and going forward.

Miss GONZÁLEZ-COLÓN. Thank you, professor. I yield back to the Chairman.

The CHAIRMAN. Thank you. Mr. Graves, you are recognized for 5 minutes. Mr. Graves? Let me ask the Ranking Member, is Mr. Graves available?

Mr. GRAVES. Yes, he is. I'm sorry, sir.

The CHAIRMAN. Thank you. You are recognized, sir.

Mr. GRAVES. Mr. Chairman, I apologize. I've been in and out of the hearing today, and I'm trying to listen as best as I can. I want to thank all the witnesses for being here. I have a couple of questions. One, I heard one of the previous Members talking about treating Puerto Rico as a colony, and disrespecting the citizens.

Look, I want to remind everybody here today that in the aftermath of the just awful, awful hurricanes that the island experienced that we provided billions and billions of dollars for the island, for restoration and disaster recovery efforts that Congresswoman González-Colón fought for to make sure that the citizens of Puerto Rico would be treated properly. Let's be clear that these dollars were well beyond the capability of the Puerto Rican government, and we were there, and no one was disrespecting that fact, and I think if you were to go through and do an analysis of the cost per capita, it is probably one of the highest allocations in history in terms of dollars per person that was provided, and that's a direct result of Puerto Rico's delegates' hard efforts up in Congress. Governor, it is nice to see you again. I hope you are doing well.

I want to ask you a very quick question, because I have some other ones. Can you just briefly respond, how will the Puerto Rican citizens respond to Federal taxation that they would be open to, and just being the Governor, could you kind of maybe just briefly explain, you have control over that now. You have the ability to tax at whatever rate you want effectively, and if now the Federal Government is going to come in and tax as well, is that a benefit? How would the citizens respond? Could you just briefly respond to that?

Governor PIERLUISI. Yes. Because of our income levels, a considerable number of our residents wouldn't pay Federal income taxes. Actually on the mainland, about 46 percent of the population does not pay Federal income taxes. So, Puerto Rico would be higher than that. At the corporate level, we would have to transition. We would have to transition this issue, and obviously Congress would have to step in the way.

It makes no sense to admit a territory into the Union and to affect the territory. You would be assisting the territory in joining the Union. As an incorporated territory, we do not pay Federal income taxes on income we earn in Puerto Rico. We pay payroll taxes, and a lot of the American corporations doing in Puerto Rico actually pay Federal income taxes because they operate through divisions in Puerto Rico.

On the manufacturing side, they're basically treated as foreign, and they are treated like investing in Puerto Rico is like investing in Ireland, or in Singapore. That's an area in which we would have to transition, but the tax uniformity clause of the U.S. Constitution shouldn't be viewed as static. In a circumstance like Puerto Rico is facing for a transition, and that's what I envision happening here.

Mr. GRAVES. Sure. Thank you, Governor. I appreciate that answer. I also was just trying to listen, I hope that I caught all this accurately, but Governor Acevedo-Vilá, you campaigned against statehood, and you had run an election, and didn't win that election, but it seems as though——

Mr. ACEVEDO-VILÁ. Sorry, can you repeat, because I lost the audio for a bit. I'm hearing you now, but I lost you in the middle of questions.

Mr. GRAVES. OK, I'm sorry about that. I was saying that you campaigned against statehood, and didn't win on that platform, and I'm trying to understand the official representative of the Popular Democratic Party, as I understand, Jose Dalmau is actually on record against H.R. 2070, yet I think you may be advocating differently, and I'm just trying to understand kind of the political complexities there.

Mr. ACEVEDO-VILÁ. No, the Popular Democratic Party is against H.R. 1522. H.R. 2070, I'm not here on behalf of the Popular Democratic Party. I guess he was going to be invited, but I just want to make a clarification. Yes, I ran on the last election. I lost the election. I have heard here a lot of people say that statehood got more votes than any of the elected officials. But you know what? The vote against statehood—the no vote got more votes than any of the elected officials. People voted more against statehood than they voted for Resident Commissioner González and Governor Pierluisi. That only shows that we are divided on this issue, and that the process of November 2020 was not really a balanced and fair process.

Mr. GRAVES. Mr. Chairman, thank you. I know I'm over time, but I just want to make for the record, it is my understanding that the new Chairman of the Popular Democratic Party, Jose Dalmau, was actually on record against H.R. 2070. I yield back.

The CHAIRMAN. Thank you, Mr. Graves. The gentleman yields. Anyone else to be recognized? I will take my opportunity now to ask a couple of quick questions, and then in some of the overtime, maybe indulge the Members with a couple of points.

First of all, it was brought up once, and it was brought up in the communication from Ms. González-Colón, and from the Ranking Member, Mr. Westerman, about doing in-person meetings insofar as those become important. And that that's the way to go, and that we could be much more productive, etcetera. Well, I don't disagree. The first thing that I would love to do is to have in-person meetings so that these discussions could occur. The issue for all the Members to know is that despite the deployment of vaccines, COVID cases continue to rise. In some parts of the country, cases are surging. In the last 7 days, the CDC has reported over 450,000 new COVID cases, and the Office of the Attending Physician continues to adamantly recommend that we maximize the utilization of remote work. We don't know the vaccine status of our Members and staff, and that's another reason.

So, as this horrific situation that we all find ourselves in—not just Congress—we will begin to accelerate and put in the protocols necessary to have more in-person meetings. I am not enjoying the process that we have now, but this is the process we have, and the issue of Puerto Rico's status was something that—there was criticism that we were delaying this, or that it wasn't getting done. Well, it was getting done.

So, the reason we did it, and we did it remotely, is that we need to expedite this and have this discussion, and begin the deliberations that I think are critical to dealing with this question. The other part that's critical in dealing with this question, my friends, is that there's a division. Not only a division in Puerto Rico in terms of opinion about statehood or another status, but also a difference of opinion within Congress, and a difference of opinion in the U.S. Senate, a difference of opinion in the House of Representatives. So, going forward, these kinds of discussions and deliberations are critical. Like it or not—and sometimes I like it less—Congress has a critical role in this decision, and how it is going to be made.

And I recognize the difficulty for some Members, but I also recognize that there's going to come a point where we're going to have to move forward on it, and I find it interesting that, just hypothetically, whichever one of these bills the House passes, that there will be a significant difference of opinion in the U.S. Senate. We've been communicating with the Biden White House through their Insular Affairs, and the Domestic Counsel, and other leadership in the White House, and asking for the Justice Department to issue an opinion on both pieces of legislation, and those will be forthcoming, and some of the constitutional issues that were brought up by the professor are part of the log of questions that we asked, including the binding nature in terms of us moving forward in terms of the vote that happened in November in terms of pro-statehood by the percentage that Mr. Graves pointed out. Nevertheless, that's where we're at, and that information will be shared with everybody.

I have two quick questions. Mr. Natal, let me ask you a question. As we were going through this discussion, I heard a couple of things today, and many of the other questions that I would have asked that were on my list, other Members took care of. H.R. 2070, the public process, the stakeholder involvement, the community-based process. In support of that process, we heard today from primarily other panelists, and some of my colleagues up here on the dais that if you support this process, you are not acknowledging the clear cut decision that was made in November in that election. That it is an excuse to delay, and for Congress to be—I think the Governor put it to not to be courageous and make a decision. And that there's unconstitutionalities associated with one, and that a definitive answer has been made.

So, my question to you, which is a question that is directly and indirectly posed to you through most of this hearing is, why not just let us have an up-or-down referendum on the question, and go forward from there? Why is this process of public engagement so critical? And let me put it to you for whatever answer, and then I have one more question, and I'm done.

Mr. NATAL-ALBELO. Yes. Thank you, Chairman. The quick answer is this is not the first time that a referendum like this has taken place. Just to give you an idea, in the last 16 years, 10 different bills have been presented regarding the statehood issue in the United States. We have had at least three referendums, and regardless whether the statehood supposedly got 97 percent or 55 percent, a process that's borne out of the lack of participation, out of exclusion, out of the imposition by one of the political parties, is a process whose outcome lacks democratic legitimacy, and that's why it doesn't matter if statehood got 97 percent 3 years ago, or it got 51 percent this time around.

It is a process that was borne out of the exclusion, and that's why it is so necessary that this Congress allows the people of Puerto Rico to put forward a participative and inclusive process of all non-colonial options, and I would just use this analogy, Chairman. Most individuals, and I respect that members of this Committee have yielded their time, either to Congresswoman Velázquez, or Congresswoman González, because they understand that as Puerto Ricans, they know more about this than maybe they do.

The CHAIRMAN. Yes.

Mr. NATAL-ALBELO. And that's what they should do with this vote, and our support of H.R. 2070 yields the decision to the people of Puerto Rico, and let Puerto Ricans decide.

The CHAIRMAN. The other question—and if I may, Mr. Fuentes, given your extensive experience, the work that you've done in Puerto Rico, the work that you did with the previous administration on issues related to Puerto Rico, the hypothetical I asked earlier in my comments, the last time around—the last 4 years, there was nothing definitive coming from the previous administration. We hope to get opinions soon, and there was no movement at all in the Senate with the previous leadership at that point.

In fact, part of the Senate leadership at that point said, over my dead body, or we're going to do it with discretion of statehood or status for Puerto Rico. And then you have, like I said, the differences of opinion both in the House and in the Senate.

How do you respond to the fact that we need to come to some closure, and how do we do that, given the dynamics, given the history, and given the fact that this issue is not an issue that can readily be dealt with in one vote, that it is going to require, I think, some level of deliberation, and consensus, but I leave that question to you. How do you see the progress going forward?

Mr. FUENTES. Well, Chairman Grijalva, thank you very much for this hearing, which is very important. The way I see it, politics are playing a role in this process that is really unacceptable. As we've discussed previously, political forecasting is even worse than weather forecasting, but as we see Puerto Ricans leaving the island, and moving to the mainland to get better quality of life, what we now have is 3 million Puerto Ricans living on the island, 6 million living in the mainland in one of the 50 states.

So, that starts to create political power, and as that political power starts to be recognized, I believe that other voices are going to start understanding it and changing, and I would point out that Senator Scott and Senator Rubio in the U.S. Senate, both of whom recognize the importance of the Puerto Rican vote in central Florida, and both of whom have expressed themselves in favor of statehood, but need to create the basis for them to launch the effort in the Senate. It will happen.

The CHAIRMAN. So, it still comes down to that—regardless of the discussions about what the Senate or the House can do, I think that Congress can pass legislation whether it is H.R. 1522 or H.R. 2070, and that becomes the law, and we could project and talk about estimating what the constitutionality or non-constitutionality of it is, but once the decision is made by this body, and the other body, hopefully that question then becomes moot. All right. I want to thank all of the witnesses. I'd appreciate it if there are written questions that Members did not get to, that they would be forwarded to you. I appreciate it, Governor, thank you, Mr. Vélez. And the meeting is adjourned. Thank you very much.

Miss GONZÁLEZ-COLÓN. Mr. Chairman——

The CHAIRMAN. We are done with the meeting.

Miss GONZÁLEZ-COLÓN. No, I was just introducing 12 letters for the record, Mr. Chairman. That was all I had.

The CHAIRMAN. Without objection, ma'am.

Miss GONZÁLEZ-COLÓN. Thank you, sir.

The CHAIRMAN. The meeting is adjourned.

[Whereupon, at 4:40 p.m., the Committee was adjourned.]

[ADDITIONAL MATERIALS SUBMITTED FOR THE RECORD]

SUBMISSIONS FOR THE RECORD BY RESIDENT COMMISSIONER GONZÁLEZ-COLÓN, SENADO ESTADO LIBRE ASOCIADO DE PUERTO RICO

Hon. RAÚL GRIJALVA,
Chairman,

Hon. BRUCE WESTERMAN,
Ranking Member,
House Committee on Natural Resources

Dear Chairman Grijalva, Ranking Member Westerman:

In the last couple of years media have made well known the situation of the island of Puerto Rico and its relationship with the United States. Puerto Rico was acquired from the Kingdom of Spain after the United States won the Spanish-American War in 1898. Since then, it's been treated as a possession with no intentions from the three branches of government to giving statehood to the island. In 1898, U.S. Army General Nelson Miles entered to the southern part of the island promising all Puerto Ricans not only to liberate them from Spanish tyranny, but also to give them the freedom from which the United States once were founded. A hundred and twenty-three years later Puerto Ricans, American Citizens from the island, are still waiting for that promise to be fulfilled.

Today President Joe Biden and the Democratic Party are defending minority values. Their campaign was all about Black Lives Matters, minorities rights, anti-nationalism and fascism and the situation of Puerto Rico is not different for what Americans are living in the mainland. The federal government systematically discriminate against American Citizens, not only on the island, but in all the five populated territories. As other fellow statehood supporters from the island and the mainland, we don't want to talk more about the referendum results were statehood won by a significate majority, but for what we want to underline is about credibility and the future of the Democratic Party itself.

In half of the 20th Century, the United States used Puerto Rico as a democracy showcase to Latin America and the Soviet world to demonstrate that American values, American living and dreams were the right direction for the world. We were on that road and we still believe in those values. Let's take the sword as once the young American Republic started to lead the free world, as General Nelson Miles once did to overcome tyranny in this strange times we are living and make example of how democracy works in times were the People's Republic of China, the Russian Federation and other autocratic states are taking advantage of that world that we once knew.

Hon. Keren Riquelme Cabrera,
Senator at Large, Puerto Rico

Statement for the Record, Puerto Rico Young Republican Federation

On Wednesday, April 14, 2021, the Committee on Natural Resources Office on Insular Affairs held a remote Full Committee Legislative Hearing on the following bills:

- H.R. 1522—To provide for the admission of the State of Puerto Rico into the Union. *Puerto Rico Statehood Admission Act*. This bill was introduced earlier

this year by Congresswoman Jenniffer González-Colón (R-PR-AL) and Congressman Darren Soto (D-FL-9) following the overwhelming results of the latest political status plebiscite held in Puerto Rico.
- H.R. 2070—To recognize the people of Puerto Rico's right to call a status convention through which the people would exercise their natural right to self-determination and establish a mechanism for congressional consideration of such decision for other purposes. *Puerto Rico Self-Determination Act of 2021*. This bill was introduced after H.R. 1522 by Congresswoman Nydia Velazquez (D-NY-7) in clear opposition of H.R. 1522 and the Puerto Rican people's electoral mandate to become the 51st state of the Union.

Through this statement the Puerto Rico Young Republican Federation would like to unequivocally express its support for bill H.R. 1522 and its repudiation of bill H.R. 2070.

Achieving statehood for the islands has been a top priority for the Puerto Rico Young Republican Federation since the day of its emergence. Puerto Rico became a U.S. territory as a result of the Spanish-American War of 1898, and its people have been American citizens for nearly as long. Puerto Ricans have significantly contributed to the well-being of the United States. Thousands of Puerto Ricans have served in the U.S. Armed Forces and fought in every major war since World War I. Tens of thousands currently serve. Puerto Rico statehood is simply the only right and moral political status option. It is long overdue for Puerto Ricans to attain the equality they deserve.

Furthermore, the people of Puerto Rico have reiterated their rejection of the island's current territorial status by supporting statehood at the ballot box, not once, not twice, but three times in the last ten years. Nonetheless, H.R. 2070 seems to ignore fair and clean election results by disguising its opposition to Puerto Rico statehood and its furtherance of the colonial status using an obscure definition of "self-determination." H.R. 2070's call for "self-determination" is a fallacy since it does not consider the choice of Puerto Rican voters and relies on a so-called "status convention" through which the people would exercise their natural right to "self-determination." More so, that won't be enough to change Puerto Rico's political status. H.R. 2070 calls for congressional consideration of the decision.

How is congressional power over the political status a form of "self-determination"? To make matters worse, H.R. 2070 was introduced by elected representatives who represent citizens of other jurisdictions outside of Puerto Rico and in an electoral process in which Puerto Ricans are not allowed to participate because of the current territorial status.

Let us be clear, Puerto Rico held fair and clean elections on November 3, 2020, where the latest political status plebiscite took place. Statehood won fair and square. Therefore, it is clear that Puerto Ricans have exercised their right to self-determination, and it is time for the U.S. Congress to honor their will.

We commend Congresswoman González-Colón's efforts that have led to the introduction of H.R. 1522 and resulted in attaining bipartisan support for this crucial piece of legislation.

We firmly believe that providing the people in Puerto Rico with the equal treatment they seek and deserve as proud citizens of the United States of America is long overdue, and we urge every single Member of Congress, both Republicans and Democrats, to acknowledge this most pressing matter by joining representatives González-Colón and Soto in supporting H.R. 1522.

Governor of Puerto Rico
Pedro R. Pierluisi
April 8, 2021

Hon. Nancy Pelosi
Speaker
U.S. House of Representatives
Washington, DC

Hon. Mitch McConnell
Republican Leader
U.S. Senate
Washington, DC

Hon. Charles Schumer
Majority Leader
U.S. Senate
Washington, DC

Hon. Kevin McCarthy
Republican Leader
U.S. House of Representatives
Washington, DC

Dear Speaker Pelosi, Majority Leader Schumer, Republican Leader McConnell, and Republican Leader McCarthy:

As the Governor of the 3.2 million American citizens living in Puerto Rico, I write to urge you to respect my constituents' right to self-determination, which has been exercised three times during the last decade. On November 3, 2020, in a straight-forward Yes or No vote, a clear majority of voters expressed—in no uncertain terms—that statehood is their preferred option to end over 100 years of colonialism. The November 3rd vote reconfirmed what my constituents had already expressed in the November 2012 plebiscite, in which a clear majority rejected the current political status and chose statehood as their preferred political status option.

I therefore ask that you respond to the will of the United States citizens of Puerto Rico with legislation that will initiate the admission of Puerto Rico as a state. Any proposal that would prolong a territorial status that has been flatly rejected by the voters in the guise of promoting a complicated and superfluous process of self-determination that ignores our people's vote must be rejected.

The territorial relationship between Puerto Rico and the United States has been the subject of extensive study and debate. It is time for Congress to begin the admission process that Puerto Rico's voters clearly favor.

The appropriate response to the American citizens of Puerto Rico is the enactment of H.R. 1522, "The Puerto Rico Statehood Admission Act" sponsored by Representative Darren Soto and Resident Commissioner Gonzalez-Colon, and S. 780 in the Senate sponsored by Senator Martin Heinrich. Under this legislation Congress would set forth the terms and conditions under which Puerto Rico would be admitted as a state of the Union, and the voters of Puerto Rico would be given the opportunity to accept or reject such admission in a final referendum before it is proclaimed.

When you consider H.R. 1522, I ask you to think about how your own constituents would feel if their full rights as Americans were still in question after being citizens of the United States for well over a century and after voting for statehood. How would they feel if the response from Congress was to set aside their expressions of self-determination with legislation that would delay the end of their territorial status?

Your support for H.R. 1522 and S. 780 will reaffirm the most sacred principles upon which our system of government was founded and will strengthen our democracy.

Sincerely,

Pedro R. Pierluisi

April 12, 2021

Hon. Nancy Pelosi
Speaker of the House
U.S. House of Representatives
Washington, DC

Hon. Mitch McConnell
Senate Republican Leader
U.S. Senate
Washington, DC

Hon. Charles Schumer
Senate Majority Leader
U.S. Senate
Washington, DC

Hon. Kevin McCarthy
House Republican Leader
U.S. House of Representatives
Washington, DC

Dear Speaker Pelosi, Majority Leader Schumer, and Leaders McCarthy and McConnell:

We, the undersigned legal and constitutional scholars, write to express our strong opposition to the Puerto Rico Self-Determination Act, H.R. 2070, and its Senate companion bill, S. 865, and to register our equally strong support for the Puerto Rico Statehood Admission Act, H.R. 1522, and its Senate companion bill, S. 780.

Like all Americans, we support self-determination. But unlike the supporters of the Puerto Rico Self-Determination Act, we believe that genuine self-determination requires the United States to offer Puerto Ricans a real choice. By "real," we mean *constitutional* and *non-territorial*. Puerto Rico's self-determination options must be *constitutional*, for the obvious reason that neither Congress nor Puerto Rico has the power to implement an unconstitutional option. And they must be *non-territorial*, because a territorial option is not self-determination.

There are two, *and only two*, real self-determination options for Puerto Rico: statehood and independence. Yet the Puerto Rico Self-Determination Act defies constitutional reality by calling upon Puerto Ricans to define other non-territorial options. *There are no other non-territorial options.* For many decades, advocates of "commonwealth" status argued that it was non-territorial. They argued that when Puerto Rico made the transition to commonwealth status in 1952, it ceased to be a U.S. territory, became a separate sovereign, and entered into a mutually binding compact with the United States. But they were wrong. Quite simply, Congress does not have the power to create a permanent union between Puerto Rico and the United States except by admitting Puerto Rico into statehood. Lest there be any doubt, the U.S. Supreme Court has repeatedly and recently refuted the controversial "compact theory." In *Puerto Rico v. Sanchez Valle* (2016), the Court ended seven decades of debilitating debate over the question of whether Puerto Rico's common-wealth status created a permanent union between two separate sovereigns with an unequivocal "no": as the Court made clear, Puerto Rico is, and always has been, a U.S. territory, and Congress retains plenary power to govern the island under the Territory Clause of the Constitution (Art. IV, § 3, cl.2). And in *Financial Oversight and Management Board of Puerto Rico v. Aurelius*

Investment LLC. (2020), the Court went on to explain that Congress's creation of a federal board with substantial powers over Puerto Rico's local government was a permissible exercise of Congress's plenary power over a U.S. territory. In short, as long as Puerto Rico is neither a state of the Union nor an independent nation, it will remain a territory. By inviting Puerto Ricans to define non-territorial options other than statehood or independence, the inaptly named Puerto Rico Self-Determination Act disserves its purported goal by perpetuating the pernicious myth that such options exist. They do not.

Despite longstanding political division within Puerto Rico, Puerto Ricans have long shared an overwhelming consensus on two key points: They reject territorial status and they wish to remain U.S. citizens. But while both statehood and independence would fulfill the goal of self-determination, only one of those options would guarantee U.S. citizenship: statehood. Last November, in an unmistakable effort to determine their political future, a clear majority of Puerto Ricans voted "yes" in their own referendum on statehood. Now that Puerto Ricans have publicly and officially asked for statehood, it is time for the United States officially to offer it. The Puerto Rico Statehood Admission Act does just that.

Proceeding respectfully, cautiously, and pragmatically, the Puerto Rico Statehood Admission Act responds to the November referendum with an offer of statehood and sets the terms for admission, but it makes admission contingent on a *second* referendum in which Puerto Ricans would ratify their choice. Were they to do so, the President would issue a proclamation admitting Puerto Rico as a state within one year of the vote. If they were to reject statehood, then the island would remain a territory with the option to pursue sovereignty at any time in the future—so the Act does not force statehood on Puerto Rico in any way. In other words, the Puerto Rico Statehood Admission Act respects the result of Puerto Rico's referendum by responding with concrete action, while ensuring that Puerto Ricans have the first and last word on their future.

In the 123 years since the United States annexed Puerto Rico, Congress has never offered Puerto Ricans the choice to become a state. Instead, the United States has allowed Puerto Rico to languish indefinitely as a U.S. territory, subjecting its residents to U.S. laws while denying them voting representation in the government that makes those laws. We strongly support a congressional offer of statehood to Puerto Rico, and we urge Congress to pass the Puerto Rico Statehood Admission Act immediately.

Signed,*

**University affiliations listed for identification purposes only.*

Jack M. Balkin
Knight Prof. of Const. Law
Yale Law School

Christopher P. Banks
Professor, Political Science
Kent State University

Evelyn Benvenutti Toro
Professor of Law
InterAmerican Univ. of
Puerto Rico School of Law

Jessica Bulman-Pozen
Betts Professor of Law
Columbia Law School

Kathleen Burch
Professor of Law
Atlanta's John Marshall
Law School

Guy-Uriel E. Charles
Professor of Law
Duke Law School

Erwin Chemerinsky
Dean and Jesse H. Choper
Distinguished Prof. of Law
U.C. Berkeley School of Law

Cornell W. Clayton
C.O. Johnson Distinguished
Prof. of Political Science
Washington State University

David S. Cohen
Professor of Law
Thomas R. Kline School of Law,
Drexel University

Andrés L. Córdova
Professor of Law
InterAmerican Univ. of
Puerto Rico School of Law

Erin F. Delaney
Professor of Law
Northwestern Pritzker
School of Law

Walter Dellinger
Douglas Maggs Emer.
Prof. of Law
Duke University

Carlos Dias Olivo
Professor of Law
Univ. of Puerto Rico
School of Law

Michael C. Dorf
Robert S. Stevens Professor of
Law Cornell Law School

Stephen M. Feldman
Distinguishe Prof. of Law
University of Wyoming

Martin S. Flaherty
Leitner Family Prof. of Intl. Law
Fordham Law School

Barry Friedman
Jacob D. Fuchsberg Prof. of Law
New York Univ. School of Law

Luis Fuentes-Rohwer
Professor of Law
Maurer School of Law,
Indiana Univ.

Lauren Gilbert
Professor of Law
St. Thomas Univ.
College of Law

Leslie F. Goldstein
Judge Hugh M. Morris
Prof. Emerita University
of Delaware

David Golove
Hiller Family Foundation
Prof. of Law
New York University
School of Law

Mark A. Graber
Univ. System of Maryland
Regents Professor
Univ. of Maryland,
Francis King
Carey School of Law

Jonathan Hafetz
Professor of Law
Seton Hall Univ. School of Law

Helen Hershkoff
Professor of Constitutional Law
New York Univ. School of Law

Gary J. Jacobsohn
H. Malcolm Macdonald Prof.
University of Texas at Austin

Randall L. Kennedy
Michael R. Klein Prof. of Law
Harvard Law School

J. Andrew Kent
Prof. of Law & John D. Feerick
Research Chair
Fordham Law School

Mark R. Killenbeck
Wylie H. Davis Distinguished
Prof. of Law
University of Arkansas

Stephen R. Lazarus
Associate Professor of Law
Cleveland-Marshall College of Law

Lawrence Lessig
Roy L. Furman Prof. of Law
Harvard Law School

Sanford V. Levinson
Professor of Government
University of Texas at Austin

Ira C. Lupu
Prof. of Law Emeritus
George Washington Univ.
Law School

Martha Minow
300th Anniversary Univ.
Professor
Harvard University

Samuel Moyn
Henry R. Luce
Prof. of Jurisprudence
Yale Law School

Christina D. Ponsa-Kraus
George Welwood Murray Prof.
of Legal History
Columbia Law School

David Pozen
Charles Keller Beekman
Prof. of Law
Columbia Law School

Richard Primus
Theodore J. St. Antoine Coll. Prof.
Univ. of Michigan Law School

Kermit Roosevelt
Professor of Law
Univ. of Pennsylvania
Law School

Lawrence Sager
Alice Jane Drysdell Sheffield
Regents Chair
University of Texas at Austin

Rogers M. Smith
Christopher H. Browne
Distinguished Profesor
University of Pennsylvania

Girardeau A. Spann
Professor of Law
Georgetown University Law Center

Kate Stith
Lafayette S. Foster Prof. of Law
Yale Law School

Geoffrey R. Stone
Edward H. Levi Dist. Prof. of Law
University of Chicago

Nelson Tebbe
Jane M.G. Foster Prof. of Law
Cornell Law School

Laurence H. Tribe
Carol M. Loeb
University Professor and
Prof. of Const. Law
Harvard Law School

Stephen I. Vladeck
Charles Alan Wright Chair in
Federal Courts
Univ. of Texas School of Law

Kenji Yoshino
Chief Justice Earl Warren Prof. of
Constitutional Law
New York University School of Law

March 18, 2021

Hon. Raúl Grijalva Hon.
Chairman
House Committee on
Natural Resources

Bruce Westerman
Ranking Member
House Committee on
Natural Resources

Hon. Joe Manchin
Chairman
Senate Committee on Energy
& Natural Resources

Hon. John Barrasso
Ranking Member
Senate Committee on
Energy & Natural
Resources

Dear Chairman Grijalva, Ranking Member Westerman, Chairman Manchin, Ranking Member Barrasso:

For over one-hundred years, the U.S. citizens of Puerto Rico have been disenfranchised in federal elections and subjected to unequal treatment across federal programs. Last November, voters stood up to change that when an absolute majority of 53% demanded statehood in a locally sponsored referendum. The Puerto Rico Statehood Admission Act, H.R. 1522 and S. 780, directly respond to that mandate, and we urge you to support it and help get it approved as soon as possible. Puerto Rico's referendum was historic because it is the first time that statehood received unquestionable majority support on the island with a simple "YES" or "NO" vote. The 117th Congress is therefore presented with a unique opportunity to make history and put an end to America's inherently colonial rule over Puerto Rico, which runs counter to America's values of democracy, equal justice under the law, and government by the consent of the governed.

We recognize there are some in Congress, such as Rep. Nydia Velázquez (NY) and Sen. Robert Menendez (NJ), who oppose statehood for Puerto Rico and have completely ignored the results of the referendum held last November. Today, they will be submitting a counter-proposal, the Puerto Rico Self-Determination Act (PRSDA), which has faced criticism from representatives of all status options.

The most significant concern, across party lines, is that the PRSDA is ultimately non-binding. Under the bill, Congress would be under no obligation to implement whichever status option is chosen by the convention and later voted on by the electorate. This would represent a huge setback for voters in Puerto Rico who have engaged in multiple acts of self-determination over the last decade and have shown, with increasing clarity, that Puerto Rico's voters reject the current territory status and favor statehood above all non-territory options.

Beyond the will of the people on the island, however, Puerto Ricans stateside also favor statehood by wide margins. For example, recent polls show 81% of Puerto Rican residents in Florida and 69% of those in New York favor the admission of the island as a state. A majority of Americans have also supported the idea for decades according to Gallup. This is a settled issue on the island as well as across the Nation, and Congress has a moral obligation to act.

The only legislative option that respects the will of the people of Puerto Rico, and ensures a binding process of self-determination is H.R. 1522 & S. 780, the Puerto Rico Statehood Admission Act. By offering statehood, stipulating the terms of admission, and requiring a ratification vote, Congress would finally open the door to full equality and democracy for the U.S. citizens of Puerto Rico while leaving the ultimate choice in their hands. If a majority opposes statehood at that point, then the island would remain a territory with the capacity to pursue independence or free association through the procedural mechanism of their choice, including a status convention. Congress has a moral obligation to let the people of Puerto Rico decide their own self-determination process.

Our organizations represent the majority of voters in Puerto Rico, as well as their allies stateside. We believe it's time to put an end to the dysfunctional, outdated, and undemocratic territory status to which Puerto Rico has been subjected. We call on Congress to open the door to full enfranchisement and equality for our fellow U.S. citizens in Puerto Rico by supporting and passing the Puerto Rico Statehood Admission Act. America can and must do better.

Sincerely,

George H. Laws Garćıa
Executive Director
Puerto Rico Statehood Council

Annabel Guillén
President
Igualdad, Futuro Seguro

Irma R. Rodriguez
President
Puerto Rico Escogió Estadidad

Kathianie Banchs
President
Young Professionals for
Puerto Rico Statehood

José Cabrera
Chair
Puerto Rico Star Project

Hon. César Méndez-Otero
President
Coalicion Pro Derechos
E Igualdad

Dr. Zayira Jordan
Founder
Frente Estadista

Jesús Pérez
Executive Director
52 States of America

Dr. José Vicente
President
Alianza Pastoral por Puerto Rico

Hon. Iván D. Hernández
Chairman
Consejo de Ex Alcaldes
de Puerto Rico

Harry Márquez Rodrıguez
President
Organizaćıon de Pensionados Estadistas

Hon. Kenneth McClintock
President
Puerto Rico Equality Forum

Hon. José Aponte-Hernandez
Executive Director
Instituto Misión Estadista

Brig. Gen. Victor Pérez (Ret.)
Director
Organización de Veteranos Progresistas

Luis Dávila Pernas
National Committeeman
Democratic Party of Puerto Rico

Ricardo Aponte
Executive Director
Republican Party of Puerto Rico

Gabriela M. Medina Marrero
President
Young Democrats of Puerto Rico

Josué Rivera
Chairman
Puerto Rico Young Republican Federation

Hon. Luis Berrios-Amadeo
Former Shadow
U.S. Representative
Puerto Rico Statehood Commission

Frankie Martınez-Blanco
Former Associate Member
President's Task Force on Puerto Rico's Status

Hon. Milagros López
President
Votar es Poder

Ken Oliver
Director
U.S. Council for Puerto Rico Statehood

Elvin Méndez Rosa
President
Movimiento Revolućıon Estadista

Luis Matos
President
Renacer Ideológico Estadista

Jorge I. Rodriguez Feliciano
President
Puertorriqueno Pro Union Permanente

Wilfredo Rivera
President
Impulso 51/Estado Igualdad

Joel Salgado
Administrator

Ricardo Marrero Passapera
President

La Suprema Definición
Gerardo Ramirez
Director
Movimineto Estadista
Puertorriqueño

Ahora SíPuerto Rico
Javier de la Luz
Founder
Boricuas con Kamala

Ruth Marrero
President
Senior 51

José A. Correa Alvarado
Outreach Coordinator
We The People

Alexander Acevedo
Spokesperson
Democratas Activaos

Hon. Roberto Lefranc Fortuño
President
Juventud Estadista de Guaynabo

Emilio Ruiz
Lead Organizer
Puerto Rico Statehood Supporters
of Florida & USA

Kemuel Delgado
Founder & Lead Organizer
Junte Estadista de Puerto Rico

Dess Soto
Coordinator
Coalicion Pro Derechos
E Igualdad PR51
Florida Chapter

Margarita Vives
President
Coalicion Pro Derechos
E Igualdad PR51
Guaynabo City Chapter

Elizabeth Reyes
Spokesperson
Puerto Rico Equality Coalition,
Massachusetts Chapter

Eric Cardona
Spokesperson
Puerto Rico Equality Coalition,
Florida Chapter

Doralice Matta
Founder & President
Las Avispas Azules

Pedro Luis Hernandez Gomez
Lead Orgnizer
Bateador Estadista

Edgardo Vargas Moya
Spokesperson
Isabelinos por la Igualdad

Iván G. González
Editor & Chief
Inside The Colony

Reina Davis Pérez
President
Statehood Educational Group

Nilka Marrero Garcia, M.Div
President
Misión Solidaria de Amor

Kevin Romero
President
Instituto de Politica Pública
y Estadidad

Benny Ortiz
President & CEO
Los Latigos Azules

Francisco "Pompy" González
Presidente
Estado PRUSA

Cristóbal Berrios
President
Acción Civil Para El Status

Samuel Rodríguez
CEO
Borinqueneers Congressional Gold
Medal Ceremony Natl. Committee

STATEMENT FOR THE RECORD, JOSÉ F. APONTE-HERNÁNDEZ, FORMER SPEAKER AND REPRESENTATIVE AT LARGE, PUERTO RICO HOUSE OF REPRESENTATIVES, ON H.R. 1522

Thank you to the Committee leadership for convening this hearing and allowing me to speak in support of H.R. 1522.

I am a former Speaker and current member of the Puerto Rico House of Representatives. More importantly, I am an American citizen since birth who has been denied his most fundamental democratic rights by virtue of living in a U.S. territory. My statement before this honorable body supporting H.R. 1522 pertains to both of these inseparable aspects of my reality. It is also backed by the freely expressed will of a majority of Puerto Rico residents and supported by more than two hundred and fifty (250) years of philosophical and legal precedent that serve as the foundation for this Nation.

My fellow citizens on the Island have defended these values with their blood, sweat, and tears. Even our veterans are deprived of equal and dignified treatment after fulfilling their obligations abroad, after fighting elsewhere for the fundamental rights they lack. I have first-hand knowledge of these challenges and inequalities. My father and brother are veterans, the former of the Second World War and the latter from the Vietnam War.

This information is not novel. One hundred twenty years have created a formidable record on which this Congress should feel obliged. We have endured over a century of self-serving discriminatory and contradictory legal interpretations and constant rule changes contrary to basic democratic principles and the very concept of civil rights.

I respectfully must point out that this Congress and this Committee are not oblivious to the injuries perpetrated but have been one of its leading promoters, either by action or omission. Hundreds of public hearings such as this one have been held. The same arguments and facts are rehashed every couple of years without concrete steps. This inertia is the best available evidence of the inherent disadvantages of our political condition.

Political discourse is only transcendent when it is accompanied by action. When principles are treated as a catchphrase, we must not forget that they lose their value and become mere propaganda. Thus, in its analysis, this political body must also face its obligations and decide its current and prospective roles in upholding this Nation's ideals. It must choose between the usual comforts of "neutrality" and the tensions associated with fulfilling a demand for justice.

As the public record reflects, on election day, November 3, 2020, the American citizens of Puerto Rico were presented with a question identical to that used by former territories admitted as a state: *Should Puerto Rico be immediately admitted into the union as a state?* The result reiterated the public expression on multiple previous electoral events (See Appendixes A-1/A-3). *A majority of the people of Puerto Rico supported statehood.* Specifically, and as certified by the Puerto Rico State Elections Commission: The YES option received 655,505 votes which amount to 52.52%, and the NO alternative received 592,671 or 47.48% of the votes. Democracy and the political process have clear and specific rules of engagement and interpretation. These are the cornerstones of the social contract. Under our voting system, the votes duly emitted are the ones that are counted. The majority of those is recognized as the people's will. Otherwise, legitimacy and stability are impossible to achieve. That is democracy; that is the rule of law. This exercise is much simpler in a case like the plebiscite held on Tuesday with a well-crafted question and simple (yes/no) alternatives.

Of course, there is always a segment of the political opposition who resort to after-the-fact interpretations, rule changes, and political spin in a way that discredits the people's will. Demagoguery under the guise of objectivity is nothing new.

Some have succumbed to an easy out in their analysis of our aspirations. Some feel that financial stability is a precondition to a change in political status. Their position fails to recognize the very nature of the problem. The total disenfranchisement and unequal treatment of the people of Puerto Rico are the cause and not the effect of our current socioeconomic condition.

The impact of a territorial system, which deprives American citizens of their fundamental civil rights, permeates all aspects of our lives. We hear every day the public cry for equal treatment as American citizens, but what does that mean? It is impossible to address the individual rights issue without simultaneously addressing the collective structural issue.

Ignoring the impact of political subordination and unequal treatment devalues civil rights and democratic principles to the point that it renders them subsidiary to financial or fiscal constraints. This argument is reminiscent of poll taxes, where financial solvency was a prerequisite to the exercise of voting rights. It seems as if some Members of Congress keep blurring and moving the "finish line" to avoid its obligations toward the American citizens of Puerto Rico.

Others have resorted to encumbering the process so that their positions prevail regardless of the people's will.

A false equivalence has been created between two legislative projects (H.R. 1522 and H.R. 2070) dealing with the Puerto Rico status issue that must be questioned and challenged. Let there be no doubt, these two projects that differ in intent, philosophy, and legitimacy. However, their joint discussion pretends to give the impression that both positions are equally situated. That there is no majority expression. This action is akin to a legislative poison pill whose victims are the people of Puerto Rico and only benefits a minority expressly rejected by the people of Puerto Rico. Congress cannot make feasible a process that reinforces colonial theories and recriminations.

At the helm of this legislative strategy are Congresswomen Nydia Velazquez and Alexandra Ocasio-Cortez of New York, who historically have been affiliated to the parties who promoted the losing proposition in the plebiscite. We respect them and are aware of all Congressmen and women's authority to file bills that transcend their districts' limits. However, we reject using their authority as a subterfuge to impose their will against a clear, direct, and forceful expression of the people. Regardless of their ancestry, they do not represent the American citizens of Puerto Rico; they represent districts in New York. Unlike Jennifer González-Colón *(proponent of H.R. 1522*), who was elected by the majority of the voters in Puerto Rico (512,697 votes), the distinguished Congresswomen from New York have never received a single vote in Puerto Rico. Let there be no doubt, the weight of their opinions stems from the Territorial Clause and not from the freely and democratically stated will of the people on the Island. Their opinions are not representative of the views of a majority of my fellow citizens in the Islands but rather an imposition from New York. That is precisely the very definition of colonialism.

Besides the vote's outcome, it is essential to recognize that this majority resulted from an open process. As seen from the official filings before the Puerto Rico State Elections Commission (See Appendixes B-1/B-3), all major political parties in the Island expressed an official position regarding the proposed alternatives. One of the groups that actively campaigned in favor of the NO option was an organization named "Boricuas Unidos en la Diaspora."

One of its leaders was former governor Anibal Acevedo-Vilá, who was also the resident commissioner candidate for the main opposition party (Popular Democratic Party) and whose candidacy was decisively rejected by people of Puerto Rico in these past elections. Attached you will find a copy of his plebiscite campaign ad for that group (See Appendixes C-1/C-4, more information available at https:// m.facebook.com/watch/?v=730377810883381&□rdr). Who were among the other active participants in this group? Not surprisingly, Congresswoman Nydia Velazquez and Alexandria Ocasio-Cortez, and former Congressman Luis Gutierrez. Precisely, the architects and promoters of H.R. 2070.

Similarly, and as expected, newly created "citizen" organizations pretend to flood the legislative record with alternative and discredited theories. Some of these "new groups" serve as the alter egos of politicians who the people of Puerto Rico expressly rejected. Precisely those who actively campaigned in favor of the NO option in the plebiscite.

H.R. 1522's legitimacy was not manufactured politically, behind closed doors, but is the product of democracy itself, by the voice of our people. It represents the aspirations of the majority, those who have to suffer from its implications.

It is a contradiction to proclaim the virtues of democracy and then work hard to hinder it. Consistency and credibility are intertwined. No amount of political spin can discredit democracy and the fact that the American citizens of Puerto Rico demand statehood. The status issue is not a matter of personal loyalties but legitimacy. We, the people of Puerto Rico, have spoken.

You have a historic opportunity to help rectify the state of structural disadvantage that has placed millions of American citizens in a subordinate position. The United States is a nation founded on principles of justice and the dignity of all. Statehood would not only be consistent with these principles, and thus, in the best interests of the Nation, but the recognition of our will.

Congress has a moral, political, and legal obligation to resolve Puerto Rico's political status. Our Island has voted and opted for Statehood three times in the last decade. Accordingly, I strongly support H.R. 1522 and urge all members of this Committee to recommend its approval.

A-1

STATE ELECTIONS COMISSION OF PUERTO RICO

FINAL CERTIFICATION AMENDED PLEBISCITE FOR THE FINAL DEFINITION OF THE PUERTO RICO'S POLITICAL STATUS

WHEREAS: The *Law for the Final Definition of the Puerto Rico's Political Status*, Puerto Rico Act No. 51-2020, was approved "to create the rules for a plebiscite that will be held on November 3, 2020 to resolve a century-old problem of Puerto Rico's status as a territory of the United States of America; to guarantee the U.S. citizens of Puerto Rico their right to self-determination and their right to demand the Federal Government for redress of grievances; provide the conditions for conducting this plebiscite pursuant to Public Law 113-76 of 2014 and the pertinent congressional reports, House Report 113-171 and House Report 116-101; to appropriate funds; and for other related purposes."

WHEREAS: The *Law for the Final Definition of the Puerto Rico's Political Status*, Puerto Rico Act No. 51-2020, establishes on its Article 1.3 (h), as Public Policy: "After more than a century of being at a disadvantage due to our territorial status, and after the conclusive result of the Plebiscite of 2012 in which the current territorial status was rejected, Congress and the President approved an appropriation of $2.5 million in the "Consolidated Appropriations Act," Pub. L. 113-76 (2014), to fund an "objective, nonpartisan education campaign for the plebiscite voters, about the alternative options that would resolve Puerto Rico's future political status." This "Law to Define Puerto Rico's Final Political Status" is consistent with the parameters established by the aforementioned Federal Act and the statements made in congressional House Report 113-171 and House Report 116-101"

WHEREAS: Article 5.9 (e) of the *Law for the Final Definition of the Puerto Rico's Political Status*, Puerto Rico Act No. 51-2020, establishes that "The status option printed on the ballot that is favored by a majority of one hundred percent (100%) of the votes defined as "Adjudicated Ballots", shall be certified by the Puerto Rico State Elections Commission as the winning option and the legitimate expression of self-determination of a majority of voters to resolve Puerto Rico's territorial status."

THEREFORE: According to Article 5.9 (e) of the *Law for the Final Definition of the Puerto Rico's Political Status*, Puerto Rico Act No. 51-2020, the Puerto Rico State Elections Commission certifies the final result of the Plebiscite for the *Final Definition of the Puerto Rico's Political Status*, held on November 3, 2020:

QUESTION: **Should Puerto Rico be admitted immediately into the Union as a State?**

POLITICAL STATUS FIGURE VOTES PERCENT PREFERENCE STATEHOOD

YES	▲	**655,505**	**52.52 %**
NO	●	**592,671**	**47.48 %**

Enacted in accordance with Article 5.9 (f) of the *Law for the Final Definition of the Puerto Rico's Political Status*, Puerto Rico Act No. 51-2020.

In San Juan, Puerto Rico, on February 12, 2021.

FRANCISCO J. ROSADO-COLOMER
Chairman

I CERTIFY: That on this same date I have sent copy of this certification to the Governor of Puerto Rico, to the Resident Commissioner in Washington DC, the presiding officers of the Legislative Assembly, the U.S. President, the presiding officers of Congress, and the U.S. Attorney General, in accordance with Article 5.9 (f) of the *Act to Define Puerto Rico's Ultimate Political Status*, Act No. 51 of May 16, 2020.

In San Juan, Puerto Rico on February 12, 2021.

ROLANDO CUEVAS COLÓN
Secretary

A-2

PUERTO RICO STATE ELECTIONS COMISS.

FINAL CERTIFICATION

PLEBISCITE FOR THE IMMEDIATE DECOLONIZATION OF PUERTO RICO

Pursuant to Article X, Section 3 of the *Puerto Rico Immediate Decolonization Act*, Act Num. 7 of February 3, 2017, as amended, the Puerto Rico State Election Commission certifies the final result of the Plebiscite for the Immediate Decolonization of Puerto Rico held on June 11, 2017.

These results constitute the legitimate expression of self-determination of a majority of United States citizens of Puerto Rico. Furthermore, these results meet the conditions imposed by the U.S. Congress and the President of the United States upon the approval of Public Law 113-76, 'Consolidated Appropriations Act, 2014'; the corresponding Congressional report on said Federal law, and the position of the U.S. Department of Justice as stated on April 13, 2017. Any other interpretation of these results would be contrary to the rights of a majority of United States citizens of Puerto Rico who cast a valid vote in accordance with the law, and the case law of the Supreme Court of Puerto Rico.

STATUS ALTERNATIVE	DEFINITION	FIGURE	VOTES	PERCENT
Statehood	With my vote, I reiterate my request to the Federal Government to immediately begin the process for the decolonization of Puerto Rico with the admission of Puerto Rico as a state of the United States of America. I am aware that the result of this request for Statehood would entail equal rights and duties with the other states, and the permanent union of Puerto Rico with the United States of America. I am also aware that my vote claiming Statehood means my support to all efforts towards the admission of Puerto Rico as a state of the Union, and to all state or federal legislation aimed at establishing equal conditions, congressional representation and the presidential vote for the American citizens of Puerto Rico.		508,862	97.13%
Free Association/ Independence	With my vote, I make the initial request to the Federal Government to begin the process of the decolonization through: (1) Free Association: Puerto Rico should adopt a status outside of the Territory Clause of the Constitution of the United States that recognizes the sovereignty of the People of Puerto Rico as a complete an unencumbered Independence. The Free Association would be based on a free and voluntary political association, the specific terms of which shall be agreed upon between the United States and Puerto Rico as sovereign nations. Such agreement would provide the scope of the jurisdictional powers that the People of Puerto Rico agree to confer to the United States and retain all other jurisdictional powers and authorities; (2) Proclamation of Independence, I demand that the United States Government, in the exercise of its power to dispose of territory, recognize the national sovereignty of Puerto Rico as a completely independent nation and that the United States Congress enact the necessary legislation to initiate the negotiation and transition to the independent nation of Puerto Rico. My vote for Independence also represents my claim to the rights, duties, powers, and prerogatives of independent and democratic republics, my support of Puerto Rican citizenship, and a "Treaty of Friendship and Cooperation" between Puerto Rico and the United States after the transition process.		7,981	1.52%
Current Territorial Status	With my vote, I express my wish that Puerto Rico remains, as it is today, subject to the powers of the Congress and subject to the Territory Clause of the United States Constitution that in its Article IV, Section 3 states: "The Congress shall have Power to dispose of and make all needful Rules and Regulations respecting the Territory or other Property belonging to the United States; and nothing in this Constitution shall be so construed as to Prejudice any Claims of the United States, or of any particular State".		7,048	1.35%

Therefore, it is the legitimate expression of a majority of United States citizens of Puerto Rico that a process of transition into, and proclamation of Statehood immediately begins.

REGISTER AND NOTIFY: In San Juan, Puerto Rico on August 17, 2017.

MARÍA D. SANTIAGO RODRÍGUEZ
Acting Chairwoman

I CERTIFY:

That on this same date I have sent copy of this certification to the Honorable Ricardo Rosselló Nevares, Governor of Puerto Rico, to the Resident Commissioner in Washington DC, to the Legislative Assembly, and the Secretary of State of Puerto Rico.

In San Juan, Puerto Rico on August 17, 2017.

ÁNGEL L. ROSA BARRIOS
Secretary

A-3

CERTIFICACIÓN DE RESULTADOS OFICIALES
CONSULTA DE ESTATUS POLÍTICO DE PUERTO RICO
-PRIMERA PREGUNTA-

De conformidad con la Ley para Disponer la Celebración de una Consulta Sobre el Estatus Político de Puerto Rico, Ley Núm. 283 - 2011 y por los Artículos 10.009 y 11.010 del Código Electoral de Puerto Rico para el Siglo XXI, Ley Núm. 78 de 1 de junio de 2011, según enmendada, la Comisión Estatal de Elecciones informa y certifica los resultados oficiales de la Primera Pregunta de la Consulta Sobre el Estatus Político de Puerto Rico del 6 de noviembre de 2012.

CONDICIÓN POLÍTICA TERRITORIAL ACTUAL
RESULTADOS ISLA

NO	970,910	53.97%
SÍ	828,077	46.03%

TOTAL: 1,798,987

OTROS	
EN BLANCO	67,267
PROTESTADAS Y NO ADJUDICADAS	12,948
PARTICIPACIÓN	
INSCRITOS UNIDADES REPORTADAS	2,402,941
VOTANTES SEGÚN LISTA	1,878,960
PARTICIPACIÓN	78.19%
TOTAL DE INSCRITOS	2,402,941

COLEGIOS REPORTADOS: 7,755 DE 7,755 PARA UN 100.00%

En esta certificación, la Comisión Estatal de Elecciones declarará los resultados oficiales para la Primera Pregunta de la Consulta Sobre el Estatus Político de Puerto Rico del 6 de noviembre de 2012.

REGÍSTRESE Y NOTIFÍQUESE:

En San Juan, Puerto Rico a 31 de diciembre de 2012.

Héctor J. Conty Pérez
Presidente

CERTIFICO: Que en esta misma fecha he enviado copia de esta certificación al Honorable Luis G. Fortuño Burset, Gobernador de Puerto Rico.

En San Juan, Puerto Rico a 31 de diciembre de 2012

Walter Vélez Martínez
Secretario

CERTIFICACIÓN DE RESULTADOS OFICIALES
CONSULTA DE ESTATUS POLÍTICO DE PUERTO RICO
-SEGUNDA PREGUNTA-

De conformidad con la Ley para Disponer la Celebración de una Consulta Sobre el Estatus Político de Puerto Rico, Ley Núm. 283 - 2011 y por los Artículos 10.009 y 11.010 del Código Electoral de Puerto Rico para el Siglo XXI, Ley Núm. 78 de 1 de junio de 2011, según enmendada, la Comisión Estatal de Elecciones informa y certifica los resultados oficiales de la Segunda Pregunta de la Consulta Sobre el Estatus Político de Puerto Rico del 6 de noviembre de 2012.

OPCIONES NO TERRITORIALES

RESULTADOS ISLA

ESTADIDAD

834,191 61.16%

ESTADO LIBRE ASOCIADO SOBERANO

454,768 33.34%

INDEPENDENCIA

74,895 5.49%

TOTAL: 1,363,854

OTROS	
EN BLANCO	498,604
PROTESTADAS Y NO ADJUDICADAS	16,744
PARTICIPACIÓN	
INSCRITOS UNIDADES REPORTADAS	2,402,941
VOTANTES SEGÚN LISTA	1,878,969
PARTICIPACIÓN	78.19%
TOTAL DE INSCRITOS	2,402,941

COLEGIOS REPORTADOS: 7,755 DE 7,755 PARA UN 100.00%

En esta certificación, la Comisión Estatal de Elecciones declarará los resultados oficiales para la Segunda Pregunta de la Consulta Sobre el Estatus Político de Puerto Rico del 6 de noviembre de 2012.

REGÍSTRESE Y NOTIFÍQUESE:

En San Juan, Puerto Rico a 31 de diciembre de 2012.

Héctor J. Conty Pérez
Presidente

CERTIFICO: Que en esta misma fecha he enviado copia de esta certificación al Honorable Luis G. Fortuño Burset, Gobernador de Puerto Rico.

En San Juan, Puerto Rico a 31 de diciembre de 2012

Walter Vélez Martínez
Secretario

B-1

COMISION ESTATAL DE ELECCIONES DE PUERTO RICO
OFICINA DEL PRESIDENTE

9 de junio de 2020

Lcdo. Lind O. Merle Feliciano
Comisionado Electoral PPD

SOLICITUD DE CERTIFICACIÓN PPD EN REPRESENTACIÓN ALTERNATIVA NO

Estimado Lcdo. Merle:

Vista, su carta de 3 de junio de 2020, dirigida a este servidor, le informo que no tengo nada que proveer. La CEE acordó por unanimidad, hace once (11) días, que la representación principal del NO le corresponde "al Partido Independentista Puertorriqueño" véase, Acuerdo de Comisión CEE-AC-20-130-A, que fuera revisado, a solicitud del propio Comisionado del PPD, y notificado el 29 de mayo de 2020.

Ante la existencia de un Acuerdo de Comisión unánime, este servidor no tiene jurisdicción sobre la materia para atender la petición esbozada en su carta del 3 de junio de 2020. Véase, Art. 3.004 del Código Electoral, 16 LPRA Sec. 4014.

Con el testimonio de mi estimación,

JUAN ERNESTO DÁVILA RIVERA
PRESIDENTE

RECIBIDO
Oficina del Secretario
Fecha: 9/6/20 Hora: 8:45
Firma:

C. COMISIONADOS ELECTORALES
SECRETARIO DE LA CEE

PO BOX 195552 SAN JUAN PR

Certifico que este documento es copia fiel y exacta del original que obra en la Comisión Estatal de Elecciones y a petición de la parte interesada, expido la presente en San Juan, Puerto Rico hoy [illegible]

B-2

COMISION ESTATAL DE ELECCIONES DE PUERTO RICO
OFICINA DEL PRESIDENTE

Juan E. Dávila Rivera
Presidente

9 de junio de 2020

Ángel L. Rosa Barrios
Secretario
Comisión Estatal de Elecciones

SOLICITUD DE NOTIFICACIÓN

Estimado señor Rosa Barrios:

Previo cumplimiento con el Capítulo VI de la Ley Núm. 51, le instruyo a que proceda de inmediato con la certificación de los representantes de las alternativas del NO y el SI, según consta en el Acuerdo de Comisión CEE-AC-20-130A, notificado el viernes, 29 de mayo de 2020.

Con el testimonio de mi estimación,

Juan E. Davila Rivera

C. Comisionados Electorales

RECIBIDO
Oficina del Secretario
Fecha: 9/6/20 Hora: 8:45
Firma:

Certifico que este documento es copia fiel y exacta del original que obra en la Comisión Estatal de Elecciones y a petición de la parte interesada, expido la presente en San Juan, Puerto Rico, hoy 12 de NOV de 2020

PAN · TIERRA · LIBERTAD

C. E. E.
COMISIONADO P. N. P.

JOSÉ ARIEL NAZARIO ÁLVAREZ
SECRETARIO GENERAL

B-3

CERTIFICACIÓN

La honorable **Junta de Gobierno del Partido Popular Democrático** ha avalado, en votación mediante referéndum electrónico efectuado el sábado 16 de mayo de 2020, la autorización al presidente del Partido, Aníbal José Torres, para realizar todos los procedimientos requeridos en la Ley 51-2020, conocida como *"Ley para la Definición Final del Estatus Político de Puerto Rico"*, a los fines de que nuestra colectividad política participe como el **representante principal** del "NO" en el referéndum establecido en la mencionada Ley.

En el referéndum electrónico participaron 25 de 32 miembros con derecho al voto conforme a nuestro Reglamento, **todos avalando** la propuesta.

En San Juan, Puerto Rico, sábado 16 de mayo de 2020.

José Ariel Nazario Álvarez

PO BOX 9020436 SAN JUAN, PR 00902-0436
secretariogeneral@ppdpr.net
Tel. (787) 721-2000

Certifico que este documento es copia fiel y exacta del original que obra en la Comisión Estatal de Elecciones y a petición de la parte interesada, expido la presente en San Juan, Puerto Rico, hoy ___ de ___ de 20__

C-1

Videos

Aníbal Acevedo... - Boricuas Unidos en la Diáspora - BUDPR
Facebook
Oct 7, 2020

Boricuas Unidos en la Diáspora - BUDPR... - Boricuas Unidos en la...

Facebook · Boricuas Unidos en la Diáspora...

C-2

m.facebook.com
BORICUAS UNIDOS EN LA DIASPORA
Boricuas Unidos en la Diáspora - BUDPR
· Follow
October 7, 2020 at 11:44 AM
Aníbal Acevedo Vilá: "Yo voy a votar que no en este plebiscito porque la estadidad... More
Aníbal Acevedo Vilá and 65 others
36 Comments 32 Shares
Like
Comment
Share

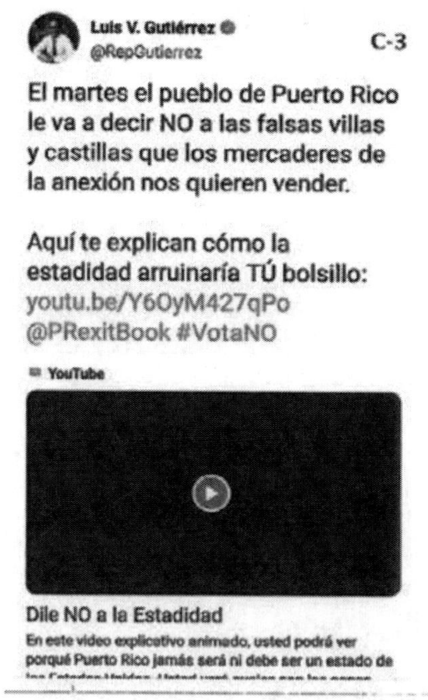
Luis V. Gutiérrez
@RepGutierrez
C-3
El martes el pueblo de Puerto Rico le va a decir NO a las falsas villas y castillas que los mercaderes de la anexión nos quieren vender.
Aquí te explican cómo la estadidad arruinaría TÚ bolsillo: youtu.be/Y6OyM427qPo @PRexitBook #VotaNO
YouTube
Dile NO a la Estadidad
En este video explicativo animado, usted podrá ver porqué Puerto Rico jamás será ni debe ser un estado de

C-4

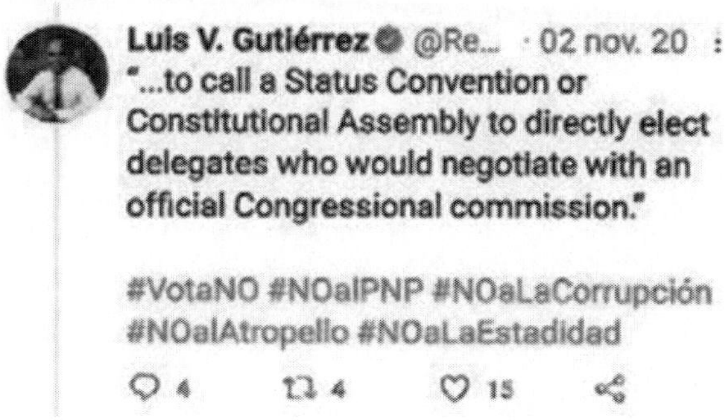

CIVIL RIGHTS COALITION FOR PUERTO RICO STATEHOOD

April 13, 2021

Hon. Raúl Grijalva
Chairman
House Committee on
Natural Resources

Hon. Bruce Westerman
Ranking Member
House Committee on
Natural Resources

Hon. Joe Manchin
Chairman
Senate Committee on Energy &
Natural Resources

Hon. John Barrasso
Ranking Member
Senate Committee on Energy &
Natural Resources

Dear Chairman Grijalva, Ranking Member Westerman, Chairman Manchin, Ranking Member Barrasso:

For over one hundred years the U.S. Citizens of Puerto Rico have been disenfranchised and treated unequally while most fellow citizens were unaware of this civil rights violation. Hurricane Maria opened the eyes of our great nation to the poverty, lack of representation and rights of those of us living in the oldest colony in the world. Last November voters in the island once more stood up to change the discriminatory treatment that we have been summited to. With an absolute majority, 53%, our people demanded statehood for Puerto Rico. There is nowhere to hide anymore, this Congress has the responsibility to act, and act now.

The United States, the beacon of democracy for the rest of the world, has a blind spot to justice in that it has more than 3.1 million of its own citizens living in a colony, denied of their civil rights and treated as less than equal.

We respectfully must insist that this hearing and all urgent congressional proceedings in 2021 meant to eradicate this civil rights inequality should be about accelerating the necessary steps to admit Puerto Rico to the Union. Any other dilation of duty, distraction, inertia or barrier to the democratic will of those of us living the second-class citizenship of colonial rule, is not in line with democracy and the better interests of the Republic. There are some simple truths that the honorable members of this Congress are duty bound to confront. The status quo is dead and the democratic will of the people of Puerto Rico is undeniable. If this hearing is to do nothing yet again and kick the can to another generation, I respectfully must warn that you would be telling the 3.1 million citizens of Puerto Rico that democracy does not apply to us by virtue of our location, ethnicity, and lack of power at this time.

The fact that some powerful politicians and business leaders keep opposing our civil and inalienable right to equality, vote, and representation despite the expressed democratic will of our fellow islanders, is outright un-American. Democracy will not be denied. Democracy will be served either by a George Washington-inspired understanding of what is fair and just by the honorable members of this committee or it shall be sought by the cries of our demands for our civil rights to be respected and our standing as equal to be honored. We will accept no less and you should aspire to no less. After all, isn't the American Experience about freedom and equality? 123 years is a long time to wait for it and the consequences have been devastating.

The Supreme Court Justices in the Insular Cases of 1901 denied our right to equality and statehood because we were, quoting their own words, "savages." If you choose to perpetuate this inequality, what do you tell your children? What shall be inscribed in the Congressional record? How will history judge members who in the face of a thrice-expressed democratic vote, deny the most Americans of rights? We are watching. The world is watching to see if our civil rights will continue to be violated and by whom. There are no two sides of equal merit or validity anymore. Members must choose to either be for democracy and support statehood now or for Jim Crow colonialism and either do nothing or support a decades long convoluted effort to have a few chosen people decide the fate of those who believed in the one wo(man), one vote pillar of American Democracy. Inertia can't be an alternative anymore. It's over and the time is now, today, AHORA, to do what is right or forever be a civil rights denier. The status quo died with the last plebiscite.

The perpetuation of the colony is a Jim Crow era legacy that subjugates US residents of the island and robs us of the civil rights you enjoy. At this moment of great expectations, I can't describe in any other way than outright shameful that some fellow US citizens (and particularly Latinos and Puerto Rican-Americans that enjoy the equality of living the prosperity of statehood but know our reality and advocate to keep us poor and under anti-democratic submission without vote or voice), lend their names and voices to sustaining an anti-American and anti-democratic structure for perpetuation of the poverty of rights and means that is colonial rule. The idea of more study, further delay of democracy, and outright denial of what just happened is not in line with the ideals of the

Federalist Papers or the Constitution. To those who oppose granting our civil rights and delaying justice via a subterfuge of no action or acting to put further hurdles in front of the democratic will of our people must hear our voices now. Make no mistake, Puerto Rico is watching carefully.

I ask your indulgence to provide frightening statistics that cruelly paint the civil rights deficit as experience in the daily lives of the US citizens of Puerto Rico. Facts tell the truth and give us a stark reminder that this blind spot of democracy under the US flag creates suffering every day.

Facts about Puerto Rico that tell the story of inequality:

- Over 5 million Puerto Ricans have moved stateside over the decades and 3.1 million are left on the island. Are you waiting for the island to be empty to finally grant statehood? Why? Why empty paradise? Why so few come back to the island?
- In 2019, 66,021 island residents "voted" by buying a one-way ticket to statehood with their suitcases in tow, and left Puerto Rico (that is 180 good-byes per day, every single day). Insensitive delay tactics are breaking our families apart every single day. It is shameful and un-American.
- An average family in Puerto Rico makes $25,338 per year which is 39% of the US average of $65,712. We are relatively worse off as compared to the national average than we were in 1952, when what was ironically called Free Associated State in Spanish in Puerto Rico and the gentrified "Commonwealth" sold to Congress and the United Nations, was established as the perpetuation of the oldest colony in the world (continuous civil rights deficit since 1492).
- Over 45% of our residents are living under the poverty level (1 in 2!)
- We have a very high dependency on welfare.
- Puerto Rico suffers the worst inequality under the US flag with a GINI rate (where 1 is equal) of 0.5509.
- In addition to low wages, we endure a high cost of living including government sponsored regressive taxation of our poorest people that should put to shame liberals and conservatives alike.

No wonder, again today, another airplane full of our smart and hardworking people hugged their mom's good-bye and left our island for good. Delaying the democratic cry for statehood of our island would accelerate this. Is anyone in your committees wishing to sentence another generation of Puerto Ricans to broken families and certain poverty? Do you want another plane to leave tomorrow? May it weigh on your conscience, as it does on my heart every day, and may you please see that decisions to act or delay have consequences and these affect real and decent citizens of these United States. Delay and anti-democratic practices create more suffering. Those of you enjoying your civil rights stateside don't seem to understand that you are playing with our lives and our rights as if this was 1901 and we were the "savages" still written in the rulings used to this day to deny us equal rights. The time for patient study, delay tactics, committees, and task forces is over. Democracy has spoken. Let her live! Our veterans and their sacrifices should remind all that if we are equal in battle, we must be equal in voting and civil rights.

For 69 years, the argument to do nothing is that we can't agree on a solution. The scaffolding to that argument has been carefully crafted by those who benefit at the local and stateside level from colonial rule and the funds that arrive for this purpose. Great resources have been spent to maintain the status quo. This has given the colonial elite carte blanche to keep the oligarchic power base intact and have motivated anti-democratic forces from the region, historical enemies of the United States, to invest and promote instability in our democracy in Puerto Rico. The combination of extremists on the Left and Right have denied what our veterans so valiantly fought for: democracy.

The November 2020 vote, with similar language to Hawaii's and Alaska's vote, was a victory for statehood despite tactics that included scaring older voters saying that a vote for statehood would mean they would lose their homes to taxes, false advertising saying that if Congress did not legislate, the plebiscite was useless, and a strong campaign to say that even if you favored statehood, not to vote to punish the statehood party in power. The fact that 40% more voters said yes to statehood than the accumulated votes of any gubernatorial candidate, means that this is not a political issue and rather a civil rights issue that goes beyond politics. The democratic exercise of one wo(man) one vote chose statehood even when all these tactics were used to derail the will of the people. And yet, these same forces keep seeking to delay statehood. What are the motivations if not economic and the pursuit of power for power's sake?

The project sponsored by the Honorable Congresswoman Velazquez intends to keep the colony afloat and running for decades to come and to perpetuate the civil rights deficit that exists. It is an endless loop that intends to stop majority rule and democracy from happening finally. There is no other goal but to perpetuate the oligarchic rule on the island and it will lead to another plane tomorrow leaving with our best and brightest, and the next day and so forth. Where is the democratic will of the people in that? Hurricane Maria showed the Nation that we are an island of great people with a civil rights deficit. It also taught our citizens that we must claim our rights as equals and not have to beg for every right, program or law. We are the largest group of Americans without representation in Congress or presidential vote in the history of the Nation. There is no answer to the question of why that does not include discrimination and a civil rights issue.

There are no two sides to democracy. Either you are for it or against it. The time to be for democracy and voting rights is now. Which side will you be on? Puerto Rico has earned in over 123 years contribution, the right to be equal among many as a state of our great Union. We shall join our fellow disenfranchised Americans of the District of Columbia in asserting our rights to equality, voting rights, and democracy.

The only legislative option that respects the will of the people of Puerto Rico, and ensures a binding process of self-determination is H.R. 1522 & S. 780, the Puerto Rico Statehood Admission Act. You have the perfect opportunity to be on the right side of history now, to do the right thing. We will accept no less, for doing so would be un-American and unfair. The time is now. Our civil rights battle will be won here or elsewhere but it will be won. George Washington would have been on our side and so should you.

Respectfully,

Dr. Evelyn Abreu,
Co-Founder/Secretary Treasurer

Jaime Fortuño,
Co-Founder/President

PUERTO RICO ESTADIDAD

Hon. Raúl Grijalva
Chairman
House Committee on
Natural Resources

Hon. Bruce Westerman
Ranking Member
House Committee on
Natural Resources

Hon. Joe Manchin
Chairman
Senate Committee on Energy &
Natural Resources

Hon. John Barrasso
Ranking Member
Senate Committee on Energy &
Natural Resources

Dear Chairman Grijalva, Ranking Member Westerman, Chairman Manchin, Ranking Member Barrasso:

As U.S. citizens from Puerto Rico, we are coming together to express our support for the Puerto Rico Statehood Admission Act, H.R. 1522 and S. 780, and to call on Congress to pass this legislation as quickly as possible.

Puerto Ricans have been part of the U.S. for over one hundred and twenty years and we have made countless contributions to the betterment of American society. During that time the population of Puerto Ricans stateside has grown to close to six million. Yet for the three million U.S. citizens that remain on the island, we remain disenfranchised in federal elections and subjected to unequal treatment in federal laws and programs.

This reduces economic development has robbed our poor and elderly of lifesaving healthcare, and every day breaks up our families and communities as people feel forced to move stateside to seek out better opportunities and quality of life for themselves and their children.

Congress must immediately end its inherently colonial territorial rule over Puerto Rico, because it violates America's values of democracy, equal justice under the law, and government by the consent of the governed. Beyond that, it doesn't serve either America or Puerto Rico to prolong an outdated, dysfunctional and morally corrupt form of government which its own citizens have now rejected on multiple occasions.

On November 3, 2020, an undisputable majority of 53% of Puerto Rico's voters demanded change in a locally sponsored referendum calling for full democracy and equality through statehood. While some bills in Congress, like H.R. 2070 & S. 865, seek to delay, confuse and distract from this electoral majority mandate in the name of "self-determination," only the Puerto Rico Statehood Admission Act acknowledges and responds to the freely expressed will of the people.

A majority of voters in Puerto Rico have requested statehood, now Congress must respond by officially offering it and allowing voters on the island to ratify their choice in a binding vote. To turn around and tell voters to go back to the drawing board and re-define multiple other options which the majority has rejected three times in the last eight years in favor of statehood, would not only be insulting to us, but effectively serve as a form of voter suppression. That is simply unacceptable and un-American.

We are natural born U.S. citizens and want an equal seat at the table in the federal government that writes and implements the laws that we live under. We want our full voting rights as American citizens, and would challenge any voting Member of Congress that would deny that to us to answer if their constituents would accept the second-class citizenship that we are subjected to under territory status.

We are proud to be Puerto Ricans, and also proud to be U.S. citizens, and know that there is no law that limits us from being both. So, don't let anyone tell you that statehood will somehow diminish our cultural pride and heritage. If anything, the economic progress that statehood would unleash will allow Puerto Rico to flourish in ways that will mutually benefit the Island and the States.

If you really believe in democracy, justice, government by the consent of the governed, you must not hesitate any further or give any more excuses. Congress must grant us the equal rights and equal responsibilities that we have earned with the blood of our veterans and the tears of their mothers, wives, children and families. Pass the Puerto Rico Statehood Admission Act as soon as possible and together we can help make America a more perfect Union.

Sincerely,

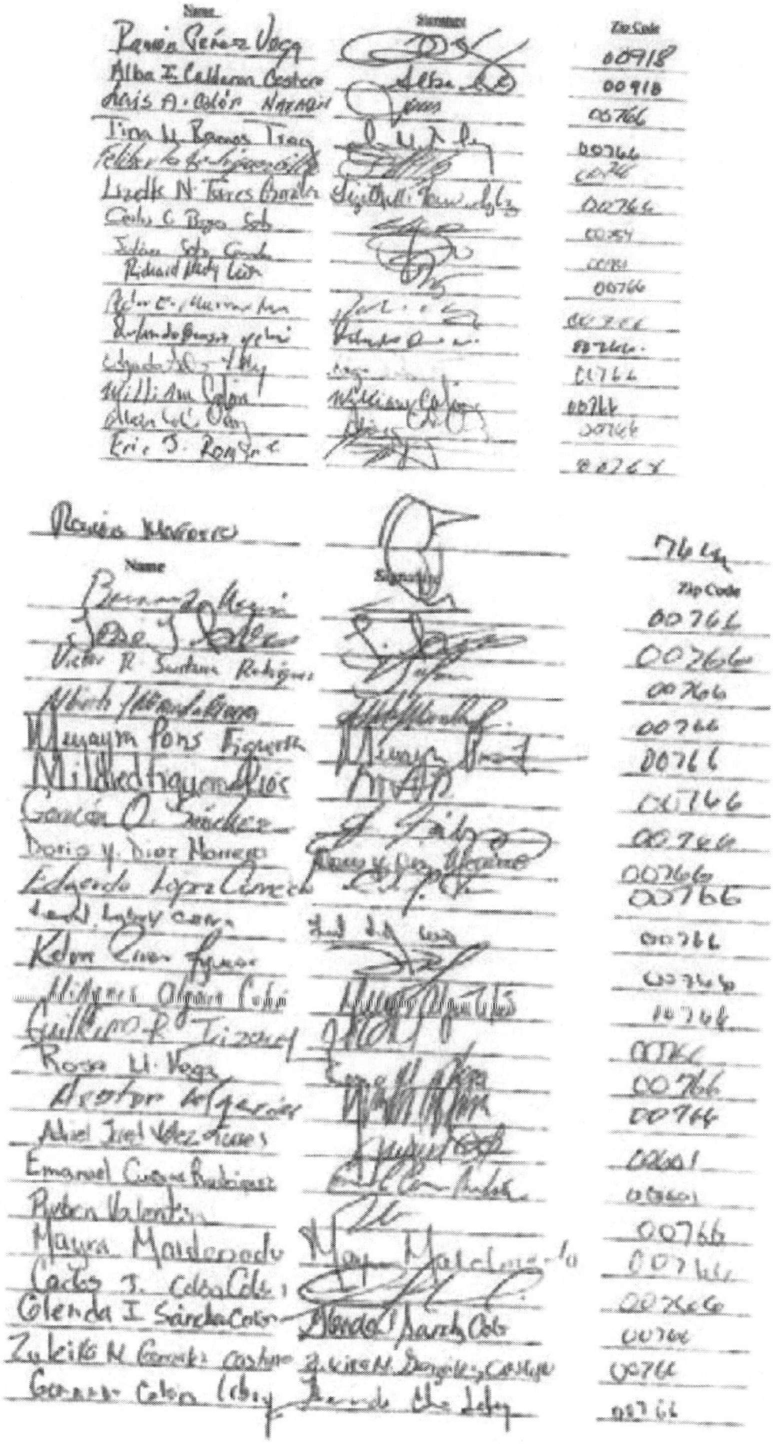

Name	Signature	Zip Code
Angel Torres	[signature]	00766
Miguel Rodriguez	[signature]	00766
Eidylamar Dedoccio Vega	[signature]	00766
Krystal H. Torres González	[signature]	00766
Elizabeth Rivera	[signature]	00766
Carla Rios Torres	[signature]	00766
Loida E. Zapata Meléndez	[signature]	00766
Keyla E. Torres Santos	[signature]	00766
Ada M. Burgos Colón	[signature]	00766
Anthony J. Alvarado	[signature]	00766
Gabriel Rivera [illegible]	[signature]	00766
[illegible]	[signature]	[illegible]
José G. Hernández Cruz	[signature]	00766
Marilyn Rosario	[signature]	00766
José A. Santana Torres	[signature]	00720
[illegible]	[signature]	[illegible]
Beatriz [illegible]	[signature]	00714
Adrián L. Cordero	[signature]	[illegible]
Ferdinand Soto	[signature]	00601
Antonio Vera Montero	[signature]	00601
Lidia Maldonado	[signature]	00601
Marta Rivera Ruiz	[signature]	00601
José Torres Rodríguez	[signature]	00601
Evelyn [illegible]	[signature]	00601
Ana R. Castrillo	[signature]	00601

Name	Signature	Zip Code
Karla Javier	[signature]	00660
Sonia N. [illegible]	[signature]	00601
Víctor J. Pérez [illegible]	[signature]	00727
[illegible] López	[signature]	00601
Omar [illegible] Torres	[signature]	00601
Noralys Lamboy López	[signature]	00601
Mary Tessa Pagán [illegible]	[signature]	00601
Migdalia Torres [illegible]	[signature]	00601
Daniel [illegible] Ross	[signature]	00601
Wanda Q. Maldonado	[signature]	00601
Jessica Castrillo	[signature]	00601
Maria Ortiz Rivera	[signature]	00601
José [illegible]	[signature]	00601
Ana Martínez	[signature]	00601
Carmen Ana Pérez Nieves	[signature]	00601
[illegible] Vélez	[signature]	00601
Jacqueline [illegible] Rodríguez	[signature]	00601
Andrea Torres	[signature]	00601
[illegible]	[signature]	00601
[illegible] Alvarado	[signature]	00601
Ely Quiñones	[signature]	00601
Franklin [illegible]	[signature]	00601
[illegible] Rodríguez	[signature]	00601
Enrique A. Ruiz Ramos	[signature]	00601

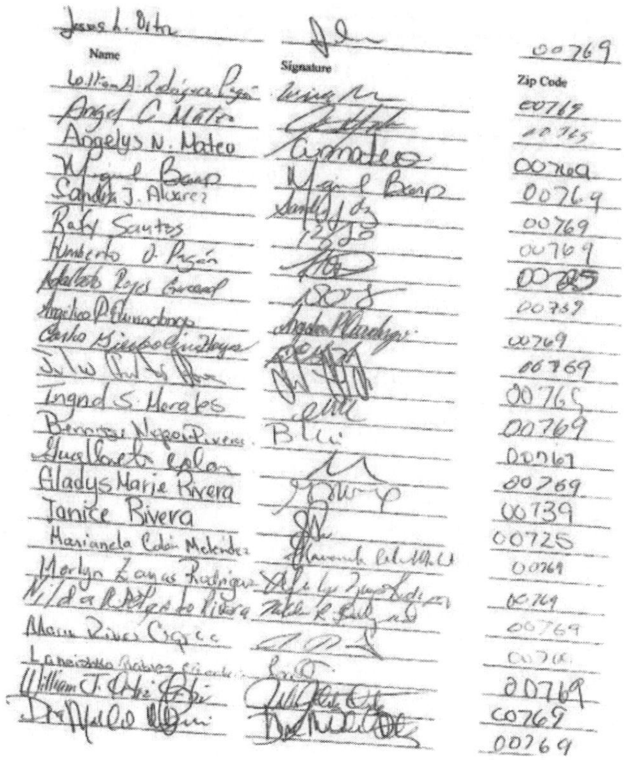

Statement for the Record, Hon. Milagros G. López Campos, Municipal Legislator of Carolina, Puerto Rico

Blessing to you, and Member of Congress. I am writing to you as a Legislator of the municipality of Carolina, where I represent over 186,000 persons and 104,378 voters.

For over one-hundred years, the U.S. citizens of Puerto Rico have been dismissed from federal elections and subjected to unequal treatment across federal programs and civil Rights that make Last November, move thousands of voters and stood up the change to obtain an absolute majority of 53% demanding statehood for Puerto Rico in a locally sponsored referendum. The Puerto Rico Statehood Admission Act, H.R. 1522 and S. 780, directly respond to that mandate, and we urge you to support it and help get it approved as soon as possible.

Puerto Rico's referendum was historic, because it is the first time that we request as a US Territory a statehood unquestionable mandate with the majority support of the people on the island with a simple "YES" or "NO" vote. The 117th Congress have therefore a unique opportunity to make history to end America's inherently colonial rule over Puerto Rico, which is the most respected American values of democracy, equality, justice and civil right under the law.

We recognize that are some Congresswoman such as Rep. Nydia Velazquez (NY) and Sen. Robert Menendez (NJ), who oppose statehood for Puerto Rico and have completely ignored the voice of the people's in the results of the referendum last November. Therefore, they will be submitting a counter-proposal, the Puerto Rico Self-Determination Act (PRSDA), which has faced criticism from representatives of all status options.

The most significant concern, across party lines, is that the PRSDA is ultimately non-binding. Under the bill, Congress would be under no obligation to implement whichever status option is chosen by the convention and later voted by the electors of PR. This would represent a huge setback for voters in Puerto Rico who have engaged in multiple acts of self-determination over the last decade and have shown, an increasing clarity, that Puerto Rican' s voters reject the current territory status and have favor statehood over all non-territory options.

Beyond the will of the people on the island, Puerto Rican's stateside also favor statehood for PR by wide margins. For example, recently polls show 81% of Puerto Rican residents in Florida and 69% of those in New York favor the admission of Puerto Rico as a state. Also, the majority of Americans have also supported the idea for decades according to Gallup.

This is a issue on the island as well as across the Nation, and Congress has a moral obligation to act promptly.

For that reason we only recommend the legislative option that respects the will of the people of Puerto Rico, and ensures a binding which is a process of self-determination and that is H.R. 1522 & S. 780, the Puerto Rico Statehood Admission Act. By offering statehood, stipulating the terms of admission, and requiring a ratifi-cation vote. Congress would finally open the door to full equality and democracy for the U.S. citizens of Puerto Rico while leaving the ultimate choice in their hands. If a majority opposes statehood at that point, then the island would remain a territory with the capacity to pursue independence or free association through the procedural mechanism of their choice, including a status convention. Congress has a moral obligation to let the people of Puerto Rico decide their own self-determination process for admission.

I request Congress to open the door to a full emancipation and equality for our fellow Americans in Puerto Rico by supporting and passing the Puerto Rico Statehood Admission Act. The United States should understand they can and must do better for our fellow Americans.

STATEMENT FOR THE RECORD, GREGORIO IGARTUA, DOMESTIC AND INTERNATIONAL LEGAL ADVICE, LLC, ON PUERTO RICO'S TERRITORIAL STATUS

Dear Congressman Grijalva:

I was born in Puerto Rico, U.S.A., and, I am an American citizen resident of Puerto Rico. I am sending this written testimony in opposition to the proposed "Self Determination Act," which is not constitutionally viable, and to support the Puerto Rico Statehood Admission Act. It is the only political alternative that fits in the U.S. Constitutional Framework, and it is 122 years overdue.

As you know, Puerto Rico has been a part of the United States since 1898. For 122 years we have been under the U.S. Government discriminatory practice of being denied the right to vote in Federal Elections, and of government without the consent of the governed. (3.4 million American Citizens by birth). We are also subject to unequal treatment in economic policies implemented by Congress for the states, which have moved Puerto Rico into bankruptcy. Moreover, for some cases the Federal Courts apply the U.S. Constitution, and not for others. Ironically, we pay more than $3 billion dollars a year in federal taxes, more than some states and many state regions. (IRS Highlights 2020).

The Committee of Natural Resources you preside, has expressed interest in pursuing Congressional action in the issue of the political status of Puerto Rico. I suggest that you consider as the most viable alternative that Puerto Rico be certified as an incorporated territory first, which de facto it is. Notwithstanding incorporation is not permanent, therefore Congress should simultaneously resolved to move Puerto Rico in transit to statehood at a definite date. Certification of Incorporation would make the U.S. Constitution fully applicable, and would give us parity with federal funds as if Puerto Rico were a state. We qualify for incorporation by having been assimilated more than any other U.S. Territory before becoming a state. Although there may be conflicting views of what is the political relation of Puerto Rico to the United States, due to the reality that we are still not a state, Congress has assimilated us gradually since 1898 into a federalist relation to be like a de facto incorporated territory.

(See: G. Igartua, The "de facto" Incorporated Territory U.S. of Puerto Rico. A copy of the Book was mailed to you a few months ago, and one is being mailed to the Committee with this letter).

I respectfully suggest that you consider proposing to Congress to declare Puerto Rico officially an Incorporated Territory of the United States in transit to statehood. (See Petition enclosed—Annex A). It is the only political alternative that fits into the U.S. Constitutional framework, it is 122 years overdue. Rather than holding more hearings on what we could hypothetically be, which is discriminatory, our political and civil rights must be recognized by Congress based on what we are, 3.4 American citizens by birth residents of a de facto incorporated territory. Incorporation was recently supported unanimously by the National Association of U.S. Mayors. (Annex B). (*See also, Consejo de Salud Playa de Ponce v Rullan, 586 FS 2nd 22 (2008)*).

No one in Puerto Rico wants independence, nor continue to be confused with political status alternatives which do not fit within the U.S. constitutional framework. No one in Puerto Rico wants to renounce their American Citizenship. A Republic of American citizens would be a matter of national security concern. (3.3 million residing in Puerto Rico, 5 million residing in states). Many are confused by the daily practice of uncertainty brought by the questioning about what our rights are as American citizens, or could be. Consider within this context the "Puerto Rico Self Determination Act" proposed for American citizens after 122 years under our American flag. Were African-Americans subjected, or should be subjected, to hearings on whether they would like to be slaves again, or be moved to a Country in Africa? Should Mexican-Americans be asked whether they would like to renounce their American Citizenship to Mexican and be moved back to Mexico, or should their American citizenship status be questioned, as your Committee is doing with us in Puerto Rico in 2021?

Consider as constitutionally viable only to start holding hearings on how the American Citizens residents of Puerto Rico can have equal rights and government by the consent of the governed. (U.S. Constitution Amendments XIV and XV). Congressman Grijalva, statehood for you, for Congresswomen Velazquez and Ocasio, for all the members of your Committee, for all Congressmen, and statehood for us the American citizens residents of Puerto Rico. Time is of the essence.

I respectfully request to be allowed to participate in the April 15, 2021, hearing your Committee has scheduled on this subject, and in support of our American Citizenship rights.

Annex A

PETITION

ADDRESSED TO THE CONGRESS OF THE UNITED STATES OF AMERICA TO CERTIFY PUERTO RICO WITH A JOINT RESOLUTION AS AN INCORPORATED TERRITORY OF THE UNITED STATES IN TRANSIT TO STATEHOOD

WHEREAS: Puerto Rico became a United States of America territory in 1898 by the Treaty of Paris, which provided that: "... *the civil rights and political status of the native inhabitants of the territories hereby ceded to the United States shall be determined by Congress.*" Immediately the native inhabitants became Nationals under the Custody and "*Parens Patriae*" of the United States of America.

WHEREAS: In 1917, the residents of Puerto Rico were granted United States American citizenship, by their own free and voluntary election, and after 1941 by birth, as disposed by Congress, enacting laws to such effect. To this date, three point four millions United States American Citizens reside in Puerto Rico and five millions have moved their residence to the mainland, were they have worked and are still working in building our Nation.

WHEREAS: Since 1917, the United States American Citizens of Puerto Rico have demonstrated their loyalty to the United States of America and to democracy by serving with dedication and honor in all armed conflicts in the Armed Forces of our Country, without the right to vote for their Commander in Chief, including many of them by dying in these conflicts.

WHEREAS: In 1952, the United States American Citizens of Puerto Rico constituted themselves into a Republican form of government in compliance with Article IV, Section 4, Constitution of the United States of America, similarly as the process used for former territories to become states of the Nation. In the Constitution of 1952, the citizens by direct vote swore their loyalty to their United States American citizenship, to the Constitution the United States of America and accepted to be under the Supremacy Clause of the Constitution, with reference to the National Government as are states under federalism.

WHEREAS: The United States American Citizens of Puerto Rico are subject to the jurisdiction of all three Branches of the Government of the United States of America. The Puerto Rico Federal Courts are Article III of the U.S. Constitution.

WHEREAS: All income from sources outside of Puerto Rico is subject to federal taxation, and the United States American Citizens residing in Puerto Rico contribute billions of dollars to the Federal Treasury paying more in federal taxes than residents of various regions in the fifty states without representation.

WHEREAS: In the quadrennial elections, held since 1964, ninety five percent (95%) or more of the voters have chosen permanent union with the United States of America. The independence has been rejected by the voters to such an extent that the Independence Party has been politically disqualified in quadrennial election.

WHEREAS: Two of the local political parties, supported by more than ninety six percent (96%) of the total voters, participate in National Politics as members of the Republican and Democratic Parties.

WHEREAS: The Government of the United States of America has been actively promoting democracy, universal suffrage, and human rights all over the world. (Presently very actively un Venezuela).

WHEREAS: The U.S. Constitution has been judicially applied to the American Citizens of Puerto Rico as if it were a state, but the non-incorporation status is being used by the Federal Courts and by Congress to switch "on and off" its applicability discriminatorily, costing more than ten billion dollars annually in federal transfers.

WHEREAS: Puerto Rico is a de facto incorporated territory of the United States because since 1898 it has been gradually moved to be legally treated and assimilated like a state more than any other U.S. Territory before being certified as incorporated. Moreover, the degree of incorporation of Puerto Rico to be like a state can be considered by implication as strong as to exclude any other view than that it is an incorporated territory of the United Sates. (See, *Consejo de Salud Playa de Ponce v Rullan, 585, FS 2nd 22 (2008)*). It has met all the requirements adopted for the Northwestern Ordinance.

WHEREAS: The First Amendment to the Constitution of the United States guarantees the right of the American Citizens to "... *petition the Government for a redress of grievances* ..." in order to ensure liberty, general welfare, and to protect their rights and privileges as American Citizens.

WHEREAS: It is the duty of Congress to protect the constitutional rights of all American citizens. The present degree of legal assimilation of Puerto Rico to the United States under domestic and international law supports this Petition to certify it as an incorporated territory of the United States in transit to statehood.

THEREFORE:

I, an American Citizen resident of Puerto Rico, respectfully request Congress to adopt a Resolution certifying Puerto Rico as an incorporated Territory of the United States in transit to statehood.

Signed this April / 2 / 2021

PETITIONER SIGNATURE

Box 3011, Aguadilla, Puerto Rico 00605
ADDRESS

(787) 891-9040 - Office (787) 379-5085 - Celular
TELEPHONE

bufeteigartua@yahoo.com
E-MAIL

Annex B

The United States Conference of Mayors
1620 EYE STREET, NORTHWEST
WASHINGTON, D.C. 20006
TELEPHONE (202) 293-7330
FAX (202) 293-2352
URL: www.usmayors.org

87th Annual Meeting
Honolulu, Hawai'i

Puerto Rico as an Incorporated Territory of the United States

WHEREAS, Puerto Rico became a United States of America territory in 1898 by the Treaty of Paris, which provided that: "... the civil rights and political status of the native inhabitants of the territories hereby ceded to the United States shall be determined by Congress." Immediately the native inhabitants became Nationals under the Custody and "Parens Patriae" of the United States of America; and

WHEREAS, Since 1917, The United States American Citizens of Puerto Rico have demonstrated their loyalty to the United States of America and to democracy by serving with dedication and honor in all armed conflicts in the Armed Forces of our Country, without the right to vote for their Commander in Chief, including many of them by dying in these conflicts; and

WHEREAS, In 1917, the residents of Puerto Rico were granted United States American citizenship, by their own free and voluntary election, and after 1941 by birth, as disposed by Congress, enacting laws to such effect. To this date, three point four millions United States American Citizens reside in Puerto Rico and four millions have moved their residence to the mainland, were they have worked and are still working in building our Nation; and

WHEREAS, In 1952, The United States American Citizens of Puerto Rico constituted themselves into a Republican form of government in compliance with Article IV, Section 4, Constitution of the United States of America, similarly as the process used for former territories to become states of the Nation. In the Constitution of 1952, the citizens by direct vote swore their loyalty to their United States American citizenship, to the Constitution of United States of America and accepted to be under the Supremacy Clause of the Constitution, with reference to the National Government as are states under federalism; and

WHEREAS, The United States American Citizens of Puerto Rico are subject to the jurisdiction of all three Branches of the Government of the United States of America. The Puerto Federal Courts are Article III of the U.S. Constitution; and

WHEREAS, All income from sources outside of Puerto Rico is subject to federal taxation, and the United States American Citizens residing in Puerto Rico contribute billions of dollars to the Federal Treasury. The United States American Citizens residing in Puerto Rico pay more in federal taxes than residents of various regions in the fifty states; and

WHEREAS, In the quadrennial elections, held since 1964 ninety five percent (95%) or more of the voters have chosen permanent union with The United States of America. The independence has been rejected by the voters to such an extent that the Independence Party has been politically disqualified in quadrennial election; and

WHEREAS, Two of the local political parties, supported by more than ninety six percent (96%) of the total voters, participate in National Politics as members of the Republican and Democratic Parties; and

WHEREAS, The Government of the United States of America has been actively promoting democracy, universal suffrage, and human rights all over the world. (Presently very actively un Venezuela); and

WHEREAS, The Constitution of the United States of America has been judicially applied to the United States American Citizens of Puerto Rico as if it were a state, but the non-incorporation status is being used by the Federal Courts and by Congress to switch "on and off" the applicability of the U.S. Constitution discriminatory, costing more than five billion dollars annually in federal transfers; and

WHEREAS, Puerto Rico is a de facto incorporated territory of the United States of America, because since 1898 it has been gradually moved to be legally treated and assimilated like a state more than any other U.S. Territory before being certified as incorporated. Moreover, the degree of incorporation of Puerto Rico to be like a state can be considered by implication as strong as to exclude any other view than that it is an incorporated territory of the United Sates; and

WHEREAS, The First Amendment to the Constitution of the United States of America guarantees the right of United States American Citizens to u... petition the Government for a redress of grievances ... " in order to ensure liberty, genera' welfare, and to protect our rights and privileges as United States of America Citizens; and

WHEREAS: It is the duty of Congress to protect the constitutional rights of all American citizens. The present degree of legal assimilation of Puerto Rico to the United States under domestic and international law supports this Petition to certify it as an incorporated territory of the United States,

NOW IT THEREFORE, BE IT RESOLVED, that the members of The U.S. Conference of Mayors, respectfully request Congress to adopt a Resolution certifying Puerto Rico as an Incorporated Territory of the United States. Copies of this document will be forwarded to the following Federal and States Public Bodies, and/or other parties; President of the United States America, Hon. Donald Trump; Vice President of the United States of America, Hon. Michael R. Pence; Speaker of the United States of America House of Representatives, Hon. Nancy Pelosi; Governor of Puerto Rico, Hon. Ricardo Rossello; and, to the Resident Commissioner of Puerto Rico, Hon. Jennifer Gonzalez.

Hon. Raúl Grijalva,
Chairman

Hon. Bruce Westerman,
Ranking Member,
House Committee on Natural Resources

Dear Chairman Grijalva, Ranking Member Westerman:

Puerto Rico has been a territory for more than 500 years, first of Spain and now of the United States. Therefore, it should not be foreign to our will that the status is an issue that moves Puerto Ricans. As a result of the discussion on the status, five (5) plebiscites have been held to decide between the options of Statehood (annexation), Independence (separation) or Commonwealth (current status), as well as the approval of evaluation committees on the status of Puerto Rico.

Puerto Rico became a possession of the United States as a result of the Spanish-American War, which culminated in the Treaty of Paris of December 10, 1898 between Spain and the United States. The Treaty of Paris set a precedent, as it was the first time that the United States acquired territories without the intention of making them states. The expansionist policy of the United States in the 19th century, before the Spanish-American War, reflected a theory: that of incorporation as a territory in preparation for statehood. All territories acquired multiplied their original population and dissipated borders with a view to integrating them as members of the American nation. The Treaty of Paris provided that the political conditions and civil rights to be conferred on the territories acquired under the treaty would be determined by Congress. This idea practiced by the United States in the colonization of Puerto Rico was contrary to the value it preached as a Nation, since it was precisely on those principles that it based its independence.

The Foraker Act of 1900 formally represented the non-incorporation of the territory as a state, thus granting greater powers to Congress and the President to administer the territory. This unequal treatment over the other states of the nation led to the argument that Puerto Rico was treated as territory and not as part of the union. Under this premise and through the insular cases of *Downes v. Bidwell* (1901) and *De Lima v. Bidwell* (1901), and later in the case of *Balzac v. People of Puerto Rico* (1922), the legal creature of the U.S. Congress, the so-called "unincorporated territory" was established and validated, maintaining as a foundation that we belong to, but are not part of the United States. This doctrine was validated by Associate Justice Edward Douglass White in his opinion offered in the case of *Downes v. Bidwell*, for the controversy that asserted whether it was constitutional for Congress to impose through the Foraker Act a tariff on trade between Puerto Rico and the continental United States, in light of the Uniformity Clause. Justice White's opinion held as follows:

> "The result of what has been said is that in an international sense Porto Rico was not a foreign country, since it was subject to the sovereignty of was owned by the United States, it was foreign to the United States in a domestic sense, because the island has not been incorporated into the United States but was merely appurtenant thereto as a possession."

The great changes resulting from the military conflicts between the countries of Western Europe, and the intervention of the United States in these conflicts, led to changes in the civil and political order in Puerto Rico. President William Howard Taft took the initiative to propose the granting of American citizenship for Puerto Rico, which culminated in the filing of the Jones-Shaforth bill, which was finally approved in the House of Representatives on May 23, 1916. It then passed the Senate on February 20, 1917 and was finally signed by President Woodrow Wilson on March 2, 1917. This bill was the product of great controversy, due to the conditions that were imposed, since it would grant citizenship without the character of admitting Puerto Rico as a state.

This act leads us to argue about the violation of the value of equal treatment of American citizens. The first violation we must recognize is not having the right to vote for those members of Congress who pass federal laws that apply to Puerto Rico, not having fair representation in Congress, and not being able to vote for the President of the United States. Recognizing what is expressed in Articles 1 and 2 of the U.S. Constitution, we must recognize that in interpreting the articles there is a clear basis for political discrimination against U.S. citizens residing in Puerto Rico. Articles 1 and 2 of the U.S. Constitution provide that:

> Article 1. Section 2. "The House of Representatives shall consist of members elected every two years by the inhabitants of the several States, and the electors shall possess in each State the qualifications requisite for electors of the most numerous branches of the local legislature."
>
> Article 1, Section 3. "The Senate of the United States shall consist of two Senators.from each State, elected for six years by the legislature thereof, and each Senator shall have one vote."
>
> [. . .]
>
> Article 2, Section 1: "The executive power is hereby vested in a President of the United States. He shall hold office for a term of four years, and shall, together with the Vice President appointed for the same term, be chosen as follows:
>
> Each State shall appoint; in such manner as its legislature may direct, a number of electors equal to the whole number of Senators and Representatives to which the State may be entitled in Congress, but no Senator, Representative, or person holding an honorary or salaried office of the United States, shall be appointed an elector."

Interpreting what is expressed in the Constitution of the United States, this closes the doors to the millions of Puerto Ricans residing on the island, to have full equality as the rest of their fellow citizens, by applying federal laws without the consent of the governed, with the argument that the right to vote will be recognized only to the residents of the states.

As a result of this issue, legal analyses have emerged that result in the deprivation of the right to equality for American citizens residing on the island. Under the colonial condition imposed on us and not being a state, Puerto Rico does not have the right to the electoral college because the territories do not meet the requirements established by Amendment XIV, which establishes that: "All persons born or naturalized in the United States and subject to the jurisdiction thereof are citizens of the United States and of the States in which they reside. [. . .]," so the territories are not part of the United States for constitutional purposes.

Under this premise presented by the Congress, we allude to international law on the establishment of the "International Covenant on Civil and Political Rights" ratified by the General Assembly in its resolution 2200 A (XXI) of December 16, 1966, which in its Article 3 mentions: "The States Parties to the present Covenant undertake to ensure the equal right of men and women to the enjoyment of all civil and political rights set forth in the present Covenant," as well as in its Article 25, which states:

> All citizens shall enjoy, without any of the distinctions mentioned in Article 2, and without undue restrictions, the following rights and opportunities:
>
> a) To take part in the conduct of public affairs, directly or through freely chosen representatives.

b) To vote and lo be elected at genuine periodic elections which shall be by universal and equal suffrage and shall be held by secret ballot, guaranteeing the free expression of the will of the electors;
c) To have access, an general terms of equality, to public service in their country.

Under the Treaty of Paris, the Congress of the United States is granted plenary powers over the territory, and it was provided that it would have the responsibility not only to determine the civil rights, but also the political status of its inhabitants. In this matter we must mention that Congress has not taken forceful action to define Puerto Rico's status under the regimes of international law and the U.S. Constitution.

These rights began to be discussed after the approval of the Universal Declaration of Human Rights on December 10, 1948, adopted by the United Nations (UN). This declaration emphasizes the equality of rights that all human beings should enjoy. Article 2 states: "No distinction shall be made on the basis of the political, jurisdictional or international status of the country or territory to which a person belongs, whether it be an independent country, a territory under trusteeship, non-self-governing or under any other limitation of sovereignty. By this declaration Puerto Ricans residing on the island should have equal rights and duties as citizens residing in one of the fifty (50) states.

This statement has been used as an argument to establish that Puerto Rico is already fully defined after the approval of Act 600, which gave way to the creation of the Commonwealth on July 25, 1952. We must mention that the precedents set in cases subsequent to the creation of the Commonwealth create ambiguity in the fact that Congress continues to have plenary powers over and above the sovereignty that was recognized to Puerto Rico in 1952. The final determination made by the Supreme Court in the case of *Puerto Rico v. Sanchez-Valle*, and the establishment of the PROMESA Act, which creates the Fiscal Oversight Board, demonstrate the permanence of Puerto Rico as a territory subject to the plenary powers of Congress, which violates international agreements on the self-determination of peoples and the value of equal rights.

One of the flaws that we can identify about our civil and political order is the lack of recognition of the vote for the President of the United States, and equal representation in Congress therefore we don't have equal justice under the law. The articulated premise, has been in other jurisdictions, as in the case of Washington DC, the product of legal actions to grant equal right of representation and presidential vote for its citizens. In the case of Washington DC, the decision of the Human Rights Commission was forceful when it concluded that the fundamental rights of American citizens are above any law that limits them.

To address the status issue, regarding the feasibility of integrating presidential voting rights into the current political relationship between the United States and Puerto Rico, studies have been conducted and status review committees have been presented. On July 25, 1962, the then President of the United States, John F. Kennedy, in his response to a letter from then Governor Luis Muñoz Marín, affirmed the need to consult the people of Puerto Rico on their preference regarding their political status formula.

As a result of this exchange, the Government of Puerto Rico submitted to the Legislative Assembly a bill ordering the holding of a referendum. Public hearings were held for six weeks in which approximately 80 people testified. The discussion of the bill concluded in the need to clarify the definition of the Commonwealth before holding a referendum and the need to obtain a declaration from Congress on the formula it is willing to approve in order to hold a meaningful and binding referendum.

Pursuant thereto, H.R. 5945 is approved, with the purpose of establishing a Commission to study the Agreement between the United States and Puerto Rico. The Commission would be composed of twelve (12) members, four appointed by the President of the United States, four by the Governor of Puerto Rico, two by the President of the U.S. Senate, and two by the Speaker of the House of Representatives. Bill H.R. 5945, when passed, became Public Law 88-271. Among its considerations, the committee contemplated the issue of equal rights and conditions for Puerto Rico to have the right to vote for the President of the United States, which gave it political power and greater importance in the national affairs of the island.

Finally, we would like to allude to the Constitution of the United States, where in its preamble establishes the expression "We the People of the United States, in Order to form a more perfect Union, establish Justice, ensure domestic Tranquility, provide for the common defense, promote the general Welfare, and secure the Blessings of Liberty to ourselves and our Posterity, do ordain and establish this Constitution for the United States of America."

This declaration marks the core value of the nation's constitution and the intent by which it is created. The cases brought to abolish slavery in the nation, as well as other movements such as the suffragettes petitioning for women's right to vote, used this consensus to argue that the term "We the people" refers to the inclusion of all American citizens in the rights outlined in the U.S. Constitution.

Therefore, we believe it is meritorious to take action on what this resolution proposes, to promote equal rights and social justice for U.S. citizens residing in Puerto Rico, so that they may enjoy the right to vote for the President of the United States. It is important that the U.S. Congress take action on the referred case and enforce the rights of the Constitution for all U.S. citizens equally.

The bills before the House Committee on Natural Resources, chaired by Congressman Grijalva, allude to taking action in favor of the freedom of determination of the people of Puerto Rico on the future of their relationship with the United States. Certainly, the guarantee of the right to self-determination of the people of Puerto Rico has been guaranteed in all the processes of expression of the people through the various plebiscites held since 1967, until the last one held on November 3, 2020. But in order for the value of the people's right to self-determination to be realized, Congress has the duty to take action in favor of the democratic expression of Puerto Ricans residing on the island.

H.R. 1522, introduced by our only congressional representative, Jenniffer Gonzalez, and Congressman Darren Soto, for consideration by the U.S. Senate and the U.S. House of Representatives, sets precedents in the history of the admission of territories as a state of the union. It also ensures concrete action on the mandate sent by the people of Puerto Rico last November 3 favoring statehood, with the ratification of the results and the approval of the President of the United States.

In contrast to H.R. 2070, presented by Congresswomen Nydia Velazquez and Alexandria Ocasio, who present a bill that seeks the creation of a status convention that is unprecedented in the processes of admission of territories to the nation, and historically only the colonies that have wished to betray themselves toward the formation of an independent Republic, have accepted it.

With much respect to this Congress and members of the House Committee on Natural Resources, I submit that H.R. 2070 does not represent the will of the people and I request that it not be taken into consideration. The only piece of legislation that provides the tools for the advancement of the Puerto Rican people and that represents the will of the majority of the Puerto Rican people is H.R. 1522.

Sincerely,

Ricardo Marrero-Passapera,
Candidate, Puerto Rico Congressional Delegation

DEMOCRATIC PARTY OF PUERTO RICO

April 6, 2021

The Honorable Joaquin Castro
U.S. House of Representatives
Washington, DC 20515

Dear Representative Castro:

We 'Write to you as leaders of the Democratic Party of Puerto Rico to respectfully request that you not further support H.R. 2070—a bill that disrespects the people of Puerto Rico and their self-determination, including their choice of equality as Americans. We assume you supported this bill in good faith. We join our new Democratic Governor, Pedro Pierluisi, who previously served eight years in the U.S. House in opposing this undemocratic bill.

Last year, Puerto Rico's elected representatives approved a law for a plebiscite on statehood, a vote conducted by many territories that became States. Held along with November's 2020 general elections, virtually as many people voted in the plebiscite as voted for any local public office. The participation percentage was greater than similar votes in many territories. A solid majority voted for statehood after vigorous campaigns for and against it. The plebiscite followed two other status votes held in 2012 and 2017 that included all of the status options Congress' committees and successive administrations have said are possible. Majorities chose statehood in those votes as well. There can be no purer self-determination process than the people voting on questions posed by their elected representatives.

- H.R. 2070 would ignore the free and fair votes of Puerto Ricans, upheld by the Federal court as well as the insular Supreme Court. It attempts to pressure the territory into conducting a status process that the Government of Puerto Rico has declined to adopt for decades. Democrats respect democratic election results and should respect Puerto Rico's self-determination as well.
- The bill's process can include status proposals that are not possible, prolonging the territory status the people specifically voted against in 2012 and that H.R. 2070 purportedly wants to replace. Impossible proposals have confused the issue, preventing resolution. The bill's House author has written that the options can include independence, free association (nationhood in an association with the U.S. that either nation can end), "and any other non-territorial status." The committees of jurisdiction of both houses of Congress and successive administrations have repeatedly determined that there can be no other option than statehood, independence and free association.
- The bill proposes a congressional commission to make recommendations to Puerto Rico on its culture, language, and other matters as a State or a nation that are not within the jurisdiction of the U.S. Government under the Constitution and international law. This would be anti-Latinx, offensive, colonial, xenophobic, and cultural imperialism: all of which are unthinkable for Democrats.
- The bill would amend many Federal laws as unilaterally drafted by a convention in Puerto Rico without the committees of jurisdiction of either house in Congress being able consider the changes or Congress being able to amend the legislation. Both houses would effectively be forced by the bill's rules changes to vote up or down on the Puerto Rico-drafted changes in Federal laws.
- The bill could change Puerto Rico's status to one that is not the first choice of a majority of the territory's voters and one with even less votes than a plurality choice. The territory's status should be a majority first choice.
- The bill's status convention could be called by Puerto Rico's legislature without the enactment of a law in the territory, ignoring the Governor in this process. It

would be disrespectful and undemocratic for Congress to disregard the elected Governor of the territory.

- The members of the bill's convention would serve indefinitely without having to face re-election no matter how long the bill's process takes. Elected officials serving indefinite terms is undemocratic.

These are just some of the deficiencies. Most important, the bill would set aside the absolute majority choice of Puerto Ricans—Americans by birth—for equality within our Nation. It attempts to thwart our self-determination and impose a choice process on Puerto Ricans, suppressing the majority vote. It would allow for an outcome that would perpetuate a colonial status under which Puerto Rico is treated worse than a State, precluded from having votes in the government that makes its local laws when that government so wishes as well as votes in making the laws to which the whole Nation is bound.

Please do not further support the mockery of self-determination reflected in H.R. 2070.

By contrast, we and the Governor of Puerto Rico support H.R. 1522 by Representative Darren Soto and 57 others. We ask you to support this bill that respects Puerto Ricans, democracy, and self-determination.

With deepest thanks for your consideration of the request of the majority of the people of Puerto Rico, we are,

Sincerely,

Charles A. Rodríguez, Chair
Democratic Party of Puerto Rico

Johanne Vélez, Vice Chair
Democratic Party of Puerto Rico

María "Mayita" Meléndez,
Committeewoman
Puerto Rico Democratic
National Committee

Luis Dávila-Pernas,
Committeeman
Puerto Rico Democratic
National Committee

SUBMISSIONS FOR THE RECORD BY REP. SOTO, STATEMENT FOR THE RECORD, STENY H. HOYER, HOUSE MAJORITY LEADER

Chairman Grijalva and Ranking Member Westerman, thank you for this opportunity to share my thoughts with the Committee regarding the political status of Puerto Rico, which has been a very important priority for me throughout my time in Congress.

For generations, Puerto Ricans have been an integral part of the American family, and millions of people born in Puerto Rico or of Puerto Rican heritage. The 3.2 million people living on the island are our fellow American citizens, and they contribute mightily to our common defense, and the social and cultural life of our nation. Puerto Rico's fragile economy, still in the midst of restructuring unsustainable levels of debt, has been hit hard by recent hurricanes, earthquakes, and the COVID-19 pandemic, and the prior Administration did not live up to its responsibility to extend help to our brothers and sisters on the island during their time of hardship and recovery. That was unfortunate, because it does not reflect what I believe is a deeply genuine sense of common purpose and common destiny that binds Puerto Rico to the rest of the United States. We take care of one another.

While Puerto Rico is served ably in Congress by my dear friend, the Resident Commissioner Jenniffer González-Colón, can any of us truly say Puerto Rico would have been treated this poorly in the wake of these disasters had it been a state and afforded full representation in Washington? The answer is self-evident.

I believe that the best path forward to resolve questions of Puerto Rico's political status is statehood, but that is a decision that must be left to Puerto Ricans themselves. I have long supported statehood for the people of Puerto Rico, but more importantly I believe in their right to self-determination. The people of Puerto Rico deserve the opportunity to chart their own future, and in my view, the people of Puerto Rico have told us time and time again, through multiple plebiscites in recent years, that they choose statehood. As recently as this past November, the people of Puerto Rico chose statehood in a simple up or down vote. I think that we in Congress would be wise to listen to what the people of Puerto Rico are telling us.

Statehood would afford the people living on the island all the rights, privileges, responsibilities, and equal treatment under federal programs that the current fifty states enjoy—everything from application of the federal minimum wage to access to Medicaid, supplemental nutrition assistance, and countless other federal programs. Most importantly, the people of Puerto Rico would have a greater say in determining the course of our nation's future, with equal representation in the Congress, including two senators, and a role in choosing our national leaders.

With a population greater than 20 of the U.S. states, there ought to be no impediment to admitting Puerto Rico as a state if they choose that course. To my friends on the other side of the aisle, who might presume from the outset what political party the people of Puerto Rico might favor in electing their representatives to the Congress, I would remind them that we were certain with the admission of Hawaii and Alaska to the Union that Hawaii would reliably elect Republicans and Alaska would be a stronghold for Democrats. Only the people of Puerto Rico will know the answer to that question. As my friend Rep. Don Young can attest, we ought to be careful about making decisions about the merits of the legislation before the Committee today with those presumptions in mind.

Our history with the people of Puerto Rico is complex, with over a century of their mistreatment as second-class citizens. It is time to right that wrong.

I thank the Committee for holding this hearing today and for considering bills introduced by my dear friends Reps. Velázquez and Soto. I hope the Committee will give a full and fair hearing to their respective pieces of legislation on the future of Puerto Rico's political status, and I appreciate the many efforts they have taken to craft their bills with care. I apologize that a prior commitment prevented me from being with you today in person, and I look forward to reading the statements of testimony and transcripts from this hearing—in addition to looking forward to continuing our work together in the Congress to ensure that Puerto Ricans have their voices heard loudly and clearly in this House as we address matters important to our common future.

SUBMISSIONS FOR THE RECORD BY REP. VELÁZQUEZ, STATUS, OUR PEOPLE AND RIGHT TO VOTE, BY VICTORIA MUÑOZ MENDOZA AND HÉCTOR LUIS ACEVEDO

> "The political status is to serve the quality of life that the Puerto Rican people want to create for themselves. The political status, we should repeat it a hundred times over and over again, is to serve those human ideals, not to deviate our people from the paths to fulfill them." Luis Muñoz Marín

The people of Puerto Rico agonized for decades with the dilemma between statehood and independence. Our energies were diluted in these struggles and the problems of our people took a back seat. From this crisis emerged a creative agenda that recognized that our people are the top priority and not status. For decades we grew inside and out.

The Commonwealth was created without sacrificing our culture. Harmonizing the values of affirmation of our own culture and personality with American citizenship and its freedom of movement, promoting economic, educational and social development never seen or repeated in our history.

Today our people face great challenges that diminish their quality of life and their options for the future. These challenges must be overcome. The pandemic, closed schools, lack of jobs, debt, fictitious budgets and our government's inability to combat corruption. Interposing the status debate on the road to recovery does not seem prudent or correct at this point. The day will come, but it is not here yet. It will come when we overcome the pandemic crisis, the Fiscal Control Board and resume our economy of hope.

This month, two bills were filed with the U.S. Congress on status. One pretends to impose statehood despite our people being divided in half, to impose a status of assimilation as a federal state that has no going back. In 1995 the status struggles led the government of Puerto Rico to request, contrary to its electoral program, the elimination of Section 936, which led to the loss of more than 100,000 jobs. A good part of our current economic problems is due to this action product of status fanaticism.

Another bill, based in good faith, seeks to impose a statehood or independence dilemma, removing Commonwealth from the ballot. It's like going back to the 1930s and the struggles faced at that time when nationalists and pro-US forces fought violently against each other. It is not possible to speak of inclusion by excluding one of the two main options in our country. It is not possible to speak of self-determination and not respect the freedom of the people of Puerto Rico to choose their preferences through their constitutional right vote. One cannot speak of democracy if the rights of the Puerto Rican people are not respected. Taking away the right to vote from the Puerto Ricans that believe in the Commonwealth is an error of principle and of the practical realities of liberty.

It is our belief that Puerto Rico's priorities should be directed toward creating consensus and a common ground that allows us to address the health, education and work crisis in which we are immersed.

We need to start a dialogue so that, in due course, all options are included, respecting differences, not trying to define an adversary's preference, much less take them off the ballot. Puerto Ricans must be able to decide, without a conflict between our quality of life and its democracy. We must forge understandings to be able to dedicate our best energies to our people.

March 25, 2021 *El Nuevo Día*, page 35.

[LIST OF DOCUMENTS SUBMITTED FOR THE RECORD POST-HEARING AND RETAINED IN THE COMMITTEE'S OFFICIAL FILES]

Submissions for the Record by Hon. Acevedo-Vilá

- Frente Puertorriqueñista (Puerto Rican Front) (signed by 115 stakeholders)—Manifesto and Letter of Support
- Views on Political Status Among Puerto Rican Voters, Hart Research Associates—Results of 2020 Telephone Survey

Submissions for the Record by José Fuentes

- Republican National Committee, Zoraida Fonalledas, National Committeewoman for Puerto Rico—Letter of Support for H.R. 1522, dated April 21, 2021

Submissions for the Record by Dr. Ponsa-Kraus

- Collection of three letters: Letter signed by 47 Legal and Constitutional Scholars supporting the Puerto Rico Admission Act of 2021 and opposing the Puerto Rico Self-Determination Act, submitted by Rep. González-Colón; a response to this letter from Constitutional Law Professors based in Puerto Rico; and Dr. Ponsa-Kraus's reply
- "Political Wine in a Judicial Bottle: Justice Sotomayor's Surprising Concurrence in *Aurelius*," by Christina D. Ponsa-Kraus, September 21, 2020, *Yale Law Journal Forum*
- "The Battle Over Puerto Rico's Future," by Christina D. Ponsa-Kraus, April 21, 2021, Constitutional Law Blog— Balkinization

Submissions for the Record from People's Hearing on Puerto Rico Self-Determination

- Maria de Lourdes Guzmá: Letter
- Marina Aleman: Letter of Support (H.R. 2070)

Submissions for the Record by VAMOS Puerto Rico

- Alejandro Torres Rivera: Informational Brief
- Alliance for Free Association (ALAS), José Ortiz Daliot: Letter of Support (H.R. 2070)
- Antonio J. Fas Alzamora, former President of the Senate of Puerto Rico: Letter of Support (H.R. 2070)
- Democratic Socialists of America, Austin González: Letter of Support (H.R. 2070)
- Eduardo Villanueva Muñoz: Letter to the Committee
- Gladys Franco, Co-Founder of the Boricua Solidarity Movement: Letter of Support (H.R. 2070)
- Javier Smith Torres: Letter to the Committee & Chairman Grijalva
- Justin Maldonado: Letter of Support (H.R. 2070)
- La Mesa Boricua of Florida, María Revelles: Letter of Support (H.R. 2070)
- María J. Torres-López: Letter of Support (H.R. 2070)
- Organización Puertorriqueña de la Mujer Trabajadora (OPMT), Alice Colón Warren: Letter of Support (H.R. 2070)

- Our Revolution Puerto Rico (ORPR), Maruxa Cárdenas: Letter of Support (H.R. 2070)
- Paul Figueroa: Letter of Support (H.R. 2070)
- Raquel M. Gonzalez-Sparks: Letter of Support (H.R. 2070)

Miscellaneous Letters/Statements in Support of H.R. 1522

Individuals

- Alba Calderon
- Andrés L. Córdova, Commissioner in Puerto Rico's Civil Rights Commission
- Dennis O. Freytes, U.S. Army (Ret.)
- Derick Leon
- Enid Acevedo
- Eugenio Matías Pérez
- Francisco Ortiz Berlingeri
- Gene Roman: Collection of News Stories, Pro-Statehood
- Joaqúın A. Márquez
- Jose Avilés
- José Vicente, Filadelfia IDDPMI Santiago Iglesias
- Luis Matos
- Manuel De Jesus Lopez Alamo
- María C Robles-Torres
- Norika Rodríguez Carmona
- Sara Muñoz Meléndez
- Virgilio Sánchez Figueroa

Groups

- National Puerto Rican Equality Coalition
- Puerto Rico Escogió Estadidad, Inc.
- Puerto Rico-USA Foundation
- Young Professionals for Puerto Rico Statehood (YPPRS)

Miscellaneous Letters/Statements in Support of H.R. 2070

- ELA de Puerto Rico-Defensores Inc.
- Puerto Rican Action Movement (MAP)—Informational Brief

Miscellaneous Letters to the Committee

- John Ward Llambias
- José Luis Dalmau, President of the Senate of Puerto Rico and of the Popular Democratic Party
- Melissa Richardson
- Zayira Jordán Conde

Other Submissions for the Record

- Professors of Constitutional Law at ABA approved law schools in Puerto Rico
- H. Con. Res. 1, House of Representatives of Puerto Rico, 19th Legislative Assembly
- Emilio Pantojas Garćıa—Metro.pr, Opinion: El mito de una mayoría estadista
- Puertorriqueños Unidos en Acción (PUA), Manuel Rivera, Letter to Chair Grijalva and the Committee
- Diálogo Por Puerto Rico

In: Legislation to Address Puerto Rico's Political Status ISBN: 978-1-68507-404-3
Editor: Alvaro Campoy

Chapter 2

H.R. 1522, "Puerto Rico Statehood Admission Act"; and H.R. 2070, "Puerto Rico Self-Determination Act of 2021," - Part 2*

Committee on Natural Resources

Legislative Hearing on H.R. 1522, to Provide for the Admission of the State of Puerto Rico into the Union, "Puerto Rico Statehood Admission Act"; and H.R. 2070, to Recognize the Right of the People of Puerto Rico to Call a Status Convention through Which the People Would Exercise Their Natural Right to Self-Determination, and to Establish a Mechanism for Congressional Consideration of Such Decision, and for Other Purposes, "Puerto Rico Self-Determination Act of 2021"—Part 2

Wednesday, June 16, 2021
U.S. House of Representatives
Committee on Natural Resources
Washington, DC

* This is an edited, reformatted and augmented version of Legislative Hearing, before the Committee on Natural Resources, U.S. House of Representatives, One Hundred Seventeenth Congress, First Session, Serial No. 117–5, dated June 16, 2021.

The Committee met, pursuant to notice, at 1:01 p.m., via Webex, Hon. Raúl M. Grijalva [Chairman of the Committee] presiding.

Present: Representatives Grijalva, Sablan, Huffman, Gallego, Porter, Leger Fernández, Stansbury, Velázquez, McEachin, Soto, San Nicolas, García, Case, Cohen, Tlaib, Trahan; Gohmert, McClintock, Gosar, Graves, Hice, Radewagen, Webster, González-Colón, Fulcher, Stauber, Tiffany, and Boebert.

Also present: Representative Ocasio-Cortez.

The CHAIRMAN. Thank you very much, Mr. Robles, and the Committee will come to order. The Committee is meeting today to receive testimony on two bills to resolve Puerto Rico's political status.

Under Committee Rule 4(f), any oral opening statements at the hearing are limited to the Chair and the Ranking Minority Member or their designees. This will allow us to hear from our witnesses sooner and help Members keep to their schedules.

However, for today's hearing, we will allow the bill sponsors to make a statement in support of their legislation before we turn to the rest of the witnesses.

I therefore ask unanimous consent that all other Members' opening statements be made part of the hearing record if they are submitted to the Clerk by 5 p.m. today or the close of the hearing, whichever comes first.

Hearing no objection, so ordered.

Without objection, the Chair might also declare a recess subject to the call of the Chair. As described in the notice, statements, documents, or motions must be submitted to the electronic repository at HNRCdocs@mail.house.gov. Additionally, please note that as with in-person meetings, Members are responsible for their own microphones. As with our in-person meetings, Members may be muted by staff to avoid inadvertent background noise. Finally, Members or witnesses experiencing technical problems should inform the Committee staff immediately, and that phone number was in your information. We are going to begin opening statements.

The Chair will now recognize the Vice Ranking Minority Member for Insular Affairs and Ranking Member designee with respect to her opening statement and with respect to H.R. 1522, legislation sponsored by herself and Representative Soto. With that, Representative González-Colón, the time is yours.

STATEMENT OF THE HON. JENNIFFER GONZÁLEZ-COLÓN, A RESIDENT COMMISSIONER IN CONGRESS FROM THE TERRITORY OF PUERTO RICO

Miss GONZÁLEZ-COLÓN. Thank you, Mr. Chairman. Today, the Committee is holding a second hearing to address Puerto Rico's political status following the

November 3 referendum in which a clear majority of voters on the island chose statehood. Also, I think, 2 days ago, the Department of Justice issued a report on the constitutional and legal perspective of the bills before us.

H.R. 1522, the Puerto Rico Statehood Admission Act, which I introduced with Congressman Darren Soto from Florida, recognizes and respects that Puerto Rico has, through the ballot box, exercised its right to self-determination, rejected the current territorial status, and voted for statehood.

H.R. 1522 will constitute Congress' response to my constituents on the island. It makes a formal offer of statehood to the American citizens living in Puerto Rico, which would have to be ratified in a federally sponsored referendum. As the DOJ recognizes, H.R. 1522 does not impose or force statehood on the people of the island. It empowers, as we would have the final say on the matter through our vote, the only true and proven self-determination process. The bill follows the precedent established for Alaska and Hawaii, setting forth a binding, self-executing process to admit Puerto Rico as a state should a majority of the voters favor it.

The other bill, H.R. 2070, blatantly ignores the will of the people of Puerto Rico and the voters and has serious constitutional flaws according to the Department of Justice.

During our last hearing, it also became clear that this bill attempts to mislead voters in Puerto Rico by establishing a complicated status convention process in which just a few delegates could come up with fanciful or unconstitutional status options. It even goes as far as saying that Congress would be required to ratify whatever option comes out of this process, something Congress cannot constitutionally bind itself to do, as the DOJ report has explicitly pointed out.

The DOJ also stated that the only two non-territorial status options consistent with the U.S. Constitution are statehood and independence. We don't need a status convention to tell this to Congress or to the people of the island. Any other option that this convention may come up with would be incompatible with the U.S. Constitution.

Mr. Chairman, a few days ago, on a separate matter, the Department of Justice announced that it would defend before the Supreme Court the constitutionality of the law that excludes Puerto Rico residents from the Supplemental Security Income, or SSI, as we know the program. Some Members of Congress, including members of this Committee, rightfully denounced this decision, calling for a legislative solution and a permanent fix to this unequal treatment.

It is true that Congress can pass legislation to give Puerto Rico access to SSI and to other Federal programs under which we are excluded. As the island's sole representative in Congress, I have introduced multiple bills to achieve this and will continue to advance these efforts. But it is similarly true that a future Congress could take away that access, and that is because as a territory, we will always be at Congress' mercy.

Mr. Chairman, the so-called parity is not equality, and it is not a permanent solution. And that is why we must respect Puerto Rico's vote and support H.R. 1522, because statehood will guarantee full and permanent equality for the 3.2 million citizens living on the island. And only statehood guarantees constitutional citizenship.

Now, as we discuss a path forward in this Committee, we must also make a choice. Are we going to ignore the will of the voters on the island and pretend that we know better than them, or are we going to stand with the fellow citizens living in Puerto Rico and respect their vote for full equality and for statehood?

I assume we are going to do the correct thing and assure that H.R. 1522 is going to be passed. Thank you, Mr. Chairman, and I yield back.

[The prepared statement of Miss González-Colón follows:]

PREPARED STATEMENT OF THE HON. JENNIFFER GONZÁLEZ-COLÓN, A RESIDENT COMMISSIONER IN CONGRESS FROM THE TERRITORY OF PUERTO RICO

Thank you, Mr. Chairman.

Today the Committee is holding a second hearing to address Puerto Rico's political status, following the November 3rd referendum in which a clear majority of voters on the Island chose statehood. Also, 2 days ago the Department of Justice (DOJ) issued a report on the constitutional and legal perspective of the bills before us.

H.R. 1522, the Puerto Rico Statehood Admission Act, which I introduced with Congressman Darren Soto, recognizes and respects that Puerto Rico has—through the ballot box—exercised its right to self-determination, rejected the current territorial status, and voted for statehood.

H.R. 1522 would constitute Congress's response to voters on the Island. It makes a formal offer of statehood to the American citizens of Puerto Rico, which would have to be ratified in a federally sponsored referendum. As DOJ recognizes, H.R. 1522 does not impose or force statehood on the people of Puerto Rico. It empowers us, as we would have the final say on the matter through our vote, the only true and proven self-determination process. The bill follows the precedent established for Alaska and Hawaii, setting forth a binding, self-executing process to admit Puerto Rico as a State should a majority of voters favor it.

The other bill, H.R. 2070, blatantly ignores the will of Puerto Rico's voters and has serious constitutional flaws, according to DOJ.

During our last hearing it also became clear that this bill attempts to mislead voters in Puerto Rico by establishing a complicated, status convention process in which a few delegates could come up with fanciful or unconstitutional status options. It even goes as far as saying that Congress would be required to ratify whatever option comes out of this process, something Congress cannot constitutionally bind itself to do as the DOJ report has explicitly pointed out.

DOJ also stated that the only two non-territorial status options consistent with the U.S. Constitution are statehood and independence. We don't need a status convention to tell this to Congress or to the people of Puerto Rico. Any other option that this convention may come up with would be incompatible with the Constitution.

Mr. Chairman, a few days ago, on a separate matter DOJ announced that it would defend before the Supreme Court the constitutionality of the law that excludes Puerto Rico residents from the Supplemental Security Income (SSI).

Some Members of Congress, including Members of this Committee, rightfully denounced this decision, calling for a legislative solution and a permanent fix to this unequal treatment.

It is true that Congress can pass legislation to give Puerto Rico access to SSI and other Federal programs under which we are excluded. As the Island's sole representative in Congress, I've introduced multiple bills to achieve this and will continue to advance these efforts.

But it is similarly true that a future Congress could take away that access. And that's because as a territory, we will always be at Congress's mercy. Mr. Chairman, so-called "parity" is not equality, and it's not a permanent solution.

That's why we must respect Puerto Rico's vote and support H.R. 1522. Because only statehood will guarantee full and permanent equality for the 3.2 million Americans on the Island, and only statehood guarantees constitutional citizenship.

Now, as we discuss a path forward in this Committee, we must also make a choice: are we going to ignore the will of voters in Puerto Rico, and pretend that we know better than them? Or are we going to stand with our fellow citizens on the Island and respect their vote for full equality, for statehood?

Thank you. I yield back.

The CHAIRMAN. The gentlelady yields, and thank you, Miss González-Colón, for your statement.

The Chair now recognizes the sponsor of H.R. 2070, the gentlelady from New York, Representative Velázquez, for 5 minutes. Ms. Velázquez, you are recognized.

Statement of the Hon. Nydia M. Velázquez, a Representative in Congress from the State of New York

Ms. VELÁZQUEZ. Thank you, Mr. Chairman, to you and the Ranking Member for holding this second hearing on the issue of statehood for Puerto Rico. There is a popular saying in Spanish that goes like this. "El rio siempre vuelve a su cauce," which translates to, “The river always makes it to the delta.” And here we are today with newly issued reports from the U.S. Department of Justice confirming what we have been saying all along.

The past plebiscites have never produced any permanent results, that statehood is not a done deal, and that Puerto Ricans need to freely vote on all possible options. And more importantly, that the DOJ only explicitly supports my bill and not H.R. 1522, the statehood bill. So, here we are at the delta. After reading DOJ’s reports, it is now more clear than ever that the Puerto Rico Self-Determination Act is the inclusive democratic approach to solving Puerto Rico’s status, while the Statehood Admission bill is a one-sided, undemocratic bill that does not even achieve the aim it supposedly purports. I want to thank Chairman Grijalva for requesting these reports, which revoke the token points on statehood that had been pushed by politicians and lobbyists to the tune of about $12 million since 2013. For years, Puerto Rican statehood leaders have used the promise of admission as a state for their own political and electoral purposes.

They have lied time and again about how close statehood for Puerto Rico really is. They allege massive support it has and all the benefits of this option, at times downplaying the responsibility it will carry. H.R. 1522 is not different, and the DOJ agrees. First and foremost, H.R. 1522 proponents argue this bill is self-executing and that statehood is automatic. That is false.

The DOJ report clearly states that the bill itself will not admit Puerto Rico as a state and, in fact, recommends a new name for this bill and, I quote, “the Department recommends that the title of the bill be the “Puerto Rico Statehood Determination Act” or simply the “Puerto Rico Statehood Act,” so as not to imply that admission of Puerto Rico as a state is a fait accompli.” So, even the name of the bill is misleading.

Secondly, H.R. 1522 has been advertised on the full premise that Puerto Ricans already decided in favor of statehood. Wrong. The DOJ questions the validity of the past plebiscite by noting that the ballot propositions in 2012 and 2017 contain inaccuracies and were potentially misleading and that the premise of the 2020 plebiscite was faulty. Finally, opponents of H.R. 2070 argue that my bill is too complex. Wrong again. DOJ notes that it is in line with the Constitution to provide the voters of Puerto Rico with clear notice of what they will be approving. My bill is the only bill that offers a clear, transparent, inclusive, and democratic way for Puerto Ricans to be informed on the consequences of becoming a state or on any other future status.

In fact, my bill creates an educational campaign and allocates money for such purposes. It also requires transitional plans accompany options during a vote. A decision to become a state of the Union binds Puerto Ricans forever. The voters in Puerto Rico have the right to know, understand, and vote upon the terms and condition for each of the status options. My bill offers Puerto Ricans the opportunity to define for themselves the status option that they will vote for.

Bear in mind that after the statehood option loss in 1993 plebiscite, the Statehood Party vowed never to allow others to present their own status options and instead craft subsequent plebiscite and status options on their own accord. That explains the one-sided, undemocratic referendum we have had today. If we truly want to solve the issue of status for the island, we need to give Puerto Ricans the tools to design a true self-determination process. Thank you, Mr. Chairman. I yield back.

The CHAIRMAN. The gentlelady yields, and I thank the gentlelady for her statement.

Madam Ranking Member, is Mr. Westerman going to be here to make a statement, the Ranking Member, or not?

Miss GONZÁLEZ-COLÓN. No, sir.

The CHAIRMAN. OK. Thank you.

Let me now recognize myself for an opening statement.

STATEMENT OF THE HON. RAÚL M. GRIJALVA, A REPRESENTATIVE IN CONGRESS FROM THE STATE OF ARIZONA

The CHAIRMAN. As was stated, we are meeting today for a second day of hearings on H.R. 1522, the Puerto Rico Statehood Admission Act, and H.R. 2070, the Puerto Rico Self-Determination Act of 2021, both of which are seeking to conclusively address the island's future political status after 123 years as a territory of the United States.

When we met for the first hearing in April, we heard from elected officials from Puerto Rico, including the Governor and the Speaker of the House of Representatives, who urged passage of the bill they supported. Today, we will hear from academics, residents of Puerto Rico, and mainland leaders, who will also address their preferred solution to Puerto Rico's political status.

The journey to address Puerto Rico's political status began in 1952, when the United States enacted legislation establishing the current relationship between Puerto Rico and the United States. Since then, there has been a series of plebiscites to find out whether the residents of Puerto Rico were satisfied with the current territory status or if they wanted to change it. The most recent of these plebiscites yielded support in favor of statehood, which led to the introduction of the two bills that are before us today.

At our last hearing, there was debate and discussion of whether the residents of Puerto Rico desire a permanent union with the United States that guarantees their U.S. citizenship and equal rights and responsibilities as Americans residing in the 50 states. We also heard arguments insisting that the residents of Puerto Rico are still unsure of agreeing to a permanent union and should therefore be allowed to debate and discuss all the non-territory status options available through a status convention.

As you are all aware, we reached out to the Biden administration's Department of Justice for an assessment of the two bills. I want to thank the Department for submitting the information to the Committee in a timely manner so it could be available to all of us for this meeting. And, in summary, the official reports indicate that the Department of Justice supports providing the people of Puerto Rico the opportunity to vote on whether to become a State of the Union, as H.R. 1522 would do. Also, the Department would support H.R. 2070, if it facilitates a choice among three constitutionally permissible status options: statehood, independence, and territory status.

We anticipate today's hearing will be similar to our first hearing but also a focus on DOJ's opinions on the two pieces of legislation before us today. Once again, I want to be straightforward with the residents of Puerto Rico and my colleagues on this Committee. This issue is a divisive issue in Congress for both parties. There is uncertainty around what would happen if there were a Committee or Floor vote on either of these bills.

Nevertheless, I recognize this Committee's responsibility in playing a leading and constructive role in resolving this issue, which is a priority for the people of Puerto Rico. For this reason, I am committed to moving this process forward. The Committee is approaching a decision-making point, which is what the residents of Puerto Rico expect and deserve.

[The prepared statement of Mr. Grijalva follows:]

PREPARED STATEMENT OF THE HON. RAÚL M. GRIJALVA, CHAIR, COMMITTEE ON NATURAL RESOURCES

We are meeting today for a second day of hearings on H.R. 1522, the Puerto Rico Statehood Admission Act and H.R. 2070, the Puerto Rico Self-Determination Act of 2021; both of which are seeking to conclusively address the island's future political status after 123 years as a territory of the United States.

When we met for the first hearing in April, we heard from elected officials from Puerto Rico—including the Governor and Speaker of the House of Representatives—who urged passage of the bill they supported. Today, we will hear from academics, residents of Puerto Rico, and diaspora leaders, who will also passionately advocate for their preferred solution to Puerto Rico's political status.

The journey to address Puerto Rico's political status began in 1952 when the U.S. enacted legislation establishing the current relationship between Puerto Rico and the United States. Since then, there has been a series of plebiscites to find out whether the residents of Puerto Rico were satisfied with the current territory status or if they wanted to change it. The most recent of those plebiscites yielded support in favor of statehood, which led to introduction of the two bills before us.

At our last hearing there was a spirited debate and discussion of whether the residents of Puerto Rico desire a permanent union with the United States that guarantees their U.S. citizenship, and equal rights and responsibilities as Americans residing in the 50 states. We also heard arguments insisting that the residents of Puerto Rico are still unsure of agreeing to a permanent union and should therefore be allowed to debate and discuss all the non-territory status options available to them through a status convention.

As you are all aware, we reached out to the Biden Administration's Department of Justice for an assessment of the two bills. I want to thank the Department for submitting the information to the Committee. In summary, the official reports indicate that the Department of Justice supports providing the people of Puerto Rico the opportunity to vote on whether to become a State of the Union, as H.R. 1522 would do. Also, that the Department would support H.R. 2070, if it facilitates a choice among three constitutionally permissible status options—statehood, independence, and territory status.

We can anticipate that today's hearing will likely be as lively as the first hearing. Once again, I want to be straightforward with the residents of Puerto Rico, this is a divisive issue in Congress—for both delegations—and there is great uncertainty around what would happen if there were a Committee or Floor vote on either of these bills.

Nevertheless, I recognize this Committee's responsibility in playing a leading and constructive role in resolving this issue, which is a priority for the people of Puerto Rico. For this reason, I am committed to moving this process forward. The Committee is approaching a decision-making point, which is what the residents of Puerto Rico expect and deserve.

With that in mind, I want to welcome our witnesses. I also want to welcome our former colleague, former Representative Luis Gutiérrez. I look forward to receiving all your testimonies.

The CHAIRMAN. I want to welcome our witnesses. I also want to welcome our former colleague, former Representative Luis Gutiérrez, who is here with us today. I look forward to receiving all your testimonies, and I will begin.

I will now turn to our witnesses. Before introducing them, I will remind the witnesses that they are encouraged to participate in the witness diversity survey created by the Congressional Office of Diversity and Inclusion. Witnesses may refer to their hearing invitation materials for how to access that information.

Let me remind the witnesses that under our Committee Rules, they must limit their oral statements to 5 minutes, but that their entire statement will appear in the hearing record. When you begin, the timer will begin, and it will turn orange when you have 1 minute remaining. I recommend that Members and witnesses use "stage view" so they can pin the timer on their screen.

After your testimony is complete, please remember to mute yourself to avoid any inadvertent background noise. I will also allow the entire panel to testify before questioning witnesses. And that questioning process will occur based on seniority of those Members in that category that are present with us today.

With that, let me begin by formally inviting our former colleague and dear friend of mine, the Hon. Luis Gutiérrez, Former Representative of Illinois' 4th District from Chicago.

Congressman, you are recognized for 5 minutes, sir.

Mr. Gutiérrez.

STATEMENT OF LUIS GUTIÉRREZ, FORMER REPRESENTATIVE, ILLINOIS' 4TH DISTRICT, CHICAGO, ILLINOIS

Mr. GUTIÉRREZ. Thank you, Chairman Grijalva, Ranking Member Westerman, and members of the Committee. Puerto Rico is a nation, a colonized nation, but a nation nonetheless. As colonization began first under the Spanish Empire in 1493 and then under the U.S. imperialism in 1898, Puerto Rico's identity and nationality was born in resistance to colonialism that today continues to manifest itself rightly in the ongoing struggle for decolonization and for self-determination.

Two brilliant and visionary Puerto Rican women have proposed a bill to end the over 122 years of U.S. colonization of Puerto Rico. Representatives Nydia Velázquez and Alexandria Cortez are the embodiment of Lola Rodríguez de Tióand Mariana Bracetti. Their bill outlines a careful and inclusive mechanism, whereby Puerto Ricans could establish a constitutional assembly to openly discuss, debate, and ultimately select a non-territorial status option.

The Puerto Rico Self-Determination Act of 2021 represents the only genuine democratic legislation about Puerto Rico's status before the 117th Congress. I would like to say that it seems to me that democracy and the foundation is based on the pillars of allowing for dissent, allowing for different opinions, of allowing people to debate and discuss and for all of those opinions to be respected. The only bill that does that is the bill presented by Congresswoman Nydia Velázquez and Ocasio-Cortez. The statehood bill, we could not say the same of it.

I just want to quickly go back to 2017. In 2017, there was a plebiscite in Puerto Rico. The Statehood Party controlled the House, the Senate, and the Governorship. They determined all of the definitions of all of the statuses and they defined all of the statuses. And guess what happened. They got a whopping 97 percent. They did so good that they had to do a repeat 4 years later because no one thought—because not even Putin gets 97 percent of the vote.

But why did they get 97 percent of the vote? Mr. Chairman, members of the Committee, because people boycotted the process, because the people of Puerto Rico felt that this was an imposed process on them. And how did they demonstrate their rejection of the plebiscite? Through a boycott.

Now, let's remember that is what Gandhi did to bring down the empire of Britain. That is what the Civil Rights Movement did under Martin Luther King to bring about justice and fairness and civil rights. It is what the farmworkers did in saying we will boycott the lettuce and Cesar Chavez led to fairer working conditions.

It is a political tool that has been used by the resistance ad memoriam. And it is one that the Puerto Rican people used in 2017. So, let's just discard that. Nobody believes they got 97 percent, not even the proponents of the statehood bill. Why? They figured they had to do it all over again. And what did they do? They said next time we are going to force people to have to vote.

But guess what they did. This time they said that the only thing we are going to allow the people of Puerto Rico to consider is statehood, yes or no. We are not going to allow them to consider independence. We are not going to allow them to consider free association. We are not going to allow them to consider any other option, non-territorial. That is what Nydia Velázquez's bill does because Nydia Velázquez's bill is based on the pillar of what? Respecting other people's opinion and bringing about consensus so that we can move forward, not the statehood bill.

Listen. I think I might be only one of very few here that was actually in Puerto Rico during the last November election that we celebrated last November. Guess what. The people in Puerto Rico didn't take that referendum seriously. The Department of Justice didn't take the referendum seriously. They promised the people of Puerto Rico that if they voted for statehood and they won, that Congress would immediately allow them to enter as the next state.

I know that is not what they say here, but there is a duality of what they say before the Congress of the United States and what they say on the island of Puerto Rico. I have lived there for the last 21⁄2 years, and I have heard it plenty. I want everyone to understand that when they got a whopping 52 percent—wow, just imagine. You exclude all your opposition. You only give the people one alternative, your alternative, and you get a whopping 52 percent, not quite the mandate I think we would all consider, especially when you get to win because you are the only alternative.

Nydia Velázquez and Ocasio-Cortez allow the people of Puerto Rico to define the status issues, non-territorial, in conjunction with this Committee and with the Congress of the United States so that when it finally happens, it happens for real. And Mr. Chairman, I campaigned for Biden. I campaigned for Biden all across the country. Biden won the election. Biden campaigned for President of the United States saying that he would not listen to that plebiscite, that he would ensure that the only plebiscite he would listen to is one that heard all the different voices. And that is in spite of the fact that he supports statehood for Puerto Rico.

He said, no, I am only going to promote and accept and campaign on the basis of people of Puerto Rico being allowed to freely accept and promote a status that they determined, always and when multiple different versions and the referendum are put before the people of Puerto Rico. You know what? That is Nydia Velázquez's bill. Maybe we should amend it to the Biden bill because it reflects in its entirety what President Biden campaigned on for the people of Puerto Rico.

Listen. The people of the United States of America elected that man, Biden. We should respect the will of the people of the United States of America and allow the people of Puerto Rico to have a free and open discussion. Two other things that I think are important. The proponents of statehood demand that we respect, according to them, their civil rights. But they do not respect the civil rights of the LGBT community in Puerto Rico.

Homophobic slurs are abundant in the rhetoric of the Statehood Party in Puerto Rico. They do not respect the rights of women and her reproductive rights in the legislation in Puerto Rico. They recently had a bill in which they say we will protect the unborn. Everybody knows what that means. Women don't get to decide about their reproductive rights. They went even further, Mr. Chairman, members of the Committee, in saying to the LGBT community, apart from the homophobic slurs that are abundant, they went and said, you know what—We are going to debilitate the right of a gay couple to have a child when they reformed the legislation.

This is a party that demands and says we come before the Congress of the United States demanding equal rights and demanding that our civil rights are protected, but they don't protect the civil rights and the human rights of the people of Puerto Rico. And lastly, let's be clear. The false premise on the basis of which the people of Puerto Rico—they said vote for statehood, and poverty will vanquish. Well, Mr. Chairman, we know since 1971, the 15th Congressional District of the State of New York has had a Puerto Rican in the leadership. That district is the iconic Puerto Rican district. And guess what? Unfortunately and tragically and sadly, it is the poorest congressional district of 435. They have lived statehood for the last 50 years, and yet they are still the poorest. Statehood does not eliminate poverty. What eliminates poverty is the fight against income inequality, raising the minimum wage, and fighting for social justice.

[The prepared statement of Mr. Gutiérrez follows:]

PREPARED STATEMENT OF FORMER CONGRESSMAN LUIS V. GUTIÉRREZ ON H.R. 2070 AND H.R. 1522

Thank you, Chairman Grijalva, Ranking Member Westerman, and members of the House Committee on Natural Resources for this invitation.

Puerto Rico is a nation, a colonized nation. Its colonization began, first under the Spanish Empire in 1493, and then under the U.S. empire in 1898. Puerto Rican identity and nationality was born in resistance to colonialism, and today continues to manifest most brightly in the ongoing struggle for decolonization and self-determination.

Two brilliant and visionary Puerto Rican women have proposed a bill to end the over 122 years of U.S. colonization of Puerto Rico. Representatives Nydia Velazquez and Alexandria Ocasio-Cortez are the embodiment of Lola Rodríguez de Tióand Mariana Bracetti. Their bill outlines a careful and inclusive mechanism whereby Puerto Ricans could establish a constitutional assembly to openly discuss, debate, and ultimate select a non-territorial status option. The Puerto Rico Self-Determination Act of 2021 (H.R. 2070) represents the only genuinely democratic legislation about Puerto Rico's status before the 117th U.S. Congress.

The same cannot be said of the Puerto Rico Statehood Admission Act, which has the support of the pro-statehood party, the Partido Nuevo Progresista (PNP). The proponents of that bill claim that the Puerto Rican people, en masse, support Puerto Rico's admission into the union. But this is not true. While they are quick to report that statehood won the November 2020 referendum with 52% of the vote, they routinely omit that a mere 55% of the Puerto Rican electorate took part, one of the lowest turnouts in recent Puerto Rican history. Like the Statehood Admission Act, the referendum, excluded other non-territorial options. It is now clear that they must exclude to achieve a so-called "majority." You cannot lose if you allow no competition. The 2020 referendum was the second referendum that the PNP steamrolled in the past legislative cycle. In 2017, the PNP put before the Puerto Rican people another exclusionary referendum on statehood, which received an unprecedented 97% for support. Even though they trumpeted this result, no one in Washington or Puerto Rico took it seriously because the referendum was boycotted by nearly 80% of the Puerto Rican electorate. Unable to advance their cause, these zealots for statehood tried a do-over in 2020. In both cases, the PNP controlled house, senate, and governorship disregarded the principled opposition of the Popular Democratic Party, the Puerto Rican Independence Party, and other local political parties. Unsurprisingly, these referendums were widely seen by Puerto Rican civil society as an illegitimate and undemocratic imposition of annexation.

The Partido Nuevo Progresista translates in English to the New Progressive Party. However, there is little progressive about this party. Although it paints itself in Washington as a champion of civil rights, the PNP has often stood against, and at times systematically opposed, civil rights in Puerto Rico. It has long been a bastion of religious fundamentalism and has contributed what one prominent LGBT rights advocate has rightly labeled, "institutionalized homophobia." The PNP was responsible for delaying the extension of anti-discrimination protections to the LGBT community and reluctant to oppose conversion theory. In 2017, as a Member of Congress, I denounced on the House floor the homophobic and transphobic slurs and policies of Thomas Rivera Schatz, the President of the Puerto Rican Senate and a leader of the PNP.

Successive PNP governorships remained silent on the issue of femicide on the island and ignored the demands of women's rights and feminist movements. Only in January of this year, thanks to aggressive activism, did a PNP governor finally declare a state of emergency on femicides against cis- and trans-women. We cannot forget that the ousted and disgraced former governor Ricardo Rossello called former speaker of the New York City Council Melissa Mark Viverito a "puta."

On matters of race, the PNP has little to celebrate. In 2020, a PNP representative used the N-word in the Puerto Rico chamber. After his remarks were challenged, one of his colleagues proposed a resolution that compared him to the great African American civil rights leader, Rosa Parks. It was not that long ago that Heidi Wys Toro, the advisor to Jenniffer Gonzalez, then the President of the Puerto Rico House of Representatives, unleashed a series of racist tweets against then President Barack Obama and first lady Michelle Obama. In one tweet in 2012, Wys Toro wrote: "Who cares? Take her to Burger King, buy her a sundae with double banana, take her to your homeland, Kenya!"

The PNP's leadership, they wish us to forget, expressed fealty to Donald Trump time and time again. But the people of Puerto Rico have not forgotten how Governor Rossello co-signed Trump's minimization of the death toll after Hurricane Maria, in which likely over 4,000 persons lost their lives. The fact that Trump called Mexican immigrants rapists and bad hombres, characterized Central American, Caribbean, and African countries "shitholes," and embolden white supremacists did not stop the resident commissioner of Puerto Rico from becoming the Republican Chairwoman for Latinos for Trump.

The PNP today knows that its electoral influence is waning. It will not soon recover from the historic protests that ousted then Governor Rossello in 2019, after a series of misogynistic, homophobic, and classist messages between him and his advisors were leaked. Perhaps without parallel, over one-third of Puerto Rico's population of three million at some point took to the streets in protest against Rossello and his corrupt administration. What informs the PNP's fanatical and fundamentally anti-democratic quest to impose statehood on Puerto Rico now is not its electoral strength but its fragility. Isn't ironic that Rossello, who was forced to flee the island as governor, was recently elected to become a paid lobbyist in Washington for Puerto Rican statehood to the tune of over $150,000. How is there plenty of money for this disgraced and ousted governor of Puerto Rico while thousands of children go without classrooms and thousands of families on the island go without roofs?

Today, I doubt that proponents of statehood will address these issues. Instead, they will double down on myths they have grown fond of telling. I have already dispelled one of those myths—the claim that statehood has majority support on the island. Again, that is simply not true and must be openly questioned.

Another myth the PNP has told is that statehood is a panacea for Puerto Rico. But it is not. Matters are much more complicated. If Puerto Rico were admitted today into the union, it would become, by far, the poorest of the 51 states. I once asked a Democratic Congressman from Mississippi on our way to vote, why he supported statehood? His response was: "I'm tired of Mississippi being called the poorest state. That honor will now go to Puerto Rico." Even so, the PNP love to tell the Puerto Rican people that statehood would end poverty. As a matter of fact, a leading advocate for statehood and former resident commissioner and governor of Puerto Rico, the late Romero Barcelo authored a book titled, *Statehood is for the Poor*. Yet, they do not offer an explanation as to why Puerto Ricans in the diaspora remain among the poorest and most marginalized populations in U.S. society after having lived statehood for several generations. On many occasions, statehood supporters have told those of us who live in the U.S. that we have enjoyed the benefits of statehood by living in a state, benefits we would denied them. It saddens me that after 50 years of Puerto Rican congressional representation—Herman Badillo, Robert Garcia, JoséSerrano, and today Richie Torres—the 15th Congressional District in the Bronx remains the poorest district of all the 50 states. Unsurprising, the 2020 referendum offered voters no details about what statehood would entail, economically or culturally. Unlike the Admission Act, the Puerto Rican Self-Determination Act explicitly demands that voters receive detailed information about each of the status options and their implications for Puerto Rican society.

The PNP has also expressed a most damaging myth: Puerto Ricans and Puerto Rico are just any other group of Americans. They deny that Puerto Rico is a nation, that Puerto Ricans are a people. Kenneth McClintock, one of the senior statesmen of the PNP, recently made this point to me at a debate in Puerto Rico. It should then come as no surprise that the PNP is willing to sell off Puerto Rico, its beaches and historic buildings, to the highest binder and openly calls for the privatization of public utilizes and social services. Contrary to this self-hating and colonial position, I affirm that Puerto Ricans have a language, a history, a culture, and a proud legacy of resistance against both Spanish and U.S. colonization. If Puerto Rico were not a nation, what explains the swiftness of the response of Puerto Ricans in Chicago, Orlando, and New York after Hurricane Maria? Why do Puerto Ricans, wherever they happen to reside, raise their mono-starred flag and take pride in the athletic, musical, and intellectual achievements of their fellow Puerto Ricans. Throughout Puerto Rico and its diaspora, schools and colleges are named after individuals that affirmed Puerto Rican identity and self-determination, such as Julia de Burgos, Eugenio Maria de Hostos, Josêde Diego, and Albizu Campos. Eighty-four years after Rafael Hernández Marín composed and penned "*Preciosa*," the song still stirs the hearts of Puerto Ricans. I remember my parents singing, "*Preciosa te llaman los bardos/Que cantan tu historia/No importa el tirano te trate/Con negra maldad*." The same is true about the lament, "*En Mi Viejo San Juan*." Decades from now, our children may add Bad Bunny's "*Estamos Bien*" to this patriotic catalogue.

We are a nation, and many of us refuse to relinquish or cancel our nationality, as the PNP seems to desire. All these myths rest on a peculiar and distorted history of Puerto Rico. It is a history that downplays the painful reality of U.S. colonization. There is no accounting for the history of political persecution, assassinations, massacres, imprisonments meted out to those that believe and struggle for Puerto Rican independence and self-determination. Look up "La Ley de la Mordaza," which made it illegal to advocate and organize for Puerto Rican independence. They say nothing about the mass sterilization of Puerto Rican women or the bombing in Vieques, which has led to high levels of cancer among the population. Are we to forget that when the U.S. invaded Puerto Rico, our Caribbean archipelago had already secured a Charter of Autonomy between itself and Spain and that American conquistadors believed Puerto Ricans were incapable of self-rule? Can we forget how the U.S. divided up the island among U.S. sugar barons and made English the official language? Can we forget how the Jones Act imposed U.S. citizenship on Puerto Rico, against the expressed will of the only Puerto Rican representative body on the island at the time, and how citizenship gave us the "right" to die in foreign wars? Should we forget the series of Organic acts and Supreme Court decisions that determined that Puerto Rico belonged to but was not a part of the United States, a position based racist and eugenicist ideas about a "mongrel" race?

In conclusion, we cannot decolonize Puerto Rico without a genuinely democratic and inclusive process. That is precisely what Nydia Velazquez and Alexandria Ocasio-Cortez's Puerto Rico Self-Determination Act offers. We have had 500 years — over half of a millennia—of colonial oppression. However, today, the PNP opposes this measure and seeks to impose annexation and force assimilation. They claim to have a mandate but over two-thirds of the Puerto Rican electorate voted against their gubernatorial candidate. The PNP refuses to come to the table and collaborate, in good faith, with the other parties and political orientations to resolve the status of Puerto Rico. Instead, they have told many myths and falsehoods in airwaves in Puerto Rico and in the halls of Congress. Both Congress and Puerto Rico deserve better. Thankfully, we have an alternative path. I urge the U.S. Congress to endorse the Puerto Rican Self-Determination bill. It is a bill that can help ensure a better, more just, and decolonized future for Puerto Rico. And that is the future I will continue to fight for.

Thank you, Chairman Grijalva, Ranking Member Westerman, and members of the House Committee on Natural Resources for your time and consideration.

The CHAIRMAN. The gentleman yields. Thank you, and to the other folks, I will provide the courtesy of extending time.

Let me now recognize Dr. Rafael Cox Alomar, Professor of Constitutional Law at the University of the District of Columbia. Doctor, you are recognized.

STATEMENT OF RAFAEL COX ALOMAR, PROFESSOR OF CONSTITUTIONAL LAW, UNIVERSITY OF THE DISTRICT OF COLUMBIA, WASHINGTON, DC

Dr. COX ALOMAR. Mr. Chairman, thank you so much. Due to the fact that the DOJ only recently published its legal opinions on both bills, I find it necessary to devote my opening statement to addressing some of the more salient conclusions put forward by the Department of Justice in its legal memoranda. Observation No. 1, while highly persuasive, DOJ opinions on territorial issues are not binding or controlling on Congress.

Congress alone possesses constitutional authority to make all needful rules and regulations respecting the territories. When the framers assembled in Philadelphia in the summer of 1787, they agreed to delegate the exclusive authority over the territories to the legislative branch, not to the executive branch. This Committee should be mindful of this nuance because it goes to the heart of America's separation of powers arrangement.

Observation No. 2, along similar lines, the Supreme Court alone and not the DOJ is the final interpreter of the Federal Constitution. Chief Justice Marshall hinted that in *Marbury v. Madison.*

Observation No. 3, international law in the words of Justice Gray in the Paquete Habana case is part of our law. Under both the United Nations charter and the International Convention on Civil and Political Rights, the United States is bound to decolonize Puerto Rico if its people so choose. The Department of Justice's opinions leave this aspect of the conversation untouched.

This is highly problematic because, after all, Puerto Rico came under U.S. sovereignty pursuant to an international treaty, namely the Treaty of Paris of 1899, and the United Nations has never fully relinquished its authority to revisit the Puerto Rico case per its authority under the charter, which is an international agreement which was ratified by the U.S. Senate.

Observation No. 4, while it is true as the Department of Justice so addressed, that the territory is a constitutional option, nothing in the Constitution requires its inclusion in the ballot. The inclusion or rejection of the territorial option is a matter of policy. It is not a matter of constitutional law.

Observation No. 5, although free association shares important foundational elements with full independence, it must be distinguished from independence in significant respects as the International Court of Justice has intimated in the Namibia and Western Sahara cases. No one could possibly suggest that Palau or the Republic of the Marshall Islands are on an equal footing with East Timor, now fully independent from Indonesia, or that Greenland's legal status is identical to that of Denmark or that Curacao or St. Martin enjoy the same political arrangement as the independent Republic of Suriname, also a former Dutch colony. Under free association, Puerto Rico would be sovereign in an international sense but still be bound to the United States on the basis of a unique relationship carved out by both contracting parties in light of their geostrategic needs and realities.

This Committee should be well-advised to look at the various free association arrangements around the world, in particular the British, the Dutch, the Danish, and the Finnish. There is no one-size-fits-all approach with respect to free association as the DOJ appears to suggest.

Observation No. 6, and finally, the DOJ's contention that PROMESA is not incompatible with statehood raises very tough questions of first impression under the so-called Equal Footing Doctrine. In the final analysis, if history has taught us anything, it is that the resolution of the Puerto Rico status conundrum is not so much a constitutional issue as it is an issue of political will or lack thereof. Thank you so much, Mr. Chairman.

[The prepared statement of Dr. Cox Alomar follows:]

Prepared Statement of Rafael Cox Alomar, Professor of Law, David A. Clarke School of Law, University of the District of Columbia, Washington, DC

Introduction

Chairman Grijalva, Ranking Member Westerman, and distinguished members of the Committee on Natural Resources. Thank you for inviting me to testify today. I am a professor of law at the David A. Clarke School of Law of the University of the District of Columbia in Washington, DC, where I teach Constitutional Law and Public International Law, among other topics. Furthermore, this coming Winter I will teach a course on American Constitutionalism and the Insular Cases at Harvard Law School. I am, moreover, the author of *The Puerto Rico Constitution* (Oxford University Press, 2022) (forthcoming) and *Revisiting the Transatlantic Triangle: The Constitutional Decolonization of the Eastern Caribbean* (Ian Randle Publishers, 2009). I am also the co-author of *The Law of the U.S. Territories* (Carolina Academic Press, 2023). I appear regularly as a constitutional law analysist for CNN *En Español*, France 24, and NTN24.

Congress' Constitutional Power to Chart a Decolonizing Path for Puerto Rico

The time is ripe for Congress to take stock of the seminal lessons stemming from the long string of failed attempts at disentangling Puerto Rico's political status conundrum.

The first lesson that must be clearly understood is that the Constitution vests in Congress plenary power to chart, along with the people of Puerto Rico, a path for achieving the island's decolonization. The language chosen by the founders in Philadelphia leaves little room for equivocation: "The Congress shall have power to dispose of and make all needful rules and regulations respecting the territory or other property belonging to the United States." (U.S. Const. Art. IV, Sec. 3, Cl. 2). Thus, it is not incumbent on the judiciary or the executive branches to articulate a decolonizing solution for Puerto Rico. Only Congress bears that constitutional responsibility. Decolonizing Puerto Rico is both a moral and legal imperative, consistent with the corpus of anti-colonial values leading the founders to overthrow (in the words of Jefferson) George III's "absolute tyranny"[1] in order to form a "more perfect union."[2] Decolonizing Puerto Rico, moreover, is consistent with the treaty obligations of the United States pursuant to the International Convention on Civil and Political Rights[3] and the U.N. Charter.[4]

Puerto Rico Presents a Unique Territorial Case-Study

The second lesson that must be clearly understood is that the case of Puerto Rico finds no parallel in the territorial architecture of the United States.

Puerto Rico is not the District of Columbia nor is it similarly situated to the Native American nations.

The District is a community culturally and linguistically intertwined to the mainland, devoid of a sovereignty movement, which came to life upon the founding of the Republic per the strictures of Article I, Section 8 of the federal Constitution. Puerto Rico is unlike the Virgin Islands. By the time the United States signed the treaty of cession with the Danish Kingdom in 1916,[5] the Virgin Islands were subject to an excessively centralized colonial system devoid of any quantum of self-government under the Danish colonial statute of 1863.[6] Puerto Rico, to the contrary, was a fully autonomous overseas province of the Spanish Kingdom[7] upon the U.S.'s invasion in 1898; remaining to this day a more

[1] Refer to the text of the 1776 Declaration of Independence.

[2] U.S. Const. Preamble.

[3] 99 U.N.T.S. 171 (1966). Note that the U.S. Senate ratified the Convention on Civil and Political Rights on June 8, 1992—subject to a series of reservations. Refer to 138 Cong. Rec. S4781-01 (1992). Of significance is the fact that the U.S. Senate, in exercising its constitutional prerogative of advice and consent, explicitly established that Articles 1 through 27 of the Convention are not self-executing. This notwithstanding, the United States is legally bound to the self-determination principles enshrined in the Convention.

[4] Refer to Articles 2, 55 and 56 of the U.N. Charter. Note that the U.S. Senate ratified the U.N. Charter on July 28, 1945.

[5] For the ratification instruments refer to 39 Stat. 1706 (1917). Note that the U.S. Senate ratified the cession treaty with Denmark on September 7, 1916. The Danish Kingdom, for its part, followed suit on December 22, 1916.

[6] For the metes and bounds of the 1863 Danish colonial legislation see, for instance, Virgin Islands: Hearing, Committee on Insular Affairs, H.R. 7183 and H.R. 8517 (1926), 1 et seq.

[7] Carta Autonómica de 1897 (Charter of Autonomy of 1897), issued by Spanish Queen María Cristina de Habsburgo y Lorena, on the advice of her Council of Ministers, on November 25, 1897.

complex political jigsaw puzzle than its immediate neighbors—hostage, as it is, to a wide universe of ideological movements on constant collision against each other.

On that same token, Puerto Rico is not Guam. While the Spanish Crown transferred its sovereignty over both jurisdictions to the United States pursuant to the 1898 Treaty of Paris,[8] in Guam there was no civil government until 1950[9] and it has, since then, been governed "not by a formal constitution but by an organic act"[10] of Congress—free from the ideological balkanization that has torn apart Puerto Rico's political milieu since 1898.

Puerto Rico, furthermore, is not American Samoa. Since their annexation to the United States, following the signing of the 1899 Tripartite Convention among Great Britain, Germany and the United States,[11] the people of American Samoa have plodded along a different territorial path than Puerto Rico—devoid of U.S. citizenship, governed by an organic act of Congress and still in the United Nations' List of Non-Self-Governing Territories.[12]

Puerto Rico, moreover, is unlike the Commonwealth of the Northern Mariana Islands and, most noticeably, dissimilar to the Republic of the Marshall Islands, the Republic of Palau, and the Federated States of Micronesia. These jurisdictions, originally placed under the fiduciary care of the U.N. Trust Territory of the Pacific Islands (which came to life in 1947 under the aegis of the U.N. Security Council), deserve separate analysis. By the time the U.N. Security Council appointed the United States as their trustee,[13] Puerto Rico was at the verge of electing its own governor (pursuant to the 1947 Elective Governor Act)[14] — soon to convene a Constitutional Convention for drafting an internal constitution of its own making.[15] Against this background, it is safe to conclude that history, geography, culture, language, politics, demographics, and economics have conspired to make Puerto Rico a unique case study within the U.S.'s wider territorial tapestry. Thus, Puerto Rico's unique location within the U.S.'s territorial topography requires a unique decolonizing solution—not inconsistent with the United States'

---

[8] 30 Stat. 1754 (1898).

[9] See Arnold Leibowitz, *Defining Status* (2013), 307.

[10] 48 U.S.C. §§ 1421–24.

[11] For the text of the Tripartite Convention, concluded on November 7, 1899, see Malloy, Treaties, Conventions, International Acts, Protocols and Agreements between the United States and Other Powers 1776-1909, Vol. II, 1576 (1910).

[12] Puerto Rico was removed from the U.N.'s List of Non-Self-Governing Territories in 1953. Refer to G.A. Res. 748 (VIII), U.N. GAOR, 8th Sess., Supp. No. 17, at 25, U.N. Doc A/2630 (Nov. 27, 1953).

[13] Refer to the statement made by the U.S. Representative to the U.N.'s Security Council on presentation of the Trust Agreement, available at 2 U.N. SCOR (113th mtg.) 410 (1947).

[14] 61 Stat. 770 (1947).

[15] 64 Stat. 319 (1950) (most commonly known as Public Law 600). Public Law 600 was enacted "in the nature of a compact" between Congress and the people of Puerto Rico. Following its ratification in a local referendum held on June 4, 1951, the constitution-making process began in earnest. Delegates to the Constitutional Convention were elected on August 27, 1951. The newly drafted Constitution, while ratified by the people of Puerto Rico on March 3, 1952, was unilaterally modified by Congress—which finally ratified it on July 3, 1952. The Commonwealth's Constitution was finally inaugurated on July 25, 1952. PROMESA has significantly eviscerated the vitality of the 1952 Constitution.

constitutional arrangement, but carefully designed to address the unique characteristics of the Puerto Rican landscape.

Designing a Binding Procedural Mechanism Is of the Essence

All federal initiatives for disentangling Puerto Rico's colonial knot have so far foundered, in no small measure, due to flawed procedural mechanisms. That is why there can be no serious talk of self-determination without first discussing process.

Therein lie the failed experiences of the 1959 Fernós-Murray bill,[16] the 1963 Aspinall bill[17] (leading President Johnson to appoint the failed status commission of 1966),[18] the 1973 Ad Hoc Advisory Group on Puerto Rico's Status appointed by President Nixon,[19] the 1989–1991 Bennett Johnston-Ron De Lugo bills,[20] the 1997 Young bill,[21] along with the more recent bills authored by the island's resident commissioner and various members of the U.S. House.[22] Furthermore, none of the 5 local plebiscites held in the island prior to 2020 (namely in 1967,[23] 1993,[24] 1998,[25] 2012[26] and 2017[27]) have led anywhere. And the 2020 "statehood yes or no" vote will also die a quiet death much like its predecessors.

Those who forget the lessons of history, in the words of the Spanish essayist Jorge Santayana y Borrás, are condemned to repeat their mistakes. Thus, fresh thinking is of the essence. The path leading to local (or *criollo*) referenda must be irrevocably discarded. These are but exercises in the dark, not binding on Congress. Under this mechanism, the

---

[16] A bill to provide amendments to the compact between the people of Puerto Rico and the United States, H.R. 5926, 86th Cong., 1st sess. (1959).

[17] To establish a procedure for the prompt settlement, in a democratic manner, of the political status of Puerto Rico, H.R. 5945, 88th Cong., 1st sess., (1963).

[18] United States-Puerto Rico Commission on the Status of Puerto Rico, Report of the United States-Puerto Rico Commission on the Status of Puerto Rico (Washington, DC.: Government Printing Office, 1966).

[19] See Report of the Ad Hoc Advisory Group on Puerto Rico, October 1, 1975. Also consult H.R. 11200, 121 Cong., 1st sess. (1975) (To approve the Compact of Permanent Union between Puerto Rico and the United States). Memorandum from Jim Cannon to President Gerald Ford (Office of the Domestic Policy Advisor, October 28, 1976) (Ford Presidential Library).

[20] To provide for a referendum on the political status of Puerto Rico, S. 712, 101 Cong., 1st sess. (1989); Puerto Rico Status Referendum Act, S. 244, 102 Cong., 1st sess. (1991); To enable the people of Puerto Rico to exercise self-determination, H.R. 4765, 101 Cong., 2nd sess. (1990).

[21] United States-Puerto Rico Political Status Act, H.R. 856, 105th Congress (1997).

[22] H.R. 2070 (along with its sister bill in the U.S. Senate) and H.R. 1522.

[23] July 23, 1967: "Enhanced" Commonwealth 60.41%, Statehood 38.98%, Independence 0.60%. Note that the Puerto Rico Independence Party boycotted the 1967 plebiscite.

[24] November 14, 1993: "Enhanced" Commonwealth 48.89%, Statehood 46.64%, Independence 4.47%.

[25] December 13, 1998: None of the Above 50.46%, Statehood 46.63%, Independence 2.55%, Free Association 0.29%, Territorial Status 0.06%.

[26] 54% voted against the territorial status quo. A sizable proportion of voters abstained from casting their ballots on the plebiscite's second question, following the Popular Democratic Party's boycott of that aspect of the local process. Against that background, Statehood 61.16%, so-called Estado Libre Asociado Soberano 33.34%, Independence 5.49%.

[27] June 11, 2017: following the boycott of the Popular Democratic Party and the Independence Party, voter turnout plummeted to 23%. Against that background, Statehood received 97% of those ballots cast.

people of Puerto Rico would cast their ballots without knowing what each formula entails. How can the people of Puerto Rico seriously exercise their inalienable right to self-determination in a *referendo criollo* if they do not know for what they are voting for? It is well settled that defining the substantive scope of the status formulas requires Congress' active participation in the process. Thus, from a procedural perspective, there are only 2 viable options for Puerto Rico. On the one hand, a federal plebiscite (with detailed definitions already agreed upon with Congress) and, on the other, a status convention (also referred as the constitutional convention). It is essential to note that these procedural options are not, necessarily, mutually exclusive. The federal plebiscite option would require, moreover, voting resolutions in Congress for the expedited consideration, and subsequent execution, of the results. Due to the tight timetable of biannual congressional elections, putting in place the expedited consideration mechanism will infuse the necessary continuity to a process that might take several years. The option of the federal plebiscite, however, would be patently incomplete without a congressional bilateral negotiation commission insulated from the vagaries of congressional elections and local politics. Because the life of the status convention would be independent from Congress' and Puerto Rico's electoral cycles, it achieves the twin goals of stability and continuity more effectively than the federal plebiscite option. The Committee on Natural Resources would be well advised to seriously consider the status convention approach delineated in the Velázquez-Ocasio Cortés Bill.

Far from silencing those voices opposing statehood, the Velázquez-Ocasio Cortés Bill opens the door to an inclusive and democratic mechanism for all ideological movements. Pursuant to H.R. 2070, Congress acknowledges the inherent authority of Puerto Rico's Legislature to call a status convention and, moreover, commits itself to consider the self-determination option chosen by the people of Puerto Rico in a final status referendum. This new procedural approach avoids the mistakes of the past, while opening the door to in-depth deliberations and negotiations between the people of Puerto Rico and the political branches in Washington. Far from un-American, the status convention is the most American of all plausible procedural mechanisms.

Congress Ought Not Act upon the Results of the November 2020 Referendum

The November 2020 referendum was not a legitimate exercise of self-determination. Puerto Rico Law No. 51 of May 16, 2020 was an empty statute. It did not define a path to statehood. It failed to describe the transitional period for the application to Puerto Rico of the Tax Uniformity Clause, which requires that "all Duties, Imposts and Excises shall be uniform throughout the United States." (U.S. Const. Art. I, Sec. 8, Cl. 1). Puerto Rico

Law No. 51 left the people of Puerto Rico (and those legal persons established under the laws of the Commonwealth) in the dark, with respect to their tax liabilities under statehood. Nowhere did it address the phasing out of the various tax preference programs currently in full force and effect in Puerto Rico. Equally importantly, Puerto Rico Law No. 51 remained silent as to which specific provisions of the Puerto Rico Constitution, and the Federal Relations Act, might be preempted by the full application to Puerto Rico of the federal Constitution; nor did it enumerate the federal statutes currently not applying to Puerto Rico but that would apply to the island under the federal Constitution's equal footing requirement. Similarly, the cultural, linguistic, and debt-restructuring aspects of the equation were left untouched. As Deputy Attorney General Jeffrey Rosen correctly concluded, Puerto Rico Law No. 51 is not compatible with the Constitution, laws, and policies of the United States.[28] It is a "decidedly pro-Statehood"[29] bill, designed to further the governing party's political interests at the 2020 local election. Unsurprisingly, the referendum was held on election day— namely November 3, 2020.

Non-Territory Status Options[30]

Non-Territory Status options, by definition, are not susceptible to Congress' plenary powers under the Territory Clause (U.S. Const. Art. IV, Sec. 3, Cl. 2). Clearly, independence is a non-territory status option. Needless to say, upon the proclamation of the Republic of Puerto Rico all obligations and responsibilities of the U.S. Government, arising under the 1898 Treaty of Paris, shall cease. Sovereignty, in the international sense, will devolve to the people of Puerto Rico. Independence, however, will require a bilateral transition commission addressing a host of seminal matters pertaining to the public debt, monetary policy, foreign relations, defense and security, international commerce, accession to multilateral financial institutions, citizenship, the phasing-out of a number of federal programs, among others. The precedents of Cuba (1902)[31] and the

[28] Letter authored by Deputy Attorney General Jeffrey Rosen, dated July 29, 2020.

[29] *Id.*

[30] Mindful that the Committee on Natural Resources has requested an opinion with respect to status options outside the reach of the Territory Clause, the author has refrained from discussing in extenso whether it is constitutionally viable for Congress and the people of Puerto Rico to enhance their current relationship through the devolution of further political authority to Puerto Rico within the federal framework. Pursuant to this formulation, sovereignty would not be transferred to Puerto Rico, but the island would no longer be subject to Congress' plenary powers under the Territory Clause. The constitutionality (let alone the desirability from a public policy perspective) of Congress' partial disposition of its powers under the Territory Clause has been the subject of intense debate. The DOJ's answer to this legal question has been far from consistent. (Compare the legal opinions rendered by the DOJ in 1960, 1963, 1975 with the ones issued in 1991 and 1994.) This notwithstanding, the recent concurrent opinion of Justice Sonia Sotomayor in *Financial Oversight and Management Board v. Aurelius*, 590 U.S. (2020), bringing to the fore the glaring discontinuities and inconsistencies surrounding this debate, justifies revisiting this legal issue in light of Justice Sotomayor's observations.

[31] Note that Cuba never belonged to the United States. Pursuant to a Joint Resolution of Congress (commonly referred as the Teller Amendment), the United States had made it clear that the people of Cuba "are, of right

Philippines (1946)[32] are inapposite to the Puerto Rican context. The uniqueness of the Puerto Rican landscape, bound to the United States through common citizenship in the midst of a highly interdependent global economy, will require a different transitional approach to the one applied in the cases of Cuba and the Philippines.

Statehood is yet another non-territory status option. It is well settled that states are sovereign entities within the Republic's federal design. Each state accedes to the Union on an equal footing with its sister states, retaining for itself an inviolable quantum of sovereignty, as Madison acknowledged in his drafting of the 10th Amendment. State sovereignty, moreover, is not commensurate to "international sovereignty." As the Supreme Court has suggested on various occasions, states are "autonomous political entities, sovereign over matters not ruled by the Constitution."[33] The path to statehood, as suggested above, will also require a well-defined transitional period. If Puerto Rico chooses to bear the economic burdens of statehood, it must do so on the basis of an informed decision.

Besides independence and statehood, free association is the third non-territorial option. Seldomly explored, the concept of free association deserves serious analysis. Free association, as a legal construct, is not foreign to federal constitutional law or to public international law. Yet, neither legal order offers detailed guidance on the substantive content of free association. Bearing in mind that the decisions of the International Court of Justice (ICJ) constitute sources of public international law,[34] it is worth noting that in its advisory opinion in the case of Western Sahara[35] the ICJ found that "free association with an independent state" was a legitimate decolonizing formula. U.N. Resolution 1541(XV) throws little light on the metes and bounds of free association. It only establishes that free association must be "the result of a free and voluntary choice by the people of the territory concerned," that the associated territory retains for itself both "the freedom to modify its status through the expression of its will," and "the right to determine its internal constitution without outside interference."[36] Public international law does not explicitly establish any further requirements. Thus, it is up to the contracting parties to carve out a free association model not inconsistent with their respective domestic legal orders and public policy imperatives. Under a free association arrangement, Congress would relinquish its sovereignty over Puerto Rico—devolving it

---

ought to be, free and independent." H.J. Res. 233 (1898). In the aftermath of the Spanish-American War, the United States formally occupied Cuba from January 1, 1899 until May 20, 1902. Yet, the process leading to the drafting of the 1901 Cuban Constitution, including the incorporation of the so-called Platt Amendment to Cuba's constitutional text, was heavily influenced by the United States.

[32] The 1916 Philippines Organic, different from the 1917 Jones Act, did not extend U.S. citizenship to the nationals of the Filipino archipelago.

[33] *Rodríguez v. Popular Democratic Party*, 457 U.S. 1, 8 (1982).

[34] For the sources of public international law see, for instance, Article 38 of the Statute of the International Court of Justice. Also refer to Section 102 of the Restatement (Third) of the Foreign Relations Law of the United States.

[35] Western Sahara, Advisory Opinion, I.C.J. Reports 1975.

[36] Declaration Guiding the Determination of Self-Government, G.A. Res. 1541 (XV) (Annex) of December 15, 1960, 15 U.N. GAOR, Supp. (No. 14), U.N. Doc. A/4684.

to the people of Puerto Rico. Consequently, the United States' international obligations, under the 1898 Treaty of Paris, would come to an end. Simultaneously, Puerto Rico (in the exercise of its newly devolved sovereignty) and the United States (through the political branches' exercise of their constitutional powers under the Treaty Clause (U.S. Const. Art. II, Sec. 2)) shall enter into a new constitutional order—where Puerto Rico would reserve for itself authority over some matters, while delegating to the United States authority over other areas. Defining the various fields of legal responsibility (i.e., economic relations, foreign affairs, defense, and security) will require in-depth study and comprehensive negotiation between the parties. The final associational agreement, moreover, would be embodied in an international treaty subscribed by both contracting parties. Whether the treaty of association ought to be self-executing or non-self-executing, requiring Congress to enact enabling domestic legislation, should be determined by the parties in the course of their negotiations. The Department of Justice's (DOJ) superficial reading of free association must be taken to task. Seeking refuge in the compacts of free association of the Marshall Islands, Palau and the Federated States of Micronesia with the United States, the DOJ has tossed aside free association as a "type of independence."[37] This uncritical approach has led to a rather skewed notion of how to superimpose to the Puerto Rican landscape a free association arrangement. A close perusal of the various free association models available around the globe renders the DOJ's analysis patently incomplete. There is no fixed approach to free association nor is there a fixed model. Each model is autochthonous, thus, adjusted to the specific realities of the partners. Construing a viable free association model for Puerto Rico requires a thorough exploration of the ways in which other jurisdictions have structured similar arrangements. Contrary to conventional wisdom, the Micronesian model is inapposite to the Puerto Rican scenario. The Micronesian archipelago, unlike Puerto Rico, was part of the territories entrusted to the U.N. Trust Territory of the Pacific Islands in the early stages of the postwar period. Consequently, its politico-constitutional relationship with the United States is completely different to Puerto Rico's. As a threshold matter, no common citizenship binds the Micronesian archipelago to the United States, while issues pertaining to geography, demographics, culture, language, and economics further sets it apart from Puerto Rico. Against this background, it is essential to explore the associational models engineered in other jurisdictions. More specifically, the associational models articulated by Denmark,[38] Finland,[39] the Netherlands,[40] and Britain[41] in decolonizing their territorial peripheries deserve special attention. The process of carving out an associational model for Puerto Rico will necessarily entail resolving

[37] See, for instance, Report by the President's Task Force on Puerto Rico's Status (Washington, D.C.: White House, 2011), 25.

[38] Act on Greenland Self-Government, Act. No. 473 of June 12, 2009 (Green.).

[39] Act on the Autonomy of A° land, 1991/1144 (1991) (Fin.).

[40] Statuut voor het Koninkrijk der Nederlanden [Charter for the Kingdom of the Netherlands], Stb. 1954 (Neth.).

[41] Statute of Westminster, 1931, 22&23 Geo. 5, c. 4 (Eng.). Also consult the West Indies Act of 1967, 11&12 Eliz. 2, c. 4 (Eng.).

complex legal and policy issues. In so doing, Congress should not limit itself to the "one size fits all" approach the DOJ proposes with respect to free association.

Conclusion

The resolution of Puerto Rico's status is not so much a legal issue, as it is a political one. This is not a legal question for the U.S. Supreme Court to decide, as the high court itself recently intimated in *Financial Oversight and Management Board v. Aurelius*,[42] but rather a political question that will require a political compromise between Congress and the people of Puerto Rico. Achieving this goal necessarily requires a new procedural approach. The time for non-binding local plebiscites is over. Only a status convention, with equitable participation from all Puerto Rican stakeholders, will command sufficient legitimacy in Washington, San Juan, and around the world, to jumpstart Puerto Rico's decolonization. Because H.R. 2070 offers the appropriate procedural vehicle for achieving that aim within the context of an inclusive political mechanism, this Committee ought to support it.

The CHAIRMAN. The gentleman yields. Thank you very much, Doctor.

The next witness is the Director of the Caribbean Institute of Human Rights in San Juan, Puerto Rico, Ms. Annette Martínez-Orabona. Five minutes are yours.

STATEMENT OF ANNETTE MARTÍNEZ-ORABONA, DIRECTOR, CARIBBEAN INSTITUTE OF HUMAN RIGHTS, SAN JUAN, PUERTO RICO

Ms. MARTíNEZ-ORABONA. Good afternoon, Chairman Grijalva, and members of the Committee. My name is Annette Martínez-Orabona, and I am an international human rights law professor at the Inter American University of Puerto Rico School of Law. This is not the first time that Congress engages in a discussion of the political future of Puerto Rico. But one fundamental aspect that is repeatedly missing in this discussion is that self-determination is first and foremost a fundamental human right, which is well-defined by specific international norms.

This set of norms has been accepted by the United States when it signed and ratified one of the most important international human rights treaties, the International Covenant on Civil and Political Rights, which very clearly establishes, under Article 1, the right to self-determination. This means that self-determination is not a matter of purely internal or domestic jurisdiction.

[42] *Financial Oversight and Management Board v. Aurelius*, 590 U.S. ____ (2020).

It is actually a matter of international relations, and it is important to emphasize this particular difference. This is not a matter of minority rights, but a matter of a distinct people with a distinct identity, a distinct territory under colonial rule for over 123 years.

H.R. 2070 actually does include this recognition of the international law as a matter of importance for this discussion. What this also means is that administrative states are not free to decide when and how self-determination is to be exercised. Under international law, self-determination is a legal entitlement recognized to peoples in colonized territories. And its valid exercise entails obligations of conduct and obligations of outcome.

In terms of the duty of conduct, we are talking about conditions present in the territory at the time of the exercise of self-determination, as well as the process itself, which needs to be transparent, participatory, and it needs to reflect the clear understanding of what the options are and the level of participation that leaves no doubt as to the will of the people.

And it is important to recognize as well that the conditions present in a territory may affect the legitimacy of a process. A process of decolonization should not be presented as a desperate possibility of survival. Administrative states have a responsibility of a fiduciary character, which requires the adoption of measures designed to advance the economic, social, and cultural freedoms of the peoples in these territories.

Conditions of economic freedom and stability are necessary so that political self-determination does not become a futile, invalid exercise. In other words, economic dependency, poverty, and starvation may inhabilitate the free exercise of this right. In this sense, I may say the imposition of the Financial Oversight Board was a step in the wrong direction and runs contrary to the international obligations of the state which require more independent, democratic means of governance, not less.

Secondly, decolonization is a matter that requires an environment of mutual trust where both parties interact as equals, each exercising their full autonomy and sovereign powers. In that sense, the United States needs first to rectify the record of what happened in 1952, providing accurate and up-to-date information on the current status of Puerto Rico to the United Nations and secondly, recognizing that the people of Puerto Rico are a distinct nation with a sovereign right to self-determination.

In terms of the options identified under international law as acceptable decolonization outcomes, there are three very straight-forward, clear alternatives which are independence, free association, and integration with another state. It should be clear, though, that the right to self-determination does not allow for a colonial relationship to remain intact. This means that in the case of Puerto Rico, any inclusion of an option of a territorial character that will maintain the status quo is not a valid option of decolonization. International law explicitly prohibits colonialism by consent.

In the case of integration, the international community has always been suspicious of a non-self-governing territory's integration into its former colonial power for very obvious reasons. In fact, of the approximately 100 non-self-governing territories that have been placed on the U.N. list since 1945, around 70 have gained independence and integration with the former colonial power.

To finalize, I would like to add that any process of decolonization must be accompanied by a transitional plan that expels out the international responsibility of the United States and guarantees measures of redress with concrete reparations for the multiple human rights violations committed during its colonial rule.

Thank you.

[The prepared statement of Ms. Martínez-Orabona follows:]

PREPARED STATEMENT OF ANNETTE M. MARTÍNEZ-ORABONA, ADJUNCT PROFESSOR OF INTERNATIONAL PUBLIC LAW, INTER-AMERICAN UNIVERSITY OF PUERTO RICO, SCHOOL OF LAW

Good afternoon, Chairman Grijalva and members of the House Committee on Natural Resources, my name is Annette Martínez-Orabona, and I am an International Human Rights lawyer and Professor at the Inter-American University of Puerto Rico, School of Law. I hereby submit my written statement on the international public law aspects of decolonization and the United States' responsibility to respect and guarantee Puerto Rico's right of self-determination, as a fundamental aspect of human rights law.

Introduction

For decades, there have been numerous discussions and debates on the political future of Puerto Rico, some of which have led to local referendums, legislative efforts, a presidential task force, many congressional hearings, among others, and none of them have provided any meaningful result.

It is my view that these efforts have been flawed from the start. All of them repeatedly ignored a basic and fundamental aspect of political determination in international law. That is, that the exercise of self-determination is first and foremost an exercise of sovereignty, and should be guided by the international normative framework on decolonization.

Additionally, in the case of Puerto Rico, as well as has happened with many former colonies, the exercise of colonial rule has been accompanied with the erosion of the rule of law, allowing for the unilateral exploitation of natural resources, the imposition of inadequate economic standards, commercial impediments, land appropriation, and environmental degradation, which often results in internal displacement, contamination, discriminatory practices, inequality, poverty and overall conditions of vulnerability for present and future generations.

The reason why I am including these two areas in my exposition is because they are inextricably interrelated. The fact that the United States has limited Puerto Rico's exercise of its own economic and sovereign powers has led to a distinct result with regard to the practice of self-determination, but it has also had an effect on the human rights and the dignity of all Puerto Ricans. Colonial rule, only operates for the benefit of the colonial power, and that is why the practice of colonialism has been strongly rejected by international law.

The Right to Self-Determination, Decolonization and Acceptable Options for a Non-Territory Status

The right to self-determination has many manifestations, but its most robust legal content is found in the decolonization context. Under international law, self-determination is a legal entitlement recognized to all colonized peoples. This right is considered a general principle of international law, as well as a customary norm that has been expressly incorporated into multiple human rights treaties. Furthermore, the International Court of Justice has reiterated its erga omnes character.[43] Today it is widely considered a norm of *ius cogens*.[44]

Art. 1 of the International Covenant on Civil and Political Rights,[45] which is binding on the United States, expressly recognizes this right and imposes specific duties for its realization. Specifically, Article 1(3) expresses that all States that assumed "responsibility for the administration of Non-Self Governing and Trust Territories, shall promote the realization of the right of self-determination, and shall respect that right, in conformity with the provisions of the Charter of the United Nations."[46]

This obligation is two-fold: first, it imposes the responsibility to guarantee the realization of the right of self-determination, and second, it incorporates as a legal obligation the provisions of the United Nations Charter regarding Non-Self-Governing Territories.[47] Under article 73 of the U.N. Charter, administrative States have a non-

---

[43] *Legal Consequences of the Separation of the Chagos Archipelago from Mauritius in 1965*, Advisory Opinion, I.C.J. Reports 2019, p. 139, para. 180; *Case Concerning East Timor (Portugal v. Australia)*, Judgment, I.C.J. Reports 1995, p. 102, para. 29.

[44] M. Nowak, U.N. Covenant on Civil and Political Rights. CCPR Commentary (Engel, Kehl, 2005) p. 9; A. Cassese, *Self-Determination of Peoples: A Legal Reappraisal* (Cambridge University Press, Cambridge, 1995), p. 319–320; H. Gros Espiell, The Right to Self-determination: Implementation of United Nations Resolutions, E/CN.4/Sub.2/405/Rev.1 (United Nations, New York, 1980) par. 70.

[45] "All peoples have a right to self-determination. By virtue of that right they freely determine their political status and freely pursue their economic, social and cultural development."

[46] *International Covenant on Civil and Political Rights*, 999 U.N.T.S. 171 (1966).

[47] There are two Chapters of the U.N. Charter that regulate the responsibility of administrative States toward dependent territories (Chapters XI and XII). For a detailed analysis, see: Steven P. Lausell Recurt, *The Song*

delegable duty to: administer the dependent territory in the best interest of its inhabitants, ensuring the practical achievement of their political, economic and social advancement, adopting measures to promote their development, and assisting them in the development of self-government, the full realization of their political aspirations and the achievement of their free political institutions.

In summary, colonial powers have a responsibility to support these territories in varying ways with the purpose of achieving self-government and independence. Professor Steven Lausell refers to this obligation as one with a "clear fiduciary character," reminiscent of general institutions of trusteeship whereby one party has a duty to forego its own personal interests and act solely in the interests of another."[48] By definition, the obligations identified under the U.N. Charter, must be temporary. The late honorable, international expert Antonio Cassese, defined it as "a temporary legal regime that must of necessity lead to the eventual extinction of legal title."[49] In other words, under International Law, colonial rule has to have an expiration date, and the ultimate obligation of administrative States is to take all necessary steps to guarantee the required conditions for a decolonization process. This process can only be achieved if the rights to economic, social and cultural freedom are protected, as intrinsic to the achievement of political freedom.[50]

It is important to emphasize that under international law, all people living under colonial rule must achieve a "full measure of self-government" in order to extinguish their status as non-self governing territories.[51] This also means that a valid decolonization process requires an environment of mutual trust, where both parties interact as equals, each exercising their full autonomy and sovereign powers. We should bear in mind, that any decolonization process is a matter of international relations. In that sense, the responsibility falls on the United States to rectify the record of what happened in 1952, providing accurate and up to date information on the real current status of Puerto Rico to the United Nations, which will set into motion a valid process of status determination under international law.

Now, having discussed the general obligations of the colonial State. Let me turn now to the discussion of the options identified under international law as acceptable decolonization outcomes. The normative content of the right to self-determination and its outcomes is defined mainly in three U.N. General Assembly Resolutions, these are,

---

Remains the Same, The United States' Fiduciary Duty to Puerto Rico as a Basis for Legal Responsibility. Master Thesis. Spring 2016.

48 Steven P. Lausell Recurt, *The Song Remains the Same, The United States' Fiduciary Duty to Puerto Rico as a Basis for Legal Responsibility*. Master Thesis. Spring 2016.

49 A. Cassese, *Self-Determination of Peoples: A Legal Reappraisal* (Cambridge University Press, Cambridge, 1995) pp. 186–187.

50 Id. at footnote 52, citing: H. Gros Espiell, *The Right to Self Determination: Implementation of United Nations Resolutions*, E/CN.4/Sub.2/405/Rev.1 (United Nations, New York, 1980), par. 113.

51 Steven P. Lausell Recurt, *supra note* 5, p. 17.

Resolution 1514 (XV) of 14 December 1960,[52] Resolution 1541 (XV) of 15 December 1960,[53] and Resolution 2625 (XXV) of 24 October 1970.[54] Resolution 1541 identifies three alternatives for achieving a full measure of self-government, which are: independence, free association, and integration with another State.[55] In regard to the option of free association, Resolution 1541 offers some clarity, indicating that it should be the result of the free, voluntary and informed decision of the people, that it entails the recognition of the associated territory's right to internal self-government without outside interference, and that a free associated state should retain the right to re-negotiate or modify the terms of the association at any time.[56] Apart from the three established options for decolonization, U.N. Resolution 2625 also makes reference to "any other political status freely determined by a people." The Resolution however, offers no clarity as to what that could mean in practice. What is undoubtedly clear, however, is that the meaningful exercise of the right to self-determination does not allow for a political relationship of a colonial nature to remain intact. Therefore, U.N. Resolution 2625 cannot be used to justify 'colonialism by consent'. In sum, all valid options for decolonization have three main pre-conditions: (a) recognition of the free and independent sovereignty of both parties, (b) elimination of colonial rule; and (c) the free and informed participation of the people.

Self-Determination and the Right to Reparations under International Human Rights Law In 1953, the United States falsely claimed in front of the United Nations that it had entered into a "mutually agreed association" with Puerto Rico, which effectively ended its colonial status. Today, it is unambiguously clear that contrary to that assertion, Puerto Rico has never been allowed to meaningfully exercise its right to self-determination.

Furthermore, it is evident that the United States government has historically acted in favor of its own interests in Puerto Rico and not in favor of Puerto Rico's development as mandated by Article 73 of the U.N. Charter. Decolonization requires that conditions of economic freedom and stability are met so that political self-determination does not become a futile exercise. If a colonial power conducts itself in a way that undermines the possibility of greater development and economic independence, then those actions are compounded violations of the human right to self-determination.

As explained earlier, the right to self-determination is a fundamental principle of human rights law, one that, as any other human right generates obligations, including the duty to redress and repair the effects of its violations. In this sense, the process of

---

[52] General Assembly Resolution 1514 (XV), *Declaration on the granting of independence to colonial countries and peoples* (14 December 1960).

[53] General Assembly Resolution 1541 (XV), *Principles which should guide Members in determining whether or not an obligation exists to transmit the information called for under Article 73e of the Charter* (15 December 1960).

[54] General Assembly Resolution 2625 (XXV), *Declaration on principles of International Law concerning friendly relations and cooperation among States in accordance with the Charter of the United Nations* (24 October 1970).

[55] Principle VI, UNGA Resolution 1541 (XV).

[56] Principle VII, UNGA Resolution 1541 (XV).

decolonization in Puerto Rico must be accompanied by the United States' formal recognition of international responsibility, and the identification of necessary steps to redress and repair the compounded effects of multiple human rights violations perpetrated during its colonial rule in Puerto Rico. The United States has breached its international human rights obligations to the people of Puerto Rico through direct and indirect action, for 123 years of colonial rule in the territory.

To give an example, the outstanding debt that Puerto Ricans are being forced to pay is in itself a violation of the human right to their survival as peoples, and runs contrary to the fiduciary obligations that the U.S. has over the territory.[57] As long as Puerto Rico remains a colonial territory and its economy, and even its Constitution, is by design made to work for the benefit of the administrative power, the accumulated debt is the sole responsibility of the colonial authority in control. Sovereignty and responsibility go hand in hand. In this sense, the imposition of the Oversight Control Board is a step in the wrong direction, and runs contrary to the international obligations of the State, which requires more independent, democratic means of governance, not less.

The reality is that Puerto Rico's colonial status has led to its economic, social and environmental regression. This relationship between the colonial status and the territory's poor living conditions, was most recently recognized by the Special Rapporteur on Extreme Poverty and Human Rights, Mr. Phillip Alston. During his official visit to the United States in December 2017, which included visits to Puerto Rico, he concluded that poverty and the absence of political rights are inextricably linked in Puerto Rico.[58]

It should also be mentioned that poverty, inequality and environmental degradation have also been the result of inadequate policies applied in Puerto Rico by federal rule, which were exacerbated by the impact of hurricanes Irma and María, and the inadequate and discriminatory response by agencies in charge. All of these conditions, as well as a the imposition of PROMESA and the Oversight Control Board, are examples of the United States' violations of its basic responsibilities toward the people of Puerto Rico and shows a lack of willingness to advance a project of true self-determination.

Conclusion

In conclusion, the issue of self-determination is ultimately a question of human dignity, a question of freedom in its most basic form, and a fundamental element of the notion of human rights. This is why self-determination is included at the very beginning of the two main international human rights treaties, and is considered a fundamental

[57] On the relationship between debt and human rights in Puerto Rico, see: U.N. Independent Expert on Foreign Debt and Human Rights, Press release: "*Puerto Rico debt crisis: "Human rights cannot be sidelined"—UN Expert Warns,*" Geneva, 9 January 2017.

[58] Report of the Special Rapporteur on Extreme Poverty and Human Rights on his mission to the United States of America. A/HRC/38/33/Add.1, 4 May 2018, pars. 22–24.

aspect of international relations. Today, the right to self-determination is considered not just an issue of political determination, but a condition that affects all aspects of human dignity and the possibility for achieving its full development.

All previous "decolonization" efforts have failed to recognize: (1) that self-determination is a fundamental human right and an issue of international relations; that the United States has forsaken and limited the exercise of this right for 122 years; and, (3) that under human rights law, these limitations have resulted in multiple violations of substantive human rights norms.

After Puerto Rico was removed from the United Nations' list of non-self governing territories in 1953, the United States has maintained that the islands of Puerto Rico have no sovereign powers of their own and that its internal autonomy could be revoked by the U.S. Congress at any moment. This position—albeit wrong, racist and discriminatory—was endorsed and regarded as correct, by the U.S. Supreme Court in *Commonwealth of Puerto Rico v. Sanchez Valle*, 136 S. Ct. 1863 (2016). See also: *Financial Oversight and Management Board v. Aurelius Investment*, 590 U.S. (2020). According to the Court, the 1952 exercise of constitutional drafting and approval was merely an authority "conferred" by Congress, which makes "Congress the original source of power for" Puerto Rico (at pp. 1875–1876). This historical and juridical conclusion will need to be re-addressed and corrected in order for any process of true self-determination to take place. No legitimate exercise of self-determination can take place, without an express recognition of the U.S. government that the people of Puerto Rico are entitled to exercise their sovereign power and to decide on their own terms, and without interference, their political, economical, social and cultural future.

As a final remark, I would also like to mention that, the legitimacy of any decolonization process depends heavily on its honesty and transparency. All discussions on this subject, including this hearing and any other in the future, as well as all legislative actions, executive orders, policies, drafts and laws concerning Puerto Rico's future will never be really transparent and open for meaningful public debate, if they continue to be held in English, without simultaneous translation to Spanish. This very simple change, is one of utmost importance, when the discussion deals with the future of people that cannot effectively participate in any of the debates since it is designed, discussed, amended and debated in a language they do not understand. All these procedures are incomplete and violate the fundamental right of meaningful participation when they continue to be held and written in English, leaving those who are the rightful protagonists of this discussion out of the conversation. This is in itself another example of a colonial decision that affects the legitimacy of these efforts.

Thank you.

QUESTIONS SUBMITTED FOR THE RECORD TO ANNETTE MARTÍNEZ-ORABONA, DIRECTOR, CARIBBEAN INSTITUTE OF HUMAN RIGHTS AND PROFESSOR OF LAW, INTER AMERICAN UNIVERSITY OF PUERTO RICO

Ms. Martínez-Orabona did not submit responses to the Committee by the appropriate deadline for inclusion in the printed record.

Questions Submitted by Representative Sablan

Question 1. As a State, Puerto Rico would be on equal footing with states to receive key federal resources like Supplemental Security Income, which is currently not available for residents of the island. An estimated 436,000 residents of Puerto Rico— who are aged, blind, and disabled, and with very low incomes—would benefit every year. Funding would also increase for federal programs including Medicaid, Medicare, and the Supplemental Nutritional Assistance Program. Why shouldn't Congress move to support statehood for Puerto Rico?

The CHAIRMAN. Thank you. The gentlelady yields.

Let me now turn to Rev. Carmen Cabrera, President of the League of United Latin American Citizens Faith Council. Reverend, 5 minutes are yours.

STATEMENT OF CARMEN CABRERA, PRESIDENT, LEAGUE OF UNITED LATIN AMERICAN CITIZENS (LULAC) FAITH COUNCIL, HATILLO, PUERTO RICO

Rev. CABRERA. Good afternoon, distinguished members of the Committee on Natural Resources. I am honored today to join you in this hearing of H.R. 2070 and H.R. 1522. I appear before you today in representation of the Puerto Rico Chapter of the League of United Latin American Citizens, also known as LULAC, the oldest and most widely respected Hispanic civil right organization in the United States of America.

I also appear before you in representation of the majority of voters in Puerto Rico like, as me, voted last November to choose statehood as the permanent political status for the island. I was born, raised, and have lived in Puerto Rico all of my life. I know firsthand the geography, culture, politics, and the faith in God of the Puerto Rican people. I also know firsthand that the people of Puerto Rico's hope is to soon wake up in a place where justice and equality shine upon all more than the sun at noon, in a place where the limbo of territorial second-class citizenship has been abolished, and where full democracy and voting rights at the Federal level prove our equality as American citizens.

Puerto Ricans have incredible talents and skills, and make countless contributions to America in fields like music, art, sports, and science. We even have a proud Puerto Rican astronaut in NASA, Joseph Acaba, a true patriot hero, yet these contributions pale in comparison to the sacrifice and bloodshed by our Puerto Rican soldiers who had fought and died defending America's liberty and democracy. The value of their lives and the sacrifices of the families who have seen their loved ones come back in flag-draped coffins can never be fully repaid by America, yet the least that Congress can do is to respect the will of the majority of voters of Puerto Rico that have demanded equality and extend a formal offer of statehood so that island residents can make a final choice.

As a leading national civil rights organization, LULAC advocates for all American citizens, including those in Puerto Rico, to have equal rights and equal opportunities. But the simple truth is that as long as the island remains a territory, Congress will continue to treat Puerto Rico unequally and deny them full rights and representation at the Federal level.

For these reasons, here in Puerto Rico, we endorse H.R. 1522 by Representative Darren Soto and Resident Commissioner Jenniffer González-Colón, which respects the will of the majority of voters in Puerto Rico and we oppose H.R. 2070. Why? Because H.R. 2070 seeks to present the perspective on the historic feelings and suffering of the people of Puerto Rico if we were a separate nation. And in doing so, it pays to give a definite solution to the vast majority who treasured our American citizenship. Instead, H.R. 1522 offers proven medicine that will put an end to citizen disenfranchisement and inequality to Puerto Rico.

If Puerto Rico had already been a state and not just a territory when the island was ravaged by Hurricane Maria, shaken by the earthquake, and enveloped by the COVID-19 pandemic, the Federal Government's response would have been very different when dealing with these life-and-death events that have greatly affected our island and its people.

If we had already been a state and not just a territory, the disaster relief would have come more quickly, saved more lives, and the ongoing post-disaster reconstruction would have made much more progress than it has in the last 4 years. We already voted to choose statehood. Congress needs to act now. Thank you for the privilege of speaking here today.

I truly believe that God has placed in your hands the opportunity to do justice by the people of Puerto Rico, and I humbly ask that in considering this issue, not only use your minds and your reason but that you look into your hearts for the right things to do.

May God bless you all and enlighten you to understand and pass

H.R. 1522. Thanks.

[The prepared statement of Rev. Cabrera follows:]

Prepared Statement of Rev. Carmen G. Cabrera, League of United Latin American Citizens (LULAC), Puerto Rico Chapter

Good afternoon distinguished members of the Committee on Natural Resources. I am honored to join you in this hearing on H.R. 2070 and H.R. 1522.

I appear before you today in representation of the Puerto Rico Chapter of the League of United Latin American Citizens also known as LULAC, the oldest and most widely respected Hispanic civil rights organization in the United States of America. I also appear before you in representation of the majority of voters in Puerto Rico, which last November chose statehood as the permanent political status for the Island.

I was born, raised and have lived in Puerto Rico all of my life. I know first-hand the geography, culture, arts, politics, and the faith in God of the Puerto Rican people. I also know first-hand that the People of Puerto Rico's hope is to soon wake up in a place where Justice and Equality shine upon all more than the sun at noon. In a place where the limbo of territorial second-class citizenship has been abolished, and where full democracy and voting rights at the federal level prove our equality as American Citizens.

Puerto Ricans have incredible talents, skills and make countless contributions to America in fields like music, art, sports, and science. We even have a proud Puerto Rican Astronaut in NASA, Joseph Acabá, a true patriot hero. Yet, these contributions pale in comparison to the sacrifice and bloodshed by our Puerto Rican soldiers who have fought and died defending America's liberty and democracy. The value of their lives, and the sacrifices of the families who have seen their loved ones come back in flag draped coffins, can never be fully repaid by America. Yet the least that Congress can do is to respect the will of the majority of voters in Puerto Rico that have demanded equality and extend a formal offer of statehood so that island residents can make a final choice.

We are in a moment of reckoning in Puerto Rico. For the first time in my life, people are not afraid to be honest and call Puerto Rico's relationship with the U.S. what it is. Puerto Rico is a colony. A possession. We are done with the "Commonwealth" label. It is time to fix it. The Constitution is clear: Congress makes the final decision on how to resolve the current undemocratic arrangement. Both proposals pending before Congress involve a vote by the people of Puerto Rico. However, H.R. 2070 imposes on the people of Puerto Rico a Constitutional convention before we hold a referendum vote. The people of Puerto Rico have not asked for this Constitutional convention. The convention would be imposed on us. This is not democracy. As a Puerto Rican voter, I urge Congress to be direct. If Congress cannot guarantee my continued U.S. citizenship, I need to know that now. The answer is available now. We don't need a convention to find out. Congress and the White House have considered this issue for decades. As voters, Puerto Ricans have made their choice. We want statehood now.

As a leading national civil rights organization, LULAC advocates for all American citizens, including those in Puerto Rico to have equal rights and equal opportunities, but the simple truth is that as long as the island remains a territory Congress will continue to treat Puerto Ricans unequally and deny them full rights and representation at the federal level.

For these reasons we endorse H.R. 1522 by Rep. Darren Soto and Resident Commissioner Jennifer González-Cólon, which respects the will of the majority of voters in Puerto Rico, and oppose H.R. 2070. H.R. 1522 would put an end to citizen disenfranchisement and the racialized oppression of unincorporated territory status. The solution for this citizen inequality is for Puerto Rico to finally become a state of the Union.

If Puerto Rico had already been a state, and not just a territory, when the island was ravished by Hurricane Maria, shaken by earthquakes and enveloped by the COVID-19 pandemic, the Federal Government's response would have been very different when dealing with these life and death events that have greatly affected our island and its people. If we had already been a state, and not just a territory, the disaster relief would have come more quickly, saved more lives, and the ongoing post disaster reconstruction would have made much more progress than it has in the last four years.

Thank you for the privilege of speaking here today. I truly believe that God has placed in your hands the opportunity to do justice by the People of Puerto Rico, and I humbly ask that in considering this issue you not only use your minds, and your reason, but that you look into your hearts for the right thing to do. May God bless you all, and enlighten you to understand and pass H.R. 1522.

Questions Submitted for the Record to Carmen Cabrera, President, League of United Latin American Citizens (LULAC) Faith Council

Questions Submitted by Representative Sablan

Question 1. Like my district, the Northern Mariana Islands, Puerto Rico was recently devastated by powerful storms resulting in loss of life and billions of dollars in damages. How do you think the federal response would have been different had Puerto Rico been a state in 2017?

Answer:

- First, Puerto Rico is a territory of the United States under the Territorial Clause of the Constitution.

- Puerto Rico belongs to but is not part of the United States.
- Being that the case, the U.S. Congress can discriminate against American Citizens on the island because they are not subject to the same rights and laws as in the mainland.
- This is a problem because Puerto Ricans cannot decide their fate and can't oblige the President nor Congress to act respecting public policy and quick responses, like is the case of the federal response soon after hurricane Maria.
- States like Texas and Louisiana didn't have these issues.
- They are states with full rights and are subject to all the guarantees of the Constitution, differently from the case of Puerto Rico.
- Today the Government of Puerto Rico is battling in the court equality with Medicaid and Social Security.
- We have the same problem with those issues as with the federal funds of hurricane Maria.
- The President can block funds without any consequence because he can do it.
- There's now law to prohibit it but on contrary, he can discriminate because we are not a state.
- In overall, if Puerto Rico were a state in 2017, the situation could have been totally different.
- Immediately we would have received the approval of funds and would be illegal for the President to block them.
- Also, the people of Puerto Rico could have expressed themselves in the ballots in 2020 for their best interest and benefits.

The CHAIRMAN. Thank you, Reverend.

Let me now invite Dr. Christina Ponsa-Kraus—welcome back. She was at the last hearing—Professor of Constitutional Law at the Columbia University from New York, New York.

Doctor, you are recognized for 5 minutes.

STATEMENT OF CHRISTINA PONSA-KRAUS, PROFESSOR OF CONSTITUTIONAL LAW, COLUMBIA UNIVERSITY, NEW YORK, NEW YORK

Dr. PONSA-KRAUS. Thank you and good afternoon. I am Christina Ponsa-Kraus. I am a Law Professor at Columbia University and a scholar of Puerto Rico's constitutional status, and I am Puerto Rican. I testified at the hearing in April, and I appreciate the invitation to appear again today.

At the April hearing, I explained why I support H.R. 1522 and oppose H.R. 2070. Today, I will comment on the DOJ's legal analysis, with which I agree. I will take issue with one policy conclusion in the DOJ report, and I will respond to several criticisms of H.R. 1522 that have been made by its opponents.

In April, I identified two flaws in H.R. 2070: that it opens the door to unconstitutional status options and that it purports to bind Congress to ratify whatever option the people of Puerto Rico choose. The DOJ report confirms the existence of both of these flaws. On the first flaw, the DOJ report confirms that by failing to specify the available options, H.R. 2070 implicitly includes non-territorial commonwealth, which is not a constitutional option.

On the second flaw, the DOJ confirms that H.R. 2070 makes an illusory promise by stating that Congress "shall approve" a joint resolution ratifying whatever option Puerto Ricans choose following a convention. The DOJ explains that, instead, Congress may offer one or more constitutionally valid options to Puerto Rico and give Puerto Ricans the option to accept or reject such an offer.

That, of course, is exactly what H.R. 1522 does. As this last point suggests, the DOJ approves of two basic approaches to Puerto Rican self-determination, a referendum, which is a yes/no vote on one option, or a plebiscite, which is a vote among all the options. I agree. However, I disagree with the DOJ's policy conclusion that a plebiscite must also include the current territorial status, and clearly I am not alone.

The DOJ defends this conclusion on the ground that it is simply adhering to the long-standing executive branch policy of neutrality among the legally permissible options. But the fact that an option is legally permissible does not mean that it is legally required. The sole purpose of both bills is to end Puerto Rico's perpetual territorial status. With all due respect to the executive branch, it is nothing short of incoherent to insist that a territorial status be included among the options for ending it.

The executive branch should remain faithful to the principle of democratic equality for all U.S. citizens and abandon its neutrality toward continued colonialism. The United States should enthusiastically support the ending of Puerto Rico's territorial status while remaining neutral among Puerto Rico's constitutional non-territorial options: statehood and independence with or without free association.

Finally, I will respond to three criticisms of H.R. 1522. First, critics of H.R. 1522 argue that Congress should not respond to the November referendum with an offer of statehood because voter turnout was too low and the margin of victory was too slim. These objections are factually baseless. Neither turnout nor margin, nor the margin of victory, was abnormally low.

But even if they had been, the objections are a red herring. Neither international law nor U.S. domestic law predicates the legitimacy of a democratic vote, including a self-determination vote, on turnout or supermajority requirements. It is not a coincidence that H.R. 2070 includes neither.

Second, critics of H.R. 1522 argue that it is not inclusive, whereas H.R. 2070 is. But criticism fails to recognize that H.R. 1522 is merely one step in a longer, larger process, including a fully inclusive debate in Puerto Rico that led to the election of a government that ran on a platform of holding a vote on statehood. It also fails to recognize that a yes/no referendum is a valid self-determination process under both domestic and international law.

Third, some statehood opponents object to H.R. 1522 on the ground that Puerto Rico is a nation and that self-determination for a nation cannot include statehood. But international law itself recognizes the right of even a nation to choose integration into another nation. In sum, these criticisms of H.R. 1522 are without merit. H.R. 1522 provides a clear, careful, and constitutionally sound approach to self-determination, and Congress should enact it. Thank you.

[The prepared statement of Dr. Ponsa-Kraus follows:]

PREPARED STATEMENT OF CHRISTINA D. PONSA-KRAUS, LAW PROFESSOR, COLUMBIA UNIVERSITY

Good afternoon. My name is Christina D. Ponsa-Kraus. I am a law professor at Columbia University and an expert on Puerto Rico's constitutional status, and I am Puerto Rican. I testified at the hearing in April and I appreciate the invitation to appear again today. At the April hearing, I explained why I support H.R. 1522 and oppose H.R. 2070. Rather than repeat those arguments today, I will respond to several criticisms of H.R. 1522.

First: Critics of H.R. 1522 argue that Congress should not respond to the November referendum with an offer of statehood because voter turnout was too low and the margin of victory was too slim. These objections are specious. As a preliminary matter, the claim of unusually low voter turnout is factually baseless. The rate of participation was about the same as for any territorial office, including that of the governor. Moreover, eligibility to vote was based on voter rolls from 2012, and it is well known that Puerto Rico lost nearly a half a million people between 2012 and 2020, which means the official turnout figures substantially understate the actual percentage of voters who reside on the island and turned out to vote. But more fundamentally, the question of voter turnout is a red-herring. Neither international law nor U.S. domestic law predicates the legitimacy of a democratic vote—including a self-determination vote—on voter turnout or supermajority requirements. In a democracy, the voters who cast ballots decide the outcome. And under the well-settled rules of democracy, a simple majority prevails absent a fairly adopted rule requiring a supermajority. Under no circumstance do those who lose get to impose a supermajority requirement after the fact. Tacitly acknowledging these elementary truths, even H.R. 2070 does not include a voter turnout or a supermajority requirement. Nor have its supporters insisted on either.

Second: Critics of H.R. 1522 argue that it is not inclusive whereas H.R. 2070 is. If they mean that every option should receive a fair hearing, the criticism fails to recognize that H.R. 1522 is merely one step in a larger process. A fully inclusive debate in Puerto Rico led to the election of a government that ran on a platform of holding a vote on statehood, which it did last November. The "No" option represented all who opposed statehood and was promoted by a vigorous campaign against statehood. Litigation against the referendum failed. The vote resulted in a majority for statehood, which H.R. 1522 would respect by responding to it with a vote on statehood under federal law, in accordance with precedents in other territories. If enough voters choose "No" this time around, they will remain free to pursue their preferred options. No option, no party, and no voter has been excluded from this process.

If critics mean instead that a self-determination process cannot be democratically legitimate unless the ballot includes all legally permissible status options, they are simply incorrect, as "Yes/No" votes on independence all over the globe and throughout history demonstrate. In fact, even the president of the anti-statehood commonwealth party called for a yes-no vote on statehood as recently as 2017, describing it as a "true and unimpeachable" method for determining the will of the people.

That said, I should add that it is not my view that a "Yes-No" vote is the only legitimate self-determination mechanism for Puerto Rico. A ballot including all of the constitutionally valid status options would be another—as long as it met additional criteria of legitimacy. These include, first and foremost, clear, accurate, and federally sanctioned definitions of the options, without which Puerto Ricans would simply be consigned to an inconclusive debate over what each option entails. For example, were such a process to include independence with a free association treaty, it would have to inform voters that such a treaty could not, under international and domestic law, provide the same guarantee of perpetual birthright U.S. citizenship that statehood would provide.

Third and finally: Some statehood opponents object to H.R. 1522 on the ground that Puerto Rico is a nation and that self-determination for a nation, by definition, cannot include the option to become a state of another nation.

Understood as a procedural argument against H.R. 1522, this "nationalism" objection fails. International law recognizes the right of a nation to choose full integration into another nation in a self-determination decision, as for example U.N. General Assembly Resolution 1541(XV) states explicitly. H.R. 1522 simply offers Puerto Ricans that choice. Understood as a substantive argument against statehood itself, it offers no ground for denying Puerto Ricans who disagree the opportunity to vote for statehood. For what it's worth, the November 2020 referendum is only the most recent evidence that a majority of Puerto Ricans see no inconsistency between their identity and the choice of statehood, which would bring them equality as citizens of the United States.

In sum, these criticisms of H.R. 1522 are without merit. H.R. 1522 provides a clear, careful, and constitutionally sound self-determination process, and Congress should enact it without further delay.

TESTIMONY OF CHRISTINA D. PONSA-KRAUS [REVISED]

[On June 14, I submitted my testimony. The same day, the Department of Justice released its analysis of the two bills. What follows is my testimony as revised in light of that analysis.]

Good afternoon. My name is Christina D. Ponsa-Kraus. I am a law professor at Columbia University and a scholar of Puerto Rico's constitutional status, and I am Puerto Rican. I testified at the hearing in April and I appreciate the invitation to appear again today.

At the April hearing, I explained why I support H.R. 1522 and oppose H.R. 2070. Today, I will comment the DOJ's legal analysis, with which I agree; I will take issue with one policy conclusion in the DOJ report; and I will respond to several criticisms of H.R. 1522 that have been made by its opponents.

First: In April, I identified two flaws in H.R. 2070: that it opens the door to unconstitutional status options and that it purports to bind Congress to ratify whatever option the people of Puerto Rico choose. The DOJ report confirms the existence of both of these flaws.

On the first flaw, the DOJ report confirms that by failing to specify the available options, H.R. 2070 implicitly includes non-territorial commonwealth, which is not a constitutional option.

On the second flaw, the DOJ confirms that H.R. 2070 makes an illusory promise by stating that Congress "shall approve" a joint resolution ratifying whatever option Puerto Ricans choose following a convention. The DOJ explains that, instead, Congress may offer one or more constitutionally valid options to Puerto Rico and give Puerto Ricans the option to accept or reject the offer. That, of course, is exactly what H.R. 1522 does.

As this last point suggests, the DOJ approves of two basic approaches to Puerto Rican self-determination: a referendum (which is a Yes/No vote on one option) or a plebiscite (which is a vote among all the options). I agree. However, I disagree with the DOJ's policy conclusion that a plebiscite must also include the current territorial status.

The DOJ defends this conclusion on the ground that it is simply adhering to the long-standing executive branch policy of neutrality among the legally permissible options. But the fact that an option is legally permissible does not mean it is legally required. The sole purpose of *both* bills is to end Puerto Rico's perpetual territorial status. With all due respect to the Executive Branch, it is nothing short of incoherent to insist that territorial status be included among the options for ending it. The Executive Branch should remain faithful to the principle of democratic equality for all U.S. citizens and abandon its neutrality toward continued colonialism. The United States should enthusiastically support the ending of Puerto Rico's territorial status, while remaining neutral among Puerto Rico's *constitutional, non-territorial* options: statehood and independence, with or without free association.

Finally, I will respond to three criticisms of H.R. 1522:

First: Critics of H.R. 1522 argue that Congress should not respond to the November referendum with an offer of statehood because voter turnout was too low and the margin of victory was too slim. These objections are factually baseless: Neither the turnout nor margin of victory was abnormally low. But even if they had been, the objections are a red-herring: Neither international law nor U.S. domestic law predicates the legitimacy of a democratic vote—including a self-determination vote—on turnout or supermajority requirements.

Second: Critics of H.R. 1522 argue that it is not inclusive whereas H.R. 2070 is. The criticism fails to recognize that H.R. 1522 is merely one step in a larger process, including a fully inclusive debate in Puerto Rico that led to the election of a government that ran on a platform of holding a vote on statehood. It also fails to recognize that a Yes/No referendum is a valid self-determination process—under *both* domestic and international law.

Third: Some statehood opponents object to H.R. 1522 on the ground that Puerto Rico is a nation and that self-determination for a nation cannot include statehood. But international law itself recognizes the right of a nation to choose full integration into another nation.

In sum, these criticisms of H.R. 1522 are without merit. H.R. 1522 provides a clear, careful, and constitutionally sound self-determination process, and Congress should enact it without further delay.

The CHAIRMAN. Thank you very much. The doctor yields.

Let me now turn to Professor Andres Córdova, Professor of Property Law at the Inter American University of Puerto Rico.

Professor, 5 minutes are yours.

Statement of Andrés L. Córdova, Professor of Property Law, Inter American University of Puerto Rico, San Juan, Puerto Rico

Mr. CÓRDOVA. Thank you, Mr. Chairman. I would like to begin by thanking the Committee for holding these hearings on the two bills addressing Puerto Rico's political status question. Any public discussion which draws attention to the political disenfranchisement of Puerto Rico's American citizens is, in itself, already a step in the right direction.

Instead of repeating what has already been so eloquently stated by others in the previous hearings, on the urgency of moving forward with H.R. 1522, I would like to focus my attention on certain fundamental aspects of H.R. 2070 which I believe require closer scrutiny. H.R. 2070 calls on the rights of the people of Puerto Rico to invoke a status convention to which they would exercise what is referred to as their natural right to self-determination.

The unexpressed assumption of the bill is that Puerto Ricans are not Americans, notwithstanding their American citizenship. From a legal perspective, this justification implicitly relies on international legal principle. At the time of its creation in 1945, the United Nations included Puerto Rico under the list of non-autonomous territories. In 1952, the U.S. Congress authorized Puerto Rico to draft its own constitution and create its own local self-governing institutions. Upon ratification, the United States informed the United Nations that Puerto Rico had acquired a level of self-government that justified its exclusion of the list of non-autonomous territories.

In 1953, the United Nations exempted the United States from presenting further reports on Puerto Rico, exemption which continues to this day. In 1960, the United Nations approved Resolution 1514, which declared the rights of national self-determination and decolonization. Those factions which favor independence have long tried to have Puerto Rico re-listed as a colonial possession subject to the jurisdiction of the United Nations, notwithstanding the consistent recommendation by the United Nations Special Committee on Decolonization led by Cuba and Venezuela. The General Assembly has rejected the committee's recommendations on 38 separate occasions.

The long-held political strategy of the pro-independence factions, for evident reasons, has been to place the status question within the context of international law to underscore the political and legal differences between the people of Puerto Rico and the people of the United States. Contrary to these efforts, the United States has historically argued, correctly in my estimation, that the issue regarding Puerto Rico's political future is a domestic matter under the jurisdiction of the Constitution and the laws of the United States.

Surely, international law is relevant but always within the constitutional context, not the other way around. It should be noted how the Department of Justice's recent comments on H.R. 2070 exclude international law from its analysis. By virtue of 1898, the Treaty of Paris, Spain ceded Puerto Rico to the United States under which terms the United States acquired the right to dispose of the civil rights of its inhabitants as accorded by Congress.

In 1990, the Foraker Act created the civil government of Puerto Rico, among other provisions. We should highlight that the people of Puerto Rico, as a legal category, is a creation of statute and not of any philosophical claim of political identity.

Although it is true that international treaties signed by the United States are part of its statutory law, as Supreme Law of the land, they are still under the Constitution. Contrary to what some would have us believe, international treaties and obligations are not above constitutional authority. When Congress exercises its plenary powers under the Territorial Clause, international provisions do not govern these actions, which in any case are not self-executing according to long-held judicial precedent.

In the *Commonwealth of Puerto Rico v. Sanchez Valle* in 2016, the Supreme Court left no doubt that Puerto Rico's sovereignty lies in the United States, in Congress, and that any sovereign claim to the contrary must pass through the Territorial Clause. The Department of Justice's comments on H.R. 2070 questioning the bill's claims of—and I quote—"the Puerto Rico legislature's inherent authority to call a status convention," is an elegant critique drawn from this same principle.

The fundamental purpose of the promoters of the status convention is to lay the legal groundwork for Puerto Rico to claim sovereignty over and against the United States and the will of the same people they claim to represent. As a matter of political reality, Puerto Ricans have been exercising their right to self-determination in every electoral process since 1952 and subsequent general elections and local plebiscites since then, albeit incompletely and inconclusively. As a matter of democratic vocation, the next step in this long-overdue process is a federally mandated referendum. I endorse H.R. 1522 with amendments, if required, and I oppose H.R. 2070. Thank you.

[The prepared statement of Mr. Córdova follows:]

PREPARED STATEMENT OF ANDRÉS L. CÓRDOVA, PROFESSOR AT INTER AMERICAN UNIVERSITY OF PUERTO RICO, SCHOOL OF LAW, SAN JUAN, PUERTO RICO

Mr. Chairman, I would like to begin by thanking the Chair and the House Committee on Natural Resources for holding these hearings on the two bills addressing Puerto Rico's political status question. Any public discussion which draws attention to the political disenfranchisement of Puerto Rico's American citizens is in itself, already, a step in the right direction.

In the previous hearing the Committee heard from various witnesses, among them Prof. Christina Ponsa-Krauss, whose statements succinctly presented the constitutional constraints and difficulties of H.R. 2070, Puerto Rico Self-Determination Act and—in contrast—of the legal and political solvency of H.R. 1522, Puerto Rico Statehood Admission Act. I fully subscribe to her views on the matter, together with my earlier remarks submitted for the written record for the April 14, 2021 hearing, which I herein include by reference.

Instead of repeating what has already been so eloquently stated by others on the urgency of moving forward with the PR Statehood Admission Act, I would like to focus my attention on certain aspects of PR Self-Determination Act which I believe require closer scrutiny.

The PR Self-Determination Act calls on the right of the people of Puerto Rico to convoke a Status Convention through which they would exercise what is referred to as their natural right to self-determination. The unexpressed assumption of this bill is that Puerto Ricans are not Americans, notwithstanding their American citizenship, and the cry for "self-determination" in this context aims to impede the electoral majority call for statehood.

From a legal perspective, its justification implicitly relies on international legal principles. At the time of its creation in 1945 the United Nations included Puerto Rico under the list of non-autonomous territories. In 1952 the U.S. Congress authorized Puerto Rico to draft its own Constitution and create its own local self-governing institutions. Upon ratification, the United States informed the United Nations that Puerto Rico had acquired a level of self-government that justified its exclusion of the list of non-autonomous territories. In 1953 the United Nations exempted the United States from presenting further reports on Puerto Rico, exemption which continues to this day.

In 1960 the United Nations approved Resolution 1514 (XV) which declared the rights of national self-determination and decolonization. Those factions which favor independence have long tried to have Puerto Rico relisted as a colonial possession subject to the jurisdiction of the United Nations. Notwithstanding the consistent recommendation by the United Nations Special Committee on Decolonization—led by Cuba and Venezuela—the General Assembly has rejected the Committee's recommendation on 38 occasions.

The long held political strategy of the pro-independence factions has been to place the status question within the context of international law, to underscore the political and legal difference between the people of Puerto Rico and the people of the United States. The PR Self-Determination Act implicitly endorses this view.

Contrary to these efforts, the United States has historically argued—correctly in my estimation—that the issue regarding Puerto Rico's political future is a domestic matter, under the jurisdiction of the Constitution and the laws of the United States. Surely International Law is relevant, but always within the constitutional context, not the other way around.

By virtue of the 1898 Treaty of Paris, Spain ceded Puerto Rico to the United States, which under the terms of the Treaty acquired the rights to dispose of the civil rights of its inhabitants by Congress. In 1900 the Foraker Act created a civil government, among other provisions. We should highlight that the people of Puerto Rico, as legal category, is a creation of this statute and not of any philosophical claims of political identity.

Although it is true that international treaties signed by the United States are part of its statutory law, as Supreme Law of the land, they are still under the Constitution. Contrary to what some would have us believe, international treaties and obligations are not above constitutional authority. When Congress exercises its plenary powers under the Territorial Clause, international provisions do not govern its actions, which in any case are not self-executing according to long held judicial precedent. The 2016 PROMESA, which created a Financial and Oversight Management Board to supervise the bankrupt government of Puerto Rico and the treatment of Puerto Rico as a foreign jurisdiction for purposes of the Internal Revenue Code are two on-going example of the exercise of this authority.

In the recent *Commonwealth of Puerto Rico v. Sanchez Valle* (2016) the Supreme Court left no doubt that Puerto Rico's sovereignty lies in the United States, in Congress, and that any sovereign claim to the contrary must pass through the Territorial Clause of the Constitution. More timely, the constitutional challenge currently before the Supreme Court in the case of *United States v. Vaello-Madero*, regarding the exclusion of SSI benefits to American citizens in Puerto Rico, assumes congressional authority to dispose of the territory without the direct participation of the people of Puerto Rico.

Any pretense of placing Puerto Rico outside of the Territorial Clause must necessarily do so either as a State or as an independent nation, in any of its guises. The continuous efforts by certain factions of trying to carve out a mythical constitutional space where Puerto Rico is not subject to the ultimate authority of Congress under the Territorial Clause has been consistently and decisively rejected by all branches of the United States government. Ironically, the PR Self-Determination Act itself is a belated recognition that Puerto Rico is under the authority of Congress and does not have the constitutional or legal right to exercise any natural law claim.

Puerto Rico is a territory of the United States, and the use of loaded terms such as "colonial" and "self-determination" are underhanded attempts to place the status question within the context of International Law instead of the United States Constitution, where it belongs. Although perfectly understandable as part of the give and take of political discourse, it is disconcerting that Congress would even consider a piece of legislation which implicitly undermines its own constitutional authority.

A Status Convention which purports to be the depositary of the will of the people of Puerto Rico would necessarily need to include all sectors of the island's political spectrum, including those that favor statehood. What exactly would a Status Convention propose that has not already been proposed in the last 122 years by the different political parties and analyzed by the political branches of the Federal Government? Invariably a Status Convention would reproduce the same positions that everybody is familiar with. Are we to believe that the delegates to such a convention are to discover any new constitutionally viable formula that has not been part of the political debate for the last century? From a practical point of view, a Status Convention would not offer any other alternative that we haven't already had before us and that can be settled by means of a plebiscite or referendum.

The fundamental purpose of the Status Convention is to lay the legal groundwork for Puerto Rico to claim sovereignty over and against the United States and the will of the same people they claim to represent. As a matter of political reality, the Puerto Ricans have been exercising their right to self-determination in every electoral event since the approval of the 1952 Constitution and subsequent general elections and local plebiscites, albeit incompletely and inconclusively. The next step in this long overdue process is a federally mandated referendum.

I endorse PR Statehood Admission Act and oppose PR Self Determination Act.

Questions Submitted for the Record to Professor Andrés L. Córdova, Professor of Property Law, Inter American University of Puerto Rico

Questions Submitted by Representative Sablan

Question 1. The people of Puerto Rico have, as recently as last November, voted in favor of statehood. The results of that vote, however, were 52.5% in favor and turn-out was 54.7% of eligible voters. How do you respond to people who say that those election results may indicate that Puerto Rican voters are not supportive enough for something as irreversible as statehood?

Answer. The central characteristic of a representative democracy is the electoral participation of its citizens in the decision-making process. There will always be differences of opinion in a society. The electoral process is precisely the manner in which we solve our differences without recurring to the use of force. There has never been a legal requirement in the history of the United States that in order for a territory be admitted as a state there has to be a given percentage of electoral approval. That is not the way democracy works. The votes that count are the ones that are cast, and the majority prevails. This is precisely what occurred in the November, 2020 election.

If in Congress has concerns as to the validity of previous plebiscites, all it needs to do is to exercise its constitutional authority and legislate a federal mandated referendum or plebiscite. H.R. 1522 does this. What should not happen is for Congress to argue that the previous plebiscites were not valid and therefore no do anything about it, using the pretext that Congress will act when Puerto Ricans come to an agreement.

The CHAIRMAN. The gentlemen yields.

Our final witness is Dr. JoséCaraballo-Cueto, Professor of Economics at the University of Puerto Rico.

Doctor, 5 minutes are yours and you are recognized.

STATEMENT OF JOSÉCARABALLO-CUETO, PROFESSOR OF ECONOMICS, UNIVERSITY OF PUERTO RICO, CAYEY, PUERTO RICO

Dr. CARABALLO-CUETO. Thank you, Mr. Chairman. Forty-four years ago arguably was the last time that Congress took a strong action to boost Puerto Rico's economy. Section 936 of the Federal tax code was enacted. After that policy, we have observed many congressional hearings but few to no positive economic policies. Some observers are betting on the new geopolitics in the Caribbean, such as the China's Belt and Road influence on Latin America, as a way for pushing Congress to favor Puerto Rico again, but that is just a theoretical scenario.

The bottom line is that no matter how much Federal funds are sent to Puerto Rico for long-term economic development, Puerto Rico needs a fundamental change in its political relationship with the United States. Fiscal, monetary, and industrial policies are key to economic development. But Puerto Rico has barely any control over this.

The monitory policy, for instance, exchange rates and interest rates imposed on Puerto Rico by the Federal Reserve, also known as the Fed, is not designed for the island, and sometimes the Fed exacerbates economic conditions of this territory. Puerto Rico has almost no representation in effect. The local fiscal policy is now handled by the Fiscal Control Board imposed by Congress, reducing the elected official authority.

Industrial policy, such as preferential taxes to manufacturing industries, have been recently managed by Congress without major considerations of Puerto Rico. For instance, the GILTI, the Global Intangible Low-Taxed Income, is also harming the remnant of the industrial sector in Puerto Rico. And if the global taxation of 15 percent is extended to the island, it will have a similar or even greater negative effect.

For some unexplained reason, Congress provides better economic tools to other territories: the U.S. Virgin Islands is exempt from the Jones Act, and the Northern Mariana Islands and Guam have a visa waiver program that boosts their tourism. The Jones Act does not just increase import costs according to most studies, moreover, it excludes Puerto Rico from international logistics.

In 2015, Puerto Rico paid in Federal taxes almost five times more than the taxes paid by other U.S. territories combined. Both sovereignty and statehood provide better economic prospect than the current status. Sovereignty will let Puerto Rico implement tailor-made fiscal, monetary, and industrial policies, for instance, protection for local businesses without being subject to the interstate commerce clause.

In addition, it will also liberate the island from the Jones Act and other regulation. But independence also has its cost. Most Federal funds received in Puerto Rico are contractual benefits, such as Social Security, Medicare, and veteran benefits. Part of the difference could be substituted from abroad. However, without the remaining Federal transfer, local government must be very efficient.

All in all, if economic actors take full advantage of the benefits of sovereignty, the disadvantages can be outweighed. In the case of statehood, fiscal, industrial, and monetary policies will not depend on the sympathy of Congress and the Fed but on the negotiation that takes place when Representatives from Puerto Rico have voting power.

Just by receiving supplemental security income and parity and nutritional assistance, the poverty rate would decrease by 14 percentage points in Puerto Rico. In addition, by being fully annexed, Puerto Rico would take advantage of its comparative edge over states in terms of wages, and would receive more investment from the United States. In the case of Hawaii, its economy or gross state product did not decline after annexation, although structural changes were felt by the population.

Statehood also carries disadvantages. First, Federal taxation will impact the middle class and small- and middle-sized enterprise of the island. Second, many multi-national manufacturers that operate as control foreign corporations in Puerto Rico will move to a third country, shrinking the industrial base even further. However, the disadvantages of statehood are probably not worse than the disadvantages of the colony.

That is why my first recommendation is to strongly oppose a recommendation of the U.S. Department of Justice to include the territorial status and to avoid specific mandates to the Federal Government. Excluding the territorial status is a consensus that I identify here. After all, this is the same Department of Justice that would oppose parity and SSI to Puerto Rico.

No. 2, both bills should specify that if statehood is not supported by either a majority of Puerto Ricans or by the Federal Government itself, the U.S. Government will end the territorial status on a specific date.

No. 3, change the PROMESA Act so that the Fiscal Control Board disappears once the debt restructuring ends.

No. 4, exclude Puerto Rico from the global tax of 15 percent and the GILTI taxation, and from any other measure that entails a greater erosion of the industrial policies of Puerto Rico.

No. 5, exclude Puerto Rico from the Jones Act and from any colonial decision.

Thank you.

[The prepared statement of Dr. Caraballo-Cueto follows:]

PREPARED STATEMENT OF DR. JOSÉ CARABALLO-CUETO, UNIVERSITY OF PUERTO RICO

Introduction

Thank you all for the invitation to testify before the Natural Resources Committee hearing on H.R. 2070, "Puerto Rico Self-Determination Act of 2021" and H.R. 1522, "Puerto Rico Statehood Admission Act." These projects are commendable efforts; my congratulations to the individuals that wrote them. Below I provide a short analysis on Puerto Rico's political status and economic development. At the end, I provide my recommendations.

Political Status and Economic Prospects for Puerto Rico

According to the world data gathered by Angus Madisson from 1955 to 1980, the economy of Puerto Rico was among the top growing economies in the world. The Gross Domestic Product per capita was 210% higher in 1980 than in 1955. Such growth doubled the world rate (83%) and would have placed the Island among the top 14 countries in the world in terms of income per capita growth.

The economic model at the time was rather simple: attract manufacturing corporations from abroad with federal and local tax incentives. In the words of Baumol and Wolff (1996): "Puerto Rico serves as an example of an extreme form of what Prebisch and his colleagues called 'dependence,' both in terms of import openness and its reliance on foreign direct investment—both almost exclusively from the U.S. mainland. Yet, because of its high investment rate and educational gains, Puerto Rico grew very rapidly, at least from the mid-1940s through the early 1970s." (Baumol and Wolff, p. 883). This was in part due to Section 936 of the federal tax code enacted 45 years ago; arguably the last time that Congress took a strong action to boost Puerto Rico's economy. After that policy, we have observed many congressional hearings but few to none positive economic policies.

The problem with such a model was its fragility: after trade liberalization and the removal of Section 936 of the federal tax code the economy of Puerto Rico collapsed (for more details, see Caraballo & Lara, 2018). This finding leads to the crucial questions: Is there a new economic model for Puerto Rico?

Policymakers attempt to implement one by increasing federal funding, providing tax incentives to attract high-income individuals (local Act 22 of 2012 and inclusion in federal designation of opportunity zones), and to promote the export of services (local Act 20 of 2012). However, such a model is insufficient in its ability to grow an economy that has not grown sustainably since 2006. Some observers are betting on the new geopolitics in the Caribbean (e.g., China's Belt & Road influence on Latin America) as a way for pushing Congress to favor Puerto Rico again, but that is just a theoretical scenario.

The bottom line is that, no matter how much federal funds are sent to Puerto Rico, for long-term economic development Puerto Rico needs a fundamental change in its political relationship with the United States. Federal funds can provide economic growth only in the short term, but they will not put Puerto Rico in its past growth path. Ilzetzki et al. (2010) found that fiscal stimulus has a low impact on economies with a ratio of external trade to Gross Domestic Product that exceeds 60%. In the case of Puerto Rico, that ratio was 156% in 2020.

Fiscal, monetary, and industrial policies are key to economic development, especially in this new century, but Puerto Rico has barely any control over these. The monetary policy (e.g., exchange rate and interest rate, among others) imposed on Puerto Rico by the Federal Reserve (Fed) is not designed for the particular business cycle of the island and sometimes the decisions taken by the Fed exacerbate the economic conditions of this territory. Puerto Rico has almost no representation in this important institution. The local fiscal policy (taxes and government spending) is now handled by the fiscal control board imposed by Congress, reducing the elected officials' authority from low to no influence on these issues: in fact, the last couple of budgets have been imposed by this board.

Industrial policies, such as preferential taxes to manufacturing industries, have been managed by Congress without major consideration of the economic situation of Puerto Rico. For instance, the current debt crisis was caused by (in addition to the exclusion of Puerto Rico from the federal bankruptcy code in 1984) the economic clash created by the removal of federal tax incentives without any alternative economic strategy: this deindustrialization reduced government revenues, increasing Puerto Rico's dependency on external funding (Caraballo and Lara, 2018). The GILTI (Global Intangible Low-Taxed Income) enacted in 2017 is also harming the remnant of the industrial sector in Puerto Rico and if the global taxation of 15% is extended to the island, it will have a similar or even greater negative effect.

For some unexplained reasons, Congress provides better economic tools to other territories: the U.S. Virgin Islands is exempt from the 1920 Jones Act and the Northern Mariana Islands and Guam have a visa waiver program that boosted their tourism.[59] The Jones Act does not just increase import costs according to most studies,[60] moreover, it excludes Puerto Rico from international logistics. For instance, a vessel departs from, say, Colombia to Puerto Rico, it cannot continue to the largest market in the region (the U.S.): either the vessel returns to Colombia or goes to another small economy. It should be pointed out that in 2015 Puerto Rico paid altogether $3.5 billion in federal taxes;

[59] https://www.guamvisitorsbureau.com/news/news-releases/philippine-arrivals-soar-in-march-2016.

[60] https://docs.wixstatic.com/ugd/5b4228_4e79040fd1b043a59df921358825334a.pdf.

almost five times more than the combined taxes paid by the U.S. Armed Service members overseas and other U.S. territories (IRS 2015).

Both sovereignty and statehood provide better economic prospects than the current status. Let me start with the case of sovereignty. In the 20th century, some economies (such as Singapore (1963), Ireland (1921), Finland (1917), S. Korea (1945), and Iceland (1944) have benefited from independence while others did not (e.g., almost all African former colonies (except for S. Africa (1910), many colonies in the Middle East, and many countries in South Asia). However, the initial conditions for Puerto Rico, in terms of infrastructure and level of income, are more favorable than many former colonies of the last century. Sovereignty would let Puerto Rico implement tailor-made fiscal, monetary, and industrial policies (e.g., protection for local businesses without being subject to the interstate commerce clause). In addition, it would also liberate the island from institutional constraints such as the Jones Act and regulations associated with product quality. Research by Caraballo-Cueto and Gautier (2020) shows that Puerto Rico export potential is limited by about $20 billion (in 2011 PPP dollars, after adjusting for transfer pricing effect) in 2016. This would represent about 17% of the Puerto Rico's GDP. This number does not consider export of services.

However, independence also has its costs to Puerto Rico. Firstly, if residents do not save more, without access to broker deposits and other instruments, interest rates would be very high, limiting households and businesses investments. Secondly, currency devaluation would be good for exporters but hurtful for consumers. Thirdly, reconstruction after disasters would be similar to other countries in Latin America, where there is a net negative effect. Most federal funds received in Puerto Rico are contractual rights such as Social Security, Medicare, and veteran benefits. In 2020, $14 billion out of $25 billion were this type of transfer. Part of the difference ($11 billion) could be substituted with remittances from abroad (Dominican Republic receives more than $3 billion in remittances). However, without the remaining federal transfers, local government must be very efficient. Otherwise, essential services would be worse than now. All in all, if economic actors take full advantage of the benefits of sovereignty, the disadvantages can be outweighed.

In the case of statehood, fiscal, industrial, and monetary policies would not depend on the sympathy of Congress and the Fed but on the negotiation that takes place when representatives from Puerto Rico have voting power. In the case of Puerto Rico, there are no current studies but in the past Jenkins and Islam (1998) found that sectors unrelated to Section 936 (both households and residents) won with statehood while local government lost funds. In 2013, if Puerto Rico were a state, small and medium size enterprises (SMEs) as well as its middle and upper classes would have paid an additional $2.9 billion in federal taxes but low-income individuals would have received an additional $3 billion in federal funds. Just by receiving parity in Supplemental Security Income and nutritional assistance, the poverty rate would decrease by 14 percentage points (Caraballo-Cueto

2019). In addition, by being fully annexed, Puerto Rico would take advantage of its comparative edge over other states in terms of wages and would receive more investments from the United States. In the case of Hawaii, its gross state product did not decline after annexation in 1959 (Schmitt 1977), though structural changes were felt by the population (Bell 2019).

Statehood also carries disadvantages. Firstly, federal taxation would impact the middle class and SMEs of the Island. Secondly, if local taxes are decreased to compensate SMEs, more painful austerity would be needed to balance the budget. Thirdly, statehood also changes the tax status of Puerto Rico and many multinational manufacturers that are now in Puerto Rico operating as a Controlled Foreign Corporation would move to a third country, shrinking the industrial base even further. However, these disadvantages of statehood are probably not worse than the disadvantages of the colony.

Both a "PRexit" or statehood will carry painful structural adjustments in the short term, but in the long term will probably be better for economic growth. There are no recent empirical studies but my colleagues and I will soon use a mathematical model to construct diverse scenarios to better inform this discussion.

Recommendations

1. Streamline the H.R. 2070 by reducing steps and establishing specific dates. I strongly oppose the recommendations of the U.S. Department of Justice to include the territorial status and to avoid specific mandates to the Federal Government.
2. In the case of H.R. 1522, it should specify that if statehood is not supported by either a majority of Puerto Ricans or by the Federal Government, the U.S. Government will end the territorial status on a specific date.
3. Change the PROMESA act so that the fiscal control board disappears once the debt restructuring ends. This would return fiscal policy to duly elected officials.
4. Exclude Puerto Rico from the global tax of 15%, the GILTI taxation, and from any other measure that entails a greater intervention from the Federal Government in the Puerto Rico economy.
5. Exclude Puerto Rico from the 1920 Jones Act.

References

Baumol, W. J. & Wolff, E. N. (1996). Catching up in the postwar period: Puerto Rico as the fifth "Tiger"? *World Development*, 24(5), 869–885.

Bell, R. (2019). *Last among equals: Hawaiian statehood and American politics.* University of Hawaii Press.

Caraballo-Cueto, J. & Lara, J. (2018). Deindustrialization and unsustainable debt in middle-income countries: The case of Puerto Rico. *Journal of Globalization and Development*, 8(2).

Caraballo-Cueto, J. (2019). *The impact of disparities in SNAP and SSI on Puerto Rico's poverty and economic growth.* Retrieved from: https://www.researchgate.net/publication/340610699_The_impact_of_disparities_in_SNAP_and_SSI_on_Puerto_Rico's_poverty_and_economic_growth.

Caraballo-Cueto, J. & Gautier, L. (2020). *Are Satellite Economies Losing Trade?* Manuscript under revision.

IRS (2015). Internal Revenue Service Data Book. Retrieved from: https://www.irs.gov/pub/irs-soi/15databk.pdf.

Ilzetzki, E., Mendoza, E.G., & Végh, C.A. (2010). *How big (small?) are fiscal multipliers?* (No. w16479). National Bureau of Economic Research.

Jenkins, G.P. & Islam, N. (1998). *Economic Consequences of Statehood for Puerto Rico: A General Equilibrium Analysis* (No. 1998-06). JDI Executive Programs.

Schmitt, R.C. (1977). *Historical Statistics of Hawaii.* Retrieved from: https://files.hawaii.gov/dbedt/economic/data_reports/Historical-Statistics-of-Hawaii.pdf.

The CHAIRMAN. I want to thank the panelists for their testimony. Next we will go to questions. Committee Rule 3(d) imposes a 5-minute limit on questions and responses. The Chair reminds Members that under the Chair's right of recognition described in Rule 3(d), the Chair can provide some reasonable additional time whenever any Member has a question for Rev. Carmen Cabrera to account for an interpreter. Members are encouraged to ask all questions in English to avoid complications with the interpretation.

The Chair will now recognize Members for any questions they may wish to ask. As I indicated earlier, we will try to do this based on seniority. Let me now turn to our colleague, Mr. Sablan.

Mr. Sablan, you are recognized for any questions or comments you might have.

Mr. SABLAN. Yes. Thank you, Mr. Chairman. Thank you very much for holding this hearing. I am going to yield most of my time, but just two general questions I would like to ask. Has anyone looked into how much Puerto Rico would gain or lose from its taxation if they are subjected to the Internal Revenue Code?

And then a question that I need to ask is, there was a recent referendum in which statehood was supposed to be approved. What was wrong with that, and could somebody eventually provide that to me in writing because I need to yield 2 minutes to the gentlelady from New York, Ms. Velázquez, please.

Ms. VELÁZQUEZ. Thank you, Mr. Sablan, for yielding. I would like to address my first question to Professor Cox. Is there anything in the U.S. Constitution that prohibits Congress from entertaining a free association agreement with Puerto Rico different from the current agreement and different from independence?

Dr. COX ALOMAR. There is no obstacle in the Constitution for that. As a matter of fact, under Congress' foreign relations powers, Congress has even more authority than when it acts domestically because it is not bound by the enumerated powers under Article I, Section 8. So, the answer, in short, is no.

Ms. VELÁZQUEZ. Thank you. And can Puerto Ricans still retain their U.S. citizenship under other status options that are not statehood?

Dr. COX ALOMAR. The answer is yes, but it needs a bit of explanation. There is a wide consensus that unilateral revocation of U.S. citizenship to those folks who already have U.S. citizenship would run afoul basic constitutional principles. The question remains— what happens with the unborn, right? And that is a question of first impression that obviously the political branches, more specifically Congress, must actually answer.

Ms. VELÁZQUEZ. OK. Thank you. And this question is important.

Mr. SABLAN. Thirty seconds.

Ms. VELÁZQUEZ. OK. I yield back.

Mr. SABLAN. Thank you, Ms. Velázquez.

Ms. VELÁZQUEZ. And thank you for yielding.

Mr. SABLAN. I would like to yield the remainder of my time, which is just about 2 minutes, to the Resident Commissioner of Puerto Rico, Ms. González-Colón. Jenniffer.

Miss GONZÁLEZ-COLÓN. Thank you to the Vice Chair of the Committee, Mr. Sablan, for yielding time. And I just want to thank the witnesses for joining us, particularly the witnesses Dr. Ponsa-Kraus from Columbia University and Professor Córdova, who teaches on the island at the Inter American University of Puerto Rico School of Law.

Given the Department of Justice has provided the Committee its analysis on the constitutionality and legality of both bills, I believe their testimony will be particularly valuable. Before going through my questions, I would like to introduce for the record letters and statements in support of H.R. 1522 from Representative Maria Mayita Meléndez, Roberto Lefranc Fortuño, and Elizabeth Torres. Same thing with the National Puerto Rican Equality Coalition, Dr. Zayira Jordan, and Mr. Juan Camilla.

[The information follows:]

PR ESTADIDAD

Hon. Raúl Grijalva	Hon. Bruce Westerman
Chairman	Ranking Member

House Committee on Natural Resources	House Committee on Natural Resources
Hon. Joe Manchin Chairman Senate Committee on Energy & Natural Resources	Hon. John Barrasso Ranking Member Senate Committee on Energy & Natural Resources

Dear Chairman Grijalva, Ranking Member Westerman, Chairman Manchin, Ranking Member Barrasso:

As U.S. citizens from Puerto Rico, we are coming together to express our support for the Puerto Rico Statehood Admission Act, H.R. 1522 and S. 780, and to call on Congress to pass this legislation as quickly as possible.

Puerto Ricans have been part of the U.S. for over one hundred and twenty years and we have made countless contributions to the betterment of American society. During that time the population of Puerto Ricans stateside has grown to close to six million. Yet for the three million U.S. citizens that remain on the island, we remain disenfranchised in federal elections and subjected to unequal treatment in federal laws and programs. This reduces economic development, has robbed our poor and elderly of lifesaving healthcare, and every day breaks up our families and communities as people feel forced to move stateside to seek out better opportunities and quality of life for themselves and their children.

Congress must immediately end its inherently colonial territorial rule over Puerto Rico, because it violates America's values of democracy, equal justice under the law, and government by the consent of the governed. Beyond that, it doesn't serve either America or Puerto Rico to prolong an outdated, dysfunctional and morally corrupt form of government which its own citizens have now rejected on multiple occasions.

On November 3, 2020, an undisputable majority of 53% of Puerto Rico's voters demanded change in a locally sponsored referendum calling for full democracy and equality through statehood. While some bills in Congress, like H.R. 2070 & S. 865, seek to delay, confuse and distract from this electoral majority mandate in the name of "self-determination," only the Puerto Rico Statehood Admission Act acknowledges and responds to the freely expressed will of the people.

A majority of voters in Puerto Rico have requested statehood, now Congress must respond by officially offering it and allowing voters on the island to ratify their choice in a binding vote. To turn around and tell voters to go back to the drawing board and re-define multiple other options which the majority has rejected three times in the last eight years in favor of statehood, would not only be insulting to us, but effectively serve as a form of voter suppression. That is simply unacceptable and un-American.

We are natural born U.S. citizens and want an equal seat at the table in the federal government that writes and implements the laws that we live under. We want our full voting rights as American citizens, and would challenge any voting Member of Congress that would deny that to us to answer if their constituents would accept the second-class citizenship that we are subjected to under territory status.

We are proud to be Puerto Ricans, and also proud to be U.S. citizens, and know that there is no law that limits us from being both. So, don't let anyone tell you that statehood will somehow diminish our cultural pride and heritage. If anything, the economic progress that statehood would unleash will allow Puerto Rico to flourish in ways that will mutually benefit the Island and the States.

If you really believe in democracy, justice, government by the consent of the governed, you must not hesitate any further or give any more excuses. Congress must grant us the equal rights and equal responsibilities that we have earned with the blood of our veterans and the tears of their mothers, wives, children and families. Pass the Puerto Rico Statehood Admission Act as soon as possible and together we can help make America *a more perfect Union*.

Sincerely,

Name	Signature	Zip Code
Juan G. Rivera Santana		
Manuel O. Claudio Rod.		00769
Zulma Reyes		00769
Francisco J. Ortiz Rodriguez Jr		00769
Gerardo Diaz Gonzalez		00729
Jose Torres		00769
Sara J. Muñoz Melendez		00769
[illegible]		00769
Merlyn J. Rivera Reyes		00769
Yajaira Alvarez		00769
Luis A. Pazo		00769
Miguel A. David Perez		00769
Limaries Torres		100769
Kenneth G. DeJesus Rodriguez		00769
Luz E Rosa		00769

Name	Signature	Zip Code
Alberto Vázquez	[illegible]	00983
Aida J. Vargas	[illegible]	00782
NICOLAS HERNANDEZ	[illegible]	00782
Maria I. Cordero	Maria I. Cordero	00782
Yamileth Márquez	[illegible]	00782
Emilio Rodríguez	[illegible]	00773
Leandro [illegible]	[illegible]	00987
Ana I. Molina Cruz	[illegible]	00782
Pedro González Rosado	[illegible]	00782
Saed Rivera Vera	[illegible]	00969
Densy Marquez Ruiz	DMR	00969
Jovanska Rodríguez	[illegible]	00782
Aida L. Rivera Rivera	[illegible]	00782
Ana L. Alejandro	A. Alejandro	00782
carmen	carmen	00782
Christian J. Alicea Cabrera	[illegible]	00782
Raul Alicea Nieves	[illegible]	00782
Cristina Oquendo	[illegible]	00983
AIDA M. MÁRQUEZ IBAÑEZ	[illegible]	00969
Janetzy Carmona Rosario	[illegible]	00782
Heemalee Aponte Velázquez	HAV	00782
Daniel Vega Ortiz	[illegible]	00795
Keila N Robo Cacas	[illegible]	00782
Lisbeth Acosto Rosario	[illegible]	00782

Name	Signature	Zip Code
Miguel Quiles		00782
Marleen Pérez Ortiz		00769
Zuleika Ziefkcle		00716
Carmen Melendez		00716
Sophya V. Mercado		00716
Ralph A. Pérez Grimmett		00680
Omar Robledo Calderon		00603
Amaryllis Pantoja Calderón		00603
Luis A. Pantoja Calderón		00603
Víctor Calderon Castro		00910
Victor Luis Calderon Ner.		00603
Ileana Calderon Castro		00603
Genaro Marcial		00603
Caleb Tully Calderon		00603
Karla P. Fuentes		00910
Ivette Yulfo Bertin		00662
Veronica Ayala		00745
Jose Ayala		00745
Betzaida Torres		00917
Jenny L. Grimmett		00680
Idaletta Pérez Pitre		00680
Gabriela Pérez Grimmett		00680
Debbie Pérez Grimmett		00623
David Ramos		00623

4

Name	Signature	Zip Code
Odermis Martinez		00677
Senén Vargas		00677
Josué C. Moreno Rivera		00677
Brendalie Arroyo		00623
Francisca Aviles Garcia		00725
José Enrique Avilés Santiago	J.EAS	00676
Gladys Martinez Lugo		00677
Tatiana Pérez		00677
Carlos Ruiz		00677
[illegible]		00677
Jorge Iván Rodríguez		00690 P.R. U.S.A.
Domingo Bonilla Felicia		00603
Melissa Vargas		00690
Ricardo Pitre		00603
Angel Miranda		00603
Natalia Riera		00603
Wilson G. Román		00603
Wilson Román López		00603
Maribell Rivera S		00951
Héctor F Morales Chiu		00676
Carlos D Ramos		00677
Zoraida Buxó		00966

There were an additional 250 pages of signatures received for this petition. A full listing of all signatures received are part of the hearing record and are being retained in the Committee's official files.

FRENTE ESTADISTA

June 10, 2021

Hon. Raúl Grijalva, Chairman,
Natural Resources Committee,
United States House of Representatives,
Washington, DC

Hon. Bruce Westerman, Ranking Member,
Natural Resources Committee,
United States House of Representatives,
Washington, DC

Dear Chairman and Ranking Member:

We hereby list, and later debunk, all the arguments put forth on the letter dated June 10, 2021 from the "Frente Puertorriqueñista" (FP) with the intention to discredit and disavow Puerto Rico's mandate for statehood and to promote the bill introduced by Representative Nydia Velázquez and Representative Alexandria Ocasio-Cortez, H.R. 2070, under consideration by the Committee of Natural Resources:

1. FP's members claim that Puerto Rico's Congressional Delegation Special Election deriving from the Commonwealth of Puerto Rico's Law 167 of 2020, calling for the election of two (2) delegates to the United States Senate and four (4) delegates to the United States House of Representatives, had low voter turnout with only 3.9% of registered voters.
2. FP's members claim that former Governor Ricardo Rosselló, of the New Progressive Party (NPP), the only pro-statehood party in the island, was rejected by the majority of the population during the Summer 2019 manifestations in which protesters stationed themselves in front of La Fortaleza asking for his resignation due to the fact that details of a chain of private text messages were revealed to the public.
3. Finally, FP's members also claim that former Governor Ricardo Rossellóis under investigation by Puerto Rico's Department of Justice regarding a statement submitted to the State Elections Commission about his domicile. Their claim is that the pending case against the former governor should immediately and permanently disqualify him from becoming a delegate in the Special Delegation under the terms of Law 167 of 2020.

Here, we present our counterarguments in response to the claims in the letter submitted by the FP:

1) Law 167 of 2020 was rejected right from the onset by the parties opposing statehood for Puerto Rico. Furthermore, the anti-statehood parties hindered the ability of the State Elections Commission at every step, most importantly, rejecting agreements for an educational campaign as demonstrated by Certification CEE-AC-21-066.[61] This, along with many other actions reflected in the State Elections Commissions' records,

---

61 https://ww2.ceepur.org/sites/ComisionEE/es_pr/Secretaria/Acuerdos/Campa%C3%B1a%20educativa%20elecci%C3%B3n%20especial%20Ley%20para%20crear%20la%20Delegaci%C3%B3n%20Congresional%20de%20Puerto%20Rico.pdf.

demonstrate the partisan approach to the enacting of Law 167 seeking to undermine the special election at every step. Invariably, the only party left to make Puerto Rico's mandate for statehood effective through this election was the NPP.

It is important to note that anti-statehood parties, namely the Popular Democratic Party (PDP), the Citizen's Victory Movement (CVM), and the Puertorrican Independentist Party (PIP), all actively promoted a No vote in the plebiscite resulting in their defeat and, therefore, do not in any way represent the Will of the People as expressed in the November 3, 2020 vote for statehood.

Despite opposition from these minority political factions, Law 167 of 2020 was enacted, by the will of the people, and by the will of democracy evidenced through our voting power. While the anti-statehood parties attempted to make a media farce of Law 167 of 2020, their attempted media hijacking and repeated attempts at blocking its implementation, proved unsuccessful. Voters, once again, honored our democracy and elected our delegates. Five of the six elected delegates: Elizabeth Torres, María (Mayita) Meléndez, Roberto Lefranc, Zoraida Buxó, and Melinda Romero, completed a lengthy and rigorous process to achieve certification for their candidacy to be able to appear in the ballot. The requirements included: submitting endorsements signed by 3,000 citizens, providing tax records for the last ten (10) years, submit a sworn and notarized statement about their interest in the position, a negative drug test, a certification to attest absence of criminal records, certifications various about absence of debts in various governmental agencies, and certifications to attest completing trainings on ethics and government budget management. Candidates in this election completed all these requirements, which go way beyond the requirements the House or Senate have, in a matter of six (6) weeks. Dr. Rosselló's path to candidacy followed a different path because his nomination came up as a matter of popular acclaim. He accepted the offer to be part of the delegation three days before the electoral event and agreed that if elected via "direct nomination" he would comply with requirements to that effect.

Claiming a low voter turnout in the Congressional Delegation's Special Election is a weak, if not altogether invalid, argument since already, and even with the COVID-19 pandemic restrictions, the majority of our people voted, unequivocally, not only for two representatives of the NPP, the only party seeking our admission into the Union, but voted in even higher numbers in the plebiscite to express their approval for an immediate admission of Puerto Rico as a state of the Union.

1,289,135 American Citizens in Puerto Rico voted yes or no to statehood in the 2020 Plebiscite. 52.52% unequivocally said yes to the question about the immediate admission of Puerto Rico into the Union as the 51st state of the United States.

If we were to address the inadmissible claim that low voter turnout constitutes in any way an argument for questioning election results, we must put this into fair perspective. The Center for American Progress states, in an article calling on ways to increase voter participation in the United States, that "[a]lmost 92 million eligible Americans did not vote in the 2016 presidential elections. In the 2014 midterm elections, an estimated 143 million eligible Americans failed to vote, marking the lowest voter participation in 72 years."[62]

Furthermore, despite the low voter turnouts in previous elections within the United States, the same democratic institutions which we resemble in our own model of democracy, the will of the majority of those who exercise their right to vote is not disregarded, or their votes made void. Democracy owes its stability to the continuation of government based on the votes that are cast, not those that are not.

2) As to the argument that former Governor Ricardo Rossellóshould be placed in controversy sequestering the Will of the People, we only wish to present the facts. Roughly 70,000 Puerto Rican voters wrote-in Dr. Ricardo Rosselló's name on the ballot to elect him as a delegate to the House, so that he, along with the other delegates, lobbies in Congress for our status to change from that of a territory to that of a State. Must those, or any of the votes for the delegates or any other elected official, be rendered void and null using any sort of questionable reasoning. But, what type of government shall we become if we were to ignore and deny the expressed Will of the People?

As to the events that transpired in the summer of 2019, these are easy to misjudge. A supposed "*majority of people*" in our Island rose to take down what they deemed untenable leadership. We must then bring to bear as evidence the necessary parallels between these and the events occurred in Capitol Hill on January 6, 2021. The entire world watched on their screens the scenes in which a group of American Citizens protested violently to undermine the nature of elections and, with it, the nature of democracy. Protesters revolted in loud proclamations and violent acts against the decision of the majority of American Citizens who voted to, as statutorily set forth by the Federal Government, complete the mandate by *which the very foundation of the United States of America is sustained.*

The majority of American Voters were nowhere near a representation of the insurrectionists who attempted to manifest through sheer brute force their claims over justice and democracy at the doorsteps of Capitol Hill. No matter how loud they screamed, no matter what force of violence they utilized, those American Citizens who participated in the January 6th insurrection, disregarding the democratic voices of the rest of the American people, stand as a seditious mob akin to that on Calle Fortaleza in the Summer of 2019. A loud minority of individuals, incited by seditious groups benefiting from the unrest, used the discontent ripped from many struggles at once to not only protest, but to vandalize businesses, homes, and churches, and instigate and commit acts of violence against the police. Former Governor Ricardo Rossellóresigned in good part due to the amount of violence these minorities used. He decided to step aside to avoid a tumultuous and violent rising of these groups who were keen to overtake La Fortaleza,

---

62 https://www.americanprogress.org/issues/democracy/reports/2018/07/11/453319/increasing-voter-participation_america/.

the Governor's residence, which stands as an emblem of our Constitution, and Democracy, and Freedom.

The questionable origins of the events immediately preceding Dr. Rosselló's resignation seem to have been forgotten by voters who have actively sought out his return to office as one of the delegates who are to further statehood in the House of the United States Congress.

3) The investigation of the claims against Dr. Ricardo Rossellóis currently underway at the Department of Justice headed by General Attorney Domingo Emmanuelli. Should the investigation find that Dr. Rossellócommitted a negligible act or acts in pursuit of a position in the Delegation under the terms of Law 167 of 2020 or any other law, the appropriate authority will advise and enact the due course of action. Only fate will decide. As we stand, the matter is in the hands of the Puerto Rico Department of Justice and the two attorneys spearheading the case. In any case, there are five (5) more delegates that will ensure the continuation of efforts to bring about statehood for Puerto Rico. They were all elected. They will go on to do their job. Their jobs and their role, our mandate and our future, must not be hijacked by unsubstantiated accusations nor will it be.

In conclusion, while the written statements submitted to Congress by the FP and co-signed by Carmen Yulín Cruz, Aníbal Acevedo Viláand Luis Gutiérrez among others, seem reasonable, not everything is as it appears. At least two of the proponents of FP's arguments, Cruz and Acevedo-Vilá, belong to the PDP party. The PDP seeks to maintain our territorial status adding more benefits brought about by the United States. A fallacy. Furthermore, both ran for office in the 2020 elections and both lost. As you may gather, Cruz and Acevedo-Viláin no way represent the will of the majority that rules democracy. Cruz ran for Mayor of our Capital city of San Juan, only to lose to Miguel Romero from the NPP, again, the candidate from the only pro-statehood party. We must further bring forth the evidence that points to Cruz's mismanagements during her eight years as Mayor of San Juan which is starting to come out as Romero audits the city's vaults. Acevedo-Vilá, on the other hand, a former governor from the PDP from 2005–2009 who also held the office of Resident Commissioner from 2001–2005 had to deal with 13 corruption charges brought against him by the Federal Bureau of Investigation. The charges were cleared through scapegoating as many under his purvue took the fall. All accused but Acevedo were found guilty. Additionally, the People of Puerto Rico have not forgotten the impeding weight of the taxation he imposed upon us, in the form of "el IVU," otherwise referred as to the Sales and Use Tax, the amount of 11% of any purchase that a person in Puerto Rico must pay when buying an item as well as the irresponsible and outrageous debt issued during his incumbency, amongst many other failures. Acevedo carries the stigma of being the ultimate statehood blocker. In 1998, Acevedo sabotaged a plebiscite to solve the status question by promoting a vote for "None of the above." In 2016, he called a boycott of another plebiscite to decide on the status question. In 2020, he asked to burn the statehood yes/no plebiscite ballots. Acevedo has wreaked havoc to effectively sabotage efforts that would forever do away with his own political agenda and stance for Puerto Rico, independence. Knowing well that support for statehood has grown with the passage of time and will continue to grow, Acevedo insists on turning a blind eye to the People's mandate.

Both, Cruz and Acevedo, oppose statehood and have sought to overturn their own political party's historical stance on status to have it embrace the ideology of independence. Both lack objectivity in their claims and have claimed in FP's own mission statement that they are against Statehood and they will fight to deter it.

As to former U.S. Representative of Illinois' 4th District Luis Gutiérrez, in an article written in the Chicago Sun on April 7th of this year by columnist Mark Brown, Gutiérrez openly stated, "*What got me into politics was the fight for the independence of Puerto Rico*." Further, the Committee should also be reminded that, during his time in the House, Gutiérrez was investigated in 2017 after having been arrested during a protest outside of the White House. After paying a fine for his misconduct, the House Committee on Ethics recommended no further action. In 2013, Gutiérrez was investigated for using funds from his Member's Representational Allowance from 2003–2013 for an unauthorized purpose—to retain an individual to provide services to his congressional office that more closely resembled those provided by an employee or consultant, rather than a contractor. In March 2018, the House Committee on Ethics reproved Gutiérrez for using his Member Representational Allowance inappropriately, albeit possibly unwittingly, and ordered him to reimburse the US Treasury for that use. On November 28, 2017, Representative Gutiérrez announced he would not seek reelection. He moved to Puerto Rico to campaign for the No in the plebiscite and push to pro-independence propaganda for a year. This year he moved back to Chicago.

"Do not cast a stone if you yourself are not free of sin," warned Jesus to the mob. These FP members have casted big stones they themselves should not, in good faith, even hold in their hands.

We must finalize by addressing the matter of HR2070's alleged benevolence in seeking Puerto Rico's self-determination while, in fact, doing the complete opposite: standing as pure election denialism. The arguments in defense of HR2070, the legislation introduced by Representatives Velázquez and Ocasio-Cortez, are corrupted in their efforts to sound democratic. While the arguments claim to pursue inclusion of all the political factions now represented throughout our Island, it denies the fact that all political factions participated and even campaigned during the time prior to the statehood plebiscite. The result is clear. The No was defeated. And HR2070 is none other than an attempt at ignoring the People's Will and blocking the passage of HR1522 and the process of democracy.

No doubt, HR2070s authors have devised a form of procedural filibuster, in the sense that they seek to prolong a never-ending rhetoric of manipulative political inclusion in order to obstruct progress and justice for the People of Puerto Rico.

Democracy is clear, when the majority votes, such is the rule of law that it requires that the minority of any political faction or any minority political opinions, no matter how desirous they are for power, should concede and abide by the Will of the People, and even assist that majority in drawing the plans for a shared future. All, in good faith, for the well-being, freedom, safety, and security of the People.

We voted. We decided. More than 600,000 US citizens in Puerto Rico expressed their unequivocal will by answering Yes to the question of statehood. Our mandate must not only be heard, it must be respected and it must be swiftly acted on. Such is the rule of the law. Such is the basis of our democracy. Where the majority elects and sits leaders and determines the direction of our future. Our democracy protects our votes. Our votes protect our democracy. We rest our case.

Respectfully,

Zayira Jordán-Conde,
Founder

Domestic and International Legal Advice, LLC, C/O Gregorio Igartua, Aguadilla, PR, June 11, 2021

Hon. Raul Grijalva
House Committee on Natural Resources
1324 Longworth House Office Building
Washington, DC

Re: WRITTEN TESTIMONY FOR COMMITTEE ON PUERTO RICO'S TERRITORIAL STATUS—P.R. SELF DETERMINATION ACT, STATEHOOD ADMISSION ACT

Dear Chairman Grijalva:

I was born in Puerto Rico, U.S.A., and, I am an American citizen resident of Puerto Rico. I am sending this written testimony in opposition to the proposed "Self Determination Act," which is not constitutionally viable, and to support the Puerto Rico Statehood Admission Act. It is the only political alternative that fits in the U.S. Constitutional Framework, and it is 122 years overdue.

As you know, Puerto Rico has been a part of the United States since 1898. For 122 years we have been under the U.S. Government discriminatory practice of being denied the right to vote in Federal Elections, and of government without the consent of the governed (3.4 million American Citizens by birth). We are also subject to unequal treatment in economic policies implemented by Congress for the states, which have moved Puerto Rico into bankruptcy. Moreover, for some cases the Federal Courts apply the U.S. Constitution, and not for others. (Consider, for example: the stance of the US DOJ in *US v. Vaello*, USSC #20-303, now before the Court, opposing equal protection treatment for Puerto Rico in the SSSI benefits; versus, President's Biden support for applicability of the SSSI; versus, the USDOJ stance in the case of *US v PR Police Dept.*, 922-FS 2nd 185 (2013), requiring Puerto Rico, under a penalty payment of 100 million dollars, to train police to secure U.S. equal protection and due process rights. Such are the constitutional contradictions the Congress is allowing for legal and economic treatment for 3.3 million American Citizens. (*See San Juan Star Article enclosed*). Ironically, we pay more than $3 billion dollars a year in federal taxes, more than some states and many state regions. (IRS Highlights 2020). Moreover, Congress grants annually billions of dollars to foreign countries, and can also implement federal taxes in Puerto Rico as to the states, at will.

The Committee of Natural Resources you preside, has expressed interest in pursuing Congressional action in the issue of the political status of Puerto Rico. I suggest that you consider as the most viable alternative that Puerto Rico be certified as an incorporated territory first, which de facto it is. Notwithstanding incorporation is not permanent, therefore Congress should simultaneously resolved to move Puerto Rico in transit to statehood at a definite date. Certification of Incorporation would make the U.S. Constitution fully applicable, and would give us parity with federal funds as if Puerto Rico were a state. We qualify for incorporation by having been assimilated more than any other U.S. Territory before becoming a state. Although there may be conflicting views of what is the political relation of Puerto Rico to the United States, due to the reality that we are still not a state, Congress has assimilated us gradually since 1898 into a federalist relation to be like a de facto incorporated territory. (See: G. Igartua, The "de facto" Incorporated Territory U.S. of Puerto Rico. A copy of the Book was mailed to you a few months ago, and one was mailed to the Committee).

I respectfully suggest that you consider proposing to Congress to declare Puerto Rico officially an Incorporated Territory of the United States in transit to statehood. (See Petition enclosed—Annex A). It is the only political alternative that fits into the U.S. Constitutional framework, it is 122 years overdue.

Rather than holding more hearings on what we could hypothetically be, which is discriminatory, our political and civil rights must be recognized by Congress based on what we are, 3.4 American citizens by birth residents of a de facto incorporated territory. Incorporation was recently supported unanimously by the National Association of U.S. Mayors. (Annex B). (*See also, Consejo de Salud Playa de Ponce v Rullan, 586 FS 2nd 22 (2008)*).

No one in Puerto Rico wants independence, nor continue to be confused with political status alternatives which do not fit within the U.S. constitutional framework. No one in Puerto Rico wants to renounce their American Citizenship. A Republic of American citizens would be a matter of national security concern. (3.3 million residing in Puerto Rico, 5 million residing in states). Many are confused by the daily practice of uncertainty brought by the questioning about what our rights are as American citizens, or could be. Consider within this context the "Puerto Rico Self Determination Act" proposed for American citizens after 122 years under our American flag. Were African-Americans subjected, or should be subjected, to hearings on whether they would like to be slaves again, or be moved to a Country in Africa? Should Mexican-Americans be asked whether they would like to renounce their American Citizenship to Mexican and be moved back to Mexico, or should their American citizenship status be questioned, as your Committee is doing with us in Puerto Rico in 2021? Insulting to the American citizens of Puerto Rico to be forced to participate in a plebiscite on whether these vote for independence, not for equality as American citizens.

Consider as constitutionally viable only to start holding hearings on how the American Citizens residents of Puerto Rico can have equal rights and government by the consent of the governed. (*U.S. Constitution Amendments XIV and XV*). Congressman Grijalva, statehood for you, for Congresswomen Velazquez and Ocasio, for all the members of your Committee, for all Congressmen, and statehood for us the American citizens residents of Puerto Rico. Time is of the essence.

I respectfully request to be allowed to participate in the June 16, 2021, hearing your Committee has scheduled on this subject, and in support of our American Citizenship rights.

Sincerely yours,

Gregorio Igartua

Annex A

PETITION

ADDRESSED TO THE CONGRESS OF THE UNITED STATES OF AMERICA TO CERTIFY PUERTO RICO WITH A JOINT RESOLUTION AS AN INCORPORATED TERRITORY OF THE UNITED STATES IN TRANSIT TO STATEHOOD

WHEREAS: Puerto Rico became a United States of America territory in 1898 by the Treaty of Paris, which provided that: "... *the civil rights and political status of the native inhabitants of the territories hereby ceded to the United States shall be determined by Congress.*" Immediately the native inhabitants became Nationals under the Custody and "*Parens Patriae*" of the United States of America.

WHEREAS: In 1917, the residents of Puerto Rico were granted United States American citizenship, by their own free and voluntary election, and after 1941 by birth, as disposed by Congress, enacting laws to such effect. To this date, three point four millions United States American Citizens reside in Puerto Rico and five millions have moved their residence to the mainland, were they have worked and are still working in building our Nation.

WHEREAS: Since 1917, the United States American Citizens of Puerto Rico have demonstrated their loyalty to the United States of America and to democracy by serving with dedication and honor in all armed conflicts in the Armed Forces of our Country, without the right to vote for their Commander in Chief, including many of them by dying in these conflicts.

WHEREAS: In 1952, the United States American Citizens of Puerto Rico constituted themselves into a Republican form of government in compliance with Article IV, Section 4, Constitution of the United States of America, similarly as the process used for former territories to become states of the Nation. In the Constitution of 1952, the citizens by direct vote swore their loyalty to their United States American citizenship, to the Constitution the United States of America and accepted to be under the Supremacy Clause of the Constitution, with reference to the National Government as are states under federalism.

WHEREAS: The United States American Citizens of Puerto Rico are subject to the jurisdiction of all three Branches of the Government of the United States of America. The Puerto Rico Federal Courts are Article III of the U.S. Constitution.

WHEREAS: All income from sources outside of Puerto Rico is subject to federal taxation, and the United States American Citizens residing in Puerto Rico contribute billions of dollars to the Federal Treasury paying more in federal taxes than residents of various regions in the fifty states without representation.

WHEREAS: In the quadrennial elections, held since 1964, ninety five percent (95%) or more of the voters have chosen permanent union with the United States of America. The independence has been rejected by the voters to such an extent that the Independence Party has been politically disqualified in quadrennial election.

WHEREAS: Two of the local political parties, supported by more than ninety six percent (96%) of the total voters, participate in National Politics as members of the Republican and Democratic Parties.

WHEREAS: The Government of the United States of America has been actively promoting democracy, universal suffrage, and human rights all over the world. (Presently very actively un Venezuela).

WHEREAS: The U.S. Constitution has been judicially applied to the American Citizens of Puerto Rico as if it were a state, but the non-incorporation status is being used by the Federal Courts and by Congress to switch "on and off" its applicability discriminatorily, costing more than ten billion dollars annually in federal transfers.

WHEREAS: Puerto Rico is a de facto incorporated territory of the United States because since 1898 it has been gradually moved to be legally treated and assimilated like a state more than any other U.S. Territory before being certified as incorporated. Moreover, the degree of incorporation of Puerto Rico to be like a state can be considered by implication as strong as to exclude any other view than that it is an incorporated territory of the United Sates. (See, *Consejo de Salud Playa de Ponce v Rullan, 586, FS 2nd 22 (2008)*). It has met all the requirements adopted for the Northwestern Ordinance.

WHEREAS: The First Amendment to the Constitution of the United States guarantees the right of the American Citizens to "... *petition the Government for a redress of grievances* ..." in order to ensure liberty, general welfare, and to protect their rights and privileges as American Citizens.

WHEREAS: It is the duty of Congress to protect the constitutional rights of all American citizens. The present degree of legal assimilation of Puerto Rico to the United States under domestic and International law supports this Petition to certify it as an incorporated territory of the United States in transit to statehood.

THEREFORE:

I, an American Citizen resident of Puerto Rico, respectfully request Congress to adopt a Resolution certifying Puerto Rico as an Incorporated Territory of the United States in transit to statehood.

Signed this April / 2 / 2021

Gregorio Igartua

PETITIONER SIGNATURE

Box 3911, Aguadilla, Puerto Rico 00605
ADDRESS

(787) 891-9040 - Office (787) 379-5095 - Cellular
TELEPHONE

bufeteigartua@yahoo.com
E-MAIL

Annex B

The United States Conference of Mayors
1620 EYE STREET, NORTHWEST
WASHINGTON, D.C. 20006
TELEPHONE (202) 293-7330
FAX (202) 293-2352
URL: www.usmayors.org

87th Annual Meeting
Honolulu, Hawai'i

Puerto Rico as an Incorporated Territory of the United States

WHEREAS, Puerto Rico became a United States of America territory in 1898 by the Treaty of Paris, which provided that: "... the civil rights and political status of the native inhabitants of the territories hereby ceded to the United States shall be determined by Congress." Immediately the native inhabitants became Nationals under the Custody and "Parens Patriae" of the United States of America; and

WHEREAS, Since 1917, The United States American Citizens of Puerto Rico have demonstrated their loyalty to the United States of America and to democracy by serving with dedication and honor in all armed conflicts in the Armed Forces of our Country, without the right to vote for their Commander in Chief, including many of them by dying in these conflicts; and

WHEREAS, In 1917, the residents of Puerto Rico were granted United States American citizenship, by their own free and voluntary election, and after 1941 by birth, as disposed by Congress, enacting laws to such effect. To this date, three point four millions United States American Citizens reside in Puerto Rico and four millions have moved their residence to the mainland, were they have worked and are still working in building our Nation; and

WHEREAS, In 1952, The United States American Citizens of Puerto Rico constituted themselves into a Republican form of government in compliance with Article IV, Section 4, Constitution of the United States of America, similarly as the process used for former territories to become states of the Nation. In the Constitution of 1952, the citizens by direct vote swore their loyalty to their United States American citizenship, to the Constitution of United States of America and accepted to be under the Supremacy Clause of the Constitution, with reference to the National Government as are states under federalism; and

WHEREAS, The United States American Citizens of Puerto Rico are subject to the jurisdiction of all three Branches of the Government of the United States of America. The Puerto Federal Courts are Article III of the U.S. Constitution; and

WHEREAS, All income from sources outside of Puerto Rico is subject to federal taxation, and the United States American Citizens residing in Puerto Rico contribute billions of dollars to the Federal Treasury. The United States American Citizens residing in Puerto Rico pay more in federal taxes than residents of various regions in the fifty states; and

WHEREAS, In the quadrennial elections, held since 1964 ninety five percent (95%) or more of the voters have chosen permanent union with The United States of America. The independence has been rejected by the voters to such an extent that the Independence Party has been politically disqualified in quadrennial election; and

WHEREAS, Two of the local political parties, supported by more than ninety six percent (96%) of the total voters, participate in National Politics as members of the Republican and Democratic Parties; and

WHEREAS, The Government of the United States of America has been actively promoting democracy, universal suffrage, and human rights all over the world. (Presently very actively un Venezuela); and

WHEREAS, The Constitution of the United States of America has been judicially applied to the United States American Citizens of Puerto Rico as if it were

a state, but the non-incorporation status is being used by the Federal Courts and by Congress to switch "on and off" the applicability of the U.S. Constitution discriminatory, costing more than five billion dollars annually in federal transfers; and

WHEREAS, Puerto Rico is a de facto incorporated territory of the United States of America, because since 1898 it has been gradually moved to be legally treated and assimilated like a state more than any other U.S. Territory before being certified as incorporated. Moreover, the degree of incorporation of Puerto Rico to be like a state can be considered by implication as strong as to exclude any other view than that it is an incorporated territory of the United Sates; and

WHEREAS, The First Amendment to the Constitution of the United States of America guarantees the right of United States American Citizens to u... petition the Government for a redress of grievances ... " in order to ensure liberty, genera' welfare, and to protect our rights and privileges as United States of America Citizens; and

WHEREAS: It is the duty of Congress to protect the constitutional rights of all American citizens. The present degree of legal assimilation of Puerto Rico to the United States under domestic and international law supports this Petition to certify it as an incorporated territory of the United States,

NOW IT THEREFORE, BE IT RESOLVED, that the members of The U.S. Conference of Mayors, respectfully request Congress to adopt a Resolution certifying Puerto Rico as an Incorporated Territory of the United States. Copies of this document will be forwarded to the following Federal and States Public Bodies, and/or other parties; President of the United States America, Hon. Donald Trump; Vice President of the United States of America, Hon. Michael R. Pence; Speaker of the United States of America House of Representatives, Hon. Nancy Pelosi; Governor of Puerto Rico, Hon. Ricardo Rossello; and, to the Resident Commissioner of Puerto Rico, Hon. Jennifer Gonzalez.

GOOD MORNING | 3

he San Juan Daily Star, the only paper with **The New York Times News Service** *in English in Puerto R*
ith a Monday, Tuesday, Wednesday and Thursday edition, along with a Weekend Edition to cover Frida

June 14, 202

publishes 7 days a wee
Saturday and Sunday.

Is the equal protection clause being applied unequally?

By THE STAR STAFF

While the U.S. Justice Department told the U.S. Supreme Court recently that the equal protection clause does not apply to Puerto Rico in cases involving the extension of Supplemental Security Income (SSI) to the U.S. territory, it has argued the opposite in previous cases, a local constitutional lawyer said Sunday.

Gregorio Igartúa, a pro-statehood attorney, said the Justice Department uses the equal protection clause when it is convenient to argue against discrimination. In the civil rights case filed against the Puerto Rico Police Department (PRPD) nine years ago, federal officials accused the local agency of violations to the equal protection clause.

"Someone is lying. Either you say equal protection applies or not," Igartúa said.

A settlement was reached in which the PRPD was ordered to deliver services equitably, respectfully, and free of unlawful bias, in a manner that promotes broad community engagement and supports effective crime prevention.

"In conducting its activities, PRPD shall ensure that members of the public receive equal protection of the law, without bias based on race, color, ethnicity, national origin, religion, gender, disability, sexual orientation, gender identity, gender expression, or political ideology or affiliation, and in accordance with the rights, privileges, or immunities secured or protected by the Constitution and laws of the United States and the Commonwealth of Puerto Rico," a settlement reached several years ago said.

In the case currently before the Supreme Court, United States vs Vaello Madero, the question parties have to answer is whether the U.S. Congress violated the equal-protection clause by establishing SSI, a program that provides benefits to needy, aged, blind and otherwise disabled individuals, in the 50 states and the District of Columbia, but not in Puerto Rico.

Under the case, the U.S. government sought to claw back some $28,081 in SSI payments that José Vaello Madero had received from the program over a three-year period after he moved back to Puerto Rico from New York in 2013. He appealed. The District Court and the Appeals Court have both ruled in favor of Vaello Madero that not extending the SSI to Puerto Rico violated the equal protection clause.

However, the federal Justice Department last week argued that Congress can discriminate against Puerto Rico in matters related to social welfare. The Justice Department says Congress, not the courts, should decide the federal government's treatment of Puerto Rico, including access, if any, to SSI benefits.

Puerto Rico's unique tax status and resulting fiscal autonomy provide a rational basis for the decision not to extend the SSI program to its residents. Residents of the island are exempt from a broad range of federal taxes, including federal income taxes.

"In practical terms, Puerto Rico's tax status means that much of the revenue that would have flowed into the federal treasury can flow into the territorial treasury instead," the federal agency said. "That is so because Puerto Rico can replace the inapplicable federal taxes with its own territorial taxes. For example, Puerto Rico has taken advantage of its exemption from federal income tax by imposing a territorial individual income tax of up to 33% for the highest bracket — well above the typical rate in the States."

President Joe Biden said the Justice Department's actions are "inconsistent with my administration's policies and values."

"However, the Department of Justice has a longstanding practice of defending the constitutionality of federal statutes, regardless of policy preferences," the president added. "This practice is critical to the department's mission of preserving the rule of law. Consistent with this important practice, the department is defending the constitutionality of the Social Security Act provision in this case."

But Igartúa said the Justice Department works under Biden and questioned the reasons why the president does not intervene.

On Wednesday, U.S. House Natural Resources Committee Chairman Raúl M. Grijalva (D-Ariz.) will oversee a hearing on legislation focused on Puerto Rico's political status. The hearing follows another one held in April.

The hearing will examine the implications of the bills. One, sponsored by Reps. Nydia Velázquez (D-N.Y.) and Alexandria Ocasio-Cortez (D-N.Y.), would "recognize the right of the People of Puerto Rico to call a status convention through which the people would exercise their natural right to self-determination, and to establish a mechanism for congressional consideration of such decision." The other, sponsored by Rep. Darren Soto (D-Fla.) and Resident Commissioner Jennifer González Colón (R-P.R.), would "provide for the admission of the State of Puerto Rico into the Union."

The hearing was slated to be held after a Justice Department opinion that has yet to be made.

"Congress needs to keep moving forward on this, because Puerto Rico can't stay in limbo any longer," Grijalva said Sunday. "The future of millions of Puerto Ricans shouldn't be a political football. This Committee takes its responsibility to address this issue seriously, and we're going to hear from experts on how best to proceed before we take any final steps."

On Friday, meanwhile, the issue of Puerto Rico's political status will be heard at the U.N. Decolonization Committee.

June 16, 2021

Hon. Raúl M. Grijalva, Chairman,
House Committee on Natural Resources,
1324 Longworth House Office Building,
Washington, DC

Hon. Bruce Westerman, Ranking Member,
House Committee on Natural Resources,
1324 Longworth House Office Building,
Washington, DC

Re: COMMITTEE HEARING ON PUERTO RICO POLITICAL STATUS BILLS H.R. 1522 AND H.R. 2070

Dear Chairman, Ranking Member, and Members of the Committee:

I write to you in support of H.R. 1522: the Puerto Rico Statehood Admission Act, and to speak against H.R. 2070, the Puerto Rico Self-Determination Act of 2021.

My reasons to support H.R. 1522 are simple: respecting the will of American citizens, enfranchising 3.3 million Americans not adequately represented in their government, and provide them with full constitutional protections and equal protection of laws.

In pursuance to solving the century-old "political status" question, Puerto Rico has held six plebiscites. The November 2020 plebiscite was different from previous ones. Together with the general elections, the ballot asked a straightforward question modeling the same proposition Alaska and Hawaii used in their plebiscites before being admitted as states: Should Puerto Rico be admitted immediately into the Union as a State? Yes or No. With 53% of the votes, *YES to Statehood* won. It received substantially more votes than any political party or candidate, including the pro-statehood party and for the offices of Governor and Resident Commissioner. Statehood won in every senatorial district on the island and in 33 of 40 representative districts. Notwithstanding, in the seven districts where the *No* option won, Yes to statehood obtained more votes than the candidate who was elected. It was also the first time when every political faction, party, or group assumed a clear position on the options.

The last plebiscite showed three things:

1. Support for statehood supersedes partisan politics. It is a multipartisan, multi-ideological movement composed of people from all around the island and backgrounds.
2. Puerto Ricans can differentiate between partisan politics and political status. Although the pro-status quo party won the majority in the local legislature, it does not erase and must not ignore that in the same elections statehood won.
3. Confirmed a trend that previous plebiscites had shown. Support for the Commonwealth option was declining and ultimately rejected, and support for statehood increased until it finally won as the preferred alternative.

To uphold the will of Americans in the last plebiscite, Congresswoman Jenniffer González-Colón (R-PR), alongside Rep. Darren Soto (D-FL), file H.R. 1522 to provide for the admission of the State of Puerto Rico. It currently has 68 co-sponsors: 17 Republicans and 51 Democrats.

The filing and cosponsorship of the bill right away tell three facts that speak for themselves:

1. It was introduced by Puerto Rico's elected representative in Congress, not by other members representing other districts that Americans on the island did not vote for.
2. It shows that admitting Puerto Rico as a state is a bipartisan effort representing a movement that, just as in the island, is diverse and encompasses people from all sides of the political spectrum.
3. The bill is cosponsored by two members who hold leadership positions in the House: Majority Leader Steny Hoyer and Republican Conference Chair Elise Stefanik.

By contrast, H.R. 2070 has only Democratic support with no House leadership involved, and the representative elected by Puerto Rico strongly opposes the bill. The Self-Determination Act is a flawed and contradictory bill.

1. Sec. 3(a) of the bill establishes that the legislature of Puerto Rico has the "inherent authority to call a status convention." However, it ignores that by that same authority Puerto Rico's duly elected politicians have called for referendums, and they must be given deference in their actions. H.R. 1522 recognizes the Puerto Rico legislature's inherent authority to call for referendums and acts on the people's choice.
2. The bill says it recognizes Puerto Rico's "natural right to self-determination." It is interesting that while it acknowledges that we have that right, H.R. 2070 completely ignores the times when Puerto Ricans themselves have exercised it. H.R. 1522 takes the self-determination option Puerto Rico voted for and provides a ratifying vote.
3. Sec. 3(a)(2)(1) states that delegates to the convention shall draft options for Puerto Rico "outside the Territorial Clause" of the U.S. Constitution. That language creates the fantasy of multiple options when there are only two: statehood and independence. A compact of free association, which is not guaranteed, would be after achieving independence.
4. H.R. 2070 is not time bounded. It does not specify the length of the convention, terms on when and how Congress or the Puerto Rico legislature may act, and no limits at all. The bill is time-open until who knows when the delegates would

draft the options, hold a referendum, and sent it to Congress. H.R. 1522 is time-specific, sets due dates the President and the Government of Puerto Rico must act.

5. The bill complicates the political status issue with unfamiliar voting formats with the intention to delude the will of the people. In addition, the voting options are prone to confusion. Sec. 5(a)(C) establishes that there could be "more than one choice with the same self-determination definition" but with different transition plans. H.R. 2070 proposed referendum suffers from the same inconsistencies some people have complained about in local plebiscites. On the other hand, H.R. 1522 is clear and will ask the people if they agree with the terms prescribed by Congress and it also details the transition from territory to state.
6. Finally, this bill tries to bind Congress to the results of the self-determination referendum. The legislative branch has absolute sovereignty in its legislative power; it cannot force itself to legislate one way or the other except by the limitations outlined in the Constitution because its sovereign power over legislative matters is complete. Much less could bind futures Congresses. By contrast, H.R. 1522 binds the Executive, a legitimate exercise of congressional authority via a statutory requirement to the President to formally proclaim, once the bill is passed and the admission act is ratified, Puerto Rico as a State of the Union.

In summary, H.R. 1522 is the bill that respects the will of Americans who voted for statehood. It has specific provisions regarding the admission of Puerto Rico into the Union, has support that is both bipartisan and reaching all sides of the political spectrum, and lets the people vote again to ratify the Admission Act. Anti-statehood opponents and skeptics say that the results of the 2020 plebiscite are not enough. I would like to remind them that 53% is the *absolute majority* of the electorate; that with lesser margins laws are passed, judicial and executive appointments are confirmed, and politicians, including presidents, are elected, shaping forever the future of the country. That is called living in a democracy.

Justice John Marshall Harlan said:

> "The idea that this country may acquire territories anywhere upon the earth . . . the people inhabiting them to enjoy only such rights as Congress chooses to accord to them is wholly inconsistent with the spirit and genius, as well as with the words, of the Constitution . . . I cannot grasp the thought that Congress, which lives and moves and has its being in the Constitution, and is consequently the mere creature of that instrument, can at its pleasure legislate or exclude its creator from territories which were acquired only by authority of the Constitution" Downes v. Bidwell, 182 U.S. 244 (1901) (Harlan, dissenting).

Justice Harlan was known as the Great Dissenter for his dissenting opinions in cases that restricted civil rights. Dissenting in *Plessy v. Ferguson*, he stated that the Constitution is colorblind and that all citizens should have equal access to civil rights. In 1954, he was vindicated in *Brown v. Board of Education*. It is up to you, members of the Committee, to vindicate once again a Justice who stood in the right side of history.

Statehood means complete protection of the U.S. Constitution to more than 3 million Americans in Puerto Rico who somehow, only for living on the island, lose equal protection in many laws. Statehood is self-governance and upholding the ideals and values the United States was founded, and for which thousands of Puerto Ricans have fought and died defending freedom and democracy. It is equal justice under the law; it is "securing the blessing of Liberty to ourselves and our posterity."

Respectfully,

Juan C. Ruiz Pinzón

June 16, 2021
Hon. Raúl Grijalva, Chairman,
House Committee on Natural Resources

Hon. Bruce Westerman, Ranking Member,
House Committee on Natural Resources

Dear Chairman Grijalva and Ranking Member:

The purpose of this letter is to urge you to act upon Puerto Rico's current colonial and/or territorial status. It is mind boggling to me and many of my Puerto Rican brothers and sisters that the land of the free, has held a colony hostage for 113 years.

Over a quarter million Puerto Rican soldiers have defended our great nation: 18,000 in WWI, 65,000 in WWII, 61,000 in the Korean War, 48,000 in the Vietnam War, 48,000 in the Gulf War and Iraqi Freedom, and 39,000 active, reserve and National Guard members; yet the home of the brave, regrettably, is not home to my Puerto Rican brothers and sisters who have bravely defended our great nation, but cannot vote to elect their Commander in Chief, nor have full representation in Congress. We have earned statehood with the blood of the Puerto Rican brothers and sisters who have proudly defended our nation.

It is unacceptable that Congress has historically chosen to ignore the express will of the American citizens living in Puerto Rico. I do not need to state Puerto Rico's history, as you are well aware of our colonial status, and how that status has kept us from fully enjoying the privileges of American citizenship. The question before you today is whether you choose to act to change that. Puerto Rico and its people certainly are.

Puerto Rico already acts like a state; we have US currency, we already pay federal taxes like Medicare, Medicaid and Social Security, we speak both English and Spanish and our government has the same structure as other state governments. That notwithstanding, we are not recognized the same the same rights as citizens who live in the other 50 states.

By supporting HR 2070 by Congresswomen Velazquez and Ocasio Cortez you will be doing the complete opposite. You would impose a course of action by Congress that ignores the will of Puerto Ricans who already voted in favor of statehood. That would be the utmost expression of Colonialism and contrary to what the United States of America stands for. Therefore, I strongly urge the Members of Congress to support HR 1522 introduced by Congressman Darren Soto and Puerto Rico's lawfully elected official Resident Commissioner Jenniffer González. This is the only bill that respects the will of the 655,505 American citizens living in Puerto Rico, 53% whom voted yes to statehood.

You have the privilege and opportunity today to take a step in the right direction. I strongly urge you to be in the right side of history. Support statehood for Puerto Rico. As American citizens, we deserve no less than our mainland brothers and sisters.

Cordially,

Roberto Lefranc Fortuño,
US Representative (Shadow), Puerto Rico

STATEMENT FOR THE RECORD, MARÍA MELÉNDEZ

Good afternoon (morning). Thank you to the Committee leadership for convening this hearing and for the opportunity to speak in support of H.R. 1522. This hearing is an essential step in the desegregation of the American citizens of Puerto Rico and the full recognition of our rights as American citizens.

As a former three-term mayor of the city of Ponce, current shadow representative, and a lifelong resident of the Island, I can attest to the dire effects the current territorial status has had on our economy, our institutions, and our people. For the past two decades we have experienced an unprecedented demographic crisis. Almost twenty-five percent (25%) of our fellow citizens have had to move from the Island to the States fragmenting our families and distressing our socioeconomic fabric. Unequal treatment and lack of political participation at the federal level have placed us in a subordinate position, a state of structural disadvantage with dire implications. We are not talking about purely theoretical or philosophical concepts but about realities that we face daily.

Effective political participation, and thus fundamental civil rights, requires the right to participate in all these public affairs that impact us. The interrelation between effective political participation and social and economic development does not arise exclusively from our experience. Instead, it constitutes a principle recognized in multiple international instruments, including the Inter-American Democratic Charter of the Organization of American States, which provides in its preamble that: ". . . economic growth and social development based on justice and equity and democracy are interdependent and mutually reinforcing." This is why we cannot isolate Puerto Rico's problems from the status discussion; they are intricately connected.

The perils of our political condition have become more visible and critical at a time when even the exercise of the most elementary rights and political prerogatives at the state level are subject to review by a federally appointed financial oversight board. The coexistence of what in essence, constitute two parallel governments has weakened public confidence in their institutions. There is an urgent need for fundamental changes! This demand is not mine, but of the American citizens of the Island that have acknowledged the harmful effects of this deprivation and have rejected the current status in free and democratic elections.

During my frequent visits after the devastation caused by Hurricane Maria, most members of this honorable Congress privately confessed that one of the biggest problems facing the Island was the lack of complete and permanent presence at the federal level. However, some of these same distinguished representatives are the first to disparage our claims publicly and distort our reality.

Let us be clear! On election day, November 3, 2020, the American citizens of Puerto Rico reiterated the public expression on multiple previous electoral events: We demand change, and we demand statehood!

Procedural arguments cannot be used as a subterfuge to impose the individual will over the collective will or extend this discussion indefinitely in the hope that the public's decision would be different in the future. If these same arguments were deemed valid and applied to the elections of most federal elected officials, their legitimacy would be questionable.

It is because of this legitimate demand by the American citizens on the Island that I urge all members of this Committee to recommend the approval of H.R. 1522.

This bill is the only one that takes into consideration the expression of the people of Puerto Rico. The form, structure, and forcefulness of that vote can hardly be questioned. Voting for statehood on a simple and direct question is a mandate for all public officials. Precisely, the bill presented makes the execution of said mandate feasible through a process similar to that followed by other territories that were admitted as states, including the holding of a ratifying vote and other transitory processes. Furthermore, this project brings with it the legitimacy of the direct vote of the people and the support of the public official who obtained the most votes on the Island.

The obligation to solve this century-old issue is reciprocal. We must close the gap between the American citizens who live in Puerto Rico and those who live on the continent. We are not requesting special considerations or exceptions; we are only asking for fair, equitable, and dignified treatment. We should not be required to abandon our families and our communities to reap the benefits of citizenship. There are no persuasive or logical arguments to support our continued treatment as second-class citizens. It is impossible to talk about effective governance without access to the rights that serve as a precondition to its exercise. It is impossible to address the issue of individual rights without simultaneously addressing the collective structural problem. Governance and legitimacy require that citizens feel that their claims are being heard, that their aspirations are part of the conversation, that democracy is not a mirage.

NAPREC—National Puerto Rican Equality Coalition

Frequently Asked Questions—Statehood for Puerto Rico

1. Was November 3, 2020, the first time that voters in Puerto Rico were asked about their political status?
   No. The U.S. citizens of Puerto Rico have been asked the question regarding the island's status three times in the last decade, with different language, and each time "statehood" has gained the majority of support.
2. What was the voter turnout and results of November 3, 2020 general election plebiscite in Puerto Rico?
   With a 54.72% participation rate, the final certified results of the plebiscite were 655,505 votes (52.52%) "Yes" and 592,671 votes (47.48%) "No," on whether Puerto Rico should join the Union as a state.
3. What was the question presented to voters?
   The plebiscite question derived by the elected representatives of Puerto Rico to voters was "[s]hould Puerto Rico be admitted immediately into the Union as a State? Yes or No."
4. Didn't the U.S. Department of Justice (DOJ) deny Puerto Rico the disbursement of $2.5 million to resolve the island's future political status?
   While the DOJ denied the disbursements of the $2.5 million, the DOJ's own disregard of congressional guidelines as to acceptable ballot materials and failure to meet congressional deadlines led to the inability to disburse funds prior to the plebiscite.
   a. House Report 116-101 (H. Rprt. 116-101) was enacted with the signing of the Consolidated Appropriations Act, 2020 (P.L. 116-93), on December 20, 2019.
   b. DOJ was required within 45 days of enactment of P.L. 116-93 "to provide the Committee, as well as the Puerto Rico State Elections Commission, with a report regarding the acceptable versions of voter education materials,

plebiscite ballot formats, and related materials that would allow the Department to obligate this funding for a future plebiscite" and to "expeditiously act upon any request for this funding."[63]

c. DOJ disregarded directives to provide acceptable plebiscite materials by the congressional deadlines to the required parties, which caused the delayed and limited timeframe for review. In April 2020, DOJ did publish the delayed report but with very limited guidance.[64]
d. Additionally, DOJ demanded that all the status options be included on the ballot, in violation of the directives in H. Rprt. 116-101 which directed that "[t]he current territorial/Commonwealth status should be excluded from any future plebiscite, since it fails to address key inequities."[65]

5. Since the DOJ did not disburse the funds does that mean the plebiscite was illegitimate?

NO, any controversy about the language of the question was resolved prior to the plebiscite by the Supreme Court of Puerto Rico ("PRSC").

a. On October 5, 2020, the PRSC upheld the constitutionality of the November 3, 2020 plebiscite, determining that it was a constitutionally valid exercise of self-determination and that those who contend the plebiscite is not neutral or is discriminatory fail to notice the legal effects of the 2012 and 2017 plebiscites.[66]
b. Additionally, the PRSC held that there has never been a single or standard process for admission as a state, and the denial by the DOJ was inconsequential since holding the plebiscite only depends on the will of the territory, not on congressional authorization.[67]

6. What are the federal legislative proposals to resolve Puerto Rico's political status?

In the 117th Congress the legislative proposals introduced to address Puerto Rico's status are as follows:

a. H.R. 1522 and S. 780, Puerto Rico Statehood Admission Act, introduced by Rep. Darren Soto (D-FL-09), Resident Commissioner Jenniffer González-Colón (R-PR At Large), and Senator Martin Heinrich (D-AZ).

---

[63] House Report 116-101, Commerce Justice, Science, and Related Agencies Appropriation Bill, 2020, https://www.congress.gov/congressional-report/116th-congress/house-report/101/1?q=%7B%22search%22%3A%5B%22House+Report+116-101%22%5D%7D&s=1&r=1.

[64] U.S. Department of Justice, Report Submitted to the House and Senate Committees on Appropriations and the Puerto Rico State Elections Commission as requested by House Report 116-101 accompanying the Consolidated Appropriations Act, 2020.

[65] House Report 116-101, Commerce Justice, Science, and Related Agencies Appropriation Bill, 2020, https://www.congress.gov/congressional-report/116th-congress/house-report/101/1?q=%7B%22search%22%3A%5B%22House+Report+116-101%22%5D%7D&s=1&r=1.

[66] *Aponte-Rosario, et al., v. President EEC, et al.*, 2020 PRSC 119 (P.R. 2020).

[67] Id.

   b. H.R. 2070 and S. 865, Puerto Rico Self-Determination Act of 2021, by Rep. Nydia Velazquez (D-NY-07) and Senator Robert Menendez (D-NJ).

7. What are the main differences between the legislative proposals?
   a. H.R. 1522 and S. 780 respect the will of voters in Puerto Rico, by mandating a binding ratification vote on the statehood "Yes" or "No" question previously presented to Puerto Rican voters and establishes the terms of admission as a state into the Union within 12 months if "statehood" is ratified.
   b. H.R. 2070 and S. 865 reject and silence the will of voters in Puerto Rico, by disregarding the electoral results and forcing the Legislature of Puerto Rico to establish a non-binding status convention composed of newly elected local delegates, supervised by a federal negotiating commission, to present a potential multitude of status options to voters with no certainty or guarantee that its proposed status option will be accepted by Congress.
8. Why are H.R. 1522 and S. 780 binding, while H.R. 2070 and S. 865 are non-binding?
   a. H.R. 1522 and S. 780 are binding because the legislation is self-executing following the direct ratification vote of Puerto Ricans on the island. If statehood is chosen again by the people of Puerto Rico, the President of the United States merely needs to execute the law and proclaim Puerto Rico as a state after 12 months.
   b. H.R. 2070 and S. 865 are non-binding because the legislation fails to establish clear timelines for choosing the self-determination option and when a referendum will take place. Also, they are non-binding since no convention can impose a status option upon Congress or mandate the automatic adoption of an unknown future resolution.
9. Puerto Rico just held a special election to choose a "Shadow Puerto Rico Congressional Delegation." What is the purpose, make-up, and term of this delegation?
   a. On May 16, 2021, Puerto Rico held a special election to choose the Puerto Rico Congressional Delegation ("Delegation"), entrusted with the duty to demand Congress honor the results of the November 3, 2020 plebiscite and admit Puerto Rico as a state.
   b. The Delegation includes two special delegates to the United States Senate and four special delegates to the United States House of Representatives.
   c. The term of the Delegation from is July 1, 2021 to December 31, 2024.
10. Opponents of statehood claim that the low voter turnout for the special election of the Delegation invalidates the vote in November. Is this correct?
   a. No. In the United States we have general elections and special elections with varying levels of voter turnout, and yet we do not disregard those results.

b. Elections are decided by ballots and votes cast, not by those who fail to vote on an issue.
c. In a time when we are protecting the right to vote and the integrity of our elections, we must not reverse or disregard the definitive will of U.S. citizens legally voting to choose their future political status.

NAPREC—National Puerto Rican Equality Coalition Support and Cosponsor H.R. 1522/S. 780: Puerto Rico Statehood, Admission Act

Historical Background

Puerto Rico was ceded to the United States by Spain at the end of the Spanish-American War in 1898. On April 12, 1900, the Foraker Act (P.L. 56-191) established the first form of civil administration of local government affairs in Puerto Rico. The Foraker Act also established the position of Resident Commissioner to represent the island in Congress. In 1917, through the Jones-Shafroth Act (P.L. 64-368), Congress extended U.S. citizenship by statute to the residents of Puerto Rico and granted further local self-government. In 1952, the Puerto Rico Federal Relations Act (P.L. 81-600) granted Puerto Rico authority over matters of internal governance when Congress approved the island's Constitution. Puerto Rico has since been known formally as the "Commonwealth of Puerto Rico," but the island is still a possession of the United States under the Territorial Clause, Article 4, Section 3 of the United States Constitution.

Since the first World War, Puerto Ricans have fought in every military conflict of the United States. From the honorable service of the Army's 65th Infantry regiment to present day, Puerto Rican service members continue to defend and protect our country honorably. However, these veterans and the U.S. citizens of Puerto Rico have no voting representation in Congress and cannot vote for their Commander in Chief. To end this inequality, we urge you to cosponsor and support H.R. 1522/S. 780, Puerto Rico Statehood Admission Act.

Facts

- In the last decade, the U.S. citizens of Puerto Rico have held three separate plebiscites to resolve their political status, and each time the majority of voters chose statehood.

- On November 3, 2020, Puerto Rico held the general election plebiscite on "[s]hould Puerto Rico be admitted immediately into the Union as a State? Yes or No."
  - Prior to the plebiscite the Supreme Court of Puerto Rico held that the question and the plebiscite to be a legitimate and constitutionally valid exercise of self-determination.[68]
- With a 54.72% participation rate, the final certified results of the plebiscite were 655,505 votes (52.52%) "Yes" and 592,671 votes (47.48%) "No."
- In the 117th Congress the legislative proposals to address Puerto Rico's status are as follows:
  - H.R. 1522 and S. 780, Puerto Rico Statehood Admission Act, introduced by Rep. Darren Soto (D-FL-09), Resident Commissioner Jenniffer González-Colón (R-PR At Large), and Senator Martin Heinrich (D-NM)
  - H.R. 2070 and S. 865, Puerto Rico Self-Determination Act of 2021, by Rep. Nydia Velazquez (D-NY-07) and Senator Robert Menendez (D-NJ).
- H.R. 1522 and S. 780 respect the will of voters and would mandate a binding ratification vote on the statehood "Yes" or "No" question previously presented to Puerto Rican voters and establishes the terms of admission as a state into the Union within 12 months if "statehood" is ratified.
- H.R. 2070 and S. 865 reject voters by calling for a non-binding status convention composed of newly elected local delegates, supervised by a federal negotiating commission, to present a potential multitude of status options to voters with no certainty or guarantee that its proposed status option will be accepted by Congress.

NAPREC
National Puerto Rican
Equality Coalition

PRSC
Puerto Rico Statehood Council

June 14, 2021

Hon. Raúl M. Grijalva, Chairman
Committee on Natural Resources
Washington, DC

Hon. Bruce Westerman,
Ranking Member
Committee on Natural Resources
Washington, DC

---

[68] *Aponte-Rosario, et al., v. President EEC, et al.*, 2020 PRSC 119 (P.R. 2020).

Dear Chairman Grijalva and Ranking Member Westerman:

We write to express our support for the bipartisan proposal H.R. 1522, Puerto Rico Statehood Admission Act, introduced by Congressman Darren Soto (D-FL-09) and Resident Commissioner Jenniffer González-Colón (R-PR At Large), which respects the will of U.S. citizens residing in Puerto Rico about their future political status. On November 3, 2020, a majority of Puerto Ricans residing on the island determined their future status and voted for equality through statehood. Now that a majority of Puerto Ricans have definitively spoken, the most appropriate response for Congress is to act on their will and extend a formal offer of admission through the enactment of H.R. 1522.

With a participation rate of 54.72 percent, the results of the November plebiscite were 52.52 percent (655,505 votes) "Yes" and 47.48 percent (592,671 votes) "No," on whether the island should be admitted as a state.[69] The plebiscite question presented by the local elected representatives of Puerto Rico to voters was "[s]hould Puerto Rico be admitted immediately into the Union as a State? Yes or No."

Not surprisingly, many of the same opponents of statehood that actively campaigned for the "No" option and lost at the ballot box, now try to argue that Congress should ignore the plebiscite results. Yet, the various reasons they provide are all easily refutable.

Plebiscite Valid Despite Failure of DOJ to Approve $2.5 million Appropriation

One common argument is that the U.S. Department of Justice ("DOJ") decided not to disburse $2.5 million in federal funds previously allocated by Congress for Puerto Rico to carry out a plebiscite to resolve its future political status when the Government of Puerto Rico requested such funds before the November 2020 vote. This argument ignores that DOJ itself disregarded congressional guidelines to provide the Government of Puerto Rico examples of acceptable ballot formats and materials. The DOJ also failed to meet congressional deadlines and then used the excuse of insufficient time as justification for their failure to disburse funds prior to the plebiscite.

Congressional guidance was provided to the DOJ in House Report 116-101 (H. Rprt. 116-101) with the enactment of the Consolidated Appropriations Act, 2020 (P.L. 116-93), on December 20, 2019. DOJ was required within 45 days of enactment "to provide the Committee, as well as the Puerto Rico State Elections Commission, with a report regarding the acceptable versions of voter education materials, plebiscite ballot formats, and related materials that would allow the Department to obligate this funding for a

[69] Puerto Rico State Elections Commission, Plebiscite Results, https://elecciones2020.ceepur.org/Escrutinio_General_93/index.html#es/default/PLEBISCITO_Resumen.xml (Last visited June 9, 2021).

future plebiscite" and to "expeditiously act upon any request for this funding."[70] However, DOJ delayed the publication of the report until April 2020, and the report itself provided very limited guidance.[71]

DOJ also demanded that all the status options be included on the ballot, in violation of the directives in H. Rprt. 116-101 which directed that "[t]he current territorial/Commonwealth status should be excluded from any future plebiscite, since it fails to address key inequities."[72] DOJ's indication that the current territory option was excluded failed to take into account that a "No" vote would effectively mean the continuation of the current territory status. Additionally, DOJ argued that the use of the word "immediately" in the question would somehow bias voters in favor of statehood without recognizing that the Government of Puerto Rico is fully within its right to ask island voters if their possible desire for statehood admission is something immediate or not.

Statehood "Yes" or "No" Is a Valid Exercise of Self-Determination

Another line of argument by statehood opponents is that somehow the statehood "Yes" or "No" question posed in the 2020 plebiscite, which would be repeated as a ratification vote in H.R. 1522, was not a legitimate exercise of self-determination. However, they ignore that this controversy was resolved prior to the plebiscite by the Supreme Court of Puerto Rico ("PRSC"). On October 5, 2020, the PRSC upheld the constitutionality of the November 3, 2020 plebiscite, determining that it was a constitutionally valid exercise of self-determination and that those who contend the plebiscite is not neutral or is discriminatory fail to account for the results of the 2012 and 2017 plebiscites where the other valid status options were presented.[73] Additionally, the PRSC held that there has never been a single or standard process for admission as a state, and the failure of DOJ to approve funding for the vote was inconsequential since the decision to hold the plebiscite only depends on the will of the territory, and did not require congressional authorization.[74]

---

[70] House Report 116-101, Commerce Justice, Science, and Related Agencies Appropriation Bill, 2020, https://www.congress.gov/congressional-report/116th-congress/house-report/101/1?q=%7B%22search%22%3A%5B%22House+Report+116-101%22%5D%7D&s=1&r=1.

[71] U.S. Department of Justice, Report Submitted to the House and Senate Committees on Appropriations and the Puerto Rico State Elections Commission as requested by House Report 116-101 accompanying the Consolidated Appropriations Act, 2020.

[72] House Report 116-101, Commerce Justice, Science, and Related Agencies Appropriation Bill, 2020, https://www.congress.gov/congressional-report/116th-congress/house-report/101/1?q=%7B%22search%22%3A%5B%22House+Report+116-101%22%5D%7D&s=1&r=1.

[73] *Aponte-Rosario, et al., v. President EEC, et al.*, 2020 PRSC 119 (P.R. 2020).

[74] Id.

The U.S. citizens of Puerto Rico have been asked the question regarding the island's status three times in the last decade, with different language, and each time "statehood" has gained the majority of support. With more than half of eligible voters casting their ballots to determine their political status, the results from this latest plebiscite have unequivocally stated the preference of the U.S. citizens that reside in Puerto Rico for statehood. Not only did statehood win by a bigger margin than the results of the U.S. Presidential race,[75] but more votes were casted in favor of statehood than for the sitting Governor of Puerto Rico, Hon. Pedro Pierluisi.[76] This confirms that the majority on the island want equality through statehood regardless of which local political party is in power.

H.R. 1522 respects the results of the plebiscite in November and provides a constitutionally valid and direct path to admission. The legislation calls for a final binding ratification vote on the statehood "Yes" or "No" question previously presented to Puerto Rican voters. If the island chooses to become a state again, H.R. 1522 establishes the terms of admission as a state to the Union and repeals all laws that are incompatible with the island's new status within 12 months. Therefore, the island's residents will have a final chance to vote "Yes" if they support statehood, or "No" if they support any of the alternative status options.

Statehood Opponents Are Engaging in Election Denial

Statehood opponents argue that their alternative to H.R. 1522 is an innocuous bill whose only objective is to be fair, neutral and democratic. Yet H.R. 2070, Puerto Rico Self-Determination Act of 2021, introduced by Congresswoman Nydia Velázquez (D-NY-07) is anything but fair and neutral because it is fundamentally based on a rejection of the voice of the people of Puerto Rico who have already voted for statehood as their future political status on three separate occasions in the past 10 years. In fact, in an action that can only be understood as election interference, just weeks before the November 3, 2020 plebiscite, a similar version of this bill was filed in the 116th Congress with the implication to island voters that the forthcoming vote was meaningless in the eyes of the bill author and its sponsors. The purpose of its introduction then, similar to its purpose now, was not to respect the will of voters in Puerto Rico, but to subvert it by ignoring the significance of the locally led self-determination efforts that have been carried out to date. As opposed to being a more fair and inclusive alternative to H.R. 1522, as written H.R. 2070 basically engages in election denial pretending as if the status plebiscite votes

---

[75] National Archives, 2020 Electoral College Results, https://www.archives.gov/electoral-college/ 2020 (Last visited June 9, 2021).

[76] Puerto Rico State Elections Commission, Governor Results, http://elecciones2020.ceepur.org/ Escrutinio_General_93/index.html#es/default/GOBERNADOR_Resumen.xml (Last visited June 9, 2021).

had not happened or as if they do not matter. This is wrong, anti-democratic, unjust and Congress must reject it.

Statehood Opponents Call for a Binding Process & Then Do the Opposite

A key argument of statehood opponents is that the mechanism for Puerto Rico's self-determination must be "binding" on Congress so that the voters on the island are empowered to make the ultimate decision and Congress will accept their choice. However, H.R. 2070, would propose that the Legislature of Puerto Rico establish a "status convention" of newly elected delegates that would create a complicated process, without any certainty or guarantee that its proposed status option will be accepted by Congress. This proposal is non-binding since no convention can impose a status option upon Congress or mandate the automatic adoption of an unknown future resolution. So, by calling itself binding, but taking the power away from voters to choose directly on the option that the majority has already favored, statehood, the bill makes promises to voters it simply cannot keep. When this is combined with the fact that the bill also fails to establish clear timelines for defining self-determination options and when a referendum will take place, it becomes clear this is less about fairness and more about blunting the momentum of last November's majority vote for statehood.

The bill sponsors have also discussed the possibility that the convention would consider options that are unconstitutional which would spoil the legitimacy of their proposed process, since real self-determination needs to be a choice between the constitutionally valid alternatives and not a flight of fancy.

Statehood Opponents Seek to Privilege International Law over the U.S. Constitution

Instead of recognizing the significance of the last three plebiscite votes, H.R. 2070 seeks to shift the footing of the debate away from the firm ground of the U.S. Constitution into the shifting sands of international law. In fact, the bill findings privilege international law over the locally led self-determination efforts that have taken place over the last decade which were all directed to address this issue within the framework of the U.S. Constitution. A notable example of this dynamic is that the bill proposes the creation of a "Congressional Bilateral Negotiating Commission," under the assumption that Puerto Rico can only exercise true self-determination under the context of international law. The reality is that "bilateral negotiations" are only needed if Puerto Rico were to choose independence with or without free association, options that have been repeatedly discarded by island voters. Statehood admission does not require such an instrument because the terms of statehood are already defined by current federal laws and the U.S. Constitution.

Ironically, the bill sponsors for H.R. 2070, who decry the undemocratic impact of Puerto Rico's Financial Oversight and Management Board (FOMB), use a similar selection mechanism to appoint members to the proposed Negotiating Commission to tell the status convention delegates and the people of Puerto Rico how they should choose their destiny. The bill implies that Puerto Ricans are unable to independently interpret federal laws and choose their self-determination options without the prescriptions of federally appointed policymakers. In spite of the bill's premise regarding the people of Puerto Rico choosing their future, H.R. 2070 is merely an unconstitutional fac¸ade of self-determination with no specific end-date meant indefinitely delay a final resolution to Puerto Rico's status.

Statehood Opponents Are Telling Congress to Discard Plebiscite Vote Results

Prominent statehood opponents including former Rep. Luis Gutierrez and former Gov. Anibal Acevedo Vilá, have argued in a recent letter to Congress that the results of the 2020 statehood vote should be invalidated and discarded because of a subsequent special election. On May 16, 2021, Puerto Rico held a special election to choose the Puerto Rico Congressional Delegation ("Delegation"), entrusted with the duty to demand Congress honor the results of the November 3, 2020 plebiscite and admit Puerto Rico as a state. Opponents claim that because there was a low voter turnout for this special election, the will of the voters in November should be disregarded. That is patently absurd. Everywhere in the United States we have general elections and special elections with varying levels of voter turnout, and yet we do not disregard the results of either. Elections are decided by ballots and votes cast, not by those who fail to participate and vote on any given issue or candidate. In a time when America must make extra effort to protect the right to vote and the integrity of our elections, Congress must not reverse the will of U.S. citizens legally voting to choose their future political status.

Conclusion—H.R. 1522 is the Appropriate & Constitutionally Viable Process for Solving Puerto Rico's Ultimate Political Status

To put an end of the island's current colonial and territorial status, and in accordance with Article 4, Section 3 of the United States Constitution, we urge the U.S. House Committee on Natural Resources to "Respect Puerto Rico's Statehood Vote" and promptly pass H.R. 1522. Statehood will guarantee the U.S. citizens residing in Puerto

Rico the same civil rights and congressional representation afforded to the U.S. citizens of the 50 states. No territory that has requested admission as a state has been denied before. Puerto Ricans have self-determined, and it is now Congress' time to listen to voters on the island and ratify their will by establishing the means of admission as a state to the Union. Only H.R. 1522 meets the principles of equality and respects the will of voters instead of rejecting and silencing them.

We thank you in advance for your attention to this matter.

Sincerely,

Martin E. Rivera, Esq.,
Executive Director
National Puerto Rican
Equality Coalition

George H. Laws Garcia,
Executive Director
Puerto Rico Statehood Council

Transcript of Video: "Statements to the Natural Resources Committee on Occasion of the 6/16/21 Status Hearings"

Link to video: https://www.youtube.com/watch?v=tzC7QwYO5dw

Introductory Remarks by Dr. Zayira Jordan

Las declaraciones que haréhoy son dirigidas al Comitéde Recursos Naturales con respecto a los proyectos de la Cámara de Representantes federal, el H.R. 1522 y el H.R. 2070, y en defensa de las voces de Puerto Rico que votaron en su mayoría en el plebiscito por la estadidad en noviembre 3 del 2020. Hoy, junio 16 de 2021, se discute en el Congreso de los Estados Unidos el futuro de todos los que habitamos en la isla de Puerto Rico. Se discute nuestro futuro y el destino de nuestro estatus. Yo había preparado un mensaje para presentar en las vistas sobre estatus en el Congreso. No estarédeponiendo en persona, pero no quise dejar que el mensaje permaneciese en silencio. Mi mensaje no solo le pertenece al Congreso, sino a Puerto Rico. Asíque hoy, 16 de junio de 2021, el mismo día que se están tomando decisiones sobre nuestro bienestar y sobre el futuro de nuestro destino, les entrego mi mensaje. Recuerden que aquíno le estaréhablando al pueblo de Puerto Rico, le estaréhablando a aquellos que tienen nuestro futuro en sus manos. Le estaréhablando a los miembros del Comitéde Recursos Naturales de la Cámara de Representantes del Congreso de los Estados Unidos para que nuestras voces sean escuchadas.

English Translation

The statements that I will make today are directed to the Natural Resources Committee regarding the bills before the U.S. House of Representatives, H.R. 1522 and H.R. 2070, and in defense of the voices of Puerto Rico who voted in their majority in the plebiscite for statehood on November 3, 2020. Today, June 16, 2021, the future of all of us who live on the island of Puerto Rico is being discussed in Congress. Our future and the fate of our status are being discussed. I had prepared a message to deliver in the public hearings in Congress. I will not be testifying in person, but I did not want to let the message remain silent. My message belongs not only to Congress, but to Puerto Rico. So today, June 16, 2021, the same day that decisions are being made about our well-being and the future of our destiny, I deliver my message to you. Remember that here I will not be addressing the people of Puerto Rico, I will be addressing those who have our future in their hands. I will be addressing the members of House Natural Resources Committee in Congress, so that our voices are heard.

Statement by Dr. Zayira Jordán

I speak to all members of the Natural Resources Committee … How did you come to be here today?

This is my first question.

Clearly, none of you were born into the positions you now find yourselves in.

Some of you might be here because you found yourself enchanted by a career in politics.

Some of you might be here because life, for some strange or unexpected reason, put you into the position you now find yourselves in.

Call it destiny, call it struggle or perseverance.

You are all here today to make decisions for tomorrow. What are we discussing today?

This is my second question.

You are all here today to make a decision as to the future of more than 3 million people, and more than them, a decision for those who are not born yet, but will be born under the terms of the decision you will make today.

What does it take?

This is my third question.

I understand clearly, as an American citizen, the difficulty of these proceedings.

Last night, on the website of https://statehood.dc.gov. I read the blueprint of Washington DC path to statehood. The website outlined what was begun by Mayor Muriel Bowser and the New Columbia Statehood Commission, and what is known as the "Tennessee Plan" and I quote, Under the Tennessee Plan, the prospective state's electorate votes on statehood and ratifies a constitution, without an enabling act, and then uses this as a basis to petition Congress for admission. This approach was pioneered by Tennessee in 1796 and used by Michigan, Iowa, California, Oregon, Kansas, and Alaska to gain admission to the Union.

Congress approved statehood for Tennessee, making Tennessee the 16th state of the Union in 1796.

In Puerto Rico, we have done every step according to the Tennessee Plan . . .

We have a constitution, ratified and put into effect since 1952. We have held a more than one referendum in which the majority of the people have voted, unequivocally for statehood. We have had "dream teams" of representatives to fight for our rights, right there on the doorsteps of Congress.

Before the new special delegates under Law 167 of 2020 swear in on July 1st of this year to defend our rights; not only statehood, but for our democracy, there was the Democracy Commission, or as we better know it, in the island *La Comision de la Igualdad*, created and put into effect by former Governor Ricardo Rossello. This commission was composed of appointees in the task of lobbying in Congress to approve Puerto Rico's request for statehood.

I ask you, what more does it take to make the will of my people be Heard? If we have done practically everything in our power to attain our Union within the United States.

Does it take sacrifice? . . .

We have sacrificed our sons, and daughters, and fathers, and mothers Since 1917, the fateful year in which we became American citizens, we have fought and sacrificed as Americans not only in World War I, but also in World War II, the Korean War, and the Vietnam War. We have fought and we will continue fighting and sacrificing in every war in which the nature of democracy and liberty is at stake. Together, side by side, with our brothers and sisters, citizens of the United States of America.

So as you see, thousands of Puerto Ricans have sacrificed to defend the American flag, which holds 50 stars, but has room to add one more singular star. If not many more.

Does it take history?

When the United States fought the cold war against Cuba and Russia, we stood as an emblem of democracy and freedom, when so many decided to turn their backs against the United States, until President Ronald Reagan proclaimed his famous words in 1987 . . .

"*Mr. Gorbachev tear down this wall.*"

I ask the same thing today as former president Ronald Reagan asked then on that fateful day. Please, tear down this wall of indifference.

Tear down this wall of anti-democracy.

Tear down this wall now, and once and for all . . .

You might be asking yourselves . . .

Maybe before I tear down this wall of indifference, it takes more suffering. Well, I'll tell you this . . .

We have suffered enough.

Hurricanes, earthquakes, the terrible imprint of the COVID-19 PANDEMIC. We have suffered, and we are used to suffering . . .

Still, We the people of Puerto Rico, stand strong. Because, United we stand, and divided we fall.

But maybe . . . just maybe . . . it does not take sacrifice, nor history, nor suffering. Maybe it takes a little bit of Politics. For one cannot be so na¨ıve, so as to think that the principles of which you stand for politically speaking, could possibly be dismissed in such a historical decision.

It lives within you, your political party, it is like the blood which keeps your heart pumping . . .

But, let me tell you something about my people . . .

They could either be democrats or republicans . . .

I'll tell you this . . .

Do not be deceived by the fact that only because we speak Spanish and we enjoy the freedoms of this United States, that the majority will immediately choose to be one way or the other; democrat or republican.

Do not be deceived by the fact that many of us are God fearing people, and enjoy the benefits of Capitalism, and hold dearly and close to our hearts our traditions, that we will be one way or the other; republican or democrat Most immigrants from Cuba who migrated to Florida after escaping the Castro dictatorship of communism, found their principles to be more attached to that of the Republican Party. But most Hispanic immigrants who migrate for economic or social issues who end up in California or New York have found their principles to be more Democratic leaning.

I have always chosen to remain bipartisan in my leanings when it comes to bringing up the issue of statehood for Puerto Rico. It is a question of simply letting go of those things which have politically bound us to think one way or the other.

Democracy, Freedom, Justice is as bipartisan as it gets . . . Truth is equally bipartisan.

We the People of Puerto Rico, American Citizens of this United States, are not willing to wait any longer. All I can tell you is that the People of Puerto Rico will hold in very high esteem those who decide to recognize our voices.

We will not forget the decision made by all of you today. A decision easy to ignore and be indifferent to. Unless your decision makes history, which it will, and so all of your names which abide by our democracy shall be remembered . . .

Before I conclude, I will ask of all of you, (Hold one finger up and keep it there)

Just one last question . . .

For all of you elected officials, whether democrat or republican, whether if chosen by destiny, or here, through your own struggles and perseverance through it all . . . If the United States does not protect the democracy of its territories, how could it possibly protect itself?

When it comes to doing the right thing, there should be no right or left. There should only be up, equality and justice, or down, indifference.

This is a court, and the decision of this jury, will decide the fate of the Island of Puerto Rico, and 3 million people, and those who are not born yet, but will be born under the terms of the decision you will make today.

The future of this Island belongs to our sons and daughters.

They will stand in place of us, who have failed them.

They are stronger than us, for they have suffered every possible ordeal capable of human suffering. They are not so easily defeated.

They will fight, and they will persevere.

I'll let them speak for themselves ... Thank You.

Statement by Mr. Juan Camilo Ruiz-Pinzon

Dear Chairman, Ranking Member and members of the Committee:

I stand in support of H.R. 1522, the Puerto Rico Statehood Admission Act, and to speak against H.R. 2070, the Puerto Rico Self-Determination Act. My reasons to support the Admission Act are simple: respecting the will of Americans as was expressed in the best self-determination mechanism a free country can offer: the ballot box, enfranchising 3.3 million Americans not adequately represented in their government, and to provide full constitutional coverage and equal protection of laws for Americans in Puerto Rico.

H.R. 1522 responds to the call Americans on the island made last November, where they voted YES to Statehood in a referendum modeled after the ones held in Alaska and Hawaii before becoming states. Statehood received more votes than any political candidate or party. It won in all senatorial districts and in 33 of the 40 representative districts. In the 8 that lost, YES to Statehood still got more votes than the candidate who was elected. The last plebiscite showed that: support for statehood overcomes partisan politics and that Puerto Ricans can differentiate between partisan politics and political status.

Although the pro-status quo party won the Legislature, that fact does not and must not erase or ignore that in the same elections, Statehood won. I would like to remind people, who object the results of the plebiscite because they say that 53% is not enough, that it is the absolute majority of the electorate. With lesser margins: laws are passed, judicial and executive appointments are confirmed and politicians, including presidents, are elected. That's called living in a democracy.

The filing and cosponsorship of the Admission Act tells 3 facts that speak for themselves:

First, it was introduced by Puerto Rico's elected representative in Congress, not by another member representing another district. Second, it shows that admitting Puerto

Rico as a state is a bipartisan effort representing a diverse movement from all sides of the political spectrum. Third, two members cosponsoring this bill hold leadership positions in the House: Majority Leader Steny Hoyer and Republican Conference Chair Elise Stefanik.

The Self-Determination Act is flawed and contradictory for the following reasons. It says that the Legislature of Puerto Rico has the inherent authority to call for a status convention but ignores that, by that same authority, our duly elected leaders have called for referendums. It says that it recognizes our natural right to self-determination, but ignores that Puerto Ricans themselves already exercised that right and chose statehood. It gives the fantasy that there are multiple options when there are only two: statehood or independence. It is not time-bounded, complicates the issue with unfamiliar voting formats and unclear definitions of choices, and tries to bind Congress in a potential exercise of legislative entrenchment; therefore making the proposed referendum non-binding.

Statehood means complete protection of the U.S. Constitution to more than 3 million Americans who somehow, just by living on the Island, lose equal protection of many laws. It means equal justice under the law; self-government; and upholding the ideals and values upon which the United States was founded, and for which thousands of Puerto Ricans have fought and died for without being able to enjoy them on the Island.

Justice John Marshall Harlan, dissenting in Downes v. Bidwell (1901), wrote:

> "The idea that this country may acquire territories anywhere upon the earth . . . the people inhabiting them to enjoy only such rights as Congress chooses to accord to them is wholly inconsistent with the spirit and genius, as well as with the words, of the Constitution." Justice Harlan was known as the Great Dissenter for his dissenting opinions in cases that restricted civil rights. Dissenting in Plessy v. Ferguson, he argued that the constitution was color-blind and that all citizens should have equal access to civil rights. In 1954, he was vindicated in Brown v. Board of Education.

And now, it is up to you to vindicate once again a Justice who stood in the right side of history.

Statement by Ms. Zuleyka Rivera

Por quéPuerto Rico debe ser estado? Puerto Rico debe ser estado porque los ciudadanos puertorriqueños tendríamos los mismos derechos que los demás estadounidenses. Asítendríamos representación en el congreso para todo lo relacionado con los programas de los diferentes departamentos, ya sea salud, educación, trabajo, seguridad, economía, entre otros. Adicional, tendríamos el derecho de votar por el presidente en las elecciones generales cada cuatro años. Esto nos ayudaría a que se defendieran nuestras ayudas, salarios, programas y asistencia en todos los ámbitos. Otro derecho sería el tener salarios justos y razonables como los tienen los otros estados. Siendo el estado 51 no nos sentiríamos discriminados por ser una isla como ocurre actualmente por no tener representación congresional. Tanto nuestros jóvenes y adultos tendríamos mejores oportunidades educativas y laborales. De esta manera nuestros policías, maestros, enfermeros y los demás profesionales estarían mejor pagados y asíno tendrían que irse de la isla.

De ser Puerto Rico un estado, no seríamos discriminados ni rechazados por ser un territorio como ocurre ahora mismo. Nuestros hombres y mujeres han servido en las fuerzas armadas y asíse sentirían bien valorados y aceptados como los demás de los otros estados; pues han sido marginados a pesar de haber dado hasta la vida en muchos frentes de batallas.

Para tener todo lo antes expuesto, es necesario que seamos el estado 51 de la nación norteamericana con los mismos derechos y privilegios que tienen los otros 50 estados. La mayoría del pueblo puertorriqueño asílo expresóen las elecciones. Llevamos más de 100 años siendo una colonia y necesitamos la igualdad. A nivel personal yo quiero quedarme aquí, quiero que mi familia y amigos regresen y quiero que volvamos a estar unidos pues se han ido a los estados a buscar un mejor porvenir. Pero y por quéirnos? si es aquídonde debemos estar y séque si logramos lo que tanto anhelamos que es convertirnos en el estado 51, sucederá.

English Translation

Why should Puerto Rico become a state? Puerto Rico should become a state because Puerto Ricans would have the same rights as other Americans. We would have representation in Congress for everything related to the programs of the different departments, either health, education, work, security, economy, among others. Additionally, we would have the right to vote for the president in the general election every four years. This would help us to defend our aid, salaries, programs and assistance in all areas. Another right would be to achieve fair and reasonable wages as the other states have. Being the 51st state, we would not feel discriminated against for being an island as it happens currently for not having congressional representation. Both our young people and adults would have better educational and employment opportunities. This way our police, teachers, nurses and other professionals would be better paid and so they would not have to leave the island.

If Puerto Rico were a state, we would not be discriminated against or rejected for being a territory as it happens right now. Our men and women have served in the military and would feel well valued and accepted like the rest of the other states; because they have been marginalized despite having given up life on many fronts of battles.

To obtain what I have expressed, it is necessary that we are the 51st state of the American nation with equal rights and privileges that the other 50 states have. Most of the people of Puerto Rico expressed this in the election. We have been a colony for more than 100 years and we need equality. On a personal level I want to stay here. I want my family and friends to come back and I want them to let us be united again because they have gone to the states to look for a better way to come.

Statement by Ms. Bianca Cardona, Esq.

Women in Puerto Rico have played an important role in the development of history. If we study women from a social context, women, as in other countries, have been marginalized in the most important sectors, such as politics, employment and equal rights. For years women in Puerto Rico were only considered for domestic work, and were prevented from being part of the development of the society in which they lived in, the culture and above all were limited to the achievement of their ambitions they had as women. However, it is important to note that, although in the first half of history women had a social boom, after the American colonization of the island, women began to capture quotas of social participation, forming an essential part of our history.

That is why today I am proud to be part of this effort, representing women, because just as we have fought in the past to advance women's rights, today I fight for the equality of all Puerto Ricans, socially, economically and politically.

The history that defines the people of Puerto Rico has been one full of stumbles, uncertainties and stagnation. While we have managed to overcome in a Puerto Rico that is suffering an economic and political recession, we must aspire to guarantee a stable future for the generations that are growing up and those to come. The political euphoria that we are experiencing at this time is the result of people who are tired of coming to a Puerto Rico with limitations and no hope for development.

The people of Puerto Rico, aware of the problem of our territorial relationship, have expressed themselves in different ways to demand that the U.S. Congress take action on our social, political and economic future. The plebiscite on Puerto Rico's status have been one of the main forums in which the people have expressed themselves on the preferential status for Puerto Rico. However, other mechanisms have also been used to raise the issue of Puerto Rico's disadvantaged status in its relationship with the United States.

Today, the United States is composed of 50 states, 48 of which are often referred to as mainland states, to differentiate them from Alaska and Hawaii, both because of their location and because of their insular nature. As are the island territories, such as Puerto Rico.

Since the independence of the thirteen British colonies on July 4, 1776, the United States did not officially stop growing until President Dwight D. Eisenhower approved the incorporation of Alaska and Hawaii as the 49th and 50th states, respectively. The construction of the country, mainly throughout the 19th and 20th centuries, was the result of various forms of territorial expansion. On one hand, much of the territory was acquired through purchases and transfers of British, French, Spanish and Mexican territories; among other examples, we find the cases of the purchases of Louisiana and Florida. On the other hand, the United States acquired some territories by conquest from other political entities, such as the Republic of Texas or the United Mexican States.

In the case of Puerto Rico, it became a part of the United States as a result of the Spanish-American War, which culminated in the Treaty of Paris of December 10, 1898, between Spain and the United States. The Treaty of Paris set a precedent for the United States as it was the first time it acquired a territory without the intention of making it a state. The expansionist policy of the United States in the 19th century, before the Spanish-American War, reflected a theory: that of incorporation as a territory in preparation for statehood. All territories acquired multiplied their original population and dissipated boundaries with a view to integrating them as members of the American nation.

The Treaty of Paris provided that the political conditions and civil rights to be conferred on the territories acquired under the treaty would be determined by Congress. This idea practiced by the United States in the colonization of Puerto Rico was contrary to the value it preached as a nation, since it was precisely on those principles that it based its independence.

[Other states have adopted admission mechanisms, such as the Tennessee Plan, which has achieved the admission of 34 territories, including the State of Tennessee.] The Tennessee Plan is a strategy that was founded in 1795 for the incorporation of Tennessee as a state of the Union. As part of the process, a referendum was held in which the majority of the people voted in favor of admitting Tennessee as a state. A law was then passed to elect a legislature with two senators and representatives, who would go to the U.S. Congress to represent the mandate of the people and achieve the incorporation of Tennessee as a State of the Union.

For its part, Puerto Rico has taken different mechanisms that emerge in the self-determination of the people to determine its political future. As part of these mechanisms, Puerto Rico passed legislation in 2017 to adopt the Tennessee Plan and held a referendum of the people, where Statehood obtained 97% of the voters' support. Accompanied by that process, the Act of Admission was filed by Resident Commissioner Jennifer González Colón. Due to the extraordinary circumstances that occurred with the atmospheric event of Hurricane María and the devastation it left on the island, unfortunately the process was hindered.

Puerto Ricans were recently granted the opportunity to express themselves again, this time under a particular plebiscite, where the people were asked if they wanted Statehood, Yes? Or No? As a result of the plebiscite, Statehood obtained 52.5% of the votes. [Following this, the legislature approved Laws No. 1654 and No. 1675, for the adoption of the Tennessee plan, this time with a delegation elected by the people of Puerto Rico. The delegation is composed of 6 members, 2 Senators and 4 Representatives, who have the duty to represent the mandate of the people of Puerto Rico expressed in the status plebiscite of November 3, 2020.]

Accompanying this process, the Puerto Rico Admission Act was filed under H.R. 1522, by our Resident Commissioner, Jennifer Gonzalez and Florida Representative Darren Soto. The bill was filed on March 2, in commemoration of the 104th anniversary of the granting of U.S. citizenship to Puerto Ricans. Since the filing of H.R. 1522, it has the support of 60 Members of Congress, including senators and representatives, such as Alaska Representative Don Young.

Finally, Puerto Rico finds itself in a historic scenario, where for the first time, after 123 years as a territory of the United States, and more than 500 years of colonialism, Puerto Rico will have the opportunity to be admitted as a State of the Union. Puerto Rico has in its favor the number of U.S. citizens residing in the territory, with approximately 3 million citizens according to the most recent census. This would represent a significant electoral weight, which would give it more political power than 25 states in the nation.

For all the aforementioned reasons, the Puerto Rico Statehood Admission Act, H.R. 1522 should be taken into consideration in order for the Puerto Rican people to be able to ratify the results of the past plebiscite.

Thank you for your time.

Statement by Mr. Ricardo Marrero-Passapera

Puerto Rico has been a territory for more than 500 years, first of Spain and now of the United States. Therefore, it should not be foreign to our will that the status is an issue that moves us as Puerto Ricans. As a result of the discussion on the status, six (6) plebiscites have been held to decide between the options of Statehood (annexation), Independence (separation) or Commonwealth (current status), as well as the approval of evaluation committees on the status of Puerto Rico.

The Foraker Act of 1900 formally represented the non-incorporation of territories as a state, thus granting greater powers to Congress and the President to administer the territory. This unequal treatment over the other states of the nation led to the argument that Puerto Rico was treated as territory and not as part of the union. Under this premise and through the insular cases the legal creature of the U.S. Congress, was named "unincorporated territory" was established and validated, maintaining as a foundation that we belong to, but are not part of [the United States]. This doctrine was validated by Associate Justice Edward Douglass White in his opinion offered in the case of *Downes v. Bidwell*, for the controversy that asserted whether it was constitutional for Congress to impose through the Foraker Act a tariff on trade between Puerto Rico and the United States, in light of the Uniformity Clause.

The great changes resulting from the military conflicts between the countries of the Western Union, and the intervention of the United States in these conflicts, led to changes in the civil and political order in Puerto Rico. President William Howard Taft took the initiative to propose the granting of American citizenship for Puerto Rico, which culminated in the approval of the Jones bill, which was finally signed by President Woodrow Wilson on March 2, 1917. This bill was the product of great controversy, due to the conditions that were imposed, since it would grant citizenship without the motivation of admitting Puerto Rico as a state.

This act leads us to argue about the violation of the value of equal treatment of American citizens. The first violation we must recognize is not having the right to vote for those Members of Congress who pass Federal laws that apply to Puerto Rico, not having fair representation in Congress, and not being able to vote for the President of the United States.

Interpreting what is expressed in the Constitution of the United States, this closes the doors to the millions of Puerto Ricans residing on the island, to have full equality as the rest of their fellow citizens, by applying federal laws without the consent of the governed, with the argument that the right to vote will be recognized only to the residents of the states.

Under the colonial condition imposed on us and not being a state, Puerto Rico does not have the right to the electoral college because the territories do not meet the requirements established by the 14 Amendment, which establishes that: "All persons born or naturalized in the United States and subject to the jurisdiction thereof are citizens of the United States and of the States in which they reside. [. . .]," so the territories are not part of the United States for constitutional purposes.

Under this premise presented by the Congress, we allude to international law on the establishment of the "International Covenant on Civil and Political Rights" ratified by the General Assembly in December 16, 1966.

Under the Treaty of Paris, the Congress of the United States is granted plenary powers over the territory, and it was provided that it would have the responsibility not only to determine the civil rights, but also the political status of its inhabitants. In this matter we must mention that Congress has not taken forceful action to define Puerto Rico's status under the regimes of international law and the U.S. Constitution.

These rights began to be discussed after the approval of the Universal Declaration of Human Rights on December 10, 1948, adopted by the United Nations (UN). This declaration emphasizes the equality of rights that all human beings should enjoy. Article 2 states: "No distinction shall be made on the basis of the political, jurisdictional or international status of the country or territory to which a person belongs, whether it be an independent country, a territory or under any other limitation of sovereignty. By this declaration Puerto Ricans residing on the island should have equal rights and duties as citizens residing in one of the fifty (50) states.

We must mention that the precedents set in cases subsequent to the creation of the Commonwealth create ambiguity in the fact that Congress continues to have plenary powers over and above the sovereignty that was recognized to Puerto Rico in 1952. The final determination made by the Supreme Court in the case of *Puerto Rico v. Sanchez-Valle*, and the establishment of the PROMESA Act, which creates the Fiscal Oversight Board, demonstrated the permanence of Puerto Rico as a territory subject to the plenary powers of Congress, which violates international agreements on the self-determination of peoples and the value of equal rights.

Finally, we would like to allude to the Constitution of the United States, where in its preamble establishes the expression "We the People of the United States" . . . This declaration marks the core value of the nation's constitution and the intent by which it is created. The cases brought to abolish slavery in the nation, as well as other movements such as the petitioning for women's right to vote, used this consensus to argue that the term "We the people" refers to the inclusion of all American citizens in the rights outlined in the U.S. Constitution.

Therefore, we believe it is meritorious to take action on what this resolution proposes, to promote equal rights and social justice for U.S. citizens residing in Puerto Rico, so that they may enjoy the right to vote for the president of the United States. It is important that the U.S. Congress take action on the referred case and enforce the rights of the Constitution for all U.S. citizens with equality.

The bills before the House Committee on Natural Resources, chaired by Congressman Grijalva, allude to taking action in favor of the freedom of determination of the people of Puerto Rico on the future of their relationship with the United States. Certainly, the guarantee of the right to self-determination of the people of Puerto Rico has been guaranteed in all the processes of expression of the people through the various plebiscites held since 1967, until the last one held on November 3, 2020. But in order for the value of the people's right to self-determination to be realized, Congress has the duty to take action in favor of the democratic expression of Puerto Ricans residing here on the island.

H.R. 1522, introduced by our only congressional representative, Jenniffer Gonzalez, and Congressman Darren Soto, for consideration by the U.S. Senate and the U.S. House of Representatives, sets precedents in the history of the admission of territories as a state of the union. It also ensures concrete action on the mandate sent by the people of Puerto Rico last November 3 in favor of statehood, with the ratification of the results and the approval of the President of the United States.

In contrast with H.R. 2070, presented by Congresswomen Nydia Velázquez and Alexandria Ocasio-Cortez, who presented a bill that seeks the creation of a status convention that is unprecedented in the processes of admission of territories to the nation, and historically only the colonies who have wished to betray themselves toward the formation of an independent Republic, have accepted it.

With much respect to this Congress and members of the House Committee on Natural Resources, I submit that H.R. 2070 does not represent the will of the people and I request that it not be taken into consideration. The only piece of legislation that provides the tools for the advancement of the Puerto Rican people and that represents the will of the majority of the Puerto Rican people is H.R. 1522.

Thank you.

Statement by Mr. Rodney Ríos

I would like to begin by stating that it is my sincere hope that this brief message helps to state the facts and clear the air regarding the issue of Puerto Rico's status. Too often in the status debate we get lost in a labyrinth of myths, contradictions and mutual recriminations, which in the end help no one and contribute little or nothing to a solution. Former president John Adams once remarked that "facts are stubborn things." I wish then to focus exclusively on the facts of this issue.

First, statehood for Puerto Rico does not entail annexation. From the historical record, it is clear that through the Treaty of Paris in 1899 the United States annexed Puerto Rico. After annexation there arose the question of what Puerto Rico's status would be in regards to the rest of the country. This question was not pertinent before 1898; before then it was understood by our founders that all territories that were acquired permanently by the United States would, eventually, become states of the union as long as they met certain criteria. The requisites for statehood are and were that the territory had a republican form of government, the resources to maintain a state government and the desire of that Territory's people to become a State of the union.

It was only after the acquisition of Puerto Rico that the idea of permanent territories, colonies to put it another way, reemerged as an option. Sadly, I believe this was so because of the stain in our country of racial discrimination, an evil which we have long fought to defeat. As such, it comes as no surprise that the Supreme Court concocted through judicial hocus pocus the idea that some territories were to be incorporated and destined for statehood, and that others were to be unincorporated and would be forever cursed to be at the mercy of the changing whims of Congress. Now, this sounds very different to the principles of self-determination that have guided this country since the Founding.

In any case, President Calvin Coolidge once stated in relation to Puerto Rico that "It would not be difficult to demonstrate that the existing status of Puerto Rico is much more liberal than any other status in its history; that its people have more control of their own affairs, with less external intervention; that its people enjoy freedom and the protection of the law." He was right. Since annexation the Puerto Rican people have been free and made great progress. Imperfect progress, but progress, nonetheless. The simple fact of the matter is that Puerto Rico is better after annexation than before.

However, one of the fundamental principles of a free society is that citizens vote for the people that make and execute their laws. There can be no freedom without popular sovereignty; in America the people govern. And here lies the crux of the issue. Puerto Ricans are American citizens; and citizenship in America is supposed to be only one. Furthermore, being citizens for more than a century, it has been long understood in American history, that a political community composed of American citizens has an inalienable right to statehood. Moreover, as former Puerto Rican Governor Rafael Hernández Colón once noted, there has never been a political entity composed of American citizens that has separated from the Union. This must also be taken together with the fact that Puerto Ricans have never favored independence. Independence, then, would not only be antidemocratic, but it contrary to our traditions and constitutional order.

This brings us to the 2020 plebiscite. For a long time it was teased by the enemies of political equality that statehooders should organize a simple yes or no vote on statehood to solve the issue once and for all. This was done in 2020, and the people voted by a majority for statehood. States, as is clear from the historical record, create themselves before admission to the Union by whatever mechanisms they deem fit.

Historically speaking, Puerto Ricans have voted only to create a local government to preserve that commonwealth status, and since 2012 the people have voted for statehood on numerous times. As such, to pretend to continue a fruitless and pointless discussion by including independence or free association in a self-determination process, is a mockery of the democratic vote of Puerto Ricans. It is also an ignorance of the history of Puerto Rico and our deep commitment to permanent union.

We in Puerto Rico are not asking for alms, or to be maintained. Do not listen to the voices of gridlock from the extreme right or left. We Puerto Ricans are not victims; we have borne the price of freedom in every war from World War One to the conflicts in Iraq and Afghanistan. We are a free, proud and noble people. What we are demanding as our right, as our heritage, is for a chance to have our political rights and powers as a State of the Union. To have equal footing, as the doctrine is called. To have the power that all other states have through voting representation and the Tenth Amendment protections of residual and shared sovereignty of a State in relation to the federal government.

In sum, Puerto Rico has an organized political system, a desire for statehood, and the resources to maintain a state government. All requirements for admission have been met; additionally, Puerto Ricans do not want independence, and they are American citizens. It would be a shame if this Congress were to end without heeding the voice of the people and it decided to side with obstructionists and in favor of the discriminatory precedents of a bygone era. We have come very far as a nation; it would be a stain in our national honor to keep citizens without representation at this day and age. I hope this Congress is wise enough to approve a federal statehood plebiscite which will resolve this issue once and for all. We are all ready and a century too late. Thank you for your time.

Miss GONZÁLEZ-COLÓN. My first question will be to Dr. Ponsa-Kraus. Have you had opportunity to read all the DOJ reports on both bills?

Dr. PONSA-KRAUS. I am sorry. Have I read the reports? Yes, I have.

Miss GONZÁLEZ-COLÓN. Did DOJ raise any constitutional issues or concerns with H.R. 1522?

Dr. PONSA-KRAUS. No. No constitutional concerns.

Miss GONZÁLEZ-COLÓN. The first part of the report says the Department of Justice supports providing the people of Puerto Rico, and I quote, "the opportunity to vote on whether to become a state of the Union, as H.R. 1522 would do."

Dr. PONSA-KRAUS. That is right.

Miss GONZÁLEZ-COLÓN. So, for you, that would mean that the Department of Justice is in support of H.R. 1522?

Dr. PONSA-KRAUS. That is how I interpret that sentence. Yes.

Miss GONZÁLEZ-COLÓN. And is the first letter of the report, correct?

Dr. PONSA-KRAUS. That is right.

Miss GONZÁLEZ-COLÓN. I will yield back the balance of my time.

Mr. SABLAN. Thank you. Mr. Chairman, I yield back my time.

The CHAIRMAN. Thank you, Mr. Sablan.

Let me now recognize Ms. González-Colón for her 5 minutes. You are recognized.

Miss GONZÁLEZ-COLÓN. Thank you, Mr. Chairman. I will continue making my questions at this time. Dr. Ponsa, when you saw that part of the report that actually is the first line of the report from DOJ, did the DOJ raise any constitutional issues or concerns with H.R. 2070.

Dr. PONSA-KRAUS. Yes, it did.

Miss GONZÁLEZ-COLÓN. Can you briefly enumerate those that concern you the most?

Dr. PONSA-KRAUS. They coincide with the ones that concerned me before. One is that the failure to specify the options opens the door to unconstitutional options. And the other is that it purports to bind Congress when that is an illusory promise. Congress can't bind itself to enact a joint resolution in the future.

Miss GONZÁLEZ-COLÓN. It has been said here in the hearing from several witnesses that H.R. 2070 will guarantee citizenship. Do you understand that other options, independence, can guarantee citizenship for Puerto Rico?

Dr. PONSA-KRAUS. No other option than statehood can guarantee citizenship in the way that the citizenship clause of the 14th Amendment does. Other options could include citizenship, but they could not guarantee it prospectively. And, in my opinion, this is not a question of first impression in the sense that it is spelled out in the citizenship clause of the 14th Amendment. It guarantees birth-right citizenship to persons born in the United States. So, if one is independent, with or without a free association, then the United States has the power to provide birthright citizenship, but it can also decide in the future to stop granting it.

Miss GONZÁLEZ-COLÓN. You read the report, as I did. And that report from DOJ says that H.R. 2070 does not recognize there are only three constitutional status options in statehood or keeping the territorial status. So, in fact, doesn't H.R. 2070 leave the door open for the convention to come up with unconstitutional status options? Dr. PONSA-KRAUS. That is right. It does. And that has been my greatest concern from the beginning, that it opens the door to such options, that it doesn't specify the constitutional options, and that means it consigns Puerto Ricans to continue having the same debate they have had for 70 years without the kind of guidance that they need from Congress to tell it here's what the constitutional options are and the ones that we would agree to.

Miss GONZÁLEZ-COLÓN. You have been hearing about nationhood and being sovereigns in Puerto Rico and many other things. Is Congress the ultimate source of the Puerto Rico government's authority?

Dr. PONSA-KRAUS. With Puerto Rico's current territorial status, yes, it is.

Miss GONZÁLEZ-COLÓN. Sadly, but it is like that.

Dr. PONSA-KRAUS. That is right.

Miss GONZÁLEZ-COLÓN. And are there other viable options under the U.S. Constitution other than statehood or independence or the territorial status?

Dr. PONSA-KRAUS. There are not. I do not believe that free association short of independence is possible. I completely agree with Professor Cox Alomar that there are lots of forms of free association, but they all involve independence with a treaty or compact of free association. Anything between independence and statehood is territorial under the U.S. Constitution.

Miss GONZÁLEZ-COLÓN. Having said that, can a constitutional convention or a status convention, as proposed in the other bill, create a new non-territorial status compatible with the U.S. Constitution?

Dr. PONSA-KRAUS. No. It cannot.

Miss GONZÁLEZ-COLÓN. Has the Federal Government previously relied on a convention to define the constitutional status options?

Dr. PONSA-KRAUS. Not to define them, no.

Miss GONZÁLEZ-COLÓN. My second question will be, is statehood the only non-territorial status option that guarantees the constitutional U.S. citizenship?

Dr. PONSA-KRAUS. Prospectively, yes. I agree that current U.S. citizens cannot be stripped of their citizenship involuntarily under any circumstance, but statehood is the only one that guarantees U.S. citizenship prospectively in the future.

Miss GONZÁLEZ-COLÓN. The Federal executive branch, the courts, and Congress have all confirmed repeatedly that Puerto Rico is a territory and that the only non-territorial options available are statehood and independence. And DOJ just reaffirmed this claim. In your opinion, do the people of Puerto Rico need a status convention to know and understand this?

Dr. PONSA-KRAUS. No. I don't think they do.

Miss GONZÁLEZ-COLÓN. Do you think that voters in the island are capable and knowledgeable enough to understand that status options are available to them and their consequences without having to resort to an assembly of a few selected—where decisions are made behind closed doors?

Dr. PONSA-KRAUS. I do believe they are capable of it, yes.

Miss GONZÁLEZ-COLÓN. Thank you. I yield back.

The CHAIRMAN. Thank you very much. The gentlelady yields.

Let me now recognize Representative Gallego for his 5 minutes. Sir, you are recognized.

Mr. Gallego?

Mr. GALLEGO. I apologize. Can you hear me now?

The CHAIRMAN. Yes. Thank you.

Mr. GALLEGO. Sorry. You would think after all these months I finally would get it together, right?

My first question is for Dr. Ponsa-Kraus. And I apologize if I mispronounced your last name. I appreciate you responding to criticisms about low levels of participation in the 2020 plebiscite. In your experience as a lawyer and a professor, have you ever seen the same argument used to dismiss results of an election in a state in the United States?

Dr. PONSA-KRAUS. I have not, no, and you pronounced my name perfectly. Thank you.

Mr. GALLEGO. Very good. And to note, I have heard this from— I said this last time. I have heard this argument in the past to also turn back plebiscites, actually, in Arizona, for example. And it is usually done by my Republican colleagues, especially when trying to do a tax increase. So, witnesses supporting both bills, including yourself, have mentioned the importance of having clear definitions of options on a self-determination ballot. In addition to the clarification around free association citizenship, what important information do you believe should be included in the definitions of statehood and independence?

Dr. PONSA-KRAUS. Well, I appreciate that question because I completely agree that there should be clarity for the voters. But I believe that a ballot can't spell every last detail of a transition out. That is unrealistic. The voters need to choose on the basic options, and then the transitions need to be developed and implemented.

So, for statehood, I think voters should understand that it gets them equal representation and U.S. citizenship now and in the future, which I believe they understand.

For independence, I believe they should understand that that is a separate sovereignty, and Puerto Rico gets to decide its own future.

And with free association, I believe it is critical that they understand that it is a form of independence and that citizenship would be within the power of the United States, that no current citizen would lose their own citizenship, but that it would be up to the United States whether to grant citizenship in the future, and it could change that policy. I believe that voters would deserve to understand that.

Mr. GALLEGO. Thank you, Doctor.

Rev. Carmen Cabrera, just a general statement, I really appreciate that you talk about that Puerto Ricans have served in the armed services. I was lucky enough to serve in the U.S. Marine Corps with a lot of Puerto Ricans, actually, and very proud Americans. Can you describe as a community leader the impact that you have seen territorial status—what it causes to our service members and their families and what a positive change would come from us having stated, for example, the reimbursement fees with TRICARE, a lot of things of that nature that is unequal?

Did I get bounced off?

Dr. PONSA-KRAUS. That question is not for me, right?

Mr. GALLEGO. No, I am sorry. I apologize. That was for Rev. Cabrera.

The INTERPRETER. Can you please repeat the question? This is Nestor Lima. I will be interpreting for her.

Mr. GALLEGO. Oh, I am sorry. Yes. [Speaking in Spanish.]

The INTERPRETER. So, in review, the question is what is the difference between specifically health care in——

Mr. GALLEGO. For veterans' benefits in general.

The INTERPRETER. Yes, veterans' health care and other benefits in the United States versus Puerto Rico for those who have served in the military?

Mr. GALLEGO. Correct.

[The following answers were delivered through an interpreter.]

Rev. CABRERA. Let me point out a few differences. For example, some that receive Social Security benefits do not receive in Puerto Rico some benefits that are received in the United States. And what we are also addressing is not just the funds and grants but also the dignity that has been negated or neglected. I can compare it to a father who pays attention to a son who does not live at home. And he allows the son to do everything, but he doesn't allow him to come back home and make decisions within his family. That is our posture for us here in Puerto Rico. This is how we feel.

So, it is not just about the benefits and about the money. And the other ones who are explaining their positions, they are doing it in a proper way as well. My position is about the heart of the Puerto Ricans, and it has to do with dignity. We have voted many times for statehood, and we don't have to keep voting for this. And I think it is time for the Congress to do what needs to be done.

Mr. GALLEGO. Thank you. And I would just like to note Puerto Rico actually has sacrificed more men and women in these last 20 years than many, many states in the United States.

Thank you. I yield back, Mr. Chairman.

The CHAIRMAN. Thank you, Mr. Gallego. The gentleman yields. It is my understanding that votes are going to be called at 2:30. It is supposed to be a lengthy vote process from what I understand. We will continue with questioning of those Members that are here or the Members that can remain at the meeting, and try to proceed that way. If it becomes cumbersome and difficult, with all due apologies to the witnesses and to my colleagues, we will call a recess until those votes are done.

With that, let me now turn to the gentleman, Mr. Gohmert, for his questions. Sir, you are recognized for 5 minutes.

Mr. GOHMERT. Thank you, Mr. Chairman. I appreciate that very much. Having studied history, gotten a degree in it, I have to express a concern. I love the people of Puerto Rico. I think they would be a wonderful addition, not just as a territory but as a state, but I know historically when language divides the country from any part of that country, it can become problematic. I understand that the generation coming up, most of them speak very good English, and I hope that is something that will continue. At this point, I want to yield my questions to my dear friend, a wonderful colleague, and that is the Honorable Jenniffer González-Colón.

Miss GONZÁLEZ-COLÓN. Thank you, Mr. Gohmert, for yielding the time. I really appreciate that. I will now make a question again to Dr. Ponsa and Dr. Córdova. A few minutes ago, we were talking about the voters and if they were capable or not to make decisions for the island. And it is Congress' plenary power such that they can approve any form status with any set of terms, any set of conditions or even benefits regardless of precedent. So, my question now will be, Dr. Ponsa, can Congress create a political relationship not contemplated in the Constitution.

Dr. PONSA-KRAUS. No. It cannot. Even its plenary power is not unconstrained by the Constitution.

Miss GONZÁLEZ-COLÓN. Can you elaborate on that?

Dr. PONSA-KRAUS. Sure. Plenary power means that Congress can govern a territory as the Federal Government and also as its local government; and it can grant or withdraw autonomy. Those powers are very much constrained by the Constitution. They don't include the power to create a status that doesn't exist and then bind the United States to it. Congress has the power to admit states. Other than that, it can recognize independent countries, and it can govern territories.

Miss GONZÁLEZ-COLÓN. Do you believe that H.R. 2070 offers a binding self-determination process?

Dr. PONSA-KRAUS. No. It is not binding.

Miss GONZÁLEZ-COLÓN. Dr. Córdova, do you think H.R. 2070 offers a binding self-determination process? Professor Córdova?

Mr. CÓRDOVA. Yes, excuse me. I forgot to unmute.

Miss GONZÁLEZ-COLÓN. OK.

Mr. CÓRDOVA. H.R. 2070 does not offer that. It is legal fiction which assumes that the people of Puerto Rico somehow will exercise their sovereignty and choose whatever path they choose, when, in fact, that sovereignty does not lie there. It lies in Congress. So, Congress is someone who is authorized to determine this, not the status convention.

Miss GONZÁLEZ-COLÓN. What about H.R. 1522? Does this bill offer a self-executing binding process should a majority of the voters on the island support statehood because this is a process? This is not forcing a solution on the voters. Actually, it needs this bill to get approved to them, be a ratification process on the island.

Mr. CÓRDOVA. Sure. And I think part of the comments of the Department of Justice precisely regarding H.R. 1522 recognizes that even the vote on ratifying the statehood in Puerto Rico would have to return to Congress. There is basically a process built in already where Congress would exercise its constitutional prerogatives. So, yes, I think H.R. 1522 does have the prerequisites to——

Miss GONZÁLEZ-COLÓN. Thank you, Professor. Dr. Ponsa, do you think that H.R. 1522 offers that self-executing binding process?

Dr. PONSA-KRAUS. It does offer a self-executing process. It offers statehood, which is something that Congress not only has the power, but the duty to do. I do believe Puerto Ricans are the ones who get to make a choice but among valid options, and Congress should offer them and has the power and duty to do that and it does so on H.R. 1522.

Miss GONZÁLEZ-COLÓN. Do you believe that a yes-or-no vote is a legitimate self-determination process?

Dr. PONSA-KRAUS. Unquestionably, it is.

Miss GONZÁLEZ-COLÓN. Do you agree that H.R. 2070 is colonial and paternalistic in nature given that it ignores the will of the people?

Dr. PONSA-KRAUS. I do. I think it is offensive that it ignores the November referendum. I think it is offensive that it provides for a bilateral negotiating commission that is neither bilateral nor negotiating. Really, I have serious problems with it, and they are not just constitutional.

Miss GONZÁLEZ-COLÓN. Thank you, Dr. Ponsa. I yield back.

The CHAIRMAN. Let me now recognize the gentlelady from New York, Ms. Velázquez, for 5 minutes. You are recognized.

Ms. VELÁZQUEZ. Thank you, Mr. Chairman.

Mr. Cox, does a status convention open the door to unconstitutional issues?

Dr. COX ALOMAR. The answer is no, and it is rather surprising that that argument could be raised. Could you imagine the framers in 1787 saying let's keep the Articles of

Confederation and not convene the convention because Washington might all of a sudden become a dictator or all of a sudden he might become a king—I mean, that is ridiculous.

The whole idea here is to have an inclusive process, a process that opens up the door for folks to actually have a meaningful, detailed conversation that has never happened since 1898.

Ms. VELÁZQUEZ. Thank you. Is Congress vested with the authority to negotiate any model of free association with Puerto Rico?

Dr. COX ALOMAR. The answer is yes. Congress has plenary authority under the Territorial Clause—I mean, has ample authority.

Ms. VELÁZQUEZ. And can you further explain why this is not an issue of constitutionality but of political will from Congress.

Dr. COX ALOMAR. That is another huge issue. I am listening to folks mixing up constitutional law with public policy. Public policy, that is something very different from—the fact that the Constitution allows for something to happen doesn't necessarily mean that Congress will actually do this. But Congress does have authority to do things, right? It is a matter of political will to decide what it wants to do.

Ms. VELÁZQUEZ. Thank you. This is 2021. Is it morally and politically correct for Congress to offer the people of Puerto Rico a status option that is subject to the plenary powers of Congress, meaning that the U.S. Congress has total authority over the island which will pose a clear continuation of the history of colonization?

Dr. COX ALOMAR. Of course not. The Senate is dealing with a John Lewis bill. All of a sudden, America is actually right now before the G7, NATO, trying to fight authoritarianism against Putin. And all of a sudden, you have folks here trying to say that America shouldn't decolonize Puerto Rico. I mean, it doesn't make any sense.

Ms. VELÁZQUEZ. Thank you. And Mr. Cox, this is a yes-or-no answer. In your opinion, would commonly known Act 2022, now renamed Act 60, that effectively creates a special tax treatment for foreigners in Puerto Rico be possible under statehood?

Dr. COX ALOMAR. No. Pursuant to the Uniformity Tax Clause, the answer would be no.

Ms. VELÁZQUEZ. OK. The DOJ report on H.R. 1522 argues that the Oversight Board is statutorily denominated part of the territorial government of Puerto Rico and will continue to do so if the island were to become a state. What should we make of Governor Pierluisi's previous statement that no state can have a fiscal board?

Dr. COX ALOMAR. Well, that is an illusory argument. Obviously, Congress has authority to impose conditions. If you go back to 1791, when Vermont acceded to the Union, all the way to Hawaii, 1959, you see that Congress has authority to make and impose conditions on territories acceding to the Union. So, Congress does have authority.

Ms. VELÁZQUEZ. And would H.R. 1522 automatically grant statehood to the island? Is statehood a done deal per the language on that bill?

Dr. COX ALOMAR. Well, no. The DOJ says it is no—there is no fait accompli. The DOJ on the first page of its opinions says this is not a done deal, right? I mean, it is pretty obvious.

Ms. VELÁZQUEZ. I would like for you to talk to us about the lessons we can learn from the pacts that were negotiated by the Pacific Islands.

Dr. COX ALOMAR. Well, the problem with those arrangements is that folks in the Pacific, they were not U.S. citizens, right? The Pacific Islands have a different history. And the other thing that people need to realize in the Committee is Puerto Rico presents a unique situation. Puerto Rico's relationship to the United States has really no parallel. We are U.S. citizens. Puerto Rico is its own nation sociologically. I hear witnesses speaking Spanish. Obviously we have a heritage that is somehow different from the Anglo heritage, and that is something that has to be dealt with by Congress. It is very, very difficult to superimpose the same solutions that have been used in the Pacific to Puerto Rico. Puerto Rico is completely different.

Ms. VELÁZQUEZ. Thank you. Congressman Gutiérrez, what does it say that in the last May election to select a shadow delegation whose only purpose is to lobby Congress, and where only 3.8 percent of voters participated, ousted Governor Rossellóhas now been elected again? Approximately 1 million Puerto Ricans marched asking for his resignation in 2019. And now with 3.8 percent of voters, he is back. Is this 3.8 percent representative of the will of the people in Puerto Rico?

Mr. GUTIÉRREZ. Absolutely not. Let's remember something. This was not part of the campaign in November. In other words, Pedro Pierluisi and the New Progressive Party did not say after the election we are going to pay six people $150,000 in spite of the fact that schools are still closed, in spite of the fact that pensions are not being paid, in spite of the fact that there are not roofs over certain people's homes.

But we are going to pay them—never said that. And think about it, Congresswoman. They elected Ricky Rossello, who was ousted by the people of Puerto Rico. You are right. A million people——

Miss GONZÁLEZ-COLÓN. Chairman, I raise a point of order.

Mr. GUTIÉRREZ [continuing]. One-quarter of the population came and marched—

The CHAIRMAN. The time is up.

Mr. GUTIÉRREZ [continuing]. Governor of Puerto Rico.

The CHAIRMAN. Mr. Gutiérrez, the time is up.

Mr. GUTIÉRREZ. I participated in that.

The CHAIRMAN. The gentleman yields back. The gentlelady yields. Let me recognize Mr. Lamborn for your 5 minutes, sir. You are recognized. Mr. Lamborn? Mr. Lamborn is not available. Mr. McClintock, you are recognized for 5 minutes.

Mr. MCCLINTOCK. Thank you, Mr. Chairman.

The CHAIRMAN. You are welcome, sir.

Mr. MCCLINTOCK. I am very disappointed with the Republican position on this issue. H.R. 1522 seems to me to be quite unambiguous. It would automatically make Puerto Rico a state upon a Puerto Rican referendum. And we have heard many reasons why this may or may not be in the interest of Puerto Rico. That is a question for Puerto Rico.

The question that Congress must decide is whether that is in the interest of the United States as a whole to admit Puerto Rico as a state. That is the responsibility that this bill would completely aggregate. I find that shocking, and I strongly disassociate myself and support that are expressed for that on behalf of the Minority. To me, this bill sidesteps fundamental questions that arise from statehood. And let's start with the impact of taxation. Many Puerto Ricans are exempt from Federal income taxes that they would have to pay under statehood. The general accounting office has estimated that the added tax burden that would accompany statehood could cause enormous job losses and additional damage to the economy of Puerto Rico. There is a question of language. The language of the United States is English, period. A common language is absolutely essential in a democracy. It is based on resolving our political differences by open debate. Open debate is impossible in a polyglot society.

Seventy-six percent of Puerto Ricans, according to one recent poll, thought it would be unacceptable that English might become their official language. As one nation, we have to be able to talk with each other. The government of Puerto Rico is a fiscal basket case, which we have been dealing with on this Committee for many years. It has far too many public employees, unsustainable pension obligations, and a long history of corruption.

Its labor participation rate is one-third less than that of the United States. An important question is does Puerto Rican statehood make America stronger or weaker. Furthermore, there has been a very unconvincing history of referenda on this issue, of six votes on the question since 1966. Three times, the people of Puerto Rico said no to statehood. The most recent vote was a narrow 52 to 48 in favor of statehood after many Puerto Ricans have already fled to the mainland. That is not the kind of convincing mandate that you decide the fundamental political relationship between Puerto Rico and the United States for all eternity. The impact of additional taxation will accompany statehood, the imposition of an official language opposed by a large majority of Puerto Rico and the strong minority sentiments in Puerto Rico for independence, free association, or our continued commonwealth status set the stage for catastrophic civil unrest if statehood should be imposed on such a slender, fragile, and perhaps transitory majority.

The question we need to ask is whether admitting Puerto Rico as a state makes our country stronger or weaker. That is the crucial question. But I am shocked and saddened to see my party content to simply ignore. This abrogates our responsibility under the Constitution and instead leaves this far-reaching and permanent decision to a simple referendum within Puerto Rico. I would appeal to my Republican colleagues to reconsider. I have no questions and I yield back.

The CHAIRMAN. The gentleman yields back. Thank you, Mr. McClintock. Let me now recognize Mr. McEachin. Sir, you are recognized for 5 minutes.

Mr. MCEACHIN. Thank you, Mr. Chairman. In the interest of time, I am going to yield the balance of my time to Mr. Soto of Florida.

The CHAIRMAN. The gentleman yields.

Mr. SOTO. I thank the gentleman. Thank you, Chairman. I thank the gentleman from Virginia for your support of the Statehood Admission Bill as well. Colleagues, last hearing, you heard about the difficult challenges facing Puerto Rico over the past few years and currently: Hurricane Maria, the deadliest natural disaster in modern history, a decade-long recession, Draconian PROMESA budget cuts, earthquakes, and now COVID-19.

As a result, Puerto Rico lost 11.8 percent of its population since 2010 according to the 2020 Census. The conclusion is obvious. The territorial status is failing Puerto Rico, and it is not surprising. Puerto Rico is just too big to be a territory anymore—3.2 million Americans there, bigger than half the states nearly, and yet they have one non-voting Resident Commissioner for the whole island. And she does her best, but she doesn't even get a vote on the Floor.

Against this backdrop, the Puerto Rican legislature passed a law to have an election, a simple statehood yes-or-no question in a high turnout general election. This is the same ballot question used by countless states to join these United States before this moment. And in November 2020, they voted yes by 52.52 percent. And the reasons are obvious. There is no question at this point that having two U.S. Senators and four voting Members of Congress would have helped them greatly through these crises. There is no question that Puerto Rico as a territory gets far less funding than states. This wreaks havoc on health care, their economy, disaster relief, child tax credits, earned income tax credits, Social Security, and countless other aspects of their lives down there. We have spent hours upon hours in this Congress and prior Congresses trying to make Puerto Rico equal in Federal program after Federal program.

In one bill and one vote, we can empower Americans in Puerto Rico to solve these inequities at once. Our bill sets up one last statehood yes-or-no question. And let me state the obvious. If they want statehood, they could vote yes. And if they do not, they could vote no. The vote would be binding, and the only action left would be approximately a year-long transition period, and then they would be admitted.

Since our last hearing, Chairman Grijalva asked the U.S. Department of Justice to submit reports on both bills. Last hearing, we told you that there were only three statuses available to Americans in Puerto Rico under the U.S. Constitution: statehood, territory, and independence. The U.S. Department of Justice agrees. The U.S. Supreme Court already ruled this last year. Last hearing, we told you that a statehood yes-or-no question was constitutional. The U.S. Department of Justice agrees.

Last hearing, we talked about the need to end the PROMESA fiscal board as part of the transition process. The U.S. Department of Justice agrees, and we will amend our bill to make it clear that the PROMESA fiscal board will be dissolved during the transition period before Puerto Rico is admitted as a state.

Last hearing, we told you that a constitutional convention could not make up new status options. The U.S. Department of Justice agrees. Last hearing, we told you that a constitutional convention could not bind future Congresses. And yet again, the U.S. Justice Department agrees. So, here we are today in the second of two historic hearings with worthy debate. This is the first time Congress has had hearings on a straight-up statehood admissions bill in our history.

It is the first time that the U.S. DOJ has weighed in timely and thoroughly on the constitutional issues and status options available to Americans in Puerto Rico. And soon under Chair Grijalva, we will have a markup. It has taken 120 years for Puerto Ricans to get to this moment, and it is time to give Americans in Puerto Rico one last binding referendum to choose whether to be admitted as a state or not.

That is the opinion backed by the majority vote in Puerto Rico. It is also backed by a bipartisan group of legislators, including their own Resident Commissioner, Jenniffer González-Colón, and House Majority Leader Steny Hoyer. For these reasons stated, I urge you all to support H.R. 1522, the Puerto Rico Statehood Admission Act. And from there, if my time is remaining, I yield back.

The CHAIRMAN. The gentleman yields. Thank you very much, Mr. Soto.

Let me now recognize Mr. Graves. Sir, you are recognized for 5 minutes. The gentleman is recognized.

Miss González-Colón, are there other people on that side of the dais that have not been recognized that need to be recognized?

Miss GONZÁLEZ-COLÓN. Yes, Mr. Chairman. I can see Ms. Radewagen on the queue.

The CHAIRMAN. OK. If Mr. Graves is not available, Ms. Radewagen, you are recognized for 5 minutes.

Mrs. RADEWAGEN. Thank you, Chairman Grijalva and Ranking Member Westerman, for holding this hearing. As a fellow Member representing a U.S. territory, I want to align myself with the statements made today by Resident Commissioner González-Colón and reiterate my support for her legislation. And, with that, I yield my time to the Resident Commissioner.

Miss GONZÁLEZ-COLÓN. Thank you, Ms. Radewagen. I just want to take the floor where Mr. McClintock left it. And I wish to respond. I strongly disagree with his position, but this is part of being part of America. Not everybody will think alike. And, again, sometimes people are misinformed. The Republican platform has endorsed statehood for more than 40 years.

So, having said that, I think this is a process to establish which bill has the constitutional base to respond to the voters or the people of the island. I may say this. If we are Americans, as we are, we should be listened to—that is the beauty of democracy. And that is the reason the people of the island have been voting many times requesting that equality that comes through statehood. This is not different from what Alaska and Hawaii did in the past.

Having said that, I would like to recognize Dr. Ponsa-Kraus. Do you want to respond to any of the statements Members——

Dr. PONSA-KRAUS. Yes, I do. I think the argument that a constitutional convention as proposed in H.R. 2070 opens the door to unconstitutional options has been misunderstood and mis-stated. The argument isn't that a constitutional convention in Puerto Rico might do something crazy. OK? It is much more precise than that, and it has a context. The context is that Puerto Ricans were led to believe for many decades that Commonwealth could be nonterritorial. They were led to believe that by the Commonwealth Party in Puerto Rico. They were told they had a compact. They were told they were no longer a territory. They voted for that under the impression they had something they did not have. That is the context in which the argument that H.R. 2070 opens the door to unconstitutional options exists.

The problem is that if Congress doesn't specify the options the way the DOJ has done, if Congress doesn't specify the options and say here are the constitutional non-territorial options that we would be willing to agree to because they are consistent with the Constitution, and they would decolonize Puerto Rico, then what they do is send Puerto Ricans back to the drawing board to have the same fight again.

It is a waste of time, and it is a delay tactic designed to defeat a statehood offer, which Puerto Ricans earned with their vote in November. So, the argument isn't Puerto Ricans might just do something crazy. OK? The argument is a specific legal argument with a context.

Miss GONZÁLEZ-COLÓN. Sorry. You just explained it. And my question will be, people argue that the current level of support for statehood is somehow not enough. Is there a constitutional threshold of support that a territory must meet in order to become a state?

Dr. PONSA-KRAUS. There is not. And can I just say that if Congress offers an option that will obviously have an impact on the support that the option has, people are voting for statehood without knowing whether Congress would grant it. And Congress is the only one that has the power to admit. So, neither is there a constitutional requirement for a threshold, nor is it sensible to think that the level of support will be the same after an offer.

Miss GONZÁLEZ-COLÓN. I am making those questions becausesometimes, I can see that for other issues, 50 percent is good enough to elect the President of the United States, but 54 percent is not enough to show the majority of the will of the island, and we must be consistent with those percentages. And you are the professor here, so I will take your opinion as the one that DOJ established.

Is a simple majority of electors required to select the President of the United States?

Dr. PONSA-KRAUS. Yes.

Miss GONZÁLEZ-COLÓN. If the U.S. Constitution only provides for statehood or independence, can the U.S. Congress enact anything else that at some external committee or convention process referring to academic theories?

Dr. PONSA-KRAUS. It cannot. And Congress' plenary power to govern territories is not relevant to Congress' power to create a free association that is anything other than independence. That is what free association is. And plenary power doesn't change it.

Miss GONZÁLEZ-COLÓN. Thank you. I yield back.

The CHAIRMAN. Thank you very much.

Let me now recognize the gentleman from Chicago. Mr. García, you are recognized for 5 minutes. Mr. García? Mr. García is not available.

I recognize the gentleman from Florida. Mr. Soto, you are recognized for 5 minutes.

Mr. SOTO. Thank you, Chairman.

[Speaking in Spanish.] Thank you Rev. Carmen Cabrera for attending this hearing. And I have just two questions for you. I really appreciate you being here and giving a perspective as someone living a second-class citizenship on the island. And I know there is going to be some interpretation, right?

The INTERPRETER. OK.

Mr. SOTO. Rev. Cabrera, why do you think more Puerto Ricans voted for statehood than any candidate on the ballot in November 2020?

The INTERPRETER. Was it 2020 or 2019?

Mr. SOTO. 2020.

Rev. CABRERA. 2020.

The INTERPRETER. OK.

Mr. SOTO. [Speaking in Spanish.]

Rev. CABRERA. We deeply appreciate our relationship with the United States of America. And the youth in Puerto Rico, they are changing their mindset. They are the children of parents who have seen the inequality. That is like a feeling that is inherited to the children, and when they come to the ballot box, they vote that way.

Mr. SOTO. Rev. Cabrera, LULAC has been a champion of Latino civil rights for many, many years in our country. Why do you think LULAC is supporting the Statehood Admission bill?

Rev. CABRERA. In the different areas that LULAC helps with civil rights, with benefits and the well-being of Latinos, they know that Puerto Rico must accept their reality as a colony. And the way of getting out of this is by getting out of the disenfranchisement in becoming the 51st state of America. Again, this is not the first time that we vote. We have voted many, many, many times. And we have given the opportunity for Puerto Ricans to vote. And time and time again, we have voted for statehood.

Mr. SOTO. Thank you, and I yield back.

The CHAIRMAN. The gentleman yields. Thank you, Mr. Soto. And let me recognize Mr. Obernolte for his 5 minutes. Sir, you are recognized.

Mr. OBERNOLTE. Thank you very much, Mr. Chairman, and thank you to the witnesses for what has been a very interesting hearing. In the interest of time, I would like to yield my remaining time to the Representative from Puerto Rico, Miss González-Colón.

Miss GONZÁLEZ-COLÓN. Thank you, Congressman, for yielding the time. I appreciate that. I will go back to some of the questions. A few minutes ago, we were talking about the contributions of Puerto Ricans to our Nation. And I think it is important to establish the numbers that are participating in our military forces. Eighteen thousand Puerto Ricans were part of World War I in our armed services. Sixty-five thousand Puerto Ricans fought in the Second World War. Forty-eight thousand Puerto Ricans fought in the Korean War, helping the United States. And then 48,000 fought in Vietnam and 61,000 in Korea. Ten thousand soldiers from the island in the U.S. Army fought in the Gulf War. And then you have more than 25,000 Puerto Ricans that are active in military service, 5,000 of them just in the reserve, more than 8,000 in the National Guard, more than 38,000 deployments in Operation Enduring Freedom. And I can go on to establish all the recognitions that are Puerto Ricans in the Armed Forces—making the ultimate sacrifice for our Nation as they were in the Korean War having the Congressional Gold Medal, among many others.

Having said that, I would like to go back to some of the questions. Dr. Ponsa, do you understand that the U.S. Constitution only provides for statehood or independence, or can Congress do anything else?

Dr. PONSA-KRAUS. The only constitutional non-territorial options are statehood and independence. Anything in between is territory.

Miss GONZÁLEZ-COLÓN. I do believe that the analysis of H.R. 1522 was particularly comprehensive and helped dispel some of the myths that are being used against statehood. For example, some of the opponents of statehood, on both sides of the aisle, claimed that Puerto Rico would first have to become an incorporated territory prior to the state. Didn't DOJ dispel this in this report, arguing that Congress could amend any bill to clarify that Puerto Rico will remain unincorporated?

Dr. PONSA-KRAUS. Absolutely. And that is clear historically and doctrinally as well. There is no requirement that Puerto Rico become incorporated before becoming a state. It is within Congress' power to say that it is unincorporated until it becomes a state.

Miss GONZÁLEZ-COLÓN. Opponents for statehood as well also claim that all Federal taxes lost will immediately apply to Puerto Rico from becoming a state. However, DOJ again dispels that, saying that, and according to the DOJ report, Congress has the power to enact legislation provided for Federal or delayed application of the constitutional or informative requirements. Is that correct or no?

Dr. PONSA-KRAUS. That is correct.

Miss GONZÁLEZ-COLÓN. Do you want to expand on that?

Dr. PONSA-KRAUS. Even the Supreme Court opinion that invented the status of unincorporated territory made clear that Congress could incorporate in certain respects and not others and be gradual in not others. And that same Court upheld what would otherwise have been a violation of uniformity just a few years later in the territory of Alaska. So, Congress does have the power to do this gradually and to incorporate one step at a time and provide for an appropriate transition.

Miss GONZÁLEZ-COLÓN. Didn't DOJ also argue that legislation provided for gradual transition to taxes and bankruptcy before Puerto Rico will be constitutional?

Dr. PONSA-KRAUS. I didn't hear the beginning of the question. I am sorry.

Miss GONZÁLEZ-COLÓN. Didn't the DOJ report also argue that legislation provided for a gradual transition to tax and bankruptcy laws, uniformity for Puerto Rico will be constitutional?

Dr. PONSA-KRAUS. Yes, it did. Yes.

Miss GONZÁLEZ-COLÓN. And according to that report of DOJ that we are looking into today, will Congress have the ability to cite economic circumstances unique to Puerto Rico as a basis for a continuation or phase-out of the tax status that treats Puerto Rico differently?

Dr. PONSA-KRAUS. Yes, absolutely. It stands to reason that Congress, with its plenary power to govern territories and its power to admit can provide for a reasonable transition. And the idea that suddenly all these oppressive things happen overnight has always been a scare tactic.

Miss GONZÁLEZ-COLÓN. Thank you, Dr. Ponsa.

I yield back, Mr. Chairman.

The CHAIRMAN. I now recognize Mr. García for 5 minutes. Sir, you are recognized. Mr. García?

Let me now recognize Mr. San Nicolas for 5 minutes. Sir, you are recognized.

Mr. SAN NICOLAS. Thank you, Mr. Chairman, and I want to first begin by thanking the Committee for convening this hearing. I am actually on Guam at the moment. I have been with the Committee since 3 a.m., and this has actually been one of the most informative hearings that I have sat through in some time. I wanted to credit all of the witnesses for definitely bringing their A-game. Everybody absolutely is making strong cases for both bills, and that is something that I think is indicative of the fact that Puerto Rico is absolutely ready to vacate its territorial status.

We have the intellect, we have the capacity, and it is time for us to move forward. I wanted to first address statements made by a colleague questioning whether or not admitting Puerto Rico as a state is something that is good for the country. I think that as long as this country maintains the hypocrisy of colonies, then we are losing our credibility internationally, and we are also undermining our credibility domestically. There should be no territories in this country ever. That is not what this country was founded upon, and it is not the future of this country.

That being said, Mr. Chairman, Guam is observing this hearing and these proceedings with great interest as we as a territory also endure the same circumstances of Puerto Rico, notwithstanding some differences in our unincorporated territorial relationship with the United States. I wanted to first posit a question to Dr. Christina Ponsa-Kraus.

You made it very clear in your testimony that the options provided to Puerto Rico, if they are going to be truly constitutional, can only be statehood or independence. Am I hearing that correctly?

Dr. PONSA-KRAUS. Yes. Independence, including free association. Statehood or independence, including free association.

Mr. SAN NICOLAS. So, free association can also be a status option on a referendum, that would be constitutionally consistent?

Dr. PONSA-KRAUS. Absolutely. My position is just that it needs to be made clear that free association is a form of independence. There is a lot of confusion. Is it two options or three options? Well, free association is a form of independence. You can count it as 2A and 2B, or 2 and 3.

Mr. SAN NICOLAS. I very much agree. I am very familiar with free association having our freely associated allies to the south of Guam in Palau, the Federated States of Micronesia and the Republic of the Marshall Islands. They are all independent countries with compacts of free association with the United States. I think it is very important for us to clearly put that on the record that free association is independence with a treaty. That is absolutely what free association is.

I also wanted to clarify some sentiments that were raised by our former colleague, Former Representative Luis Gutiérrez. Sir, you mentioned that 52 percent was inadequate for that to reflect the will of the people. I am concerned that if we put forward status options that involve multiple considerations, whether it is statehood, free association, Commonwealth or independence, wouldn't having multiple status options actually result in an outcome even worse than 52 percent? Mr. Gutiérrez?

Mr. GUTIÉRREZ. Representative, here is my point. They define the manner in which the plebiscite was going to be conducted. Who did that? They had a majority in the House, a majority in the Senate. They had the governorship. And they decided that it was going to be yes or no on statehood.

And my answer to you is the following. We are going to ultimately decide on one status. But let's remember this is irrevocable. You make Puerto Rico a State of the Union, and it is irrevocable. It should be something in which everyone participates. How is it—

Mr. SAN NICOLAS. I don't mean to be disrespectful. I need to reclaim my time, so I can make a final point. If I may reclaim my time, Mr. Chairman.

The CHAIRMAN. Mr. San Nicolas, thank you.

Mr. SAN NICOLAS. Thank you. So, my concern and just to conclude, I co-sponsored both bills, and that has to do with where I initiated my remarks. There should be no territories in this country. We need to move this issue forward one way or another. I am concerned about diluting the question again and there being some kind of undecided outcome, and no one knows how to move forward. I am also concerned about whether or not we are being very, very clear. And I think that that needs to happen regardless of what bill passes. But I will be voting for both. Thank you, Mr. Chairman, and I yield back.

The CHAIRMAN. The gentleman yields.

Mr. Graves, sir, you are recognized for 5 minutes.

Mr. GRAVES. Thank you, Mr. Chairman. I appreciate it. Congressman Gutiérrez, nice to see you again. I hope you are doing well. I first want to just make note that I want to disassociate myself with comments made earlier.

The CHAIRMAN. Mr. Graves, we are having some difficulty hearing. Is there a problem on your end in terms of——

Mr. GRAVES. Let me try to see if I can go along to—any better or no?

The CHAIRMAN. It is better. Yes.

Mr. GRAVES. All right. I am not sure if you heard me earlier. I just want to say that I first disassociate myself with comments made earlier about the appropriate litmus test or language for folks to be citizens of the United States. I don't think that is the appropriate standard and very concerning to hear those comments made.

Secondly, I want to thank all the witnesses that I have enjoyed hearing in discussion at this hearing and previous. Dr. Ponsa-Kraus, in your opinion, would it be disingenuous to tell people, the people of Puerto Rico, that there are other constitutionally viable status options other than statehood, independence, or the current territorial status?

Dr. PONSA-KRAUS. Yes, it would be, and it has happened before, and it will hopefully never happen again.

Mr. GRAVES. Is free association independent?

Dr. PONSA-KRAUS. Free association is a form of independence, yes.

Mr. GRAVES. Has the United States ever granted blanket citizenship to the residents of an independent nation?

Dr. PONSA-KRAUS. No. It never has.

Mr. GRAVES. In an independent Puerto Rico under a treaty of free association, would U.S. citizenship be granted for future generations?

Dr. PONSA-KRAUS. Congress would have the power to do so, and Congress would also have the power to stop doing so.

Mr. GRAVES. Mr. Chairman, I yield my remaining time to Congresswoman Jenniffer González-Colón.

Miss GONZÁLEZ-COLÓN. Thank you, Mr. Garret Graves, for yielding the time, and your help in many Puerto Rican issues, not just in this Committee but in the Transportation and Infrastructure Committee. And I will try to take your last question. And, again, I will go directly to Dr. Ponsa and Professor Córdova.

Following that analysis of the Department of Justice regarding H.R. 1522, some are saying that statehood is the one that is going to say whether voters of the island will have the final say, that they will have to ratify statehood also made by Congress in a referendum. Is that correct?

Dr. PONSA-KRAUS. That is correct. H.R. 1522 offers it, and the voters have a chance to vote yes or no.

Miss GONZÁLEZ-COLÓN. And that would be the way to ratify the final step in the process to gain statehood, correct?

Dr. PONSA-KRAUS. Right. Well, as H.R. 1522 provides, then the President would be required to issue a proclamation in the wake of a yes vote for statehood. There are more steps, but the final substantive stuff would be that choice of yes if the voters made it.

Miss GONZÁLEZ-COLÓN. So, the first step is actually recognizing the votes of November of last year, and that is what this bill, H.R. 1522, does, recognizing that vote, prompting the question to Congress so Congress can make the offer to the people of the island. And once this bill is approved—needs to be in the House, it appears to be approved in the Senate—if the President is to sign it, then having a Federal sponsor of a referendum in Puerto Rico with that final yes or no question—do you want to be admitted as a state? Yes or no? Thus, in that process, the "no" will mean any other option, correct?

Dr. PONSA-KRAUS. No leaves open a subsequent process. To choose any other option, we are going to vote on statehood again. I mean, "no" doesn't rule anything out. The constitutional non-territorial options remain available.

Miss GONZÁLEZ-COLÓN. So, that will mean that people that have been saying that they are excluded from the ballot, that they were excluded in the past November referendum is not correct, actually. The people who were against statehood, who were for independence, who were for free association or even the people who wanted to remain as a territory, they were paying directly for the "no" as an option. So, they were represented legally and constitutionally speaking.

Dr. PONSA-KRAUS. That is right. Opponents of statehood freely campaigned against statehood, and supporters freely campaigned for it. No party, no option, no voter was excluded.

Miss GONZÁLEZ-COLÓN. Thank you.

Mr. Chairman, I yield back.

The CHAIRMAN. The gentlelady yields. Mr. Graves yields.

Let me recognize Mr. García. Sir, you are recognized for 5 minutes.

Mr. GARCÍA. Thank you, Mr. Chairman. I am glad to overcome the technical glitches. The people of Puerto Rico have suffered too much for too long. And we can all agree that most of Puerto Rico's problems are rooted in its colonial status. As Chair Grijalva has stated, Congress needs to keep moving forward on this because Puerto Rico can't stay in limbo any longer. The future of millions of Puerto Ricans shouldn't be a political football. We have an opportunity to rectify Puerto Rico's long-standing colonial status which has resulted in its people being treated as second-class citizens. But let me be clear. It must be done correctly and transparently. Regardless of the status outcome, the people of Puerto Rico deserve a thoughtful and thorough transition plan as required in the Puerto Rico self-determination plan.

A question for Dr. Cox Alomar. In the analysis of H.R. 1522, Puerto Rico Statehood Admission Act, the DOJ concluded that its biggest concern was execution and transition. In your view, would it be possible for the people of Puerto Rico to know what a transition to statehood might look like before they vote on it? And would they know the economic and political trade-offs?

Dr. COX ALOMAR. Well, under the current bill, there is no certainty. The people of Puerto Rico would basically be in the dark. I mean, there is no certainty about whether PROMESA would stay under statehood. There is no certainty of whether Puerto Rico would become an incorporated territory or for how long. And that is the basic flaw of the bill before the House right now before the Committee, lack of certainty.

Mr. GARCÍA. So, it is not as it has been portrayed in your opinion by the statehood advocates.

Dr. COX ALOMAR. There could be no—I am sorry, sir. I mean, very quick, there can be no self-determination if there is no informed choice in the first place.

Mr. GARCÍA. Thank you, sir.

Dr. Caraballo, in their analysis, the DOJ recommends, quote, "that Congress consider providing a more tailored solution for continuity in the operations of the Oversight Board." PROMESA passed out of Congress 5 years ago last week, but seems like we are talking about it non-stop in the Committee since I got here. I think it is fair to say that resolving Puerto Rico's debt in a democratic way is a complicated political issue.

Do you think it is realistic for Congress to quickly find a tailored solution for PROMESA, and would it be possible for Puerto Rican voters to know what the solution might be before choosing statehood?

Dr. CARABALLO-CUETO. Yes. I believe that there is a quick pass through it. We just have to get rid of the Fiscal Control Board that the majority of the citizens in Puerto Rico reject. Once we do that, then we can start talking among more democratic ways to restructure the debt, especially by looking at what the civil society can do. The first thing that many people have been demanding is auditing the debt. And that is the first step that has to be done before restructuring.

Mr. GARCÍA. Thank you, sir.

And to Congressman Gutiérrez, can you talk about two things, and briefly, in a minute and 25 seconds? The first is: I understand that the FBI Director in the year 2000 offered an apology to advocates of a different political solution, those for independence for all of the repression that had been inflicted upon them for a long time. And (2), I heard a lot of talk about civil rights here from advocates of statehood. What is their practice in terms of defending civil rights on the island?

Mr. GUTIÉRREZ. No. 1, great question. No. 1, it was the FBI Director in the year 2000 in a congressional hearing who said the FBI conducted illegal searches and criminal actions against proponents of independence in Puerto Rico, and they did it for over 50 years. It wasn't just happenstance. They did it. It is called the creation of Las Carpetas where over 100,000 advocates of Puerto Rican independence were monitored. And Congressman García, we have to understand it wasn't just that they created dossiers on them. They destroyed families. They destroyed reputations. They destroyed people. And they debilitated the fundamental democracy in Puerto Rico. And secondly, look, they continued to come before the Congress of the United States to say, "Where are my human rights? Where are my civil rights?" Statehood is what gives it to us while they diminish and undermine the rights of the LGBTQ community in Puerto Rico.

The civil code was just changed recently in Puerto Rico to undermine same-sex marriages. No. 1, the right of a woman to have control over her body and her reproductive system again is debilitated. The racist notions—I mean, think about it. The Statehood Party in Puerto Rico thinks it is fine to use the N-word. They think it is fine. They have legislators who give congratulatory resolutions to journalists who are fired by Univision, one of them for using the N-word.

How can at this time in this nature—and I just want to say to you, Congressman García, look. We cannot let this go by. We cannot allow this to continue to happen. You and I have to be on the City Council together. We have to go to the Congress because black people gave up their lives so that we could have a Voting Rights Act, so that we could espouse our positions. Cox Alomar is here with us, a distinguished jurist. And when he ran for Resident Commissioner of Puerto Rico, the former——

Miss GONZÁLEZ-COLÓN. Chairman, I raise a point of order.

The CHAIRMAN. I know. Gentlemen, time is up.

Mr. GUTIÉRREZ. That is something that we should also address. Mr. GARCíA. I yield back, Mr. Chairman.

The CHAIRMAN. Thank you, Mr. García.

Let me now recognize Mr. Hice. Sir, you are recognized for 5 minutes.

Let me now go to Representative Tiffany. Sir, you are recognized for 5 minutes.

Ranking Member, Ms. González-Colón, are there additional people on your side of the dais that wish to be recognized?

Miss GONZÁLEZ-COLÓN. Mr. Chairman, some Members are on the Floor at this time, so at this time, there are no Republicans in the queue.

The CHAIRMAN. OK. I appreciate that. Thank you. If Mr. Cohen is available on the Majority side, sir, you are recognized for 5 minutes.

I think the voting is undergoing. Let me now attempt to recognize a member of the Committee, Ms. Tlaib, for 5 minutes, any comments you may make or questions?

Ms. Ocasio-Cortez, you are recognized for 5 minutes for your comments and questions.

Given the fact that people are voting at this point, we will recess for a limited period of time, hopefully 15–20 minutes, and get some of the Members that had indicated they wanted to participate and be recognized, Mr. Cohen, Ms. Tlaib, Mrs. Trahan, Ms. Ocasio-Cortez, Mr. Hice, and Mr. Tiffany. And if the Ranking Member is comfortable with that, we will recess and allow them to come back. You are right. This is a very important meeting, and I would not want to deny them their opportunity to have an opportunity to ask questions, so now we will——

Miss GONZÁLEZ-COLÓN. Mr. Chairman, I agree with you. Can we establish how much time?

The CHAIRMAN. The Committee will notify, but I will—what time is it right now?

Miss GONZÁLEZ-COLÓN. 3:20.

The CHAIRMAN. Let's say 4 o'clock.

Miss GONZÁLEZ-COLÓN. Perfect.

The CHAIRMAN. Thank you.

And to the witnesses, my apologies. The vote occurred. It is a long vote, and hopefully we will be back soon and be able to continue with this hearing and with the participation of the Members. Thank you very much. The Committee is recessed until 4 o'clock.

[Recess.]

The CHAIRMAN. Will staff please notify the Ranking Member and whomever is going to be available in terms of Members, but we need to reconvene the meeting?

Miss GONZÁLEZ-COLÓN. I am sorry, Mr. Chairman. Ready to go.

The CHAIRMAN. OK. Thank you. And before we gavel the meeting to start, let me just thank all the witnesses in particular for their endurance and their patience. I very much appreciate it.

As Ms. González-Colón knows quite well and the staff knows quite well, I get really frustrated with the hearings on the issue of status in Puerto Rico, whether it is PROMESA, because they go on for a long, long time.

And I am not frustrated today—having learned a lesson that the issue of status, the issue of the economic and human life in Puerto Rico, is of tremendous consequence to everybody that is here, to the Members and to Congress. So, having to recess, having to convene back together and having a meeting that has extended this far, I appreciate the time. But I think it is necessary time because we need to move forward. So, we are going to reconvene the meeting, and Representative González-Colón, are there any Members on your side? The sequence was the Minority's turn to have questions.

Miss GONZÁLEZ-COLÓN. Mr. Chairman, not at this time. They are still voting on the Floor. So, I understand that we should go with the next in the queue. We can continue with whatever Members are available.

The CHAIRMAN. OK. The votes were much longer than anticipated, and I want to now recognize Representative Tlaib from Minnesota if she is available for any questions or comments she might have.

Ms. TLAIB. Thank you, Chairman. I am actually from Michigan, but it is OK.

The CHAIRMAN. Michigan. I am sorry. Oh, God. And I was just on that meeting with you.

Ms. TLAIB. I do have a question. Is Representative Velázquez on? Is she logged on? I know I just saw her voting just now because I am yielding my time to her, so I just logged on to make sure that I yielded my time to her.

The CHAIRMAN. If you would hold, I am certain she is on her way, and then I can—I haven't asked questions yet, and I can utilize that time to recognize myself.

Let me ask is Mr. Cohen available for questions.

And Representative Ocasio-Cortez, is she available for questions?

OK. With that, let me ask the questions that I had intended. And thank you very much. And I want to thank all the witnesses.

Two of the witnesses had to leave, and that is unfortunate. Professor Cox Alomar, can we discuss the results of the 2020 plebiscite? If I have the numbers correctly, yes on statehood received 52.52 percent, and no was 47 percent out of a turnout of 54.7 percent of eligible voters in Puerto Rico.

Based on these results, is it accurate to say that the majority of Puerto Ricans voted in favor of statehood, which, if granted by Congress, would be irreversible and permanent? Any response to that question, sir?

Dr. COX ALOMAR. Well, Mr. Chairman, the problem really is not the numbers. The problem is that there wasn't a real informed choice. I mean, statehood wasn't fully defined in terms of its consequences. Obviously, statehood is a matter that goes into perpetuity. And we do not want to have a Brexit situation in Puerto Rico, right? We want the people of Puerto Rico to actually exercise their right to determine their future on the basis of an informed choice. And the DOJ opinion is pretty clear. I mean, there are a series of very problematic areas which are completely left undefined in the statehood bill.

What happens with PROMESA and what happens with the debt, what is the transition to tax uniformity as required under the Constitution and the Equal Footing Doctrine? So, the issue here is trying to avoid what has happened with the Brexit, what has happened in southern Sudan, what had happened in other places where people are making choices pretty much in the dark.

The CHAIRMAN. Thank you. Dr. Ponsa-Kraus, the U.S. Department of Justice submitted reports on the two pieces of legislation. It was approved by the White House. All executive branch agencies with an interest in the bills also had input. And those weren't presented to the Committee with comments on and recommendations regarding each piece of legislation. Having said that, would you support H.R. 1522 and H.R. 2070 if they were amended as recommended by the Justice Department/the Biden administration?

Dr. PONSA-KRAUS. I do support the changes suggested to H.R. 1522, which are not to its basic merits, but there are some improvements there that I don't have objections to. As for H.R. 2070, I certainly don't agree that territorial status should be part of any self-determination process at all.

The CHAIRMAN. OK.

Dr. PONSA-KRAUS. If it specified the options, that would be an improvement, but I would still object to it because I believe that Puerto Ricans have had a full, free, and fair debate for 70 years and that a constitutional convention, while it sounds nice, in the context of Puerto Rico is a delay. It doesn't move the process forward because Puerto Ricans do know what the actions are. And what they need is a campaign for options that educates them as to the basic features, but they don't need a constitutional convention. Constitutional convention is for making constitutions, and Puerto Rico has one already.

The CHAIRMAN. OK. Let me just follow up real quickly because if I may, Doctor, one of the things that I think the Members in Congress and certainly in this Committee are attuned to is unintended consequences. And I ask that question because having gone through the agony of PROMESA, having gone through the agony of relief efforts, the duality and inequality in terms of the application of whether it is Social Security, taxes, etc., benefits to the citizens of Puerto Rico by the Federal Government, and now dealing with the status issue that has been constant. You are right, it has been constant for decades.

Let's say we are going into a transition around H.R. 1522. Does the issue of the Oversight Board established under PROMESA— does that occur before or after action on H.R. 1522? Does constitutional uniformity in terms of taxation and bankruptcy laws, as an example, that single out Puerto Rico, do they occur—and that requires legislative action as well—do they occur before or after action on H.R. 1522?

Dr. PONSA-KRAUS. They absolutely occur after. I think the word "agony" is exactly right. It is 123 years of agony, and it is decades of agonizing debate. It is one thing to ask the voters to offer them options that are constitutional and non-territorial and defined in their basic features for sure, for example, statehood, guaranteed citizenship—is independent. You offer them that. But then once the voters make that choice, then you work out the details of a transition. I mean, think about free association, for example.

You cannot put to the voters a negotiated treaty of free association before they have chosen it, right? So, there is no way for every last detail to be worked out beforehand. The voters know the basic options. They should be told what their basic features are. And then the transition should be worked out. So, I don't think action should be delayed.

The CHAIRMAN. Delayed being one way, the unintended consequences being the other way to describe it, but we will go with your word, "delay," at this point.

Congressman Gutiérrez, in this whole discussion in looking at H.R. 2070 and the legislation itself, fundamental to it is a process, an engagement process, a civic engagement process, a public participation process that, as you described it and as the legislation describe it, lays the issue of status open for everyone to be able to understand exactly what happens, what intended and unintended consequences might be to that and have input and recommendations relative to that.

Can you talk a little bit about that transparency issue that you mentioned at the beginning of your discussion.

Mr. GUTIÉRREZ. Sure. Thank you, Mr. Chairman. Here is the point. There hasn't been a free debate and discussion. In 1948, they passed the Ley de La Mordaza. And for 10 years, it was illegal. You would be put in jail for displaying this flag. There are consequences to that action, as FBI Director Freeh apologized and said that the FBI conducted criminal acts of repression against those that didn't favor a permanent relationship with the United States, the independence movements.

So, you have to put that in context. What I want to say is, Mr. Chairman, I actually lived it. I watched the commercials each and every day. I was part of that campaign. We have people coming here as witnesses who weren't there, didn't see what happened, were never there. What happened was we had dirty, filthy—how would I say it—dark money.

We don't know where it came from. So, to say it was fair, Mr. Chairman, is just not true. There were at least 20——

Miss GONZÁLEZ-COLÓN. Mr. Chairman, point of order.

The CHAIRMAN. Yes. Let me reclaim my time, Mr. Gutiérrez. Yes. I have been the subject of some full-page ads here in Arizona from the pro-statehood people that I have not been able to verify who is paying for it at this point. But anyway, that doesn't bother me.

Let me recognize now Ms. Tlaib. You are recognized for 5 minutes.

Ms. TLAIB. Thank you, Mr. Chair. I would like to now yield my 5 minutes to Congresswoman Velázquez.

Ms. VELÁZQUEZ. OK. Thank you, Ms. Tlaib. Thank you so much for yielding time to me. I just want to say that time and time again, people continue to allege unconstitutionality of H.R. 2070 with complete disregard to the fact that we have the pen.

The U.S. Congress, we have this pen. We write legislation. We pass the law. So, it is up to us, to Congress, without thoroughly, precisely vested by the Constitution, to decide what type of mechanism for decolonization we should pursue. So, having a transparent process and having options, that is exactly what we need to do in order to decolonize Puerto Rico.

And we, in consultation, the Congress, with a bilateral commission, that will be the responsibility to decide what are the options that will be included. What are the terms and conditions and an education element that is so important. As I said before, this is not any election. This is an election to define and decide once and for all the colonial status of Puerto Rico, to put an end to that—2021. Mr. Cox, I would like for you to review any comments or opinions that were made before that you feel you need to address.

Dr. COX ALOMAR. Yes. I want to go back to the issue of context, and to the issue of opening doors for alleged unconstitutional options. When we talk about context, in the specific issue of Puerto Rico's status, we need not say that the sole culprit for x or y status was a local political party.

We need to go back to what the United States represented to the United Nations. We need to go back to Mason Sears, to Henry Cabot Lodge, to the First Circuit of Appeals in Boston, which basically, under Chief Judge Magruder, even Justice Breyer, when he sat in the First Circuit, actually articulated a doctrine whereby Puerto Rico was described as having acceded to a special relationship under American federalism, a mutual consent agreement covenant with the U.S. Congress.

So, it is not as if a local political party all of a sudden concocted a surreal political status. The context is very broad and obviously encompasses representations made by the Truman administration, the Eisenhower administration, the Kennedy administration, the Johnson administration, and a whole series of other administrations. As much as it is a Puerto Rican problem, this is an American problem, and it was authored by a series of administrations going back to the McKinley administration.

Ms. VELÁZQUEZ. Thank you, Mr. Cox.

Mr. Cueto, I would like to address my next question to you. How Federal taxation under statehood or an incorporated territory will affect the island's economy? How would Puerto Rico afford paying for essential services and the debt if it also must pay Federal income, excise, gas, and telecom taxes they don't pay now? Would the creation be seriously disrupted under statehood as the 2014 GAO report on the effects of statehood suggested?

Dr. CARABALLO-CUETO. Well, the worst-case scenario will be an incorporated territory because we will have taxation, but we will not have the parity in Federal programs. So, it is going to cost more to Puerto Rico. Plus we are going to lose the tax advantages that we have right now to attract investment from abroad. And under statehood, especially the middle class and the upper class will have to pay more taxes. But the low-income class will receive more benefits in the case of parity for Federal programs. So, there is a trade-off in terms of taxation in the case of statehood. But in the case of incorporated territory, that will be the worst of all scenarios.

Ms. VELÁZQUEZ. Thank you.

Mr. Chairman, I yield back.

The CHAIRMAN. Let me recognize the gentlelady from New York, Ms. Ocasio-Cortez. You are recognized for 5 minutes.

Ms. OCASIO-CORTEZ. Thank you so much, Chairman Grijalva. Thank you for taking the time to have this meeting and this hearing today, and thank you to all of our witnesses who have come to share their expertise.

I am a proud co-lead along with Representative Nydia Velázquez on H.R. 2070, which is the Puerto Rico Self-Determination Act, and as was noted by one of our witnesses, self-determination is a human right. I believe that this legislation is the best answer to the centuries-old question of Puerto Rico's status and colonial history. I am pleased that in the Department of Justice's analysis of our bill, they conclude that Puerto Rico as an island does, in fact, have a right to a fair and democratic self-determination process and that one-sided initiatives fail to grant Puerto Ricans this outcome.

However, I want to be clear that a true decolonization process exempts the current territorial status. With that said, I just want to clear up some mythologies around this bill. To Dr. Cox Alomar, very quickly as a yes or no, have former statehood plebiscites and referendums in Puerto Rico been plagued historically by electoral irregularities, inaccuracies and/or been unilaterally influenced by one party?

Dr. COX ALOMAR. The answer is yes.

Ms. OCASIO-CORTEZ. Would a constitutional assembly be the most inclusive, democratic, and just process given that history of irregularity and bias? Would a constitutional assembly be the most just process for the decolonization of Puerto Rico in your view?

Dr. COX ALOMAR. Definitely yes, and I actually invite you to take a look at the White House Task Force Report of 2011, which basically suggests that the convention is the most encompassing process.

Ms. OCASIO-CORTEZ. Thank you. Now, additionally, in our self-determination bill, does the bill oppose statehood?

Dr. COX ALOMAR. No.

Ms. OCASIO-CORTEZ. No. Our bill does not oppose statehood whatsoever. And does this bill, on the other side, too—does it impose independence necessarily on the island?

Dr. COX ALOMAR. The answer is no.

Ms. OCASIO-CORTEZ. No. It is status agnostic, and it is focused on the process. Now, let's contrast that with the statehood bill. The Puerto Rico Statehood Admission Act, if passed, would it admit Puerto Rico immediately to the United States as its supporters claim?

Dr. COX ALOMAR. The answer is no. And the DOJ says there is no fait accompli. This is no done deal. I mean, it is pretty clear——

Ms. OCASIO-CORTEZ. This bill, if passed, will not immediately admit Puerto Rico as a state. Now, would this—in your expert opinion, can voters legitimately exercise their right to self-determination without knowing fully the options that they are voting for?

Dr. COX ALOMAR. The answer is no. Take a look at Brexit.

Ms. OCASIO-CORTEZ. Thank you very much. I think that is a wonderful example of the situation that voters are in where they had a status vote, were not fully informed, and many of them regret what is happening. On that note, do you believe that Puerto Ricans on the island have ever had the benefit of being fully informed that voting for statehood also means potentially ensuring the survival of La Junta de Control Fiscal?

Dr. COX ALOMAR. No. There is no proper process of actually informing folks what is going on. No.

Ms. OCASIO-CORTEZ. So, you would say that Puerto Ricans don't know that La Junta could stay and be preserved if the statehood bill passes?

Dr. COX ALOMAR. The answer is no.

Ms. OCASIO-CORTEZ. Lastly, in the cases of Alaska and Hawaii, when they were admitted to the United States, they had a mandate that information about the legal effects of statehood and the transition be provided to those voters. Alaska and Hawaii had full information.

Does H.R. 1522, the statehood bill, have any mandate at all that information about the legal effects of statehood be granted to voters the way that they were in Alaska and Hawaii?

Dr. COX ALOMAR. The answer is no.

Ms. OCASIO-CORTEZ. So, they are being treated differently even compared to other recent communities that were most recently admitted as states into the country. Puerto Ricans deserve to have the full facts and information about what not only the statehood bill contains but also what that transition would mean because we cannot make these decisions with a lack of information and find out afterwards that there are tax implications, financial implications, and status implications that may negatively affect their lives. So, our bill, H.R. 2070, contains, guarantees, and mandates a full information campaign so that Puerto Ricans will know what they are voting for. It doesn't say no to statehood. It doesn't mandate independence. What it mandates is a fully informed and just process that Puerto Ricans deserve. With that, I thank you very much. Thank you, Dr. Cox Alomar, for your expertise, and I yield back to the Chair.

The CHAIRMAN. Thank you very much. The gentlelady yields. Madam Ranking Member, are there any Members on your side that we did not get to?

Miss GONZÁLEZ-COLÓN. They are still on the Floor.

The CHAIRMAN. OK. As we said, we are wrapping up this hearing. I want to thank all of you for the sacrifice of time and the changes you had to go through to be here, the witnesses in particular. To all of you, thank you very much. It was a very good one.

The process of decolonization of Puerto Rico and the path to self-determination is the goal. And the issue for me is full disclosure and transparency. The issue for me is the public's right to know. The issue for me is that there be a level of a public understanding and embrace on the part of the Puerto Rican people on the island as to their path toward that self-determination. And statehood is one of the options, as my colleague, Ms. Ocasio-Cortez, said very clearly. But also the process for me is to assure that those other important prerogatives that any voter, and certainly the people of Puerto Rico that have been left behind in Federal policy and Federal attention for too long, needs to have. We are going to continue to go forward.

I will work with the Ranking Member to continue a meeting. The process goes forward. These two pieces of legislation continue to be very much the focal point of what this Committee will have to deal with. And the other point I want to make is that I am going to follow up with the Department of Justice in terms of the prerogatives and the powers of Congress and our legislative responsibility in terms of what we can and cannot do. There could have been some really clear denunciations about you can't go any further than this because of constitutional limits and prohibitions.

I would like to get that opinion. I would like to get that pretty clearly as to what the prerogatives are so that that argument either continues, is validated, or is off the table. Thank you very much, Representative González-Colón. Thank you so much for your cooperation and for helping put this meeting together.

With that, the meeting is adjourned, and thank you so much.

[Whereupon, at 4:58 p.m., the Committee was adjourned.]

[ADDITIONAL MATERIALS SUBMITTED FOR THE RECORD]

Statement for the Record Department of Justice, H.R. 1522, The Puerto Rico Statehood Admission Act

Executive Summary

The Department of Justice supports providing the people of Puerto Rico the opportunity to vote on whether to become a state of the Union, as H.R. 1522 would do. The Department's concerns with the bill relate only to the manner of execution. The Department's primary concerns are (1) providing for an orderly transition of the Financial Managements and Oversight Board for Puerto Rico that was established by the Puerto Rico Oversight, Management, and Economic Stability Act ("PROMESA"), Pub. L. No. 114–187, 130 Stat. 549 (2016); and (2) addressing legal complications that would ensue from application of certain constitutional uniformity doctrines upon Puerto Rico's transition to a state. The Department stands ready to assist further in refining the legislation to address these and other concerns described in more detail below.

Section-by-Section Analysis

Section 1 (Short Title)

The stated purpose of H.R. 1522 is allow the Puerto Rican people to choose whether to become a state or remain a territory. The bill itself would not admit Puerto Rico as a state; rather, it would direct the President to issue a proclamation setting a date on which Puerto Rico will become a state if a majority of Puerto Rican voters chooses statehood in a territory-wide referendum. The Department would thus recommend that the title of the bill be the "Puerto Rico Statehood Determination Act," or simply the "Puerto Rico Statehood Act," so as not imply that admission of Puerto Rico as a state is a fait accompli.

Section 2 (Findings)

Subsection (4)

It is unclear what section 2(4) means in saying that Puerto Rico, unlike Alaska and Hawaii, has not achieved statehood "due to anomalies emanating from the 1901 *Downes* ruling and its progeny." Although *Downes v. Bidwell*, 182 U.S. 244 (1901), held that Puerto Rico was an unincorporated territory—and therefore not "surely destined for statehood," *Boumedienne v. Bush*, 553 U.S. 753, 757 (2008)—it did not hold that Puerto Rico's current status as an unincorporated territory is immutable.

Subsection (13)

As all of the current inhabited territories of the United States (the U.S. Virgin Islands, American Samoa, Guam, and the Northern Mariana Islands, in addition to Puerto Rico) are also considered unincorporated, we recommend changing "unlike territories that are parts of the United States" to "unlike incorporated territories in the past."

Subsections (15)–(19)

We note that the validity of the plebiscites identified in these findings is disputed. The Department of Justice has previously stated that the ballot propositions in the 2012 and 2017 plebiscites contained inaccuracies and were potentially misleading and that the premise of the 2020 plebiscite—that the people of Puerto Rico had conclusively rejected the current territorial status in 2012 and 2017—was one with which the Department disagreed. *See, e.g.*, Letter for Juan Ernesto Davila Rivera, Chairman, Puerto Rico State Elections Commission, from Jeffrey A. Rosen, Deputy Attorney General, *Re: Request of*

Federal Funds for Puerto Rico Plebiscite at 3 (July 29, 2020). Although the Department advised that all available status options were required to be included in the ballot for the 2017 plebiscite, we were not provided adequate time to review and approve the finalized ballot in time for the vote.[77]

Section 3 (Admission)

Section 3 provides:

> Subject to the provisions of this Act, and upon issuance of the proclamation required by section 7(c), the Commonwealth of Puerto Rico is hereby declared to be a State of the United States of America, and as such shall be declared admitted into the Union on an equal footing with the other States in all respects.

The language of section 3 is in some tension with the language of section 7(c). According to section 3, Puerto Rico would become a state upon "issuance of the proclamation required by section 7(c)." Section 7(c), however, directs the President to issue a proclamation that declares the date (no more than 12 months after the Governor's certification) on which Puerto Rico would become a state, in order to "facilitate a transition process." Under section 7(c), therefore, Puerto Rico becomes a state upon the date specified in the proclamation, not upon the issuance of the proclamation. Section 10, providing for termination of all federal and territorial laws incompatible with a status of statehood for Puerto Rico under the Constitution, similarly is tied to "the date of statehood admission proclaimed by the President under section 7(c)." We presume that one of the purposes of this transition process is to give Congress time to adjust federal law to be consistent with Puerto Rico's new status as a state (by, for instance, repealing tax and bankruptcy laws unique to Puerto Rico that might implicate the uniformity requirements of the Constitution, discussed further below). Declaring that Puerto Rico will become a state "upon issuance of the proclamation required by section 7(c)" will not afford time for these adjustments.

The Department therefore recommends that section 3 be revised as follows:

> Subject to the provisions of this Act, and upon **the date declared by the President for admission of Puerto Rico as a State in** ~~issuance of~~ the proclamation required by section 7(c), the Commonwealth of Puerto Rico is hereby declared to be a State of the United States of America, and as such shall be ~~declared~~ admitted into the Union on an equal footing with the other States in all respects.

---

[77] The Department has assumed a role in approving the ballots and voter education materials for the recent plebiscites upon Puerto Rico's requests for disbursement of funding for a plebiscite under the Consolidated Appropriations Act of 2014, Pub. L. No. 113–76, 128 Stat. 5, 61 (2014).

Section 4 (Physical Territory)

The Department has no concerns with this section.

Section 5 (Constitution)

Section 5 provides:

> The constitution of the State of Puerto Rico shall always be republican in form and shall not be repugnant to the Constitution of the United States and the principles of the Declaration of Independence. The constitution of the Commonwealth of Puerto Rico, as approved by Public Law 82–447 and subsequently amended, is hereby found to be republican in form and in conformity with the Constitution of the United States and the principles of the Declaration of Independence, and is hereby accepted, ratified, and confirmed as the constitution of said State.

This provision seems to leave open the possibility of further amendments to the Constitution of Puerto Rico that would not have been known to Congress or the President at the time this bill is enacted into law. The Department recommends that section 5 be revised as follows:

> The constitution of the State of Puerto Rico shall always be republican in form and shall not be repugnant to the Constitution of the United States and the principles of the Declaration of Independence. The constitution of the Commonwealth of Puerto Rico, as approved by Public Law 82–447 and subsequently amended *as of the date of enactment of this statute,* is hereby found to be republican in form and in conformity with the Constitution of the United States and the principles of the Declaration of Independence, and is hereby accepted, ratified, and confirmed as the constitution of said State.

Section 6 (Certification by President)

Section 6 provides:

> Upon enactment of this Act, the President of the United States shall certify such fact to the Governor of Puerto Rico. Thereupon the Governor shall, within 30 days after receipt of the official notification of such approval, issue a proclamation for the election of Senators and Representatives in Congress.

This language could be read to imply that Puerto Rico will be entitled to Senators and Representatives in Congress as soon as the bill is enacted, instead of on the date set by the President in section 7(c) for Puerto Rico's admission as a state. To avoid that implication, the Department recommends that section 6 be revised as follows:

> Upon enactment of this Act, the President of the United States shall certify such fact to the Governor of Puerto Rico. Thereupon the Governor shall, within 30 days after

receipt of the official notification of such approval, issue a proclamation for the election of Senators and Representatives *to serve* in Congress *upon admission of Puerto Rico as a State.*

Section 7 (Ratification Vote)

Subsection (a) (Ratification of Proposition)

Subsection (a) prescribes the method by which the Puerto Rican people may vote to approve making Puerto Rico into a state. It requires a ballot with the following question:

> Shall Puerto Rico immediately be admitted into the Union as a State, in accordance with terms prescribed in the Act of Congress approved [date of approval of this Act]?
> Yes No .

Because this language incorporates by reference the terms of this bill, including the territorial bounds of the new state (section 4) and other legal effects (sections 9 and 10), the Department believes it is constitutionally adequate to provide the voters of Puerto Rico with clear notice of what they would be approving. There is some tension, however, between voting that Puerto Rico be "immediately" admitted as a state and voting that Puerto Rico be admitted "in accordance with terms prescribed in the Act of Congress," since that Act provides for the President to declare a later date on which Puerto Rico would be admitted. We recommend deleting the word "immediately."

It should also be noted that the prescribed ballots for Alaska and Hawaii statehood included some additional detail about the legal effects of statehood that might have prompted voters to inspect the acts of Congress more closely. *See* Hawaii Statehood Act, Pub. L. No. 86–3, § 7(b), 73 Stat. 4, 7 (1959) ("(2) The boundaries of the State of Hawaii shall be as prescribed in the Act of Congress approved [on date of enactment], and all claims of this State to any areas of land or sea outside the boundaries so prescribed are hereby irrevocably relinquished to the United States. (3) All provisions of the Act of Congress approved [on date of enactment] reserving rights orto the United States, as well as those prescribing the terms or conditions of the grants of lands or other property therein made to the State of Hawaii[,] are consented to fully by said State and its people."); Alaska Statehood Act, Pub. L. No. 85–508, § 8(b), 72 Stat. 339, 343 (1958) ("(2) The boundaries of the State of Alaska shall be as prescribed in the Act of Congress approved [on date of enactment] and all claims of this State to any areas of land or sea outside the boundaries so prescribed are hereby irrevocably relinquished to the United States. (3) All provisions of the Act of Congress approved [on date of enactment] reserving rights orto the United States, as well as those prescribing the terms or conditions of the grants of lands or other property therein made to the State of Alaska, are consented to fully by said State and its people."). Congress might consider instructing

Puerto Rico to include similar informative language on the ballot, which might include language making clear the effect of statehood on any Federal laws found to be at odds with constitutional uniformity requirements, discussed further below.

Subsection (b) (Certified Results)

Subsection (b) prescribes a process by which the Governor of Puerto Rico would certify to the President and to Congress the results of the voter referendum in subsection (a). The Department does not recommend changes to this provision.

Subsection (c) (Presidential Proclamation)

Subsection (c) would direct the President, upon receiving the Governor's certification in subsection (b), to issue a proclamation "declaring . . . the date Puerto Rico is admitted as a State of the Union on an equal footing with all other States." In this proclamation, the President would certify that the people of Puerto Rico have voted in favor of statehood (based on a certification by the Governor of Puerto Rico to that fact) and would designate a date on which Puerto Rico would become a state. The President could declare that Puerto Rico is to be admitted as a state as much as 12 months after the certification of results by the Governor, "in order to facilitate a transition process." Confusingly, however, the final sentence of subsection (c) provides: "Upon issuance of the proclamation by the President, Puerto Rico shall be deemed admitted into the Union as a State." This contradiction is similar to the one noted above in section 3. Assuming that Congress intends for the transition process to be effective, the Department recommends deleting the final sentence in section 7(c).

Section 8 (Election of Officers)

Section 8 provides that, upon issuing the proclamation required by section 6, the Governor of Puerto Rico shall institute a process for the voters of Puerto Rico to elect Senators and Representatives. "Puerto Rico shall be entitled to the same number of Representatives as the State whose most recent Census population was closest to, but less than, that of Puerto Rico," H.R. 1522, § 8(2), and that number of Representatives would be added temporarily to the current total of 435 Representatives in the House, until the next apportionment, at which time the number of Representatives in the House would revert to 435. "Thereafter, the State of Puerto Rico shall be entitled to such number of Representatives as provided for by applicable law based on the next reapportionment." *Id.*

According to the Census Bureau's recently issued population counts and apportionments based on the 2020 Census, Puerto Rico's population in 2020 was 3,285,874. Utah was the State with the closest population that was less than Puerto Rico's, with a population of 3,275,252 and four Representatives. As a result, under section 8 Puerto Rico would be temporarily entitled to four Representatives and the

House would increase temporarily to 439 members. This arrangement would last until the next apportionment following the next decennial census, likely in 2031.

The temporary designation of Representatives for Puerto Rico based on its population count in the most recent census would comply with the constitutional requirements for apportionment of Representatives. Other than stating that "Representatives shall be apportioned among the several States *according to their respective numbers*, counting the whole number of persons in each State excluding Indians not taxed," U.S. Const. amend. XIV, § 2 (Apportionment Clause) (emphasis added), the Constitution does not prescribe a precise formula by which population is to be used in determining how many Representatives each state will receive. Exact apportionment "according to [the states'] respective numbers" is not possible, since it would yield a non-whole number of Representatives for each state, and the Apportionment Clause necessarily accords Congress some flexibility in devising a formula to distribute Representatives among the states. Congress has used a variety of methods over time to determine the number of Representatives for each state, settling on the current method of equal proportions in 1941. *See* Royce Crocker, Cong. Research Serv., *The U.S. House of Representatives Apportionment Formula in Theory and Practice*, No. R41357, at 1–2 (Aug. 4, 2013); Pub. L. No. 77–291, § 1, 55 Stat. 761, 762 (1941), *codified as amended at* 2 U.S.C. § 2a. Although the apportionment of Representatives to Puerto Rico equivalent to the number apportioned to the state with the closest, but lower, population than Puerto Rico deviates slightly from simple application of the equal proportions approach, it appears well within the range of discretion accorded to Congress by the Apportionment Clause and is consistent with historical practice when a territory is newly admitted as a state. For example, Hawaii received one Representative following its admission to statehood, and its apportionment then rose to two Representatives under the equal proportions approach after the 1960 census. *See* Cong. Research Serv., *Puerto Rican Statehood: Effects on House Apportionment*, No. R41113, at 2, 5 (Mar. 16, 2011); Hawaii Statehood Act, Pub. L. No. 86–3, § 8, 73 Stat. 4, 8 (1959).

In addition, temporarily increasing the number of Representatives to 439 would come nowhere close to contravening the constitutional requirement that "[t]he number of Representatives shall not exceed one for every Thirty Thousand." U.S. Const. art. I, § 2, cl. 3. Here, too, this approach accords with historical practice. With the admission of Alaska and Hawaii, each of which received one Representative, the House of Representatives increased temporarily from 435 to 437 members until the next apportionment following the 1960 census. At that time, the House reverted to 435 members and the newly admitted states received Representatives along with the other 48 states in accordance with the method of equal proportions.

Section 9 (Continuity of Laws, Government, and Obligations)

Subsection (1) (Continuity of Laws)

Subsection (1) would provide that laws both of the United States and of Puerto Rico shall remain in effect following Puerto Rico's admission as a state, if they are "not in conflict with this Act." Section 10, discussed next, would provide for the repeal of any law "incompatible with the political and legal status of statehood under the Constitution." To make these provisions parallel, the Department recommends that subsection (1) be modified to provide that the laws of the United States and of Puerto Rico shall remain in effect if they are "not in conflict with this Act *or with the Constitution*."

The Department additionally recommends that Congress consider providing a more tailored solution for continuity in the operations of the Financial Managements and Oversight Board for Puerto Rico ("Oversight Board"). The Oversight Board was established by the Puerto Rico Oversight, Management, and Economic Stability Act ("PROMESA"), Pub. L. No. 114–187, § 101, 130 Stat. 549, 553 (2016), *codified at* 48 U.S.C. § 2121, to approve plans for restructuring Puerto Rico's debt as well as Puerto Rico's budget and fiscal plans, *id.* §§ 201–212, *codified at* 48 U.S.C. §§ 2141–2152. PROMESA created the Oversight Board "as an entity within the territorial government for which it is established," pursuant to Congress's authority under the Territory Clause, Article IV, Section 3. Pub. L. No. 114–187, § 101(b), (c). The Supreme Court recently held that the members of the Oversight Board were local or territorial officers because they have "primarily local duties." *Fin. Oversight & Management Bd. for P.R. v. Aurelius Inv., LLC*, 140 S. Ct. 1649, 1663 (2020).

Subsection (2) (Continuity of Government)

Subsection (2) would provide that "individuals holding legislative, executive, and judicial offices of Puerto Rico shall continue to discharge the duties of their respective offices when Puerto Rico becomes a State." As the Oversight Board is statutorily denominated part of the territorial government, and the Board members are territorial officers, the Oversight Board would appear to become part of the new state government if Puerto Rico becomes a state. This would accord with historical practice, although the statehood admission acts for Alaska and Hawaii more clearly provided that, upon admission as a state, "officers not required to be elected . . . shall be selected or continued in office as provided by the constitution and laws of said State" and would "exercise all the functions pertaining to their offices" in, under, or by the authority of the government of said State. Alaska Statehood Act, Pub. L. No. 85–508, § 8(c), 72 Stat. 339, 344 (1958); Hawaii Statehood Act, Pub. L. No. 86–3, § 7(c), 73 Stat. 4, 8 (1959).

One complication, however, is that PROMESA provides that the seven members of the Oversight Board will be appointed by the President and sets out an elaborate structure whereby the President can select from congressionally provided lists, thereby avoiding the need for Senate confirmation, or can appoint "off-list" in which case Senate advice and consent is required. 48 U.S.C. § 2121(e)(2). It is unclear whether or how this appointment structure would transfer over to the state level upon Puerto Rico's becoming a state. Questions about the Oversight Board's composition might undercut its capacity to operate.

The Department thus recommends that Congress expressly provide in H.R. 1522, or in separate legislation enacted during the transition period effected by the President's proclamation of a date for admission of Puerto Rico, for an orderly transition of the Oversight Board into an entity of the new State of Puerto Rico. Alternatively, of course, Congress may decide that the Oversight Board should terminate operations if Puerto Rico becomes a state, in which case the Department would also recommend express legislation to that effect.

Section 10 (Repeals)

Section 10 provides that "[a]ll Federal . . . laws, rules, and regulations, or parts of Federal . . . laws, rules, and regulations, applicable to Puerto Rico that are incompatible with the political and legal status of statehood under the Constitution and the provisions of this Act are repealed and terminated as of the date of statehood admission proclaimed by the President under section 7(c) of this Act." This abrupt transition oversimplifies what it will take to admit Puerto Rico on an equal footing with other states. Some additional legislation will likely be required to address instances where federal law regarding Puerto Rico is not compatible "with the political and legal status of statehood."

Under current federal tax and bankruptcy law, for example, Puerto Rico is treated differently than states. *See, e.g.*, 26 U.S.C. § 933 (providing tax credit to "a bona fide resident of Puerto Rico" for "income derived from sources within Puerto Rico"); *id.* § 7653(b) ("Articles, goods, wares, or merchandise going into Puerto Rico, the Virgin Islands, Guam, and American Samoa from the United States shall be exempted from the payment of any tax imposed by the internal revenue laws of the United States."); PROMESA, Pub. L. No. 114–187, 130 Stat. 549 (2016), *codified at* 48 U.S.C. ch. 20 (providing special process for restructuring the debt of Puerto Rico). The Constitution meanwhile requires that all "Duties, Imposts, and Excises shall be uniform throughout the United States," U.S. Const. art. I, § 8, cl. 1, and authorizes Congress to make "uniform Laws on the subject of Bankruptcies throughout the United States," *id.* cl. 4; *see also id.* § 9, cl. 6 ("No Preference shall be given by any Regulation of Commerce or Revenue to the Ports of one State over those of another; nor shall Vessels bound to, or from, one State be obliged to enter, clear, or pay Duties to another."). These uniformity requirements have not applied to Puerto Rico given its status as an unincorporated territory, *Downes v. Bidwell*, 182 U.S. 244, 282–84, 287 (1901); *id.* at 291, 339–40 (White, J., concurring, joined by Shiras and McKenna, JJ.), but would become applicable upon Puerto Rico's becoming a state.

Presumably, one reason why the Act allows up to a year between a vote by Puerto Rico in favor of statehood and Puerto Rico's admission as a state is to provide a window within which Congress can address this conflict between current law and uniformity requirements, as well as any other issues implicated by Puerto Rico's transition to statehood. It is possible, however, that Puerto Rico would become an incorporated territory, and thus fully subject to the Constitution and the uniformity requirements of Article I, even before the date the President designates for Puerto Rico to be admitted as a state. Although the case law on when a territory is deemed to be incorporated is not "altogether harmonious," *Downes*, 182 U.S. at 258, one formulation the Supreme Court has frequently used is that an incorporated territory is one that is "surely destined for statehood." *Boumediene*, 553 U.S. at 757; *see also United States v. Verdugo-Urquidez*, 494 U.S. 259, 268 (1990) (an "unincorporated territory" is one "not clearly destined for statehood"). Under H.R. 1522, Puerto Rico would appear to be "surely destined for statehood" when the President of the State Elections Commission for Puerto Rico certifies under section 7(b) that a majority of Puerto Rican voters have cast ballots in favor of statehood. At that point, section 7(c) requires the President to proclaim the date on which Puerto Rico would succeed to statehood.

Attorney General Thornburgh took a similar view in 1991, regarding a bill that would have authorized a referendum on the legal status of Puerto Rico accompanied by a non-binding "commitment by Congress to implement the status receiving a majority." S. 244, § 101(e)(2). The bill contemplated that the implementing legislation would include a five-year transition period to phase out the special tax treatments for Puerto Rico that would have come into conflict with the Uniformity Clause. Attorney General Thornburgh testified that Puerto Rico "would become subject to the requirements of the [U]niformity [C]lause as soon as Congress passe[d] implementing legislation to make Puerto Rico a State," because at that point in time it would have to be considered "destined for statehood." *Political Status of Puerto Rico: Hearings on S. 244 Before the S. Comm. on Energy and Natural Resources*, 102d Cong. at 189–90 (Feb. 7, 1991) ("1991 Hearings").

We nevertheless believe that Congress should be able to enact legislation providing for a delayed or gradual application of the Constitution's uniformity requirements, including the potential delay of up to a year before these requirements apply envisioned by the combination of sections 7(c) and 10. Some case law suggests that incorporation rests on the intent of Congress as expressed in statutes (or on the intent of the President and Senate, as expressed in treaties), and not just on an independent judicial assessment of the likelihood that a particular territory will eventually become a state. *See Balzac v. People of Porto Rico*, 258 U.S. 298, 309 (1922) ("[I]n the absence of other and countervailing evidence, a law of Congress or a provision in a treaty acquiring territory, declaring an intention to confer political and civil rights on the inhabitants of the new lands as American citizens, may be properly interpreted to mean an incorporation of it into the Union[.]"); *see also Rassmussen v. United States*, 197 U.S. 516, 523 (1905)

("That Congress, shortly following the adoption of the treaty with Russia, clearly contemplated the incorportion of Alaska into the United States as a part thereof, we think plainly results from the act[s] . . . concerning internal revenue taxation, . . . extending the laws of the United States relating to customs, commerce and navigation over Alaska and establishing a collection district therein.") In *Balzac*, the Court reasoned that, "[h]ad Congress intended to take the important step of changing the treaty status of Porto Rico by incorporating it into the Union, it is reasonable to suppose that it would have done so by the plain declaration, and would not have left it to mere inference." 258 U.S. at 306; *see also id.* ("[I]ncorporation is not to be assumed without express declaration, or an implication so strong as to exclude any other view."). The Supreme Court has also highlighted the role of "practical considerations" in determining which constitutional provisions apply to a given territory, noting "a common thread" in the relevant case law: "the idea that questions of extraterritoriality turn on objective factors and practical concerns, not formalism." *Boumediene*, 553 U.S. at 757–64.

H.R. 1522 does not contain an express declaration of intent to make Puerto Rico an "incorporated" territory immediately upon certification of a pro-statehood vote. To the contrary, H.R. 1522 seems designed to postpone incorporation until the effective date in the President's declaration, at which time Puerto Rico would skip past the intermediate step of being considered an incorporated territory and be admitted directly into the Union as a state. Moreover, the immediate disruption that would result were Puerto Rico to quickly become subject to the Constitution's uniformity provisions should count strongly against such a result. To reduce the possibility of immediate incorporation even further, however, the Department recommends that Congress state expressly that Puerto Rico shall remain unincorporated until its admission as a state under section 3.

Even if the uniformity requirements of Article I were to become immediately applicable upon certification of a pro-statehood vote, we think that legislation providing for a gradual transition to tax and bankruptcy uniformity for Puerto Rico would be constitutional. In *United States v. Ptasynski*, 462 U.S. 74 (1983), the Court upheld a tax exemption for crude oil produced in a geographically defined area that encompassed Alaska and "certain offshore territorial waters" that were "beyond the limits of any State" against a uniformity challenge. *Id.* at 78. Previously, the Court had made clear that the Uniformity Clause "does not require Congress to devise a tax that falls equally or proportionately on each State" and thus had confirmed Congress's authority to draw "distinctions between similar classes" in "defining the subject of a tax," as long as the tax applied evenly "wherever the classification is found." *Id.* at 82. The Court appeared to regard the geographic classification in *Ptasynski* as a logical extension of this principle, in view of credible evidence amassed by Congress of "climatic and geographic conditions" unique to the covered geographic region. *Id.* at 78; *see id.* at 78–79 & nn. 6–7 (discussing evidence).

Although the tax exemptions for Puerto Rico in 26 U.S.C. §§ 933 and 7653 are arguably distinct in being expressly "drawn on state political lines," *id.* at 78, the reasoning of *Ptasynski* suggests that a geographic classification based on state boundaries does not violate the Uniformity Clause if Congress can demonstrate that the classification arises from genuine differences in economic circumstance that fall incidentally along state lines. In the case of Puerto Rico, the objective of maintaining the tax preferences for a short transition period would be to ameliorate the economic dislocation that would result from a sudden loss of pre-existing tax preferences accompanying the switch from commonwealth status to statehood. Attorney General Thornburgh testified to similar effect in 1991, stating that "the uniformity clause permits tax transition provisions, provided they are narrowly tailored, to prevent specific and identified problems of economic dislocation that Congress concludes would otherwise result from the transition from a non-incorporated territorial status to either an incorporated territorial or State status." 1991 Hearings at 190; *see also Puerto Rico's Political Status: Hearings on S. 712 Before the S. Comm. on Finance*, 101st Cong. at 7 (1989) ("1989 Hearings") (testimony of Shirley D. Peterson, Assistant Attorney General for the Tax Division of the Department, that the Uniformity Clause did not "disable Congress from fashioning reasonable and necessary transitional measures").

To the best of our knowledge, no court has addressed the extent to which Congress may provide for transitional disuniformity in the tax treatment of an incoming state, so any attempt to suggest an outer limit on how long the transition period could last would be speculative at best. In 1989, the Department testified that a three-year transition period to phase out special tax treatment was permissible, *see* 1989 Hearings at 7 (testimony of Peterson); in 1991, the Department intimated that five years might be too much, *see* 1991 Hearings at 189 (testimony of Thornburgh). Notably, at least one statute, retained from the period before Alaska and Hawaii were admitted as states, continues to single out portions of the routes to and from those states for a reduced tax on air transportation. *See* 26 U.S.C. § 4262(b)(2), (c)(1); 26 C.F.R. § 49.4262–2(b). It does not appear that this differential treatment has been challenged constitutionally, and this treatment may be justified by a uniform principle of reducing the incidence of the tax on routes of longer distances. By similar logic, Congress might be able to cite economic circumstances unique to Puerto Rico—perhaps, for example, patterns of investment undertaken in reliance on Puerto Rico's disuniform tax treatment—as a basis for a continuation or longer phase-out of tax statutes that treat Puerto Rico differently.

We believe a transition period should also be permissible for the special bankruptcy provisions for Puerto Rico in PROMESA. In *Railway Labor Executives Ass'n Gibbons*, 455 U.S. 457 (1982) ("Rock Island"), the Court struck down on uniformity grounds a federal law designed solely for the bankruptcy of the Rock Island Railroad, reasoning that "[t]o survive scrutiny under the Bankruptcy Clause, a law must at least apply uniformly to a defined class of debtors," and "a bankruptcy law . . . confined as it is to the affairs of one named debtor can hardly be considered uniform." *Id.* at 473. Yet the Court also stated, similar to *Ptasyski*, that the uniformity requirement "'does not deny Congress power to take into account differences that exist between different parts of the country, and to fashion legislation to resolve geographically isolated problems.' "*Id.* at 469 (quoting *Regional Railroad Reorganization Act Cases*, 419 U.S. 102, 159 (1974)). Arguably, legislation limited to Puerto Rico should be viewed not as legislation directed at Puerto Rico as a specific debtor, but at Puerto Rico as a specific region for which it is necessary to resolve "geographically isolated problems." In advising on the constitutionality of PROMESA before it was enacted, we had considerable doubts that this argument would prevail. But we believe that such an argument would be more likely to succeed as a justification for disuniformity during a transition period, given that Puerto Rico's change in status to a state is a factor distinct from its status as a debtor.

More broadly, we think a good argument can be made that PROMESA would not violate the uniformity requirements of the Bankruptcy Clause at all were Puerto Rico to become a state. PROMESA was enacted under the Territories Clause and its bankruptcy provisions would attach to any relevant debt *before* Puerto Rico becomes a state and uniformity requirements applied. Congress could also determine that it is "necessary and proper for carrying into Execution" its Article IV to fashion a broader solution for territories entering the Union, thereby avoiding the pitfall of "a bankruptcy law . . . confined as it is to the affairs of one named debtor." Rock Island, 455 U.S. at 473. "As stated by the Supreme Court in the *Railroad Rail Reorganization Cases*," the Bankruptcy Clause "'was not intended to hobble Congress by forcing it into nationwide enactments to deal with conditions calling for a remedy only in certain regions.' "1989 Hearings at 8 (quoting 419 U.S. at 159) (testimony of Peterson).

In short, regardless of whether Puerto Rico becomes subject to the uniformity requirements in Article I at the time a pro-statehood vote is certified or on the date set by the President for admission to statehood, we think there will be opportunity for Congress to enact further legislation providing for a phase-out of those tax and bankruptcy laws that single out Puerto Rico for special treatment. We recommend, however, that Congress include findings in any such bill, ideally supported by expert testimony in public hearings, explaining why a phase-out period is necessary to avoid specific economic problems unique to Puerto Rico.

Section 11 (Severability)

The Department has no concerns with this section.

STATEMENT FOR THE RECORD, DEPARTMENT OF JUSTICE, H.R. 2070, THE PUERTO RICO SELF-DETERMINATION ACT OF 2021

Executive Summary

The Department of Justice agrees that the people of Puerto Rico should be allowed to choose whether to become a nation independent of the United States, become a state within the United States, or retain the current status of a territory. Insofar as H.R. 2070 would facilitate a choice among those three options, which we believe are the three constitutional options available to Puerto Rico, the Department supports the bill. In the section-by-section analysis, the Department explains the basis for its view more fully and advises of its comments on certain sections of the bill.

Section-by-Section Analysis

Section 1 (Short Title)

The Department has no comment on this section.

Section 2 (Findings)

The Department has no comment on this section.

Section 3 (Puerto Rico Status Convention)

Section 3(a) provides that the Puerto Rico legislature will have "inherent authority" to call a status convention "for the purpose of proposing to the people of Puerto Rico self-determination options." The convention, consisting of delegates elected by Puerto Rico voters, would be tasked with "debat[ing] and draft[ing] definitions on self-determination options for Puerto Rico, which shall be outside the Territorial Clause of the United States Constitution," and presenting those options, along with at least one transition plan for each option, to Puerto Rico voters in a referendum. H.R. 2070, § 3(c). Once assembled, the convention would be "dissolved only when the United States ratifies the self-determination option presented to Congress by the status convention as selected by the people of Puerto Rico in the referendum." *Id.* § 3(a)(1).

The Department has three comments on this section.

1. The Department's first comment relates to the reference to the Puerto Rico legislature's having "inherent" authority to call a status convention. H.R. 2070, § 3(a). We surmise that this description of the nature of Puerto Rico's authority is intended to acknowledge the Commonwealth's significant autonomy and powers

of self-government. We note, however, that the use of the word "inherent" may create confusion as to the ultimate source of the Puerto Rico government's authority. As the Supreme Court recently noted, even though "Puerto Rico today has a distinctive, indeed exceptional, status as a self-governing Commonwealth," the "ultimate source" of Puerto Rico law is an enactment of the U.S. Congress. *Puerto Rico v. Sanchez Valle*, 136 S. Ct. 1863, 1874 (2016) (concluding that Puerto Rico and the United States are not separate sovereigns for purposes of the Double Jeopardy Clause). Describing Puerto Rico's authority as "inherent"—that is, "existing . . . as a permanent attribute or quality . . . indwelling, intrinsic," OED Online (Mar. 2021)—when in fact that authority derives from Congress, is legally inaccurate. The Department does not object to some sort of acknowledgment of Puerto Rico's self-governance, but to avoid confusion as to the source of the Puerto Rico legislature's authority, we recommend striking the word "inherent."

2. Second, the Department notes that section 3 appears to be in tension with the executive branch's long-standing "policy . . . to enable Puerto Ricans to determine their preference among options for the islands' future status that are not incompatible with the Constitution and basic laws and policies of the United States" and to "consider and develop positions on proposals, without preference among the options, for the Commonwealth's future status." Exec. Order No. 13183 (Dec. 23, 2000). The tension results because of the combination of several provisions: section 3(a)(1), which provides that the convention would be "dissolved only when the United States ratifies the self-determination option presented to Congress by the status convention as selected by the people of Puerto Rico" pursuant to the referendum authorized in section 5; section 3(c)(1), which expressly instructs the status convention to develop options for Puerto Rico that are "outside the Territorial Clause of the United States Constitution"; and section 3(c)(3), which provides that the convention "shall . . . select and present to the people of Puerto Rico the self-determination options that will be included in the referendum under section 5." *See also* § 5(a)(1)(B) ("A referendum vote by the people of Puerto Rico . . . may consist of choices each composed of a self-determination definition and accompanying transition plan as presented by the delegates under section 3").

   Taken together, these provisions appear to eliminate the current territorial status as an available choice for the people of Puerto Rico under the procedures in the bill. Moreover, these provisions may be read to imply that the United States has determined that the people of Puerto Rico may not decide to retain the island's current territorial status, departing from the executive branch's long-standing view that "Puerto Ricans should determine for themselves the future status of the Island" and the federal government's responsibility is to facilitate "the desire of the people of Puerto Rico to change status or to establish, for some period of time, that they have chosen no change in status." Report by the President's Task Force on Puerto Rico's Status at 23–24 (Mar. 2011) ("2011 Task Force Report"); *see also* Presidential Memorandum of December 23, 2000 ("Resolution of Puerto Rico's Status") (noting that "[s]uccessive Presidents . . . have supported the people of Puerto Rico in determining their status preference from among options that are not incompatible with the Constitution and basic laws and policies of the United States" and concluding that the executive branch has "the responsibility to help Puerto Ricans obtain the necessary transitional legislation toward a new status, if chosen"). One way to address these concerns is to remove the phrase "which shall be outside the Territorial Clause of the United States Constitution" from section 3(c)(1).

3. Finally, the Department notes that section 3 does not specify that the only constitutionally permissible status options available to the status convention—and thus the only options that Congress could subsequently adopt by joint resolution, *see* H.R. 2070, § 6—are statehood, independence, or Puerto Rico's current status as a territory. Independence is a general term that refers to the possibilities both of full independence from the United States and of a compact of free association, in which Puerto Rico would become a sovereign nation but would continue to have close ties to the United States under the terms of a mutually agreed-upon compact. *See* 2011 Task Force Report at 25. Were Puerto Rico to choose a compact of free association, it would occupy a status similar to the Republic of the Marshall Islands, the Federated States of Micronesia, and the Republic of Palau. *Id.*

As has been the Department's consistent view since 1991, we continue to believe that the Constitution limits Puerto Rico to three constitutional choices: the current territorial status, statehood, or independence. The District of Columbia aside, land under United States sovereignty must be either a state or a territory; and if land is "not included in any State," it "must necessarily be governed by or under the authority of Congress." *First Nat'l Bank v. Yankton County*, 101 U.S. 129, 133 (1879). Congress may, in its administration of non-state land, afford such a territory considerable powers of self-government, as it has already done with Puerto Rico. *See* Puerto Rican Federal Relations Act, Pub. L. No. 81–600, 64 Stat. 319 (1950), *codified at* 48 U.S.C. §§ 731b–731e. But Congress cannot constitutionally relinquish its ability to legislate with respect to that territory under the Territories Clause unless it either admits the territory as a state, U.S. Const. art. IV, § 3, cl. 1, or enacts legislation making the territory independent and no longer subject to the jurisdiction of the United States. *See Mutual Consent Provisions in the Guam Commonwealth Legislation*, Op. O.L.C. Supp., at *5 (July 28, 1994) ("*Mutual Consent*") ("The requirement that the delegation of governmental authority to the non-state areas be subject to federal supremacy and federal supervision means that such delegation is necessarily subject to the right of Congress to revise, alter, or revoke the authority granted.") (citing *Dist. of Columbia v. Thompson Co.*, 346 U.S. 100, 109 (1953), among other cases). In other words, there is no constitutionally permissible status "outside of the Territorial Clause" other than statehood or independence (including free-association agreements).

Our view on this issue also rests on the general rule that one Congress cannot irrevocably bind subsequent Congresses. *See Marbury v. Madison*, 5 U.S. (1 Cranch) 137, 177 (1803) (Marshall, C.J.) (noting that legislative acts are "alterable when the legislature shall please to alter [them]"). Although this general rule is subject to limitations imposed by the Due Process Clause of the Fifth Amendment, those limitations do not apply to protect Puerto Rico's political status from congressional revision if Puerto Rico remains a territory. *Mutual Consent* at *8–9. Territories, like states and their political subdivisions, are not "persons" for purposes of due process. *Id.* at *6–7. And a particular political relationship with the national government is not the type of vested property right that due process protects. *Id.* at *8–9 (citing *Bowen v. Public Agencies Opposed to Social Security Entrapment*, 477 U.S. 41, 55 (1986), among other cases).

In the past, Congress has purported to enter into covenants with territories that would be alterable only with mutual consent. *See, e.g.*, Pub. L. No. 24–241, 90 Stat. 263, 264 (1976) (approving the "Covenant to Establish a Commonwealth of the Northern Mariana Islands in Political Union with the United States of America," section 105 of which provides that certain provisions of the Covenant "may be modified only with the consent of the Government of the United States and the Government of the Northern Mariana Islands"); Act of Aug. 7, 1789, ch. 8, 1 Stat. 50, 52 n.a (maintaining the Northwest Ordinance, including a prefatory clause providing that the articles of the compact would "forever remain unalterable, unless by common consent"); *Mutual Consent* at *2 n.2. But in view of the foregoing principles, we believe that these provisions cannot be binding—a view to which the Department has long subscribed. *See Mutual Consent* at *13.

We note, in addition, that the principle of a current Congress's not being able to bind future Congresses would also apply to any compact of free association entered into with Puerto Rico if Puerto Rico were to choose that type of independence. As a matter of our domestic law, such a compact would necessarily be revocable or subject to revision by a subsequent act of Congress. *See Medellín v. Texas*, 552 U.S. 491, 509 n.5 (2008) ("[A] later-in-time federal statute supersedes inconsistent treaty provisions.").

Section 4 (Congressional Bilateral Negotiating Commission)

Section 4(a) would establish a "Congressional Bilateral Negotiating Commission. . . to provide advice and consultation to delegates elected" to the status convention established under section 3. H.R. 2070, § 4(a). It would be composed of a number of members of Congress, including the chairs and ranking members of the relevant congressional committees, members selected by congressional leadership, and the Resident Commissioner of Puerto Rico. *Id.* § 4(b)(1). In addition, the Commission would include "a member from the Department of Justice" and "a member from the Department of the Interior," both "with the consent of the Speaker of the House of Representatives and majority leader of the Senate." *Id.* § 4(b)(1)(H), (I).

The Commission would seem to be a legislative branch entity that reports only to congressional leadership and is limited to purely advisory functions, such as "develop[ing] recommendations regarding self-determination options on constitutional issues and policies" and "provid[ing] technical assistance and constitutional advice to the delegates during the Puerto Rico status convention." *Id.* § 4(c). Consistent with separation of powers constraints, we do not understand that policy or legal recommendations issued by the Commission would bind the Executive Branch. *See, e.g., Metro. Wash. Airports Auth. v. Citizens for the Abatement of Aircraft Noise, Inc.*, 501 U.S. 252, 276 (1991) ("If the power is executive, the Constitution does not permit an agent of Congress to exercise it."); *Buckley v. Valeo*, 424 U.S. 1, 139 (1976) (per curiam) (holding that congressional appointees may "perform duties only in aid of those functions that Congress may carry out by itself, or in an area sufficiently removed from the administration and enforcement of the public law").

Finally, we note that the name of the Commission, the "Congressional Bilateral Negotiating Commission," does not seem to be an apt description of the Commission's advisory duties. The Department does not read the duties of the Commission to include negotiations with the convention and would accordingly suggest that the name be modified to more accurately characterize the Commission's role—e.g., the Congressional Advisory Commission.

Section 5 (Puerto Rico Status Referendum; Education Campaign)

The Department has identified no legal concerns with this provision, which sets out the structure for a referendum vote on the status options developed by the convention under section 3. We note, however, that in the past Congress has sought the Department of Justice's involvement in ensuring that the options presented to the Puerto Rican people in a plebiscite are constitutional. *See* H.R. Rep. No. 113– 171, at 54 (2014). Were the legislation to provide for the Department of Justice to have a certification role here, it would help ensure that any status option developed by the convention and selected by the people of Puerto Rico would be constitutional and thus could be ratified by Congress.

Section 6 (Congressional Deliberation and Enacting Resolution)

Section 6 would provide that "[i]f the referendum under this Act is approved by the people of Puerto Rico, Congress shall approve a joint resolution to ratify the preferred self-determination option approved in that referendum vote." This provision is constitutional only if it is read to mean that Congress shall consider *whether* to approve a joint resolution ratifying the results of the referendum. If, instead, it were read to bind Congress to approve a joint resolution, it would impermissibly constrain Congress.

To address this constitutional concern, the Department recommends changing "shall" to "may" in section 6. Alternatively, section 6 could be amended to provide that Puerto Rico's status shall become whatever the people selected. The Department has concluded that contingent legislation of that type is constitutionally permissible. *See Altering Puerto Rico's Relationship with the United States Through Referendum*, 36 Op. O.L.C. 93, 93–94 (2012) (concluding that "legislation conditioning a change in Puerto Rico's political relationship with the United States on the results of one or more referenda by the Puerto Rican electorate, without subsequent congressional action, would be constitutional, insofar as the referendum . . . presented voters in the territory with a limited set of options specified in advance by Congress"). However, for this alternative approach to be available, it would be necessary for Congress to approve the options presented to the Puerto Rican people ahead of the vote (or to provide a list of acceptable options from which the status convention could choose).

March 31, 2021

Dear Congressmen and Congresswoman:

English

On November 3, 2020, we went to our voting centers for the third time in this decade to vote in favor of the YES to statehood. There have been several Annexation Acts that have been submitted to Congress and even the US citizens who live on the island have congressional action to support these acts.

The issue of Puerto Rico's political status is not a matter of political party ideals. The status issue is about citizens, about us, who suffer second-class citizenship every day. Where our elderly and disabled do not have the right to supplementary social security, because they live in a neighborhood. On our island where schools lack educational resources for students since there is no parity of funds for being a colony. Where we cannot vote for him President and we lack equal representation, with a vote in Congress and the United States Senate. And where our military, who serve our flag with so much honor, cannot vote for the person who sends them to war.

We hereby ask you to support the Admission Act for Puerto Rico HR 1522, so that all citizens who live on this beautiful island have equal rights, as US citizens.

Español

El pasado 3 de noviembre de 2020, fuimos a nuestros centres de votación, por tercera vez en esta década para votar a favor del SI a la estadidad. Han sido varias las Actas de Anexión que se han sometido al Congreso y aun los ciudadanos estadounidenses que vivimos en la isla la acción dei congreso en apoyar estas actas. El asunto del estatus de politico de Puerto Rico no es un tema de ideales de partidos político. El asunto de estatus es sobre los ciudadanos, sobre nosotros, los que cada día sufrimos la ciudadanía de segunda clase. Donde nuestros ancianos e incapacitados no tienen derecho al seguro social complementario, por vivir en una colonia. En nuestra isla donde las escuelas carecen de recursos educativos para los estudiantes, ya que no existe una paridad de fondos por ser una colonia. En donde no podemos votar por él Presidente y carecemos de representación igualitaria, con voto en el Congreso y en el Senado de Estados Unidos. Y donde nuestros militares, que con tan tanto honor sirven a nuestra bandera, no pueden votar por la persona que los envía a la guerra.

Por este media le solicitamos que apoye el Acta de Admisión para Puerto Rico HR 1522, para que todos los ciudadanos que vivimos en esta hermosa isla tengamos la igualdad de derechos, coma ciudadanos estadounidenses.

Firma,

Jimarie Martinez Baladeio

Nombre	Firma	Edad	Email, teléfono o dirección
Nancy Merced Rivera	[illegible]	58	nanmercedrivera@gmail.com
Wanda Rodríguez García	[illegible]	40	wandarodriguez@gmail.com
Efrain Calo Fernández	[illegible]	42	efraincalo@hotmail.com
Yomaira Feliciano	[illegible]	Apt 103	yomairaf343@gmail.com
Victor Robles	Victor	Apt 103	yomairaf343@gmail.com
Ricardo Rodriguez	[illegible]	Apt 103	nefti2010@gmail.com
Megan Stacy Nieves Navarro	[illegible]	18	meganstacynieves@gmail.com
Melissa Arroyo	[illegible]	20	melissaarroyoquiros@gmail.com
Cynthia E. Nazario	[illegible]	44	cynthianazario18@gmail.com
Mariángel Muñoz Martinez	Mariangel Muñoz	14	939-334-7555

Marco J. Rodríguez	x Marco	9	939-334-7555
Sonia Rojas Herrero	x Sonia Rojas Herrero	66	[illegible]
Néstor Rodríguez Ruiz	x Néstor Rodríguez Ruiz	73	787-797-1914
Néstor J. Rodríguez	[illegible]	41	nestor.rodriguez1@upr.edu
Kimberly S. Díaz	Kimberly S. Díaz	14	939-3496246
Sonia Rodríguez Rojas	S. Rodríguez	46	mabelorod@gmail.com
Vladymir Soto	[illegible]	54	vlado@hotmail.com
Melvin E. Carrero Montes	[illegible]	35	787-385-3664
Edwin J. Pérez	Edwin J. Pérez	16	787-310-9760
María M. Martínez	[illegible]		787 475 1414
Héctor Collazo [illegible]	HECTOR COLLAZO		787 475 1414
Carmen M. Baladejo	[illegible]	62	(787) 598-1136
Carmen L. Vázquez	Carmen L. Vázquez	80	(787) 293-7521
[illegible] Martínez Pérez	[illegible]	64	787-450-4114
María L. Baladejo Vázquez	[illegible]	57	(787) 201-8508
Jesús Baladejo	Jesús Baladejo	39	787-964-6525
Mildred J Baladejo	M. Baladejo	15	939-240-2179
Mildred Vázquez	M Vázquez	39	787-383-2033
Gabriela Pérez	[illegible]	22	(787) 445-1934
[illegible]	[illegible]	21	939-275-1339
Paola L. [illegible] López	[illegible]	30	787-329-1531
[illegible]	Carla I Baladejo	28	787-225-3759

Federation of Municipal Legislators of PR

April 6, 2021

Dear Chairman Grijalva, Ranking Member Westerman, Chairman Manchin, Ranking Member Barrasso:

For over one-hundred years, the U.S. citizens of Puerto Rico have been disenfranchised in federal elections and subjected to unequal treatment across federal programs. Last November, voters stood up to change that when an absolute majority of

53% demanded statehood in a locally sponsored referendum. The Puerto Rico Statehood Admission Act, H.R. 1522 and S. 780, directly respond to that mandate, and we urge you to support it and help get it approved as soon as possible.

Puerto Rico's referendum was historic because it is the first time that statehood received unquestionable majority support on the island with a simple "YES" or "NO" vote. The 117th Congress is therefore presented with a unique opportunity to make history and put an end to America's inherently colonial rule over Puerto Rico, which runs counter to America's values of democracy, equal justice under the law, and government by the consent of the governed.

We recognize there are some in Congress, such as Rep. Nydia Velázquez (NY) and Sen. Robert Menendez (NJ), who oppose statehood for Puerto Rico and have completely ignored the results of the referendum held last November. Today, they will be submitting a counter-proposal, the Puerto Rico Self-Determination Act (PRSDA), which has faced criticism from representatives of all status options.

The most significant concern, across party lines, is that the PRSDA is ultimately non-binding. Under the bill, Congress would be under no obligation to implement whichever status option is chosen by the convention and later voted on by the electorate. This would represent a huge setback for voters in Puerto Rico who have engaged in multiple acts of self-determination over the last decade and have shown, with increasing clarity, that Puerto Rico's voters reject the current territory status and favor statehood above all non-territory options.

Beyond the will of the people on the island, however, Puerto Ricans stateside also favor statehood by wide margins. For example, recent polls show 81% of Puerto Rican residents in Florida and 69% of those in New York favor the admission of the island as a state. A majority of Americans have also supported the idea for decades according to Gallup. This is a settled issue on the island as well as across the Nation, and Congress has a moral obligation to act.

The only legislative option that respects the will of the people of Puerto Rico, and ensures a binding process of self-determination is H.R. 1522 & S. 780, the Puerto Rico Statehood Admission Act. By offering statehood, stipulating the terms of admission, and requiring a ratification vote, Congress would finally open the door to full equality and democracy for the U.S. citizens of Puerto Rico while leaving the ultimate choice in their hands. If a majority opposes statehood at that point, then the island would remain a territory with the capacity to pursue independence or free association through the procedural mechanism of their choice, including a status convention. Congress has a moral obligation to let the people of Puerto Rico decide their own self-determination process.

Our organization represents Municipal Legislators from the 78 municipalities in Puerto Rico. We believe that it is time to put an end to the dysfunctional, obsolete and undemocratic status of territory to which Puerto Rico has been subjected. We call on

Congress to open the door to full emancipation and equality for our fellow Americans in Puerto Rico by supporting and passing the Puerto Rico Statehood Admission Act. The United States can and must do better.

Sincerely,

Luis Carlos Maldonado Padilla,
President

League of United Latin American Citizens

Dear Members of Congress:

LULAC is the largest and oldest Hispanic civil rights organization in the United States. The League of United Latin American Citizens (LULAC), our National President, National Board Members and one hundred and thirty thousand members and supporters nationwide are appealing to you to support the Puerto Rico Statehood Admission Act, H.R. 1522 and S. 780.

We strongly support H.R. 1522 and S. 780, the Puerto Rico Statehood Admission Act. This legislation respects Puerto Rico's right to self-determination, as expressed in previous referenda, and empowers voters on the island to have a final say on becoming a state of the union.

Puerto Ricans have been clear about their demand for statehood, most recently in a referendum held last November. Voters were asked the question "Should Puerto Rico be admitted immediately into the Union as a state?" and 53% said yes, while 47% said no. Not only did the "yes" option win, it also got more votes than any elected official on the island, including the governor and at-large delegate to Congress. This vote was historic, and ignoring it means being complicit in the continued disenfranchisement of over 3 million Hispanic-Americans.

The island has been stuck in a territorial status limbo for decades, in no small part due to partisan infighting and the convenience of simply pushing the issue to the side. LULAC believes Congress has a moral responsibility to respond to the will of the people of Puerto Rico by offering a concrete path to statehood, particularly after the results of the 2020 referendum.

In addition to those on the island, statehood for Puerto Rico has the support of a vast majority of Puerto Ricans living in different U.S. states, including Florida, Pennsylvania, and New York. Additionally, a majority both Republicans and Democrats across the nation have supported the idea of making Puerto Rico a state for decades. There is no time to waste when it comes to securing the enfranchisement of over 3 million Hispanic-Americans, and this Congress has all the reasons it needs to get it done.

Above all else, LULAC listens to the will of the people of Puerto Rico, who value their American citizenship and have clearly stated their support for the rights that only statehood can assure. We are confident that the people of Puerto Rico would ratify that decision via popular vote, and we would be proud to welcome our nation's first majority-Hispanic state.

A competing proposal in Congress is the Puerto Rico Self-Determination Act, introduced by Rep. Nydia Velázquez (D-NY) and Sen. Bernie Sanders (I-VT). LULAC stands in firm opposition to this bill as it is written, since it only offers a non-binding "status convention" as a solution rather than the binding ratification vote offered in the Puerto Rico Statehood Admission Act, H.R. 1522 & S. 780.

The only legislative option that respects the will of the people of Puerto Rico, and ensures a binding process of self-determination is H.R. 1522, the Puerto Rico Statehood Admission Act. By offering statehood, stipulating the terms of admission, and requiring a ratification vote, Congress would finally open the door to full equality and democracy for the U.S. citizens of Puerto Rico, while leaving the ultimate choice in their hands. Should a majority oppose statehood at that point, then the island would remain a territory with the capacity to pursue independence or free association through the procedural mechanism of their choice, including a status convention.

FEDERACIÓN DE ALCALDES DE PUERTO RICO, INC.

May 14, 2021

Hon. Raúl Grijalva
Chairman
House Committee on
Natural Resources

Hon. Bruce Westerman
Ranking Member
House Committee on
Natural Resources

Hon. Joe Manchin
Chairman
Senate Committee on Energy
& Natural Resources

Hon. John Barrasso
Ranking Member
Senate Committee on Energy
& Natural Resources

Dear Chairman Grijalva, Ranking Member Westerman, Chairman Manchin, Ranking Member Barrasso:

As mayors from municipalities across Puerto Rico we write to express our strong support for H.R. 1522 & S. 780, the Puerto Rico Statehood Admission Act, and to urge the U.S. Congress to approve it as soon as possible.

We represent a wide range of municipalities, from Puerto Rico's largest urban centers in the San Juan metro area to rural municipalities in the heart of Puerto Rico's central mountain range. We represent coastal towns that thrive on tourism, towns with current and former military bases, from towns with significant agriculture production to towns with advanced industrial manufacturing.

While each of our municipalities brings its own unique identity and contribution, they all share a common challenge. Under the current territory status, we are unable to provide an equal quality of life to our residents or to generate as many opportunities for our local residents as cities and towns in the states.

The reason for this is simple. Under the current territory status, the federal government is able to discriminate against Puerto Rico in the laws, programs and policies that we live under every day. This creates an unequal playing field from which it is impossible for our cities and towns to ever reach our full potential, because we are always starting at a disadvantage.

The other reason is that under territory status we are denied the right to vote for President, denied any representation in the U.S. Senate, and have only one non-voting Resident Commissioner in the House to represent a population that would normally have approximately four voting Representatives. This gap in representation means we often have to depend on officials we have no role in electing, and are not accountable to us, to advocate for the needs and advance the priorities of our communities.

This combination of structural inequality and democratic deficit means that many of our most talented, hard-working and productive residents are being forced to seek equal opportunities and full voting rights only found in the states. This is tearing apart families and communities as people in Puerto Rico feel compelled to leave the island and move stateside to seek a brighter future. Data from the U.S. Census illustrates this starkly.

According to the latest numbers Puerto Rico's population declined 11.8% (approximately 440,000 residents) in the last decade. This is not only the worse populations loss of any jurisdiction in the entire U.S., but possibly in the whole Western Hemisphere.

The current territory status is literally robbing our towns and cities of their present and future, and voter in Puerto Rico have had enough. In 2012 and 2017, voters in Puerto Rico rejected the current territory status and favored statehood among the valid non-territory options. Then last November, to eliminate any remaining doubt on whether or not the majority of Puerto Rico's voters supported statehood, 52.5% voted "YES" to the island's immediate admission as a state of the Union. These voters are calling for equal rights, equal representation and equal opportunities to those of their fellow citizens in the states.

We understand that some Members of Congress personally oppose statehood and or represent constituents that favor independence for Puerto Rico. While we respect their right to their own opinions and those of their constituents who do not live on the island, we strongly oppose any effort to disregard the will of the majority of the actual voters that live in Puerto Rico. That is shy we must also express our opposition to H.R. 2070 & S. 865, the Puerto Rico Self-Determination Act.

This bill engages in election denial by ignoring the will of the majority of Puerto Rico's voters in support of statehood and opens the door to an endless debate on an indefinite number of options, some of which are unconstitutional. That is completely reckless, and Congress must reject it.

As mayors, we have seen the issue of Puerto Rico's political status debated for decades and we know that until it is resolved we will never be able to offer our residents the rights, representation and opportunities they deserve and have earned after over 100 years of U.S. citizenship. Congress must not delay this debate any further with new commissions, false options or indefinite timelines like in H.R. 2070 & S. 865. Instead, Congress must listen to the will of the majority of Puerto Rico's voters, extend a formal offer of admission to Puerto Rico as a state, and empower voters on the island to make the final decision to ratify our desire for full equality and democracy through statehood.

As local elected officials that see and work for the 3.2 million U.S. citizens of Puerto Rico every day, we need you to take action now. We strongly urge Congress to support and pass the Puerto Rico Statehood Admission Act.

Sincerely,

Ángel A. Pérez Otero,
President

CSG East, Resolution # TR-2020-01

Resolution in Support of Congressional Action for Puerto Rico Statehood

- Whereas, the People of Puerto Rico held a plebiscite on November 3, 2020, in which this question was presented to them: "Should Puerto Rico be admitted immediately into the Union as a State?"; and
- Whereas, 96.8 percent of those who participated in the 2020 General Election also participated in the plebiscite, and
- Whereas, of those who participated in the plebiscite, 52.34 percent voted "Yes" in favor of Congress beginning the statehood process for Puerto Rico; and
- Whereas, the "Yes" column received 623,053 votes more votes than any political candidate present on the ballot in the 2020 General Election; and

- Whereas, support for statehood as the final status option has incrementally gained support throughout all six plebiscites that have been conducted (1967, 1993, 1998, 2012, 2017, 2020); and
- Whereas, both the Democratic and Republican parties' platforms are committed to respecting Puerto Rico's right to self-determination; and
- Whereas, the ultimate decision regarding Puerto Rico's future political status rests in the hands of Congress; and
- Whereas, in 1992 CSG/ERC supported a resolution asking Congress for a prompt response to the formal petition mandated by the people of Puerto Rico that would be issued as a result of the 1993 plebiscite;
- Therefore, Be It Resolved, that the Council of State Governments' Eastern Regional Conference (CSG/ERC) supports the results of the 2020 plebiscite which clearly show the will of the People of Puerto Rico; and
- Be It Further Resolved, that CSG/ERC also supports a prompt response by the United States Congress to the formal petition for statehood that was supported by the majority of Puerto Rican voters in the 2020 plebiscite; and
- Be It Further Resolved, that a copy of this resolution will be provided to the Governor-Elect of Puerto Rico, the incoming President of the Senate and Speaker of the House of Representatives of Puerto Rico, the President-Elect of the United States, the Vice President Elect of the United States, the Speaker of the U.S. House of Representatives, the President Pro Tempore of the U.S. Senate, the Majority Leader of the U.S. Senate, the Chair and members of the U.S. Senate Committee on Energy and Natural Resources and the Chair and members of the U.S. House of Representatives Committee on Natural Resources.

Puertorriqueños Unidos En Acción (PUA), Arlington, Virginia, June 11, 2021

President Joe Biden
The White House
Washington, DC

Re: UNITED NATIONS DECOLONIZATION COMMITTEE HEARINGS ON PUERTO RICO

Dear President Biden:

November 6, 2012 was a momentous day in the history of Puerto Rico and the United States. The people of Puerto Rico spoke out on this date. Fifty-five percent of the voters expressed their will to change the actual colonial relationship between Puerto Rico and the United States. Therefore, the era of colonialism by consent in Puerto Rico has ended.

As you should know, the Constitution assigns Congress the responsibility of defining the relationship between the federal government and U.S. territories. Now, more than ever, the President and Congress' role is significant in Puerto Rico's choice to end the present colonial status.

Over 1.8 million registered voters participated in this plebiscite. The numbers indicate the will of the people to change the present colonial status. However, Congress has been running counter to the United States' democratic beliefs by holding back on a meaningful process to end colonialism. The people of Puerto Rico have spoken. Now is the United States government's chance to express their will to change the current relationship between our two nations. The United States should commit to implementing the results of the 2012 referendum rejecting the actual relationship without any further referendums or delays.

As it has been stated in two Presidential Task Force Reports, "If the process produces a clear result, Congress should act on it quickly with the President's support." (See Presidential Task Force Report on Puerto Rico under President Bush, December 2007, page 23, and Presidential Task Report, March 2011, page 3 under former President Obama). The current relationship between Puerto Rico and the United States has deteriorated. Congress arbitrarily implements laws that affect the well-being of many Puerto Ricans and their livelihood, from controlling the way Puerto Ricans practice their culture and traditions to deciding the way they manage their municipal budgets. Recent examples include imposing a finance control board that oversees Puerto Rico's finances with more power than the democratically elected government and the prohibition of the cockfighting sport; a tradition practiced for over 500 years.

We have the results since 2012 that support a realistic chance to decolonize Puerto Rico. I urge the President of the United States to move forward and achieve this goal of a free Puerto Rico and, in doing such, stand by the principles of democracy. The recognition of Puerto Rico's right to self-determination and the transfer of political powers to the people of Puerto Rico is not an issue to be debated. It is Congress and the President's responsibility. It is time to speak out.

On June 18, 2021, the United Nations Decolonization Committee will consider Puerto Rico's colonial status. I urge the President to adopt this year's resolution and its recommendations, participate in the Committee's works and exhort your country's delegation to present the official position of the United States government regarding the case of Puerto Rico. The voters of Puerto Rico decided in 2012. Thank you very much for your prompt attention to this matter.

Sincerely,

Manuel Rivera

The Puerto Rico Senate, Office of the Senate President, June 15, 2021

Hon. Raúl Grijalva, Chairman
Committee on Natural Resources
U.S. House of Representatives
Washington, DC

Dear Chairman Grijalva:

I am writing to you as President of the Senate of the Commonwealth of Puerto Rico and as President of the Popular Democratic Party, the party that controls the parliamentary majority in the Legislative Assembly and the majority of Puerto Rico's municipalities.

During the past few months, the congressional committee that you lead has been evaluating two legislative bills that have the purpose of addressing the issue of Puerto Rico's political status.

The first, H.R. 2070 (The Puerto Rico Self-Determination Act of 2021) authored by Congresswomen Nydia Velázquez and Alexandria Ocasio-Cortez, as well as H.R. 1522 (The Puerto Rico Statehood Admission Act) authored by Congressman Darren Soto.

Our institution has expressed its willingness to support any Congressional initiative that seeks to seriously and responsibly address an issue as important as Puerto Rico's political status.

Both initiatives, however, contain serious deficiencies that prevent the Popular Democratic Party—the parliamentary majority of the Puerto Rican government— from supporting their content at this time. The absence of fair procedural mechanisms, the deliberate exclusion of the alternative of Commonwealth development and the unrealistic offer to convert Puerto Rico into a state of the Union within 12 months, without providing details on the impact of federal contributions on the island, make these bills unacceptable.

Consistent with our position, the U.S. Department of Justice has reiterated that any political status consultation process intended to obtain the validity of the federal government must include the Commonwealth option. Moreover, in that opinion, the DOJ only recognizes three real alternatives, namely, commonwealth, statehood and independence.

It is for these reasons that the U.S. Congress cannot ignore the demand of almost half of the island's electorate and the legal opinion of the US Department of Justice.

As we have pointed out, the bill of Congresswomen Velázquez and Ocasio-Cortez has a laudable purpose, but in its wording, it does not meet the expectations outlined, since several sections—such as the election of delegates and the one that defines the various status formulas—are far from resolving the issue, complicate it and make the process an ineffective one.

On the other hand, it is inexplicable that the congressional committee that intends to legislate or even urge the legislative branch of Puerto Rico to address this issue through future legislation, has not had the deference to listen and address the claims of the Popular Democratic Party, the party that happens to be the parliamentary majority that would have the responsibility to legislate at the local level any status proposal on the island.

However, despite this regrettable omission, I, in discharging my responsibility, proceed to submit my comments on both bills summarized in the following points:

About H.R. 2070

1. H.R. 2070 (The Puerto Rico Self-Determination Act of 2021) authored by Congresswomen Nydia Velázquez and Alexandria Ocasio-Cortez does not include the option of Commonwealth development and rules out the participation of political parties in the delegate nomination process. For the Popular Democratic Party this is unacceptable.
2. Contrary to existing legislation adopted by President Barack Obama in 2014, H.R. 2070 eliminates the requirement that the US Department of Justice must pass judgment prior to any vote on the validity of each status formula. For the Popular Democratic Party, this should be a mandatory requirement in any congressional legislation.
3. The way in which H.R. 2070 establishes the delegate selection process and the design of status options is a way to mislead voters by leading them to vote blindly for delegates without knowing in advance their status preferences or the agenda they will advance if elected. This is so because the structure of the project places voters in the dilemma of electing delegates without knowing what ideological sector they belong to or what specific proposals on status formulas they will defend. This would be granting a blank check. For the Popular Democratic Party, this is unacceptable.
4. In compliance with the terms of Act No. 51-2020 that called for the vote on statehood in the past elections, the majority of the Legislature understands that the plebiscite mandate granted to that option expires on November 3, 2021; therefore, any Congressional bill that intends to act on that vote must be approved on or before that date.
5. We reiterate that if by that date Congress has not acted—ignoring the results—and does not pass any legislation in both legislative bodies aimed at specifically responding to that result, for purposes of the Legislative Assembly of Puerto

Rico, it shall be understood that Congress has rejected that vote. Thereafter, the Puerto Rico Legislative Assembly shall route a new political status referendum invoking the existing legislation passed by Congress in 2014, which provided for an appropriation of $2.5 million. (H.R. Rep. No. 113-171, at 54 (2014).

6. Regarding the institutional position of the Popular Democratic Party on our vision for the empowerment of the Commonwealth option, it is our opinion that the same shall be part of a fair and balanced dialogue process between the people of Puerto Rico, the Congress and the White House, in accordance with the commitment made by President Joe Biden.
7. We require that any proposed congressional legislation must contain clear and detailed transition reports to be presented to the electorate prior to any vote. Specifically, voters must know answers on such important issues as: the impact of federal taxation under statehood on Puerto Rico's economy, the possibility of requiring Puerto Rico to become an incorporated territory as a preliminary to statehood, and the loss of U.S. citizenship at birth under independence options. Such answers are necessary to eliminate fanciful or misleading options.
8. For the foregoing reasons, the Popular Democratic Party recommends a substitute bill (chairman's mark) for H.R. 2070, eliminating sections 3 (selection of delegates) and 5 (design of status formulas) of the bills in their entirety and leaving the design of both matters in the hands of the Legislative Assembly of Puerto Rico.

About H.R. 1522

With regard to H.R. 1522 calling for the admission of Puerto Rico as a state, I wish to call your attention to a monumental flaw in the bill.

H.R. 1522 does not provide for assessing if Puerto Rico is prepared for statehood. It would admit Puerto Rico as a State in 12 months without first examining if the island has enough resources to meet the federal tax obligations it would be assuming and be able to raise enough state tax revenues to balance its budget, meet debt and pension obligations, and provide essential services.

In a recent brief filed before the U.S. Supreme Court, the Department of Justice pointed out that:

> Puerto Rico has taken advantage of its exemption from federal income tax by imposing a territorial individual income tax of up to 33% for the highest bracket—well above the typical rate in the States. Puerto Rico Internal Revenue Code § 1021.01(a). Puerto Rico has likewise taken advantage of its exemption from the federal corporate tax

> by imposing a territorial corporate tax of up to 37.5%—again, well above the typical rate in the States. Id. § 1022.01(b), 1022.02(b)(2).

Pet. Brief, U.S. v. Vaello-Madero, 20-303 (June 2021), 17.

The reality is that Puerto Rico, even with its particular tax rates, has not balanced a budget in over a decade. It even found itself unable to pay its general obligations in 2014, prompting Congress to legislate, two years later, the creation of a Fiscal Oversight Board, as it had previously done for Washington, D.C.

Five years after the Promesa Act, Puerto Rico still has not completed its debt restructuring and has not balanced its first of four required budgets in a row.

On this issue, in 2014, the General Accountability Office took the DOJ statement a step further and laid out what would logically occur if Puerto Rico were to become a state:

> Puerto Rico's individual and corporate income tax rates are relatively high compared to those of the states. If the Puerto Rico government wanted to maintain pre-statehood tax burdens for individuals and corporations, it would need to lower its tax rates, which could reduce tax revenues." U.S. Government Accountability Office, GAO-14-315, Puerto Rico: Information on How Statehood Would Potentially Affect Selected Federal Programs and Revenue Sources 31-32 (March 2014).

With this clear warning of reduced tax revenues under statehood falling on a jurisdiction that has experienced chronic budget deficits and an inability to meet its general obligations, the Natural Resources Committee would be remiss to consider and pass H.R. 1522 without adequate studies on the extent of the impact of statehood on Puerto Rico's tax revenues.

This is of particular importance given that debts are currently being restructured for the coming decades based on Puerto Rico's current tax revenues. If those tax revenues are reduced under statehood and debt service would remain unchanged, the impending hit of cuts would affect essential services and pensions the hardest, forcing a new default. The U.S. Congress cannot ignore this reality. For the above reasons, we call for the reject of this bill.

I hope you will give serious consideration to these remarks.

Cordially yours,

Joséluis Dalmau-Santiago,
Senate President

Statement for the Record, Miriam J Ramirez MD, San Juan, PR, Former Senator of the Commonwealth of Puerto Rico and Founder—Puerto Ricans in Civic Action

Chairman Grijalva, Members of the Committee, ladies and gentlemen:

I applaud your efforts in scheduling hearings to discuss Puerto Rico's centennial colonial problem. I have been visiting many of you for over the last 40 years; to get the United States Congress attention to resolve this embarrassing situation of having a colony of US citizens without representation in the government that rules our lives. On many occasions, we have been told the "need to get our act together." BUT it's YOU, the United States CONGRESS, which imposes rules, out of our control, which make it impossible to get our act together.

I am mentioning in my statement, just some of the many decisions that are totally under the responsibility of the United States Congress, with the hopes that you start from there. It's no use to hold more hearings on more plebiscites, when you have made decision to keep us locked under a colonial rule in order to facilitate tax evasion for CFC's, High Tech Corps, the very wealthy from Puerto Rico, the several states, and the world.

THE US CONGRESS has

Allowed Puerto Rico to be an Offshore Tax paradise,

Not allowed Representation in Congress to US Citizens

Not allowed US CITIZENS to vote for the President and Vice President, who determine to send us to wars.

Therefore, I respectfully request that my statement be included for the Record towards the Legislative Hearing on H.R. 1522 (Rep. Soto), titled "Puerto Rico Statehood Admission Act," and H.R. 2070 (Rep. Velázquez), entitled the "Puerto Rico Self-Determination Act of 2021," on Wednesday, June 16, 2021, and which explicitly says: "with the intent of receiving testimony that is primarily from legal and scholarly witnesses."

We, the US Citizens of Puerto Rico; hereby let it be known, have had extensive patience awaiting for the United States Congress to resolve the status of Puerto Rico! We, the US Citizens of Puerto Rico also want it to be known, a resolution towards the final political status of Puerto Rico is not just a matter for scholars, political parties and vested interests, whom have access to express their viewpoint before a congressional hearing. There is an essential "moral" and democratic responsibility, with a need to conduct public hearing at Puerto Rico.

The US citizens of Puerto Rico public must be heard!

We, the US Citizens of Puerto Rico, therefore request, the Natural Resources Committee of the U.S. House of Representatives submit a bill to the Floor and resolve;

the following "dilemmas" which Congress itself has created towards Puerto Rico, which are:

1. Financial Oversight and Management Board for Puerto Rico
   It is Imperative that Congress eliminate the Financial Oversight and Management Board for Puerto Rico.
   It has proven to be totally ineffective in resolving the fiscal public debt issue and has probably cost us more than what we Puerto Rican's owe.
   If they were "true and competent" experts and advisors, as it was sold to us, in the content—why have they spent millions of dollars in consulting fees and expenses?
   "Professionals have requested about $883 Million in fees and expenses through the Title III compensation process as of March 1, 2021." These are legal expenses for all parties due to litigation. Congress instructed the Board to have consensual negotiations with bondholders but instead they have litigated for over four years. [Reference; (Exhibit—See Page 2) https://drive.google.com/file/d/1RyNs4H7yvpk0P w4DtK57WeHzeZEKggXA/view?usp=sharing.]
   While the Congressional Budget Office estimated that the process should cost approximately $370 Million. [Reference; (Exhibit) https://drive.google.com/file/d/1QmLknEwU9P20zP57-SZQieBOkBqKieMa/view?usp=sharing.]
   We, the US Citizens of Puerto Rico therefore; will be over paying a cost of more than $350 Million estimated, due to the actions of the Board.
2. URGENT—United State CONGRESS Modify—IRC Tax Code towards Puerto Rico
   Puerto Rico is treated as a Foreign Entity for IRC tax purposes. Puerto Rico is a US Territory with US Citizens and should be treated as such. This participation will open the way towards our full participation within the Federal fiscal system. [Reference; (Exhibit) Source: https://howmuch.net/articles/corporate-tax-rates-around-the-world.]
3. URGENT—The United States CONGRESS MUST ELIMINATE TAX EVASION SCHEMES which has made Puerto Rico an Offshore IRC tax shelter! The very affluent rich and powerful, use our beautiful island to evade taxes and enjoy our bankrupt circumstance, while most of the population resides under the poverty level, with the lowest per-capita income under the American Flag. [Reference; (Exhibit) Source: IRS Seizes Foothold on Puerto Rico Tax Haven Movimiento Revolución Estadista Inc.Audits, https://news.bloombergtax.com/daily-tax-report/irs-seizes-foothold-on-puerto-rico-tax-haven-audits.]
   We have many more requests for this committee and suggest that it hold a hearing to allow the people whom are actually suffering the consequences of years of the inactions, report and testify. We, the US Citizens of Puerto Rico are

more than tired of observing, selected and handpicked witnesses who do not represent us, or speak for us.

I respectfully and publicly request, that the people of Puerto Rico who agree with my statement to endorse it by sign your name at the end, and ask that it be introduced for the record.

Movimiento Puertorriqueño Reunificacionista Con España—MPRE

June 16, 2021

Hon. Raúl Grijalva, Chairman
Committee on Natural Resources
U.S. House of Representatives
Washington, DC

Dear Chairman Grijalva and Members of the Committee:

My name is Manuel A. Rugama Amparo, Vice President of the Movimiento Puertorriqueño Reunificacionista con España—MPRE (Puerto Rican Reunification Movement with Spain). Today I am speaking on behalf of the MPRE, a political association which is a legally registered in the Department of State of San Juan, Puerto Rico, and all of its members.

We are requesting to consider the inclusion of the option of Reunification with Spain as one of the valid options available for the Island in this hearing and in future hearings on H.R. 1522 & H.R. 2070.

The Province of Puerto Rico was invaded by the United States in 1898 without any justification. One million of Puerto Ricans were separated from their true nation and stripped from their spanish citizenship, a citizenship that emanated from the spanish constitution of 1876 which was the current constitution of the Province of Puerto Rico at the time of the US occupation. The Province of Puerto Rico never declared its independence from Spain.

Puerto Ricans have the sacred right to claim the reincorporation of the Island to their spanish nation due to the fact that the island was separated by an act of war and the imposition of the Treaty of Paris.

Thank you for your attention,

Manuel A. Rugama Amparo,
Vice President of MPRE

STATEMENT FOR THE RECORD, PROFESSOR ROLAND BLASINI

Chairman Grijalva, and Members of the Committee:

I respectfully request my statement be included in the Committee's Hearing record on H.R. 1522 (Rep. Soto), titled "Puerto Rico Statehood Admission Act," and H.R. 2070 (Rep. Velázquez), entitled the "Puerto Rico Self-Determination Act of 2021," Wednesday, June 16, 2021, and which explicitly says: "the intent of receiving testimony that is primarily from legal and scholarly witnesses."

Some 30 years ago, on July 17, 1988; I also had submitted a written statement then to the Interior and Insular Affairs Committee—Oversight Hearing on: "The International Role of the U.S. Insular Areas" Chairman, by the late Hon. Morris K. Udall and distinguish author of that essential publication on Congress entitled: "The Role of a Congressman." I hereby request once again this statement be also posted for public discourse.

Due to the current political and legislative environment, I honestly do not foresee this process ending with a final result of a signed Presidential authorization.

On one side, is our desire to see a final solution toward the status matter. On the other side of the coin, is the current political reality—for which two additional US Senators would change the composition of the upper chamber.

Due to the highly partisanship and policy implications; James Carville, an American political consultant and LSU Mass Communication faculty, stated the predicament very clearly: "Do the Math—We Only Have a 50/50 Senate, No One Is Playing Patty-Cake" (Source: Anderson Cooper 360, CNN 8 June 21).

Since the Chairman released and made available the analysis of each bill from the Department of Justice—Memorandum—regarding the issues of constitutionality and feasibility, The DOJ states and I quote:

> ". . . agrees that the people of Puerto Rico should be allowed to choose whether to become a nation independent of the United States, become a state within the United States, or retain the current status of a territory. Insofar as H.R. 2070 would facilitate a choice among those three options, which we believe are the three constitutional options available to Puerto Rico, the Department supports the bill."

Due to the fact, the DOJ "suggest" to maintain the prevalent political regimen; I will address this "poison pill" element further on.

Since a deadlock reality is prevalent—I would like to present some different options before the Committee, in order to address some general consensus options with fundamental public policy and administrative developmental reforms, which are:

1. Via Congressional mandate—*ELIMINATE—the Financial and Management Oversight Board for Puerto Rico*

One must question; "the reliability and competency cost" on behalf of the advisors and their role, since its foundation. Thus, spending Millions of dollars from Puerto Rican taxpayers' fiscal funds in consulting fees and expenses on behalf for themselves, with ZERO end results.

One must also question, the length and duration for the Oversight Board; especially due to the past political donations received for the 2020 campaign election cycle.

Has the Oversight Board become an ATM or Gravy-Train source for elected officials? (Source: Puerto Rico Debt Vultures Give Big to 2020 Candidates as Fiscal Board Appointments Loom). See: Exhibits 1-2019-2020 Campaigns' Committees Donations; 2-2019-2020 Vulture Funds' Donations; 3-2019-2020 Vulture Law Firms' Donations.

2. Establish a *RECALL election procedure.*

All elected positions in the Commonwealth of Puerto Rico's government, would be subject to a RECALL Provision and amending the Resident Commissioner term for a two-year post.

During the summer of 2019, a governmental constitutional crisis was generated and evolved with disorderly conduct and even up to sporadic street violence, at Old San Juan. The final outcome was the Governor's resignation. Also during that "boiling" time period, various instrumental events went on, for which did not prelude toward a smooth, rapid and orderly transition.

Another factor is the local political sociological and cultural reality prevalent due to the level of "institutionalized corruption," which can easily be documented by the number of federal prosecutions of not only administrative appointments, but also elected local officials.

The insertion of a federal RECALL election procedure statute toward Puerto Rico, would safeguard an orderly transition and ensure a democratic leadership; if prior conditions were repeated once again.

3. Procedural—Pathway = Methodology for the Status Solution Process

It's time to approach a final status solution, thru an optical lens of quantitative theory analysis.

Rather than present mathematical modeling equations, let me express it in simple terms, there is a game—many have played as children call "tug-of-War." Under the classic format—there are two sides, the side with the greater force pushing, and wins. One the other side, IF a modified game model is used, where various ropes are placed thru a center and such center illustrates whom the winner is, of such interaction will be. The interaction on behalf of the participants can neutralize forces and coalitions can evolve, therefore distorting the end result.

Our political constitutional system and order, was developed and establish through a Constitutional Convention in Philadelphia. The national interest and discussions were focused on a simple two-tier model approach, in order to have a final end result on an issue. The method used for a solution on behalf this approach is commonly known as a decision-tree model.

Puerto Rico's political status dilemma has quite a different focus; since it is based on a multi-polar model, which therefore having various final solutions or various options, easily can join different options or forces together and neutralize an outcome, having then a zero-sum game. The end result being neutralize by the opposite interest for a "spoiler" option resolution.

The time has come to approach the voter-pathway electoral participation method using a "decision-tree" model, for which there would ONLY be two options or categories at a time to select from—on behalf a simple majority will of the electorate.

Pathway Method Approach—Voters Would Be Asked—For Example

a. Stage One

Do you favor maintaining the current political relationship?

___ Yes or No

If the YES option obtains the majority—simply the voter consultation would ends, until a future timeframe for another inquiry.

If the NO option, obtains the majority—then continue the pathway toward the next phase.

b. Stage Two

Do you favor maintaining "ties" with the US or breaking away from the US?

___ Relationship with US ___ Breaking Away from US

Next stage responds to which option obtained a majority

c. Stage Three

If the—Relation with US, obtains the majority.

A voter inquiry is conducted between options Congress is willing to grant—territorial, statehood—voters would select an option provided The alternative with a majority would continue, toward the next stage,

If the—Breaking Away from the US, obtains a majority.

A voter inquiry is conducted between options of Free Association or Independence-voters would select an option and the process would Continue, of whom obtained the majority of votes.

d. Stage Four

The option which obtains the majority results from stage three, would be subject toward two (2)—Yes or No voter inquiry consultation and a majority—is required—toward a pathway solution.

It is at this stage a Commission is established on both sides. One on behalf of Puerto Rico and the other on behalf the Federal government to identify, make very clear and educate voters the conditions toward the final pathway solution.

While NO methodological pathway approach is listed in either bill, the Zero-Sum Game reality will persist. The desired "suggestion" on behalf the US Department of Justice for the inclusion on behalf the current status is a clear demonstration of providing a "poison pill" toward NO solution. The Federal Government has THREE co-equal branches. Therefore, it's time to ensure the independence and individual power by each branch of government and not be subject toward a submissive stand, dictated by one branch toward another regardless of the affinity on behalf of the Executive and Legislative branches of government.

I simply cannot be silent to this institutional violation on behalf of the division of powers and foresee an obligation to denounce such. In memory of my experience and education provided, here on The Hill by academics, highly skilled staffers from all branches and even the Library of Congree personnel, but most of all—the bipartisanship institutional Members of Congress, which I have always cherished their lectures and pleasantries in the hallway, during those years here on the Hill, I cannot be silent.

4. Objection toward Procedural Usage Constitutional Assembly Method—H.R. 2070

The introduction on behalf for usage of a Constitutional Assembly method, as a matter of resolution toward the political status of Puerto Rico dilemma; came from the late Juan Mari Bras (La Asamblea Constituyente. 1962).

The strategy was first advocated within entities such as MPI-PSP (Movimiento Pro-Independencia), the Puerto Rican Bar Association or any organization for which it's leadership withheld post or control were independence advocates, in order to push such approach. The reason and strategy is very simple, The Constitutional Assembly method requires—ALL transfer of power—be vested entirely back toward Puerto Rico; therefore, it would be a sovereign nation with such process. Foreseeing a negotiation reality, of non-equals and lack of interest any intention toward any negotiation—Puerto Rico would be granted its independence by default.

The intellectual author for such approach (Mari Bras), even advocated for an "Independent Monarchy" republic for Puerto Rico.

The usage of a Constitutional Assembly also provides, opportunities on behalf of organizational managerial "mischief."

Nassim Nicholas Taleb, Ph.D., author of; "Skin in the Game: Hidden Asymmetries in Daily Life" (2018) points out in a provocative and practical manner, redefines what it means to understand the world, succeed in a profession, contribute to a fair and just society, detect nonsense, and influence others. He clearly demonstrates with vast clearly examples on how—*Minority rules—A "stubborn minority" can impose its will on the relatively disinterested majority.*

One must also add, toward this organizational nightmare forecast proposal the usage of Serge Galam "tipping point." (Ref. Serge Galam, Ph.D. and Taksu Cheon, Ph.D., "Tipping Points in Opinion Dynamics: A Universal Formulaions," CEVIPOF—Centre for Political Research, Sciences Po and CNRS, Paris, France).

"The universal formula is shown to predict the dynamics of public opinion including eventual sudden and unexpected outbreaks of minority opinions within a generic parameter space of five dimensions. The formula is obtained by combining and extending several components of the Galam model of opinion dynamics, otherwise treated separately, into one single update equation, which then deploys in a social space of five dimensions.

Four dimensions account for a rich diversity of individual traits within a heterogeneous population, including differentiated stubbornness, contrarianism, and embedded prejudices. The fifth dimension is the size of the update groups being discussed. Having one single formula allows one to explore the complete geometry of the underlying landscape of opinion dynamics. Attractors and tipping points, which shape the topology of the different possible dynamics flows, are unveiled. Driven by repeated discussion among small groups of people during a social or political public campaign, the phenomenon of minority spreading and parallel majority collapse are thus revealed ahead of their occurrence."

Just these two operational realities demonstrate a clear operational "outcome bias" toward tilting an end result in favor of one option, therefore; I come and oppose such inclusion of the Constitutional Assembly; in the proposed legislation.

In conclusion, I respectfully request my entire statement be added for the record and thank you.

2019-2020 Campaigns' Committees Donations

Candidate	Position	Party	Donation
Donald Trump	President	Republican	$182,643
Joe Biden	Presidential candidate	Democrat	$1,124,224
Nancy Pelosi	Speaker of the House	Democrat	$12,150
Chuck Schumer	Senate Minority Leader	Democrat	$1,500
Mitch McConnell	Senate Majority Leader	Republican	$81,450
Kevin McCarthy	House Minority Leader	Republican	$71,80

Figure 1.

2019-2020 Vulture Funds' Donations

Fund	Candidate	Donation
Aristeia Capital	Joe Biden	$5,600
	Donald Trump	$1,000
Aurelius Capital	Donald Trump	$14,000
	Mitch McConnell	$5,600
BlackRock		
Joe Biden	$100,044	
Donald Trump	$2,125	
Brookfield Asset Management	Joe Biden	$2,800
Canyon Capital	Mitch McConnell	$30,600
Emso Asset Management	Joe Biden	$8,150
GoldenTree Asset Management	Mitch McConnell	$28,700
Mason Capital	Donald Trump	$81,200
Oaktree Capital	Joe Biden	$68,050
Sculptor Capital	Joe Biden	$3,550
Silver Point Capital	Kevin McCarthy	$16,200
Taconic Capital	Joe Biden	$58,900
Total	N/A	**$426,519**

Figure 2.

2019-2020 Vulture Law Firms' Donations

Law Firm	Client	Candidate	Donation
		Joe Biden	$77,550
Davis Polk & Wardwell	Commonwealth Bondholder Group	Nancy Pelosi	$1,000
		Donald Trump	$3,195
		Joe Biden	$57,751
Jones Day	Employees Retirement System Secured Creditors	Nancy Pelosi	$250
		Donald Trump	$9,303
		Joe Biden	$47,080
Kramer Levin	Ad Hoc Group of PREPA Bondholders	Chuck Schumer	$1,500
		Donald Trump	$70
Morgan Lewis	QTCB Noteholders Group	Joe Biden	$134,497
		Donald Trump	$1,592
Morrison & Foerster	Ad Hoc Group of Constitutional Debtholders	Joe Biden	$67,911
		Donald Trump	$1,187
		Joe Biden	$381,526
Paul Weiss	Ad Hoc Group of General Obligation Bondholders	Mitch McConnell	$16,500
		Donald Trump	$1,975
		Joe Biden	$25,062
	Oversight Board	Kevin McCarthy	$55,600
Proskauer Rose		Mitch McConnell	$50
		Nancy Pelosi	$10,900
		Donald Trump	$65,000
Quinn Emanuel	Lawful Constitutional Debt Coalition	Joe Biden	$46,058
		Donald Trump	$942
Willkie Farr	Ad Hoc Group of General Obligation Bondholders	Joe Biden	$24,653
		Donald Trump	$1,048
Total	N/A	**$1,047,249**	

Figure 3.

Statement for the Record, Elvin Méndez-Rosa, President, Movimiento Revolución Estadista Inc.

Chairman Grijalva, Members of the Committee, ladies and gentlemen:

I applaud your efforts in scheduling hearings to discuss Puerto Rico's centennial colonial problem. I have been visiting many of you for over the last 40 years; to get the United States Congress attention to resolve this embarrassing situation of having a colony of US citizens without representation in the government that rules our lives. On many occasions, we have been told the "need to get our act together." BUT it's YOU, the United States CONGRESS, which imposes rules, out of our control, which make it impossible to get our act together.

I am mentioning in my statement, just some of the many decisions that are totally under the responsibility of the United States Congress, with the hopes that you start from there. It's no use to hold more hearings on more plebiscites, when you have made decision to keep us locked under a colonial rule in order to facilitate tax evasion for CFC's, High Tech Corps, the very wealthy from Puerto Rico, the several states, and the world.

THE US CONGRESS has

Allowed Puerto Rico to be an Offshore Tax paradise,

Not allowed Representation in Congress to US Citizens

Not allowed US CITIZENS to vote for the President and Vice President, who determine to send us to wars.

Therefore, I respectfully request that my statement be included for the Record towards the Legislative Hearing on H.R. 1522 (Rep. Soto), titled "Puerto Rico Statehood Admission Act," and H.R. 2070 (Rep. Velázquez), entitled the "Puerto Rico Self-Determination Act of 2021," on Wednesday, June 16, 2021, and which explicitly says: "with the intent of receiving testimony that is primarily from legal and scholarly witnesses."

We, the US Citizens of Puerto Rico; hereby let it be known, have had extensive patience awaiting for the United States Congress to resolve the status of Puerto Rico! We, the US Citizens of Puerto Rico also want it to be known, a resolution towards the final political status of Puerto Rico is not just a matter for scholars, political parties and vested interests, whom have access to express their viewpoint before a congressional hearing. There is an essential "moral" and democratic responsibility, with a need to conduct public hearing at Puerto Rico.

The US citizens of Puerto Rico public must be heard!

We, the US Citizens of Puerto Rico, therefore request, the Natural Resources Committee of the U.S. House of Representatives submit a bill to the Floor and resolve;

the following “dilemmas” which Congress itself has created towards Puerto Rico, which are:

Financial Oversight and Management Board for Puerto Rico

It is Imperative that Congress eliminate the Financial Oversight and Management Board for Puerto Rico.

It has proven to be totally ineffective in resolving the fiscal public debt issue and has probably cost us more than what we Puerto Rican’s owe.

If they were “true and competent” experts and advisors, as it was sold to us, in the content—why have they spent millions of dollars in consulting fees and expenses?

“Professionals have requested about $883 Million in fees and expenses through the Title III compensation process as of March 1, 2021.” These are legal expenses for all parties due to litigation. Congress instructed the Board to have consensual negotiations with bondholders but instead they have litigated for over four years. [Reference; (Exhibit—See Page 2) https://drive.google.com/file/d/1RyNs4H7yvpk0P w4DtK57 WeHzeZEKggXA/view?usp=sharing.]

While the Congressional Budget Office estimated that the process should cost approximately $370 Million. [Reference; (Exhibit) https://drive.google.com/ file/d/1QmLknEwU9P20zP57-SZQieBOkBqKieMa/view?usp=sharing.]

We, the US Citizens of Puerto Rico therefore; will be over paying a cost of more than $350 Million estimated, due to the actions of the Board.

Urgent—United State Congress Modify—IRC Tax Code towards Puerto Rico

Puerto Rico is treated as a Foreign Entity for IRC tax purposes. Puerto Rico is a US Territory with US Citizens and should be treated as such. This participation will open the way towards our full participation within the Federal fiscal system. [Reference; (Exhibit) Source: https://howmuch.net/articles/corporate-tax-rates-around-the-world.]

Urgent—The United States Congress Must Eliminate Tax Evasion Schemes Which Has Made Puerto Rico an Offshore IRC Tax Shelter

The very affluent rich and powerful, use our beautiful island to evade taxes and enjoy our bankrupt circumstance, while most of the population resides under the poverty level, with the lowest per-capita income under the American Flag. [Reference; (Exhibit)

Source: IRS Seizes Foothold on Puerto Rico Tax Haven Movimiento Revolución Estadista Inc.Audits, https://news.bloombergtax.com/daily-tax-report/irs-seizes-foothold-on-puerto-rico-tax-haven-audits.]

We have many more requests for this committee and suggest that it hold a hearing to allow the people whom are actually suffering the consequences of years of the inactions, report and testify. We, the US Citizens of Puerto Rico are more than tired of observing, selected and handpicked witnesses who do not represent us, or speak for us.

I respectfully and publicly request, that the people of Puerto Rico who agree with my statement to endorse it by sign your name at the end, and ask that it be introduced for the record.

Puerto Rico Escogióestadidad [Puerto Rico Chose Statehood]

June 17, 2021

House Committee on Natural Resources,
Washington, DC

Hello Mr. Modeste and Ms. Varela,

I wanted to write you after yesterday's hearing on the Puerto Rico political status bills because, since we met back in March, my organization has been very actively working to show Congress that it cannot ignore the will of the majority of voters in Puerto Rico.

We have driven all across the island, risking our lives during the pandemic, going from town to town, to collect signatures from average citizens on the street who don't have the means or the know-how to communicate with Congress. We have been to a multitude of municipalities, and have had people drive for hours to come to our gatherings to register their signature and send their message. In total we have collected over 5,300 signatures to date demanding that Congress listen to the will of the people and pass H.R. 1522. We have placed the letters here so you can access them, look at the signatures yourself and share them with your Committee members. These are real people who are living the injustice of territory status every day. Congress has to take this into account, and I humbly ask that you include this for the record.

My organization also worked as part of the Puerto Rico Statehood Action Network to mobilize support from our fellow citizens in the states, and last Monday I flew from Puerto Rico to DC to participate in a demonstration calling on Congress to "Respect Puerto Rico's Statehood Vote." We mobilized over 40 people to demonstrate on the

Capitol grounds, some driving from places as far away as Pennsylvania, so that Congress understands that action on this is urgent and necessary.

Please help make sure Chairman Grijalva and the rest of the Committee sees this.

Thank you,

Irma Rodriguez,
President

Figure 4.

PR ESTADIDAD

Hon. Raúl Grijalva Chairman House Committee on Natural Resources	Hon. Bruce Westerman Ranking Member House Committee on Natural Resources
Hon. Joe Manchin Chairman Senate Committee on Energy & Natural Resources	Hon. John Barrasso Ranking Member Senate Committee on Energy & Natural Resources

Dear Chairman Grijalva, Ranking Member Westerman, Chairman Manchin, Ranking Member Barrasso:

As U.S. citizens from Puerto Rico, we are coming together to express our support for the Puerto Rico Statehood Admission Act, H.R. 1522 and S. 780, and to call on Congress to pass this legislation as quickly as possible.

Puerto Ricans have been part of the U.S. for over one hundred and twenty years and we have made countless contributions to the betterment of American society. During that time the population of Puerto Ricans stateside has grown to close to six million. Yet for the three million U.S. citizens that remain on the island, we remain disenfranchised in federal elections and subjected to unequal treatment in federal laws and programs. This reduces economic development, has robbed our poor and elderly of lifesaving healthcare, and every day breaks up our families and communities as people feel forced to move stateside to seek out better opportunities and quality of life for themselves and their children.

Congress must immediately end its inherently colonial territorial rule over Puerto Rico, because it violates America's values of democracy, equal justice under the law, and government by the consent of the governed. Beyond that, it doesn't serve either America or Puerto Rico to prolong an outdated, dysfunctional and morally corrupt form of government which its own citizens have now rejected on multiple occasions. On November 3, 2020, an undisputable majority of 53% of Puerto Rico's voters demanded change in a locally sponsored referendum calling for full democracy and equality through statehood. While some bills in Congress, like H.R. 2070 & S. 865, seek to delay, confuse and distract from this electoral majority mandate in the name of "self-determination," only the Puerto Rico Statehood Admission Act acknowledges and responds to the freely expressed will of the people.

A majority of voters in Puerto Rico have requested statehood, now Congress must respond by officially offering it and allowing voters on the island to ratify their choice in a binding vote. To turn around and tell voters to go back to the drawing board and re-define multiple other options which the majority has rejected three times in the last eight years in favor of statehood, would not only be insulting to us, but effectively serve as a form of voter suppression. That is simply unacceptable and un-American.

We are natural born U.S. citizens and want an equal seat at the table in the federal government that writes and implements the laws that we live under. We want our full voting rights as American citizens, and would challenge any voting Member of Congress that would deny that to us to answer if their constituents would accept the second-class citizenship that we are subjected to under territory status.

We are proud to be Puerto Ricans, and also proud to be U.S. citizens, and know that there is no law that limits us from being both. So, don't let anyone tell you that statehood will somehow diminish our cultural pride and heritage. If anything, the economic progress that statehood would unleash will allow Puerto Rico to flourish in ways that will mutually benefit the Island and the States.

If you really believe in democracy, justice, government by the consent of the governed, you must not hesitate any further or give any more excuses. Congress must grant us the equal rights and equal responsibilities that we have earned with the blood of our veterans and the tears of their mothers, wives, children and families. Pass the Puerto

Rico Statehood Admission Act as soon as possible and together we can help make America a more perfect Union.

Sincerely,

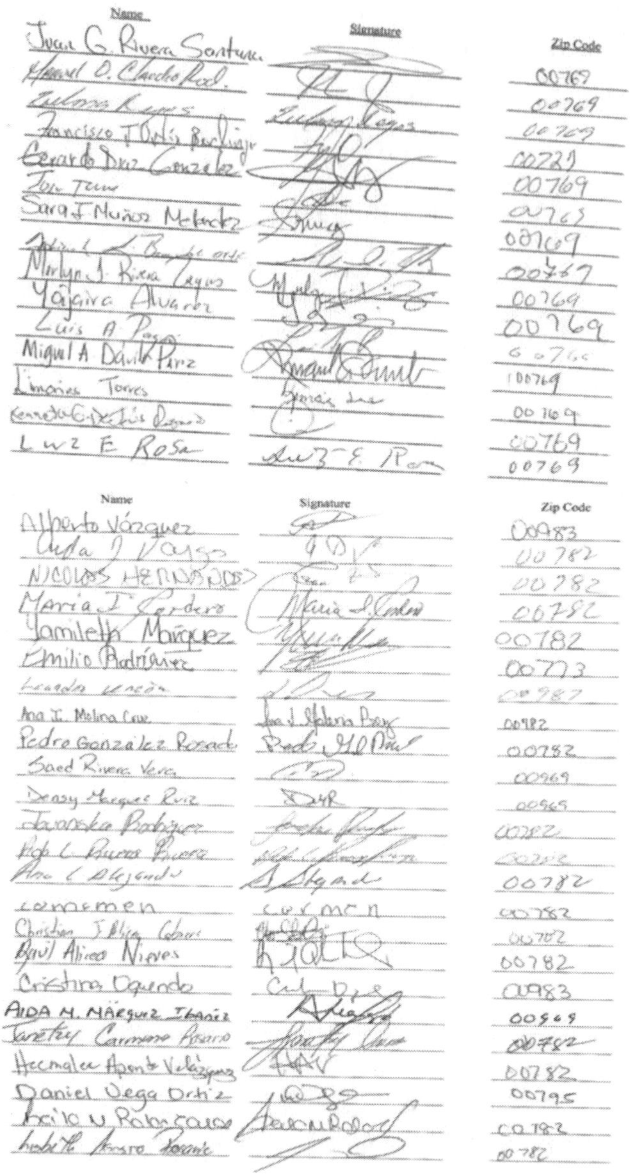

Name	Signature	Zip Code
Juan G. Rivera Santana		00769
Manuel O. Clavijo Rod.		00769
Zulma Reyes		00769
Francisco J. Ortiz [illegible]		00729
Gerardo Diaz Gonzalez		00769
Jose Torres		00763
Sara J. Muñoz Melendez		00769
[illegible]		00767
Marilyn J. Rivera Reyes		00769
Yajaira Alvarez		00769
Luis A. Pagan		00766
Miguel A. David Perez		00769
Limaries Torres		00769
[illegible] De Jesus [illegible]		00769
Luz E. Rosa		00769

Name	Signature	Zip Code
Alberto Vázquez		00983
Aida I. Vargas		00782
Nicolas Hernandez		00782
Maria I. Cordero		00782
Yamileth Márquez		00782
Emilio Rodríguez		00773
Leandro [illegible]		00787
Ana I. Molina Cruz		00782
Pedro González Rosado		00782
Saed Rivera Vera		00969
Deasy Marquez Ruiz		00969
Yaniska Rodriguez		00782
[illegible] Bueno Bueno		00782
Ana L. Alejandro		00782
Carmen		00782
Christian J. [illegible]		00782
Raul Alicea Nieves		00782
Cristina Oquendo		00983
Aida M. Márquez Ibañez		00969
Janetsy Carmona Rosario		00782
Hecmalee Aponte Velázquez		00782
Daniel Vega Ortiz		00795
Leila N. Robles [illegible]		00783
Lisbeth Amaro Rosario		00782

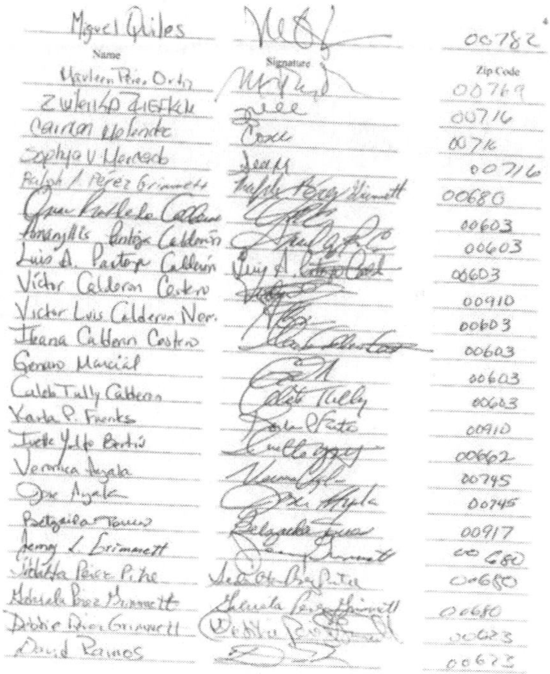

There were an additional 250 pages of signatures received for this petition. A full listing of all signatures received are part of the hearing record and are being retained in the Committee's official files.

INDEX

F

G

H

I

Q

R

V

W

Y